JIM NOBLE

JIM NOBLE

LANCASTER

M. GARBETT & B. GOULDING

Grange BOOKS

LANCASTER BOMBER *Presented to the City of Toronto by the Toronto Region of the Royal Canadian Air Force Association — on the Toronto waterfront near Ontario Place.*

The LANCASTER at WAR

MIKE GARBETT and BRIAN GOULDING

PART ONE

To those
who gave their all

This edition combines two books first
published in 1971 and 1979 by Ian Allan
Ltd under the titles "Lancaster at War" and
"Lancaster at War 2".

Published 1991 by
PRC Publishing Ltd
Kiln House, 210 New Kings Road
London SW6 4NZ

This edition published in 1999 by
An imprint of Grange Books PLC
The Grange, Kingsnorth Ind. Estate
Hoo, nr. Rochester, Kent
ME3 9ND

ISBN: 1 84013 303 1

Printed and bound in China

Contents

Photo credits

The photographs in this book have been provided by:

Foreword

by Marshal of the Royal Air Force
SIR ARTHUR T. HARRIS, Bt
GCB, OBE, AFC, LLD
Air Officer Commanding-in-Chief, Bomber Command
February 1942 – September 1945

This remarkable book is a well-deserved tribute to a remarkable aircraft and to those who designed and built her – Roy Chadwick, A. V. Roe's Chief Designer, Roy Dobson, Managing Director, and the thousands of men and women who laboured with skill and devotion to put that Shining Sword into the hands of Bomber Command crews.

The Lancaster, beyond doubt, was a major factor in beating the Nazi enemy down to defeat – as even the enemy admitted. But no aircraft, however outstanding its qualities, can be an effective weapon of war unless the aircrew that man them are also of superlative quality. That the Lancaster crews were of such a breed is evidenced by the deeds and experiences related in this book.

This country, and its allies, owe these young men – the Many that died, the Few that survived – a debt they have not met: because it can never be met in full.

It is due to them, and their kind in the other Services, that Britain today is not a mere slave market in a Nazi Empire. That was the Plan.

Never forget it.

Arthur T. Harris

Introduction

It is now over a quarter of a century since the Lancaster last flew operationally during World War II; fifteen years have elapsed since its withdrawal from the RAF in 1956, and the last users, the Royal Canadian Air Force, the French Navy and the Argentine Air Force, retired their Lancasters in 1963/4. Yet the magic of the name 'Lancaster' remains, and still there is the strongest feeling of affection for this great aircraft, 'the old Lanc', as it became so widely known. If the name Spitfire became synonymous with saving the war for Britain, so the name Lancaster became synonymous with the winning of it.

For eighteen years the Lancaster has occupied a great deal of both our lives. Neither of us was old enough to have served on them, and we cannot put our finger on what it was that sparked our interest in the Lancaster in preference to other fine aircraft. Was it the Lancaster's looks, its performance, its sound or achievements? It is impossible to say, but something about it set us off on a trail of research that has taken us thousands of miles, and brought us into contact with hundreds of nice people all over the world who were either directly connected with the Lancaster or who share our interest in it.

Our efforts have been truly a labour of love, which has cost us dearly in time and money. What started as a schoolboy interest when the Lancaster was ending its front-line RAF life has blossomed into more than a hobby, rather a way of life, which has snowballed so rapidly in recent years that it has become impossible to 'get off', not that either of us would care to do so.

This is our third book on the Lanc and in it we have endeavoured to depict the aircraft in the wartime environment for which it was designed. We trust the many who operated in them post-war – including the Canadians, French and Argentinians – will forgive their omission on this occasion. They are by no means forgotten and their stories will be told in time.

In the preparation of this book, recourse to official records has been minimal. We have, over the years, searched the files of the Imperial War Museum, Air Ministry, Defence Ministry, etc., and spent many hours in the archives of the news agencies, uncovering dusty boxes of wartime prints which had lain forgotten for years.

Some of the photographs have been published before, but in most cases, during the war on poor quality magazine paper. In this book we hope they are done full justice.

It is those photographs reproduced from private sources which, we feel, convey the true atmosphere of Lancaster operations; not the official, posed, censored shots, but those taken – albeit illicitly – by the men who flew and maintained Lancasters. Although photography was, in general, strictly prohibited until the last few months of the war, when senior squadron pilots were allowed cameras, we have nevertheless acquired several thousand prints of Lancasters and crews from men who risked a snapshot of their beloved machine; men determined to record their part in the war effort. The developing and printing of their film by 'a friend in the photographic section' would cost them dearly in bribes of cigarettes or sweets.

Somehow, thankfully, these pictures got taken despite the risks involved, and many such snapshots are used in this book. There are many more which we would like to have used, but space and quality are unavoidable constraints.

Because the British were so notoriously anti-camera during the war – perhaps understandably so in the earlier years – there are large gaps in our history. How we envy the historian writing of the Lancaster's American counterparts, the B17 Fortress and B24 Liberator, with a vast, seemingly inexhaustible supply of superb action photographs from which to choose, almost every aircraft in their daylight formations having one or more cameras aboard. We cannot match their formation pictures, their battle scenes, aircraft being hit by flak, crews baling out, combats, contrails, etc. It must also be remembered that the Lancaster operated mainly by night until the last year of the war, giving much less opportunity for photography.

Official British sources are relatively sparse. Many priceless photographs remain locked away in official archives, unavailable to the enthusiast, while thousands more are known to have been destroyed, regardless of historical significance. We would like to have shown more photographs of Lancasters downed in enemy territory; photographs which we have actually seen in official albums in London, acquired from the Germans. Unfortunately, some obscure rule can always be found to prevent these really priceless pictures being released.

And so we turned to the private sources – the ex-aircrew; the fitters, armourers, orderlies and clerks, even the WAAFs – the men who flew the Lancs and the men and women who kept them flying. It is to them that this book is wholeheartedly dedicated.

It is not possible to mention by name all those who have helped, but we extend our grateful thanks for the logbooks, photographs, diaries and other material which has so trustingly been loaned to us from all over the world. In particular we must mention the following, without whose help this book would not have been published: Chris Ashworth, Derek Monk and Ray Sturtivant, the other three members of our original 'Lancaster Syndicate'; Trevor Allen; Leslie Butson; Jack Gregson; Olive Hamilton; Harry Holmes (who we know will not mind being between two ladies); Lena Johnson; Ted Manners; Philip Moyes; Cyril Parrish; John Rawlings; Bruce Robertson, whose own Lancaster book will always remain the standard reference work on the subject; Bill Spowage; Ron Valentine; Rusty Waughman and Gerrie Zwanenburg.

Also we wish to thank: various members of *Air Britain*; the staff of Avro's, Woodford, including Jack Beatty, Derek Bowyer, Ken Foden, Bill Hannah, Sandy Jack; Jack Hilton and staff of Avro Canada; the Australian War Memorial; *Blackwood's Magazine*; Brigadier-General Bourgeois and the staff of the Canadian Armed Forces HQ; R. W. Bradford of the Canadian National Museum of Science & Technology (Aviation Division); Maurice Smith, the Editor, and staff of *Flight International*; J. F. R. Painter of Hawker Siddeley Canada Ltd.; the staff of the Imperial War Museum; L. A. Jacketts and staff of the MoD (Air Historical Branch); J. H. G. Bennett and staff of the MoD (Publicity 3); the staff of the Press Association and its photographic agencies; W. R. Collier of Rose Brothers; the Royal Australian Air Force.

The authors of the factual accounts and impressions deserve a special mention. We are grateful for having been allowed to publish such highly personal documents, most of which were written shortly after the events described. It was not always easy to persuade the authors to donate such features because of the old fear of being accused of 'line shooting'. Their individual styles have been faithfully preserved.

Our sincere thanks, therefore, to:

'Biff' Baker	Lt/Col Johnny Goldsmith, CAF
Bill Bennée	Ken Lane
Bill Breckenridge	Carl Olsson
Don Charlwood	'Blue' Rackley
Lance Connery	Capt Rod Rodley
Edward Cook	John Shelton
Jack Currie	Fred Smooker
Lettice Curtis	Stan Wells
Jimmy Griffiths	

MIKE GARBETT
BRIAN GOULDING

THE EARLY DAYS

THE START OF IT ALL *The prototype Manchester, out of which the Lancaster was born, photographed (above) at Ringway on July 24, 1939, the day of her first flight. The Manchester's engines proved unsatisfactory and the decision to replace the two Vultures with four Merlins was probably one of the most momentous of the war.*

FIRST OF THE MANY *The prototype Lancaster, BT308, clearly showing the triple fins (below), seen at Ringway in early January 1941, at about the* time of her first flight. Only this machine had the three fins, all subsequent Lancasters having the enlarged twin fins and extended tailplane.*

SHE CLIMBS LIKE A BIRD *The second prototype, DG595, in standard prototype camouflage, with yellow undersurfaces a sharp contrast to the standard bomber black, climbs away while on service trials at Boscombe Down. The ventral turret fitting is clearly seen, but it was not persevered with for long in squadron service, being of no use on night raids.*

IN PRODUCTION

THE BIRD TAKES SHAPE *Production line 1942. The scene at A. V. Roe's main plant at Chadderton, where the major manufacturing processes took place. Consisting of 55,000 separate parts, it has been estimated that half a million different manufacturing opera-* *tions were involved to produce just one aircraft.*

Peak production was achieved in August 1944 when the Lancaster Group as a whole turned out 293 machines, of which the Avro factories alone contributed 155.

HERE'S MY BODY – MY NOSE IS FOLLOWING *The Lancaster consisted of some 31 main components to permit dispersed production, and broke down into four sections for transport by road.*

A. V. Roe, the parent company, had several factories in the Manchester area which supplied components to the main plant at Chadderton. The final marriage of wings, fuselage and tail took place at Woodford or Ringway, nearly 20 miles away, from where the completed machines would be test flown.

This new BIII, ND824, is seen on Greengate, outside the Chadderton factory before starting its journey to Woodford early in March 1944.

FINAL ASSEMBLY *The huge assembly shed at Woodford, June 1942, where the major sections of the Avro and Metropolitan-Vickers-built Lancasters were finally married and the engines fitted.*

The shining sword

Jack Currie

Aircraft come and go, but few leave a lasting impression. One which attained true greatness was the Avro Lancaster.

Right from the start, A. V. Roe knew they had a winner. Watching the prototype take to the air for the first time, Sir Roy Dobson, managing director, turned to Roy Chadwick, chief designer, and said ecstatically, "Oh boy, oh boy . . . what an aeroplane! WHAT a piece of aeroplane!"

Of all the glowing tributes heaped on the immortal Lancaster, none can top that of Sir Arthur Harris, Chief of Bomber Command from 1942 to 1945. His eloquent words in his book, *Bomber Offensive*, are well known. Less known are his words in a letter to the Lancaster production group on its disbandment at the end of 1945.

"As the user of the Lancaster during the last three and a half years of bitter, unrelenting warfare, I would say this to those who placed that shining sword in our hands: 'Without your genius and your effort, we would not have prevailed – the Lancaster was the greatest single factor in winning the war.' "

Perfect in every way, a pilot's aeroplane without a single vice, the Lanc inspired confidence – evinced by the flight engineer who, having feathered two engines, pondered over the prospect of flying over several hundred miles of cold, unfriendly ocean. With deep gloom but perfect sincerity, he turned to his skipper and said, "I suppose this means we shall be bloody late for breakfast!"

Flying the Lancaster was mainly a man's prerogative, and the following impressions by Jack Currie would be echoed by most operational pilots. His enthusiasm is balanced by the views of a former ATA girl who found the Lancaster too much of a 'Gentleman's' aeroplane to test her flying skill. But then, perhaps her endearment had not been heightened by safe returns from ops!

I was a sergeant-pilot, twenty-one years old, flying Wellingtons at an operational training unit near Derby, when they told me I was going to fly Lancasters. There were two other types of heavy bomber in the command, the Halifax and the Stirling, but most people said the Lancaster was the best.

14

ROLL OUT *A. V. Roe alone employed around 40,000 people by 1943, the majority being engaged in Lancaster production. Women formed 44 per cent of the Lancaster labour force and here (facing page) a lady tractor driver tows out a brand new machine, fresh off the assembly line.*

CAREFUL, SHE'S NEW *Marshaller Walter Holland will be thinking as driver Alf Beacon brings a brand-new Lanc to the flight line after leaving the assembly sheds at Woodford. This BI, R5493, was destined to be the first Lancaster lost on operations – failing to return from a gardening sortie to Lorient on March 24, 1942.*

We finished OTU and went to Lincolnshire for heavy conversion. We did some flying in Halifaxes, and picked up a flight engineer and another gunner, which made up the crew to seven. There were some Lancasters belonging to the finishing school on the airfield, and I could hardly wait to get my hands on one of them. The Lancaster looked good because everything was well shaped and in proportion, and she had a good flying attitude. Some aeroplanes look as though they're leaning forward, and some look as though they're being pushed along from behind, but the Lancaster rode the air smoothly, easily and steadily.

You got into the Lancaster either through the main door at the back, or up a ladder into the nose. When you reached the cockpit it seemed a long way off the ground. The pilot's seat was comfortable and you could see around well. The cockpit smelled good. There was a long list of checks to go through before you could start the engines, then more checks before you got moving, and more before take-off.

It wasn't very easy to taxi along a narrow, winding track out to the runway. You turned by gunning the outer engine, and straightened up by giving the opposite outer engine a burst, but there was a lot of inertia, and you had to anticipate each turn. You had to keep a good grip on the brake lever, otherwise she would run away with you. A screened pilot sat next to me for the first take-off and landing. You opened the throttles with your right hand, palm down, leading with the thumb on the port outer to stop her swinging left. You pushed the stick forward to get the tail up as soon as you could, because then you could steer with the rudders instead of the engines.

For landing, you had to take the power right off on rounding out, or she would float on and on down the runway and never touch down. You had to remember these things on take-off and landing and get used to them. In between take-off and landing the Lanc flew herself. She was a dream aeroplane.

All the crew were happy about the Lanc and their own bit of her. The bomb aimer was down in the nose with the bombsight and release gear, and he could also man the front gun-turret. Up a step behind him you came to the cabin, where I sat on the left and the flight engineer on the right. If you wanted to get past the flight engineer, from the cabin into the nose, he had to push his foot-rest out of the way and swing his feet up, and then you could crawl under his seat. The navigator sat at a little desk behind me, facing left, with the wireless operator aft of him. The navigator could take sextant shots through the astrodome above the wireless op's right shoulder. Back down the fuselage aft of the cabin, you passed the rest-bed and came to the mid-upper gun-turret sticking out of the roof. You squeezed past that to get to the main door and the Elsan closet, and finally to the rear turret, poking out at the back between the rudders.

We heard a lot of stories about casualties on the squadrons, how this or that crew had 'got the chop', people we had been training with at OTU or HCU. Some squadrons were supposed to have better luck than others, or better leadership or maintenance. I felt confident of the Lancaster and of the crew, and I didn't pay much attention to these stories.

With full petrol tanks and a normal bombload, the Lancaster climbed slowly. You were briefed to bomb from 20,000 feet, give or take a thousand feet or so, but the last few thousand were hard to reach, especially on a warm night. On a short-range target like the Ruhr, you couldn't reach 20,000 feet by the time you got to the target even if you climbed hard all the way. So you had to climb the first 10,000 feet or so over base before setting course. The idea of hundreds of bombers circling around together over Lincolnshire was a bit fearsome, especially in cloud. One evening I saw two Lancasters collide at about 10,000 feet and they both blew up.

Once you levelled out, she settled down nicely to a steady 150 mph indicated or a bit more, and she was manœuvrable with the full load on. There was a constant volume of noise all the time. You couldn't hear anything that was going on outside the aircraft, like thunder or flak-bursts or other aircraft, unless they were very close. You did hear anything that hit you, even rain or sleet, and hail sounded very loud on the canopy. You could usually hear your own guns when they fired, and you could feel them make the aircraft throb. Over a hot target I sometimes let my seat right down, so that I could concentrate on the bombing run without being put off by all the lights and flashes.

You could tell when the bomb doors were open by the change in the noise of the slipstream. When the bomb aimer let the bombs go, the Lancaster gave a little jump.

I listened to the engines all the time. The flight engineer tried to get all four going at the same rpm with the propeller-pitch levers, and then I fiddled with them to get the sound exactly right. If there was any sort of light you could synchronise the engines by getting the shadows on the propellers all at the same angle. On the way home from a long-range target I sometimes fell asleep for a second, and immediately woke up in a cold sweat because I couldn't hear the engines in my sleep, and thought they had stopped.

The Lanc always did everything I asked her to do, and some things I couldn't reasonably have expected. Once we flew home with both ailerons broken clean off at the hinges. We got through a searchlight cone and some flak over Heligoland, crossed the North Sea and made a reasonable landing at base. I steered her with the rudders and outer engines. I told the crew it might be a good idea to bale out, but they all had enough confidence to stay on board.

Another time both port engines were out, with one propeller feathered and the other windmilling, and we had to make an emergency landing in Kent. There was an enemy raid going on, and most of the aerodrome lights were out. I misjudged the approach and had to go round again. We'd got the wheels and some of the flap down, part of the bombload still on board, and hardly enough height to try it. Going round again on two engines on the same side was never a good idea, but she made it.

Sometimes the airspeed indicator used to get iced up, and then it didn't give a true reading. It usually came unstuck once you got down below the freezing level, but once it didn't, and we had to land with it like that. The rear gunner said he could tell whether we were fast or slow on the approach by the noise of the slipstream around his turret. He was right too, because we made a better landing than usual.

You could really throw the Lanc around if you wanted to. We used to have practice scraps with the Spitfire boys, and if the gunners knew their stuff and gave you the word to go into the corkscrew at just the right moment, you could make it very difficult for the fighter to get a good shot in. Meanwhile the gunners were supposed to be shooting pieces out of the fighter. We played this game in earnest coming back from the Peenemunde raid on a bright moonlit night. A pair of Messerschmitts attacked us for ten minutes, but we got away with it, and the mid-upper gunner knocked one of them down. I was warmly dressed for a long cold trip, and the exercise and the fright made me sweat like a horse.

I always called the Lancaster the Queen of the Sky, except when she floated a few feet off the ground on and on down the runway and didn't want to land. Then I used to say, "get down, you big black bastard", but the crew would make me take that back.

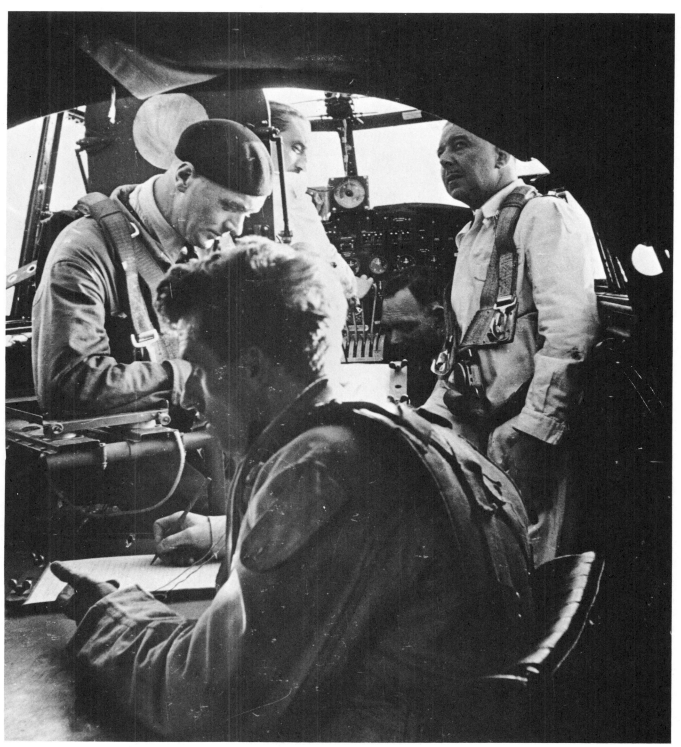

FAITH IN HIS OWN DESIGN
Roy Chadwick, the Lancaster's designer, on a test flight from Woodford in 1942. With A. V. Roe since World War I, he was to be tragically killed on August 23, 1947, in a Tudor, together with the company's chief test pilot, Bill Thorne, who is seen at the controls in this picture. Also in the flight test crew are Donald Woods (foreground), Harry Barnes (with beret) and Syd Gleave (bending). At the peak of Lancaster production Avro's maintained seven full-time flight test crews (pilot and flight engineer) at Woodford, test- and production-flying being a continuous dawn-to-dusk task, every day of the week.

17

FIRST FLIGHT *A late production BI,* PP687, *on a test flight from Vickers Armstrong's Castle Bromwich factory in March 1945.*

Known as the Lancaster Group, companies building the Lancaster comprised A. V. Roe (Manchester area and Yeadon), Metropolitan-Vickers (Manchester area), Armstrong Whitworth (Baginton), Vickers-Armstrong (Chester and Castle Bromwich), Austin Motors (Longbridge) and Victory Aircraft Canada (Malton).

Masking tape clearly shows the fuselage sections. The painting of the aircraft would be completed at either an RAF Maintenance Unit or on the Squadrons, where codes would be added.

18

ROUND THE CLOCK *As evening approaches work continues at the factories; a scene at Woodford in September 1943, as yet another new Lanc is prepared for the next day's flight, the tractor manned by two ladies, Joan Brough and Freda Turner.*

. . . and the woman's view

Miss Lettice Curtis

The Lancaster was by far the easiest of the wartime heavy bombers to fly and, as such, was not used for four-engined training in ATA. I am sure that any competent twin-engine pilot could have got into a Lancaster and flown it without any trouble.

Although up to 1943 some ATA pilots were trained on the Stirling, the majority graduated on the Halifax and in fact, after spring 1943, all training took place at Marston Moor where an ATA Halifax training flight was run in conjunction with the RAF.

Unlike singles and twins, each four-engined aircraft was endorsed on one's authorisation card separately. After ferrying ten of the type on which one had been trained, one progressed to further types by doing two trips in the right-hand seat, and one ferry trip with another pilot to see – literally, because there was no question of any dual – what went on. Then one went out and ferried one oneself. The Lanc was so straightforward it was the only aircraft on which we did not have to do these 'stooge' trips.

I was lucky enough to be the first woman to be cleared four-engines in February 1943. I flew my first Lanc in April, ED396, from Llandow to Elsham Wolds. In May 1943 I delivered ED817/G from Farnborough to Scampton, then a grass airfield. Although I suppose we knew about the dam busting we had no idea where the dam busters were based and so I had no reason to know that this was a specially modified aircraft. We flew quite a lot of /G aircraft, mostly Halifaxes fitted with H2S for the Pathfinders and Coastal Command; and, incidentally, a friend used to tell me that Bomber Command had to release the Halifax to Coastal not only because of the ASV MkII, but because the Lancs had very poor ditching characteristics. They sank in minutes if they came down in the sea.

I used to get a tremendous satisfaction from landing a Lib or from three-pointing a Stirling or a Halifax, but the Lanc was a straightforward, safe and efficient but, I fear, a rather dull and characterless flying machine!

Miss Curtis delivered several hundred aircraft while serving with the Air Transport Auxiliary.

UNUSUAL ANGLE *on Avro test pilots Sam Brown and Bill Thorne as they prepare to enter one of the early production Lancs at Woodford in the spring of 1942.*

ENTRY INTO SERVICE

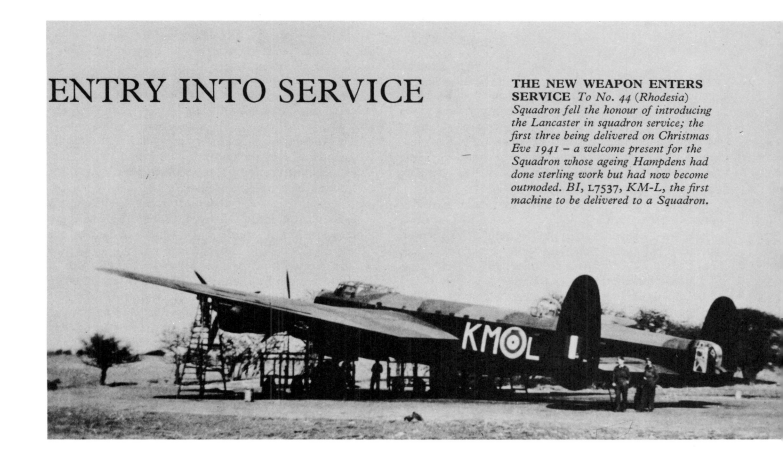

THE NEW WEAPON ENTERS SERVICE *To No. 44 (Rhodesia) Squadron fell the honour of introducing the Lancaster in squadron service; the first three being delivered on Christmas Eve 1941 – a welcome present for the Squadron whose ageing Hampdens had done sterling work but had now become outmoded. BI, L7537, KM-L, the first machine to be delivered to a Squadron.*

The tip-off

Rod Rodley

Flying a new type of aircraft is always hazardous, in wartime particularly, when new types had to be rushed into service to meet a pressing need. The Lanc, beautiful flying machine though she was, had her share of teething troubles. Never before had a bomber been asked to carry so much at so great a speed, and in the early days it was a journey into the unknown for crews and designers alike.

Some crews got away with it – many didn't. Those who did were able to contribute vital information which, pieced together, helped to make the Lanc the best bomber and one of the safest flying machines of World War II.

This story, told by Rod Rodley, who was later to survive the Augsburg raid and who still flies airliners today, shows how, by a cool piece of flying and a certain amount of good fortune, he was able to provide vital evidence of some structural weakness at an early stage, which resulted in the whole of the Lancaster force being temporarily grounded.

The operation was 97 Squadron's first with the Lancaster, only seventeen days after 44 Squadron had pioneered the first operation on Lancs.

The squadron had only had Lancasters for a couple of

months, and bombloads and fuel loads were worked out somewhere above my level in the hierarchy so, when a low-level attack on Essen was cancelled one morning because of dwindling cloud, I was very happy. Group, however, thought we should do some training and we were tanked up for a long cross-country, despite the fact that a front was giving a cloud base of 300–400 feet and visibility of half a mile in rain. (We lost three or four Lancs that day landing around the countryside.)

Suddenly, it was all changed. "Go and lay some mines along the Frisian Islands." So, six 1,500lb sea-mines were loaded by the cursing armourers, a total load, with our 2,154 gallons of fuel, well above maximum take-off weight! Not that I knew anything about that!

Poor old L7570 OF-B took off from a soaking Wood-hall somewhere about lunchtime, and I decided to stay under the low cloud to get an accurate fix as we crossed the coast, so that we would not go blundering into the defences on the other side of the sea. I was at about 350 feet when I saw houses and a cemetery come into view, and realised I was too far north and this was Boston, with its Stump* higher than we were! I im-

* St. Botolph's Church Tower.

mediately turned right and at that moment ran into some low wrack. As this cleared, I was horrified to see the ground coming up at a steep angle. I eased her up as gently as possible, not wanting to stall into the town, and we roared across the rooftops, damaging some property with our aerial-weight, which was swinging about only 35 feet below us.

Chiding myself for an atrocious turn, I climbed gingerly away, hoping no one had got my number, when my Canadian co-pilot, 'Junior' Colquhoun, turned a pale face to me and said, "Holy Jeez, Rod, d'you know your wingtips are missing?"

I looked out and on the starboard side there was just a bright jagged aluminium line where the tip used to be. On the port side, a six-foot high green and sand tip of camouflage paint stood at right angles to the wing. I noticed too that the far end of the aileron abutted on to this, and realised the danger of nipping the aileron if I slipped in on a turn.

I was frozen with horror; seven bods in a kite full of 100 octane and six mines, flying in atrocious weather and nowhere to go! I certainly couldn't fling this Lanc about trying to make a bad weather circuit. Just then we crossed the coast and I saw a beautiful flat expanse of sand, ample for my purpose, so I decided to put her down. I turned gingerly, called the crew up to crash positions and eased back the throttles.

With the wheels retracted, I flew lower and lower over the sand until I felt the tailwheel running along. Gently back with the stick as we lost speed, and then the inner props struck and we were down. We bucketed along for a couple of hundred yards and I was aware of a thumping and rolling underneath – I realised later it was the cylindrical mines – and suddenly all was quiet except for the loud crackling and tinkling of cooling engines. I pressed the fire-extinguisher for good luck and turned to crack a joke, only to find I was alone!

I opened the side window, put my head out into the rain and saw six figures disappearing into the mist. I bellowed at them to come back and they shouted to me, "Leave it, it's going to go up." We compromised and met halfway.

Opening our escape outfits, we got out our 1-in. diameter compasses and decided to strike north-west into the rain and mist to ensure we hit the coast somewhere. The sandbanks were intersected by deep runnels in which water was flowing strongly westwards, so we guessed that the tide was making. Our Sidcots and flying boots didn't help. One of us left a boot in deep mud, but we hurried on, treading carefully over all sticks because we had been warned of anti-invasion mines. My chief regret at the time was that I couldn't get the Lanc salvaged before the sea came up. She seemed undamaged except for the bomb doors she had landed on, plus the bent props.

Suddenly Merralls, my wireless op, remembered his pigeon, so we had to wait while he retraced his steps to rescue the bird.

On we went, shouting every now and then, but only the ripple of the tide and the odd sea bird answered. Then we heard running feet, labouring breath, and out of the murk appeared a Home Guard. We were saved! But, he ran past us. I shouted to him and he briefly looked at us and said, "Straight on the way you're going. Turn left at the path. I'm going to look at the crash."

We guessed it was the clock he was going to look at but pressed on, feeling rather happier, if less heroic.

We found the path, turned left and came to a pub. There we were received rather casually as we stamped in, wet and muddy, and flung our parachutes down. "Was it you just went over?" We confirmed this and then rum was produced and sunk for purely medicinal purposes and to ward off the evil eye. I needed it too, because many evil eyes were on me for a few weeks after that.

The Group Engineer Officer was good enough to doubt my word and was convinced I had deliberately low-flown and knocked my wingtips off on the roofs. However, the tips were produced, one from Boston and one from the wreck, which disproved this uncharitable theory. I was pleased to note that Air Marshal John Slessor kept a very open mind during this period.

A little while later, the squadron was visited by a high-powered committee, and to my surprise I was called to the watch office where a civilian asked me to walk on the grass with him. He introduced himself as Roy Chadwick, Avro's chief designer. He explained that Britain had sunk everything into the Lanc and he *had* to know if my story was true. He said that if I had been larking about (*sic!*) it would go no further and that production could go on. On assuring him of my veracity, he accepted it and I believe production was halted, and a campaign commenced on all the Lancs then flying. Fortunately for me, they found a weakness in the tip attachment and I was exonerated. The necessary modifications were quickly put in hand and the Lanc got into its stride once again.

That was that, except that my rear gunner had an injured foot, received when he finished up at a 'bit of a run' as we touched down before he had reached his crash position. That was Jack Crisp, now a famous modern painter.

I believe a gallant armaments officer went to the wreck later, cut a hole and crawled in to de-fuse the mines which had been made live and magnetically dangerous by the act of the sea dissolving their salt plugs.

L7578 KM-B, flies low over Waddington, the first Lancaster station. The
latter view shows clearly the layout of
a typical pre-war airfield. This photograph was taken on one of 44 Squadron's
low-level formation practices carried out
in the week before the Augsburg raid in
April 1942, KM-B being flown at the
time by S/Ldr John Nettleton and his
co-pilot P/O Pat Dorehill, both
Rhodesians. For some reason she was
transferred to 97 Squadron only two
days before the raid actually took place,
Nettleton and crew taking over a
brand-new KM-B, R5508.

23

PANORAMA OF POWER

STATION TURN OUT *With 21 Lancs in the background, sixteen crews of 12 and 626 Squadrons pose for a publicity-cum-propaganda shot on a cold and dismal day in January 1944 before setting off on yet another raid on the German capital. There is a story behind this picture. The press that day, January 20, were visiting Ludford Magna to see the workings of a bomber station and the preparations behind an operation. As the airfield housed 101 Squadron, censorship forbade publication of pictures showing the three aerials jutting from the fuselage of their special Lancs, so nearby Wickenby paraded its aircraft and crews to complete the pressmen's day. These pictures give some idea of what was involved in putting out a 'maximum effort' on one squadron alone.*

Not often did the men behind the scenes get into the picture. Here are some of those responsible for keeping the Lancasters flying. The Lanc in the background has somehow escaped the attention of the censor, though an attempt has been made to cover the nose aerial.

1. W/Os and NCOs. 2. Armourers. 3. W/T mechanics. 4. Electricians and instrument fitters. 5. Engine fitters. 6. Spark plug testers. 7. Airframe fitters. 8. Radio mechs.

Bomb load and handling crews for sending twenty Lancs to Berlin.

Some of the crews manning the petrol and oil bowsers, fire tenders, oxygen cylinders, etc.

MAKING READY

PLUG TROUBLE *A slight problem is sorted out on the starboard inner Merlin of a 622 Squadron Lanc BIII, LM511 GI-C, at Mildenhall in the summer of 1944.*

This example is a Packard-Merlin, built in the USA under licence. Ground crews particularly liked the magnificent toolkits supplied with the American-built engines.

PROP CHANGE *Changing the propellers of a Lanc was a delicate task as they each weighed around 500lb and had to be very finely balanced.*

Here, ground crew of 426 'Thunderbird' Squadron RCAF at Linton-on-Ouse show how it is done, with the aid of a special rig, while another 'erk' paints a motif on the nose. Under the letter K on the nose is painted — · — ('dah – di – dah', the letter in morse).

ENGINE SNAG *The ground crew of* KB762 *VR-J, a veteran MkX belonging to 419 'Moose' Squadron RCAF, discuss a problem with the starboard inner CSU, while two others remove the top panel. It is spring 1945 and the village church provides a sober contrast to an instrument of war at this Middleton St George dispersal.*

WHEEL CHANGE *This picture, taken at Linton-on-Ouse in 1943, gives some idea of the size of a Lancaster's main wheel and tyre assembly. No tread was deemed necessary at the time.*

In the background is a Lancaster II, DS741, OW-T of the RCAF's 426 'Thunderbird' Squadron.

GETTING GUNNED UP *Armourers slot in the four Browning .303s through the doors of the rear turret. The guns could fire a total of 1,200 rounds a minute, and although some Lancasters were later fitted with guns of .5 calibre, the .303s remained generally standard and were able to give a good account of themselves.*

IN GOES THE 'AMMO' *Feeding up .303 ammunition belts into the nose of a 617 Squadron BI, ED763 KC-Z, at Woodhall Spa in 1944. Capacity was 14,000 rounds, including reserves.*

This view shows clearly the Stabilised Automatic Bomb Sight (SABS) used only by 617.

BOOTS *Precariously poised, a ground crew bod struggles to release the cover from the front turret of a 115 Squadron Lanc BIII, ND758 A4-A, at Witchford, July 1944. The pilot's open window reveals the control locks still in place. Behind the wheel can be seen the ignition switches. The DV (direct vision) panel on the front corner of the cockpit is also open. Below the bomb motif is the later-style pitot head for the air speed indicator. Skipper of this kite was F/O Don S. McKechnie, RCAF.*

SECRET SERVICE *A hive of activity at 'Oor Wullie's' dispersal (BI, LL757), Ludford Magna, May 1944. Two masts on top of the fuselage, plus one under the nose (and barely visible here) signify No. 101 – a squadron with a difference. From October 1943 its Lancasters were fitted with special radio-jamming equipment known as ABC, or 'Airborne Cigar' and carried an eighth crew-member known as the 'Special Duties Operator'*

'Airborne Cigar' was a development of 'Ground Cigar', used by special ground signals units to jam German fighter broadcasts, but whose range was limited to a narrow band along the French and Dutch coasts.

'Airborne Cigar' consisted of a receiver and three transmitters (hence the three aerials), a table with lamp, clock, etc., and was situated on top of the bomb bay aft of the main spar on the port side. The jamming signal was an undulating, warbling, almost musical note. The receiver included a cathode ray tube which gave a visual indication of every signal within the waveband covered. As soon as a signal appeared the special operator tuned his receiver to it, and, having identified it, one of the transmitters would be tuned to the same frequency and switched on. He would then continue to search the band for other signals.

In the early days the SDOs transmitted in German but the Germans soon overcame this by broadcasting on several wavelengths. This earlier method went under the code name 'Corona', but after it was discontinued, the SDOs simply searched for – and jammed – the messages etc. Because 101 was such a top-secret unit, this photograph had to be taken from inside a ground crew hut.

WINTER COATS *Early morning at Waddington, January 1945, with two Lancs looking cold and forlorn after an overnight fall of snow. Seldom would the snow, however heavy, hold up operations for more than a night or two. It was 'all hands to the brooms and shovels' with every available man and woman on the station lending a hand to clear runways, taxiways and dispersals.*

Air and ground crews of 630 squadron hard at it, in January 1945, at East Kirkby.

BOMBING UP

'JOE LANC' *Few men could say they flew their namesake. F/Lt 'Joe' Lancaster of 12 Squadron was one who could. Here he sits astride a dark green 'cookie' with cans of incendiaries behind, before loading into his faithful kite 'R-Robert' (BI, w4366 PH-R) at Wickenby in March 1943.*

HANDLE WITH CARE *Fitting the fins to 500-pounders at Skellingthorpe in August 1944. The bombs are a mixture of British and American, the latter distinguishable by their two shackle-rings.*

CHANGE HERE FOR CALAIS
These 115 Squadron armourers hitch a ride on the bomb trolleys out to a dispersal at Witchford on a summer day in 1944. The job of fusing and loading bombs was a dangerous, exacting one, which had to be accomplished no matter what the weather or time of day or night.

SAFELY STORED 1 *A typical area bombing load (below) – a 4,000lb 'cookie' surrounded by incendiaries in the bomb bay of an 83 Squadron Lanc at Scampton in June 1942.*
  Of all the bombs dropped by Bomber Command, Lancasters dropped 63.8 per cent, amounting to 608,612 tons. Some 51,513,106 incendiaries were dropped.

SAFELY STORED 2 *A typical tactical target load (right). A 'cookie' and 500-pounders in the bay of the veteran BI, R5868 PO-S, at 467 Squadron, Waddington, in May 1944, destined for a marshalling yard in France.*

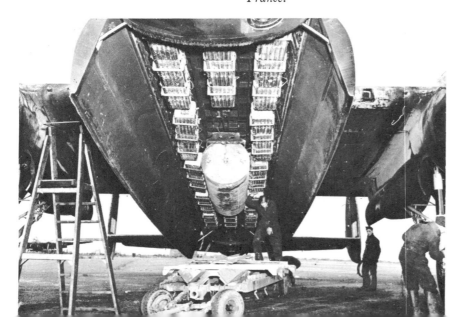

Twenty Lancasters

Carl Olsson

"RAF drops 1,500 tons on Duisburg . . ." "2,300 tons cascade on Hamburg . . ." so the newspaper headlines ran day after day.

To a great many people such headlines became just figures, a rough guide to the size and weight of a raid. Little did they realise what lay behind them – the nature of the toil, the cost and the prodigious human effort involved in reaching such plain tonnages of blast and flame.

A typical wartime airfield housed some 2,500 personnel, of which one-tenth comprised aircrew. It took dozens of men and women to send just one Lancaster on an operation. Not for them the glamour of flying and being in the public eye. Unheard and unseen to outsiders, theirs was a mundane routine job, but nonetheless vital.

An aerodrome was a township, a factory, a battle headquarters and a front-line assault point from which men sallied forth to attack the enemy. It was never at complete rest. Throughout every twenty-four hours someone was working.

Set down among the fields of home, its 2,500 men and women led an entirely independent existence from the rest of the country for weeks on end. If they became ill or were injured, treatment would be in their own hospital. Canteens, kitchens and food stores, big enough to supply a small town, fed them. They had their own recreation facilities such as playing fields, cinema, sometimes even a dance hall, with a stage for variety shows.

In the maintenance stores was a vast array of spare parts, enough to refit completely about half of the aircraft on the station's strength.

Bomber Command will always be associated with the blasting of cities like Berlin, despite its tremendous onslaughts on tactical and industrial targets. An attack on the 'big city' in the winter of 1943/4 typifies a day in the life of a station.

Take-off would be before dusk, around 16.00 hrs, so that the long journey out and home would be completed before the moon rose, or early morning fog settled down on the aerodrome.

The day began before 08.00 with the handling crews hard at work in the bomb dump at the far end of the airfield. Scores of men slithered about in the mud, bringing 100lb cases of incendiaries to a central section where they were packed into the special containers known as SBCs.

They advanced from the dump in lines of ten, with the exception of the two end men, each holding in either hand one handle of the incendiary case. Thus, at each journey the men had to carry 900lb to the packing section.

In another part of the dump other men were rolling out the great 4,000lb 'cookies' and mounting them on low bomb trolleys. Others would be loading flares and leaflets. All this work went on without a pause or break till the early afternoon, when the trolleys were driven out to the aircraft. Lunch might be a hastily eaten sandwich and a mug of tea.

Meanwhile, in another section, armament crews were working against time, feeding tens of thousands of cartridges into the ammunition belts.

At the fuel dump the great Matador 2,500-gallon capacity petrol bowsers were being filled, and the 450-gallon oil bowsers also topped up. One petrol bowser held enough to fill one Lancaster for a long-distance journey, with a mere 300 gallons to spare. So many journeys had to be made back and forth from the storage tanks to the aircraft waiting at the dispersal pens that it would be mid-afternoon before all were filled.

At the dispersals ground crews were swarming over the kites in their charge. Every part had to be checked; engines, plugs, instruments, bomb door mechanism, and a host of other things. Some snag was nearly always found in one part or another of the aircraft and had to be set right, the toiling men always working against time.

If a fault connected with the flying ability was detected it had to be put right in time for a test flight, which had to be made to ensure the fault had been rectified long before take-off on the raid.

It sometimes happened that two or three test flights were made before the sweating ground crews completed the job to the satisfaction of the Captain of the aircraft. No aircrew liked flying in someone else's Lanc for, like cars, all had their own characteristics.

Over at the hangars two or three Lancs might be getting a special overhaul to put them into full serviceability at the hands of skilled maintenance fitters and riggers. Perhaps whole engines had to be changed, or a wing or tailplane, new instruments put in, or pipelines and cables refitted.

Test flights had to be made in these cases of course, and not infrequently the maintenance crews worked on the aircraft right up to a few minutes before take-off. There were cases of skilled crews refitting an engine less than an hour before take-off, which was certainly cutting it close.

While all this sweat and toil was going on at many different points of the airfield, other special staff also worked against time.

The Intelligence Officers were getting out data on the target, such as maps and photographs, collecting information from Group Headquarters and Path Finder

Force. All had to be ready for the briefing of the crews in the afternoon.

The Meteorological Officers collected and revised up to the minute weather information from their own central channels.

In the locker rooms, other staff sorted out all the items of clothing and equipment needed by each member of the aircrew as soon as briefing ended. About fifteen articles were required by each man, ranging from life-saving Mae Wests to socks.

In the kitchen, WAAFs cut sandwiches for nearly two hundred aircrew and parcelled up rations of chocolate, fruit, chewing gum and flasks of tea or coffee.

At Station Headquarters, the CO and his staff worked out the technical data for the trip ahead. Sometimes news came through from Group, making a change of plan necessary. It could happen that this change would result in most of the morning's work being altered within half an hour of briefing.

The only personnel who had no part in this unceasing labour were the aircrew. Theirs perhaps was the worst part – the waiting from the time they were 'warned' for a raid that night, until the final take-off. It was a long wait, broken only by the briefing and then by dressing up in the crew room.

But everyone else on the station doggedly carried on until the moment came when the last Lanc was signalled down the runway and off on the long trip ahead.

Then, and only then, did the tired ground crews, the bomb teams and the others stretch their aching limbs and take their ease in the canteens or mess halls. But not for long; in an hour or two it was time for bed, to be ready for an early morning start and another long, exhausting day.

VEGETABLES FOR EXPORT
Winching 1,500lb mines aboard a 106 Squadron kite at Syerston in November 1942. Each Lanc usually carried six.

From the first days of the war, Bomber Command waged a steady sea-mining campaign and of the Command's 18,725 'gardening' sorties, 2,929 were by Lancasters, on which a total of 12,733 mines was laid.

OPS ARE ON *While the armourers prepare the SBCs (small bomb containers) of incendiaries for loading, the undercarriage locks are removed. A scene at a 207 Squadron dispersal, Langar, in early May 1943.*

FUELLING

TOPPING UP – '2154 OF PETROL PLEASE' *The Matador bowser has been skilfully backed beneath the starboard engines of this 75 New Zealand Squadron Lanc, at rain-swept Mepal in January 1945. Even before the target was known, the petrol load gave crews some indication of the likely distance involved. If it was 2,154 gallons (the maximum) then it would mean a long stooge deep into enemy territory. Lancasters consumed some 228 million gallons of petrol in the course of operations.*

'. . . AND 150 OF OIL' *As a Hercules-engined MkII of a 6 Group RCAF squadron is topped up somewhere in East Yorkshire, autumn 1943.*

READY AT DISPERSAL

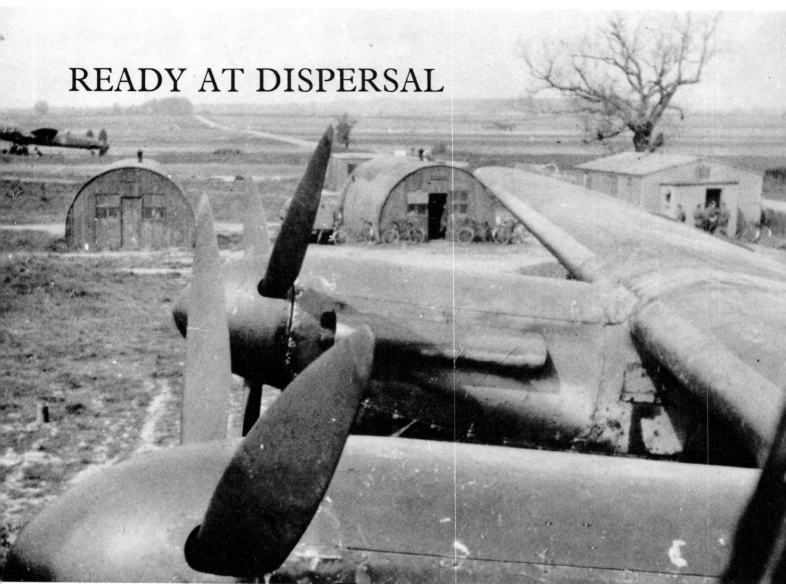

LINCOLNSHIRE SCENE 1 A bleak landscape at Kirmington in the heart of the bomber country, home of 166 Squadron, with typically spartan ground-crew huts, the inevitable collection of squadron bikes and showing how widely the Lancasters were dispersed into the countryside, sometimes two or three miles from the main airfield buildings and hangars. The airfields covered large tracts of former agricultural land and were situated in some of the remotest parts of the country, often many miles from the nearest large town.

LINCOLNSHIRE SCENE 2 With a few precious minutes to spare before an air test, F/Lt Cliff Chatten, and part of his 97 Squadron crew, give some idea of the size of a Lanc. The pilot, standing on the far wing tip, will be nearly 100 feet away from the camera.

In the background is Tattershall Castle, a landmark which became a very familiar sight to Coningsby crews.

LINCOLNSHIRE SCENE 3 *Up in the Lincolnshire Wolds, BI NX560 J-Jig² of 460 (Australian) Squadron stands quietly at dispersal on the perimeter of Binbrook in 1945.*

She has the round-ended props known as paddle blades, first introduced on the American-built Merlins, and later adopted as standard. They improved performance, particularly in the climb, and Lancs so fitted became commonly known as 'paddle steamers'. AR-J² is one of the rare BVII Interims.

RURAL SCENE *The farmhouse, the bare trees, the pale spring sunshine: a typically English backcloth, so well remembered by the thousands of Commonwealth airmen who had travelled to their mother country for the first time. Another scene at Middleton St George, Co. Durham. At dispersal is KB882 NA-R, a brand new Canadian-built BX of 428 "Ghost" Squadron. Behind the Lancaster is a protective earth blast-wall, a common sight beside far flung dispersal pans.*

THE UNSUNG HEROES

TEA-BREAK – 1944 STYLE
Smiles all around as the YMCA tea lady calls at a 617 Squadron dispersal, Woodhall Spa. The squadron dog seems to have lost all interest in the proceedings, as the lads have a 'cuppa tea and a wad'.

Women were rarely allowed at dispersal, as they were considered to be an unlucky omen. It is rumoured that some WAAFs actually had stones thrown at them by aircrew to keep them away from the aircraft!

Not all had wings

Stan Wells

On hearing I was posted to Wickenby, my first reaction was, "Where on earth is that?" No one seemed to know, but as I had been told that the squadron there had recently formed with Lancasters, it was presumably somewhere in Lincolnshire.

Having heard so much about the Lanc, I was pleased to be going to an operational squadron equipped with *the* premier weapon of Bomber Command. Word had spread that this aircraft had no vices, was a delight to fly, and what is more, was easy to service and maintain.

Poring over a map revealed a tiny village, from which the station derived its name, tucked away in the heart of rural Lincolnshire, about twelve miles from Lincoln and six from Market Rasen. Knowing a little of that county pre-war, I knew at least that the natives were a friendly lot!

Arriving on a typically cold and damp winter's day, my heart sank on seeing my new home. What a dump! Coming from a peacetime station, with permanent buildings, comfortable quarters and plenty of amenities, it was a shock to see the general drabness of the place. Ugly black steel-sheet hangars stood out like sore thumbs on the surrounding farmland. Concrete buildings with corrugated roofs and Nissen huts abounded, camouflaged and austere; purely functional.

At first sight there appeared to be no pattern at all, but on looking around the place, some thought had indeed gone into the layout. Hurriedly laid concrete paths led to each building and mud was everywhere.

However poor my first impressions were, I was to become very fond of Wickenby as the months rolled by. The dispersals were quite pleasantly situated, particularly those on the far side of the airfield, away from view and sheltered by trees. The latter were very welcome, especially when cold and bitter winds swept across the Wolds.

My Squadron, 626, had only recently formed from a flight of No. 12, a pre-war squadron, and with whom we were to share the 'drome until the end of the war.

The billets were situated some distance away and dispersed in case of air attack. Most were Nissen huts but made quite homely inside. In the centre of each was a round stove and it was a constant problem getting coal to keep them going. A good deal of 'borrowing' went on, and at night groups crept stealthily about the camp and always found a hoard somehow.

The morale of the camp was very high. Though the bulk of the men and women were British, many nationalities were represented. The Commonwealth Air Training Plan was in full swing, with increasing numbers of Australians, Canadians and New Zealanders figuring amongst the aircrew.

From all walks of life they came; some of the aircrew being pimply-faced youngsters barely out of school. Not many from the pre-war regular Air Force were to be seen, except perhaps among the ground staff. Many duties formerly handled by men were handed over to WAAFs and they did sterling work on such duties as driving tractors and crew trucks. The ground crews were, in the main, a little older than the aircrew; many were married with families and had been established in a wide variety of trades prior to hostilities. What a grand bunch they were too.

Each ground crew built themselves a hut on the edge of the dispersals. The crew which I joined had made a fine job from bits of Anderson shelter, timber and other oddments, and it was quite cosy inside. A neat garden had been laid out, though for much of the time it seemed to be a quagmire. Some crews went one better and erected rustic trelliswork, and even vegetables were planted.

We really loved our own allotted Lanc. She was fussed over like a new car, though we did not always get a brand new machine fresh from the factory. She was as much ours of course as the aircrew to whom she was assigned. She was swept and cleaned inside, and woe betide anyone who left a cigarette end around or was sick and said nothing.

Naturally, the enemy sometimes took a hand. If a kite came back from ops peppered with holes and jagged edges, we would jokingly curse the aircrew for not being more careful!

It was a proud boast to start the engines first time, regardless of the weather. However, a snag such as a sudden mag drop could not be helped. The Squadron Engineering Officer and the 'Chiefy' were always on hand to help sort out a ticklish problem. Tools were in short supply but we improvised and some ingenious concoctions resulted.

Patching and replacing parts would mean a long toil, and many were the times we worked day and night without a break, for it was a matter of pride to get one's kite back in the line as quickly as possible. The weather was perhaps our biggest enemy; soaked to the skin or blue with cold, we would be kept going with constant mugs of piping hot tea, brewed on our own stove. A wartime airfield was quite a pleasant place in summer, and on hot days we would strip down to the waist, even sunbathing when it was quiet.

In off-duty hours we made many friends with the local populace. Every evening the local pubs were packed, and the civilians were most tolerant of this huge invasion. Perhaps the favourite pub was *The White Hart* at Lissington, but with so many small villages near by, all the pubs were visited. Added to the RAF contingent were the Army, who had a camp near Wragby, and girls of the Land Army who were helping local farmers. All got on with one another surprisingly well, though a lot of friendly rivalry existed as to who could get all the girls!

Relations with the aircrews were excellent. During their tour of ops we got to know a crew very well. Often we would play cricket, football or have a round or two at cards over a brew-up at the hut when take-off was delayed. This was particularly so during the summer and autumn of 1944, when the second front opened and the daylight trips began in earnest.

In the dark grim days of 1943, with the Battle of the Ruhr in full swing, and again in the winter of 1943/4 – the Battle of Berlin – losses were heavy and few crews got past ten trips. Some were unlucky, going down on the last five. When a crew did not return there would be glum faces, but within a day or two a new crew would arrive and the whole cycle would begin again.

Once a kite was airborne we would take it in turns to wait up for her, and always there would be some of us to greet the crew when they returned. After each operation we would proudly paint on a bomb symbol with a stencil up on the kite's nose, and much friendly competition existed as to who had the kite with the most ops.

Some seemed to lead charmed lives, lasting for months on end, while others lasted but a week or two. From D-Day onwards, things became somewhat easier and kites began to tot up impressive totals. We heard a lot about veterans on other squadrons having reached a century, but the nearest we got was when 'Shiny Twelve' achieved it with their N-Nan. What a party followed!

While we would occasionally go out for a drink with a crew during their tour, there was always a free evening's beer when they finished their tour. Riotous parties at the 'Snake Pit' (officially known as the *Saracen's Head*) in Lincoln, or the *George* at Market Rasen would follow; then within a day or two they would be gone, usually being sent to an OTU or HCU as instructors. Once in a while one would lob in while on a cross-country exercise but, despite firm promises to keep in touch, one never did.

With the end of the war in Europe, the station took on a different atmosphere: gone was the old spirit. The whole camp was drastically run-down and most of us were posted. Now, 25 years on, memories of those stirring days have dimmed somewhat, but never will I forget. I would not have missed it for worlds.

CREW HUT *463 Squadron ground crew take a breather outside their gaudily-painted hut at Waddington. These huts, though crudely built, provided welcome shelter for both air and ground crews on bleak wind- and rain-swept airfields.*

Not all were of such sound construction. This one at Holme-on-Spalding Moor had been knocked together out of surplus Anderson shelter sections by 101 Squadron ground crew.

EASTER EGG *Ground crew of 424 'Tiger' Squadron RCAF send their own message to the enemy from Skipton-on-Swale, East Yorkshire. The raid was on Heide Oil Refinery, Hemmingstadt, March 20/21, 1945 and F/Lt J. F. Thomas, RCAF, and his crew having the honour of delivery (in BI, RF128 QB-V).*

BRIEFING

A HOLIDAY ABROAD *9 Squadron crews at Bardney in happy mood at briefing – in this case for Operation 'Bellicose', the first 'Shuttle Bombing' raid by Bomber Command.*

Bombing Freidrichshaven on June 20/21, 1943, 5 Group Lancs landed in North Africa and attacked Spezia on the return journey three nights later.

The hut is typical of the wartime approach to building, being completely utilitarian and functional.

Note the aircraft recognition models.

THE TENSION MOUNTS *As the large map at the end of the briefing room is uncovered revealing the target, the air is filled with deriding groans or lively chatter.*

The target is described and reason for attacking it, together with the latest gen on the weather and defences, followed by the tactics to be employed.

A 115 Squadron briefing at Witchford.

CREW CONFERENCE *Sergeant Frank Collis of 207 Squadron checks over the final route and target details with his crew. In the foreground is the navigator's Dalton computer.*

A normal Lancaster crew numbered seven – pilot, navigator, flight engineer, wireless operator (distinguished in this photo by the fist-and-sparks motif on his sleeve), bomb aimer/front gunner, mid-upper and rear gunners. Until 1943, there were isolated occasions when a crew member other than the pilot might be captain, but, subsequently, all pilots were captains, regardless of their rank.

The formation of early crews was a leftover from twin-engined bomber days and, until mid-1942, a Lancaster crew consisted of two pilots (the second doing the job later taken over by flight engineers), front gunner, observer, who navigated and dropped the bombs, first and second wireless operators, the latter being the mid-upper gunner (until mid-1942 all wireless operators were trained air gunners) and rear gunner.

In the early days of Lanc operations, with aircraft in short supply, some pilots did almost a complete tour as 'second dickey' until they were given their own Lanc and crew, when flight engineers became available. Later, a new squadron pilot would normally do his first op as flight engineer with an experienced crew.

Prelude to Hell

John Shelton

What was it like to go to war in the air? Which were the worst moments? The take-off? The outward journey? The bombing run? The ordeal of fighters, or flak?

Almost without exception those who flew bombers will tell you it was that last hour or so before the actual take-off. All along you secretly hoped for a cancellation, but the nearer loomed the time for take-off, the greater became the feeling of apprehension.

The tension really began to mount as you collected your gear, then caught the crew bus. By the time you reached your kite's dispersal, and had a last look round in the fading light, your nerves were becoming really stretched. As you climbed aboard and the door shut irrevocably behind you, the moment of truth arrived, the instant when stark reality replaced the sense of unreality which had prevailed all day since your name had appeared on the battle order.

You had really to force down the feeling of fear which now gripped you as you went through the checks, mouth dry, voice sounding an octave above normal. With engines running and take-off only moments away, the tension reached its peak. If you were going to abdicate, now was the time to do so. Once airborne and with work to do, it wasn't so bad, but oh, that last hour!

This feature, by John Shelton, describes vividly the sensations of those last minutes before a raid.

"Last night a strong force of Lancasters and Halifaxes of Bomber Command successfully attacked targets in the Ruhr. Extensive damage was done to marshalling yards and . . ."

A terse news bulletin . . . tired crews in restless sleep . . . the Merlins of dispersed Lancasters silent.

Some fourteen hours ago, the final briefings had been completed, the eggs and bacon had been downed to a backcloth of brittle cheerfulness and idle chatter. This, the prelude, was the worst of all. The whining Bedford truck arrives to transport crews to their aircraft, and all the necessary kit is carelessly slung aboard followed by a group of young, seemingly carefree men, hardly men at all and yet, because of their garb, appearing older than their years. They bear no resemblance to the young men in the streets outside; they are a race apart, a race belonging to aircraft, living in a world unreal to others. Bulbous flying jackets and boots disguise the frames within as the truck begins its jerky, unsprung journey towards the waiting aircraft at dispersal. Fresh cigarettes are lighted from the stub of a finished one as the truck heads for the expanse of tarmac and grass away from the cluster of camouflaged buildings, away from civilisation.

The airfield is quiet on this summer's evening, the sun spreading a mellow light, casting shadows many times longer than their owners. The Lincolnshire countryside personifies England, save for this plateau with its group of clinically stark buildings and hangars, and the runway running like a gigantic scar across its face. And standing at intervals around the plateau, these machines of war – the Lancasters of Bomber Command, these pregnant monsters that will give birth over the cities of Germany, in their drab coat of black stained with oil, threadbare in parts through erosion by the elements. Those two powerful looking legs supporting the aggressive body sniffing the air, its shoulders hunched, looking restless when tethered to Mother Earth, waiting for that truckload of unruly looking mortals who alone can cut its leash and allow it to soar into its natural element, where it will purr its contentment for hours on end.

Why is it the airfield always looks so much cleaner and less like an airfield in the late evening? It seems a good place to be, though not perched precariously on the side board of this infernal truck, but walking the WAAF from the ops room around its perimeter past the sleeping Lancasters, shrouded like falcons. You wish that were possible; that the truck and its noisy occupants could suddenly vaporise and leave you there alone. But its brakes suddenly project you forwards and then back and some wag shouts, "Terminus!" And you are over the side, tugging and pulling at your gear with its straps and leads and bags, and making your ungainly way to the open door. Around the aircraft are scattered those lucky dogs who will keep their feet on terra firma after you have gone, probably to walk that WAAF around to the NAAFI, the ground staff who, throughout the day, have watered and fed the beast, preparing it for its role in the ceaseless programme of destruction and fear.

Once inside you are aware of the smell peculiar to aircraft alone, a mixture of paint, dope, metal, oil – a smell that can play havoc with a delicate stomach even before take-off. There is general activity within; kit to be stowed; the pilot going through his now familiar checks and routines. The door finally closes, the ladder is stowed, and once more you are in this claustrophobic environment, the sun's rays shafting through the massive greenhouse above the pilot's cabin. You can hear the directions and instructions exchanged between the pilot and the ground crew far below, and then the first of those throbbing Merlins breaks into life, momentarily coughing and spluttering before settling into a rhythmic cycle. The instruments and radio sets vibrate slightly in their chipped, black crackle-finished mountings. One by one the four engines augment the sound that vibrates every rivet. The wash from those massive props plays around the tailplane and makes the Lancaster dance lightly on its tailwheel, and the grass behind flattens itself against the soil.

Through the window can be seen other Lancasters along the line, coming into life, and there you stand as first one engine note rises and falls and then another. Eventually the power reaches an even sustained pitch and slowly the beast moves forward. There is a squeal of protest from the brakes as the pilot steers his mount on to the perimeter track. Again the brakes squeal, and the aircraft lurches forward and then relaxes. The long taxi to the end of the active runway. A long meandering line of Lancasters weighed down by their maximum burden, appearing as clumsy as plodding elephants around a circus ring.

The shaft of sunlight through the small window beside you sweeps slowly over the scuffed floor of the aircraft as it moves slowly round the perimeter track until those brakes squeal once more and you spin round and stop, lined up on the active runway, conscious of the wash from the preceding aircraft at full power for take-off. Finally the four Merlins raise their voices in full cry and for a moment the aircraft is checked in its urgency to take flight, and then the brakes are released and she surges forward, slowly at first, so slowly it seems, gradually gathering speed. Up front the pilot plays his throttles to check and compensate the torque produced by those lashing props. The runway flashes past the window, its rubber-scarred surface looking like some gigantic endless belt. The take-off run seems to go on and on as she rises on to the main wheels and the wings flex to lift the tremendous fuel and bombload. At long last the bumps suddenly diminish and fade away and she is airborne. The boundary fence and Chance light disappear behind you, and there is the flat Lincolnshire countryside, its predominant brownness scattered with shadows. The dusk is already beginning to appear to the east as the Lancaster reaches for altitude, on course for its rendezvous with the main flock. And now you are busy and because of this the tension eases somewhat. Yes, it's that prelude which is the worst of all – it always is.

INTENSE CONCENTRATION *as F/Lt G. Murtough, bombing leader of 463 Squadron RAAF, briefs his bomb aimers at Waddington for their vital part in the night's work which lies ahead, April 1944.*

OUT TO THE KITES

THE LOCKER ROOM *Briefing over, the crews collect their cumbersome gear, watched anxiously by one of the many WAAFs who tended their kit and packed their chutes. These 9 Squadron crews are bound for Stettin on the night of January 5/6, 1944.*

IT'LL BE COLD UP THERE
F/Sgt C. T. Akers, an Aussie, on his first tour, gets a helping hand with his unwieldy heated suit from his Gunnery Leader, F/Lt Bill Hill, on his third tour.

101 Squadron, Ludford Magna, before an attack on Berlin, January 20/21, 1944. The turrets were the coldest spots in a Lancaster, particularly the rear gunner's position where, with the centre panel removed, temperatures of minus 40°C could be experienced. Frostbite was a common occupational hazard.

The gunners' kapok suits were known as 'Taylor Suits', being bright yellow and having their own built-in Mae Wests.

THE LAST RITES *A last fag and forced joke by 101 Squadron air gunners at Ludford Magna before leaving for Berlin, January 20/21, 1944.*

NIGHT SCENE *A 44 Squadron BI, veteran of 72 ops, R5729 KM-A, at Dunholme Lodge, is caught by the lights of the crew bus as it drops the crew off at the 'terminus' before a raid on Berlin, January 2/3, 1944.*

Bomb doors would normally remain open until engines were started unless there had been a last-minute run-up to clear a minor snag, or unless the load was mines.

On this night, in the hands of P/O N. J. Lyford, RAAF, and crew, she was hit by flak and had to return on three engines. Perhaps it was an omen, because only a few nights later, with a different crew, she was lost without trace over Brunswick.

48

SOME WALK *Conditions on wartime airfields could be grim, particularly during bad weather. This is a typical scene at Ludford Magna, home of 101 Squadron, more often than not known as 'Mudford Magna'.*

SOME RIDE *A last minute check of gear by 9 Squadron crews as they assemble at the trucks which will take them to dispersal. The tension is reflected in the crews' faces before one of the devastating attacks on Hamburg in July 1943 (Operation Gomorrah).*

In the foreground are two yellow pigeon carriers. Each Lancaster would take two on operations in the early days but the practice was soon discontinued.

SOME PEDAL *This 106 Squadron crew cycles out to dispersal at Syerston, Notts., on a mild autumn evening in 1942.*

Squadron bikes were standard issue and, though each station would have several hundred, they were always in short supply.

The BI Lanc in the background is W4118 ZN-Y Admiral Prune, the mount of the Squadron CO, W/Cdr Guy Gibson, and shared with his 'B' Flight Commander S/Ldr 'Dim' Wooldridge.

THANKS FOR THE LIFT *On a cold, dark winter night in January 1944, F/O A. E. Manning and his 9 Squadron crew disembark at dispersal. This is their last chance for a cigarette and, although each man appears outwardly calm, inwardly the tension mounts and the stomachs tighten. Their destination, Stettin, one of the most heavily defended targets, deep in northeast Germany on the Polish border. Nine hours of hell ahead.*

THE WAITING GAME *Crews would often have to wait around at dispersal during the summer and autumn of 1944 in particular when, with the allied armies advancing on the Continent, targets were mostly tactical and could change rapidly.*

Sometimes there would be several briefings and false alarms in one day –

a great strain on the nerves. The time would be passed by playing cricket or football, a game of cards, or just lying on the grass and waiting for the 'off'.

At Witchford in June 1944 an all-NCO crew of 115 Squadron check the target details (left) and (below) enter their kite, KO-E.

'A WELCOME CUPPA' *at the NAAFI van, always a comforting sight on a cold, blustery night, with take-off put back and crews kept hanging about at dispersal.*

Here W/Cdr Gomm and his 467 Squadron crew enjoy a hot brew at Bottesford in the winter of 1943. Of Brazilian descent, Gomm typifies the many nationalities flying with the RAF in the cause of freedom.

HERE WE GO AGAIN – ALL ABOARD *As the evening draws in, Sgt John McIntosh and his crew of 207 Squadron board their aircraft at Langar, May 1943. The series of photos which follow show the crew at their stations.*

INTERIORS

THE DREADED MAIN SPAR
Once inside, the crew grope their way along the dark narrow fuselage. Here (above left) *the wireless operator, Sgt John Hyde, negotiates the main spar, with which many a shin lost an argument.*

'NAV' IN HIS OFFICE *The navigator, Sgt Iain H. Nicholson, dons his helmet* (left). *After take off, few navs would venture outside their curtained-off compartment.*

RADIO CHECK *The wireless op checks his set* (above). *His position was the warmest in the kite, right beside the warm air outlet, and he would often be sweating when the others were shivering.*

BLIND BOMBING AID *The H2S set* (below). *The scanner was housed in a ventral radome and the trace threw a negative-style picture of the ground below on the screen. It is rumoured that it acquired its name while in the early experimental stage. A particularly high-ranking officer was somewhat suspicious of the scientists' claims and is reputed to have said, 'It smells – call it H2S'.*

EQUIPMENT CHECK *The Lancaster gave the bomb aimer the best view of any wartime bomber, particularly when the larger blister was fitted from 1943 onwards. Later in the war, a downward and rearward-sighting blister was added just below the nose. Equipment had to be thoroughly checked before take-off. Sgt Desmond Ball checks his panel (above) and front guns (below).*

For take-off and landing the bomb aimer was not supposed to stay in the nose, but many did. With parachute harness on, it was no easy job to squeeze under the flight engineer's seat to return to the front compartment.

BOX OF TRICKS *The bomb aimer's panel. Top left are the 16 bomb selector switches. Below them is the timing device for stick-bombing, the dial bottom-right being for selection of the timing interval between bombs. To the right, in the centre of the panel, is the selector box for order of dropping, it being essential to keep the aircraft balanced by correct spread of bomb-release from the 33-foot long bomb bay. Master switch and camera controls are centre top, and photo-flare releases are on the small separate panel below. Extreme top right is the 4,000lb bomb slip heater which prevented a hang-up through freezing. The bomb-release button can be seen in its stowed position, with a small guard above it to prevent accidental depressions of the 'tit'.*

THE LONELIEST PLACE *The rear gunner, Sgt Roland Middleton, closes the doors of his turret. His was a most unenviable spot – cut off from the others except by intercom. Quite the loneliest position in the kite.*

TAIL-END CHARLIES *Three stages in rear turret development. (Right) the original turret of 1942 vintage. Gunners had difficulty seeing through the centre perspex panel which often became scratched, misted or frosted up and it was removed as shown (below left) on a 186 Squadron BI, NG149 XY-G) at Stradishall, January 1945. The gunner is Sgt Jack Collins, hence the title 'Jack's Joint'.*

Though Frazer Nash turrets were standard in nose, mid-upper and tail, a new turret appeared in 1944, made by Rose Bros. It was equipped with two .5in Brownings and was large enough to house two gunners. 1 Group were the main users.

Sgt Ted Eyles of 101 Squadron in a Rose tail turret (below right) early in 1945. Under the turret is the 'Monica' radar aerial operated by the wireless operator to detect enemy fighters.

MID-UPPER *The mid-upper gunner had the best all round view. Getting into the restricted space of the turret was a difficult task; getting out in a hurry when the aircraft was in trouble could be even more difficult. It was also a highly vulnerable spot with little or no armour protection, and the roundels below were an ideal aiming point for enemy fighters from any angle.*

COCKPIT *Clean and functional – the 'office' with the pilot's position on the left and flight engineer on the right. Not an inch of space was wasted. For training, extension arms for a second control wheel and rudders could be fitted, but very few operational Lancasters were fitted for two-pilot operation.*

START UP

PRE-START CHECKS *Pilot and flight engineer checking fuel booster pumps by the ammeter before starting engines. The flight engineer's panel on the starboard side includes oil and fuel gauges, fuel tank selector cocks, booster pump switches, fuel pressure warning lights, emergency air control and oil dilution buttons. The engineer's seat hinged upwards from the side and the hard, uncomfortable back-rest hinged outwards.*

Clearly visible is the only piece of armour plating in the aircraft – the pilot's seat with extended head-plate.

THE CAPTAIN *Sgt John McIntosh checks the elevator trimmer for 'full and free movement and set to neutral'. Above the skipper's head is the quick-release panel in the roof of the cockpit – his exit in case of need. This pilot is wearing a chest-type parachute harness instead of the more usual seat type, which became standard by 1944. The latter was uncomfortable on long trips and movement was very restricted if you had to get out in a hurry, so some pilots stuck to the chest-type.*

READY TO START STARBOARD INNER *Ground/Flight switch* – On ground. *Throttles* – Set. *Pitch* – Fully fine. *Slow Running* – Idle Cut off. *Supercharger* – 'M' Gear – lights out. *Air Intake* – Cold. *Rad. Shutters* – Auto. *No. 2 Tank* – Selected – booster pump on. *Master Fuel Cocks* – On. *Ignition* – On.

  Contact!

READY TO START No. 1 *With both inner engines running, F/Lt Jock Shaw prepares to start the port outer of* Press on Regardless *prior to setting off for Dusseldorf on November 2, 1944. It was the aircraft's 100th op, his own 35th and 33rd in BIII, ED905, BQ-F, 550 Squadron North Killingholme. She was one of no less than four Lancs on that station to complete a century of operations.*

58

DUSK RUN UP 1 *With chocks still firmly in position, the Hercules engines of this MkII of 426 'Thunderbird' Squadron RCAF are 'given the gun' by the pilot until the props are almost invisible at full revs against the setting sun. Checking –*
Pressures & temperatures – All OK. *Hydraulics* – Flaps down, up and indicating. *Bomb doors* – Closed. *Booster pumps* – Off. *Rad. Shutters* – Open. *Magnetos* – Checked and serviceable.

DUSK RUN UP 2 *In the gathering dusk, anxiously watched by three ground crew, Sgt McIntosh finishes the engine checks on BIII* ED802, EM-M, *in her Langar dispersal before calling the pre-taxi checks –*
Ground/Flight switch – On flight. *Nav. lights* – On. *Altimeter* – QFE is set. *Instruments* – All serviceable. *Suction* – 4½. *Rad. Shutters* – Open. *Brakes* – Pressures OK.

First flight on ops

Lance Connery

Ask anyone who served in aircrew in the 1939–45 fracas if he remembers his first bomber operation. He will.

It's the kind of high adventure one never forgets. Even the small details stay fresh in the mind long after most other operational flights have slipped away into memory's limbo.

There's good reason for that sense of vivid recollection. The first op is a long-awaited consummation of hundreds of hours of flying training between seven young men. Up to that point nothing that has gone before seems really consequential. For many new crews, the first trip spells the ultimate difference between success and failure, life and death.

It was no secret during the war that aircrew losses on the first five operations were heavy. Bomber Command came to expect an average loss of four per cent on each trip, though individual operations sometimes cost as high as ten per cent in aircraft missing. For brand new crews the average was much higher; it was the old hands who made a habit of coming back.

At one time it was squadron custom to send a crew on leave after the first operational flight. The trouble was that when they returned to make a second trip they were apt to go missing, either from over-confidence, or because they were not perfectly fit (celebrating can be overdone!).

In my own group the rule was changed to, "No leave until five successful operations are completed." The practice cut the ratio of crew losses appreciably.

World War II may have been the last conflict in which bomber crews will operate in that fashion. The days of heavy bombers are going fast, and the guided missile promises to replace even the pilot, who may eventually become a highly-trained ground technician, rather than the airborne master of a high-flying apparatus of mass destruction.

I well remember my own first trip. It was the night of March 24, 1944, at a Lancaster station called Bardney, near the centuries-old city of Lincoln. The squadron was one of the oldest in the RAF. Its motto was, 'Throughout the night we fly', but everyone used the unofficial motto of, 'There's always bloody something', which dated back to the squadron's Wimpeys in the pioneering days of 1941.

The station wasn't a glamorous establishment like those permanent RAF bases with cut-stone manor houses for billets and messing. It was a sprawling layout of Nissen huts with a few larger buildings of the same ugly but highly functional construction. Two thousand souls called it home. Two miles away was the village of Bardney, which had only one thousand population and no fewer than seven pubs!

That day the squadron buzzed with pre-ops gossip.

Since the petrol load was a relatively large one, we knew it was going to be a long trip, but hadn't the least idea where. Not till briefing-time did we know, and the news was not conducive to morale for a sprog crew. The target was to be Berlin. Now Berlin had already been subjected to mass attacks by the RAF fifteen times, and this, though we didn't know it till later, was to be the sixteenth and last such large-scale sortie against the German capital.

There were about 900 heavy bombers ordered to fly that night, in two-minute waves of 180 aircraft each, scheduled to reach the target at various heights between 19,000 and 23,000 feet. Timing was of the utmost importance, not only to reduce the chances of collision over the target, but to swamp the defences by as concentrated an attack as possible.

After briefing we adjourned for the night flying meal, in which the squadron's happy practice was to include a precious fried egg. Other squadrons were inclined to serve the egg with the post-operational meal, but our people argued it wasn't fair, since missing crews hadn't had their eggs! That may have been consoling to some; to us it sounded positively sinister.

We took off at 19.00 hrs, climbing slowly to height in our heavily-laden Lancaster, then followed the track to the specified turning points. As we neared the target the Lancaster started to heave and pitch in the slipstream of other aircraft, and an unholy mess of flak came up from the city. Small bits clattered against our aircraft, but our bomb aimer got the load away successfully and we headed for home.

There were fighters in the offing, so we jinked about a bit in the usual evasive action, and finally settled down to the long trip back. There was low cloud over Bardney, so we were diverted to Little Snoring (those wonderful English place-names!) and flew from there to base later in the day. Seven hours and thirty-five minutes was the duration of the operation.

We'd been pretty lucky. There were 17 small holes in the aircraft, none of them bigger than an inch in diameter, and all in non-vital places. Lancasters were wonderful operational bombers; they would fly well on three engines, not badly on two, and they could land on one.

Not all first trips were so uneventful. Another crew had no fewer than seven combats with fighters on their first operation and happily came home unharmed, though with a few chunks of aircraft missing.

After Berlin, the rest was anti-climax and we had no tougher target in the tour. It's hard to recall the rest of them. There's nothing like the first.

TAXYING AND MARSHALLING

QUEUE HERE FOR KASTROP
On some occasions the fully-laden aircraft would be taxied round the peritrack to a convenient holding point and shut down until it was time to go. These Lancasters of 428 'Ghost' Squadron RCAF stand tightly packed near the runway's end at Middleton St George, all ready to go when the time comes. A gunner and two ground crew take advantage of the pause to do some last-minute tinkering. In an hour the whole area will shake as a hundred Merlins are started up. If a Lanc went u/s at this stage, it could cause chaos, and towing vehicles were always on hand to haul them clear if necessary.

The night's raid was to be on the synthetic oil plant at Kastrop-Rauxel, November 21/22, 1944, a night on which Bomber Command put up 1,100 aircraft and attacked five separate targets. The following figures may help to illustrate the magnitude of the task involved in preparing for an operation by a thousand bombers: over 2,000,000 gallons of petrol, 70,000 gallons of oil, and 5,000 gallons of coolant go into the aircraft themselves. Over 4,500 tons of bombs may be required, plus 10,000,000 rounds of ammunition for the guns. Thirty thousand bicycles, 3,500 bomb trolleys, and 6,000 other vehicles are employed. Fifteen million litres of oxygen, 8,000 pints of coffee and 6,000lb of food also go into the aircraft.

STAND BY TO TAXI *The signal given, a Lanc moves out of dispersal to queue up on the perimeter track at the end of the runway.*

Turning was achieved by giving the outer engine a burst and straightening up by using the opposite outer, keeping a hand on the brake lever to stop her running away.

This is the time of day to which the Lancaster seemed to belong – the fading light; the setting sun highlighting spinners, turrets and cockpit.

GENTLY DOES IT *Taxying a fully-laden Lancaster along the winding narrow peri-track could be a tricky business.* KB839 *VR-D, Daisy, a Canadian-built BX of 419 "Moose" Squadron RCAF, is eased gently along at Middleton St George prior to a daylight op in 1945.*

In the background can be seen a ground crew's hut, complete with the Squadron insignia.

M – MOTHER, CLEAR TO LINE UP *The Chance light guides the way as BIII* ED724, *PM-M of 103 Squadron, nears the end of the runway on a dark night at Elsham Wolds, early in March 1943.*

Paraffin-filled 'goosenecks' line the runway while a canopy of searchlights pierce the sky to show the cloudbase.

Often all the airfield lights would suddenly go out – intruders were about!

WAITING THEIR TURN *Who said the kiwi has no wings? Lancs from the No. 75 New Zealand Squadron queue up for take-off at Mepal in March 1945. (Nearest is BI,* PB820 *JN-V, F/Lt D. Clements, RNZAF, and crew.)*

By April 1945, Bomber Command could put up over 1,000 Lancs alone and an Order of Battle drawn up on the 19th shows 52 squadrons so equipped, comprising a total strength of 1,375 machines.

TAKE-OFF

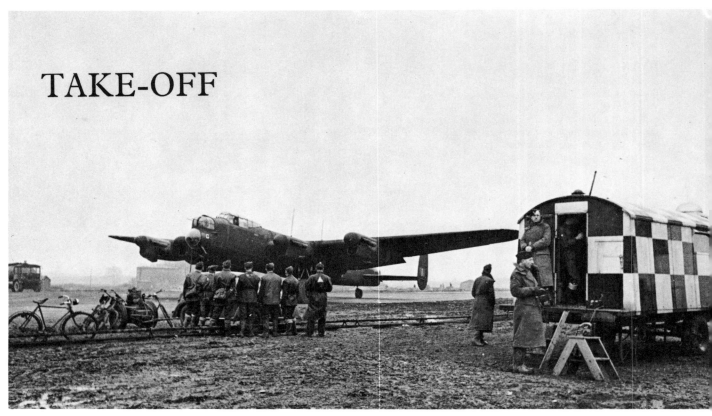

G – GEORGE – READY FOR TAKE-OFF *A spare 'trolley acc' and standby ground crew are on hand in case a kite stalls and blocks the runway. Final pre-take-off checks are made: Autopilot – Clutch in, cock out. D.R. Compass – Set and operating. Pitot heater – On. Trimmer – Elevator two forward, others to neutral. Pitch – Fully fine. Fuel – Contents checked, Master cocks on, No. 2 tanks selected,* Crossfeeds off, Booster pumps on. *Superchargers – M Gear. Air Intake – Cold. Rad. Shutters – Auto. Flaps – Set to take off and indicating.*

A green from the caravan will send 'George', BIII DV236, of 101 Squadron on its way to Berlin January 20/21, 1944, from Ludford Magna, piloted by Sgt Sandy Sandford. The FIDO pipes, looking surprisingly frail, border the runway.

ABOUT TO LIFT OFF *Right hand on the throttles, thumb advancing the port outer to stop her swinging, stick forward to get the tail up, deft use of the rudders to keep her straight, the needle creeps up to the 90 knots mark and the 'point of no return'. In the hands of 'A' Flight Commander, S/Ldr Tom Rippingale, A-Able NX573, P4-A, a brand new 153 Squadron kite, is about to become 'unstuck' at Scampton in 1945. Keen eyes will note the dorsal turret forward of the standard position, this being one of 50 BI (BVII interim) Lancs produced by Austin Motors pending the introduction of the BVII with a Martin turret.*

GOOD LUCK *There was always a gathering of station personnel to wave off each kite regardless of the weather. This is a scene (above) at Elsham Wolds on July 4, 1944, as BI* LM227

I-Item of 576 Squadron begins to roll at the end of the runway on the first of the 100 operations she was to complete by the cessation of the war in Europe.

Pilotless bomber

Jimmy Griffiths

When something went wrong on take-off it could mean disaster for an aircraft heavily laden with high-explosive and incendiary bombs.

In April 1944, P/O Jimmy Griffiths and his crew arrived at Elsham Wolds to join 576 Squadron as 'new boys'. To their dismay, they were allocated the oldest Lancaster on the station.

One week and three operations later, their Flight Commander, whose posting to PFF had just come through, yielded to their protests and let them have his new Lanc BIII, LM527 UL-U². It was a decision which very nearly cost the crew their lives.

Following the abortive take-off described below, the young Scots skipper and his crew reverted to their original BIII, ED888 UL-M², in which they went on to complete their tour. Indeed, this veteran Lanc was later to become Bomber Command's top-scoring 'heavy', with 140 operational sorties to its credit.

Briefing was over, final checks had been made on the aircraft and the crews were relaxing in the few minutes left before take-off time, on a lovely spring evening, April 30, 1944 – target Maintenon.

I was thrilled at the prospect of flying one of the latest Lancasters, so much superior to old M², the veteran aircraft I had flown on my first three operations.

The runway in use was the shortest one on the 'drome and necessitated revving up against the brakes, almost to full power, before take-off, similar to the method employed on aircraft carriers.

Time to go – always a tense moment – and we are soon lined up on the runway making the last quick cockpit check. "Rich mixture", "Propellers in fine pitch", "Flaps up", "Fuel gauges OK". Ready to go! Throttles are opened slowly against the brakes until the aircraft throbs with power, straining and vibrating until the brakes can barely hold her. Brakes are released and we leap forward. Keep straight by use of throttles and rudder and ease the control column forward to bring the tail up. "Full power!" the engineer takes over the throttles and opens them fully, locking them in that position. The tail is now off the ground, giving full control on the rudders for keeping straight, and the airspeed indicator is creeping slowly up towards the take-off speed.

Something's wrong! We are nearing the end of the runway and haven't yet reached take-off speed. We should be airborne by now! A glance at the instruments shows that, whilst all four engines are running smoothly, they are not giving maximum power. Too late to stop –

the fence at the end of the runway is right under our nose – speed is dangerously low.

I yank back on the stick and the aircraft labours painfully off the ground. We are on the point of stalling and I have to level out, praying that I'll miss the small hill beyond the fence. I have just time to shout "Wheels up!" when – *Crash ! ! !*

The aircraft shudders violently; the nose kicks up at a dangerous angle and I instinctively push the stick forward to avoid stalling. I ease the stick back quickly, flying a matter of inches above the ground which, providentially, is sloping downwards. I nurse the aircraft along, still hugging the grass. The speed slowly increases beyond the danger mark and very gradually the altimeter needle creeps away from ZERO in answer to a slight backward pressure on the stick.

I start to breathe again, brushing the perspiration from my brow and feel a cold chill up my spine as I think of the load of high explosive bombs beneath my feet hanging on their inadequate-looking hooks. "A fine start to an operation," I was thinking; but more was to follow.

We were climbing very slowly and I realised from the sluggishness of the controls that all was not well. Charlie Bint, the bomb aimer, climbed down into his compartment in the nose and was able to inform me that the starboard wheel had not fully retracted! It must have taken the full force of the impact into the hill. No amount of pumping on the emergency hydraulic hand pump would budge it either up or down, and I knew that we would be unable to continue on the mission as it was taking too much power and consequently too much fuel to overcome the drag of the damaged wheel.

I flew east, still climbing very slowly, meaning to jettison the bombload in the North Sea and return to make an emergency landing.

One hour after take-off we had reached 9,000 feet and were circling a few miles east of Grimsby, the North Sea looking cold and deserted underneath. I depressed the lever which should have opened the bomb doors but no red warning light appeared! This was serious. I dived steeply and pulled out quickly in the hope of shaking the doors open, but to no avail. The flight engineer reported that the tank for the hydraulic fluid was completely dry. It was obvious that in our attempts to retract the damaged wheel we had pumped all the fluid into the atmosphere through a broken pipeline.

There was no alternative but to return to base for instructions. It was safe to break radio silence now that the rest of the squadron had been on their way for almost two hours. The WAAF radio telephonist lost no time in passing my message to the Flying Control Officer and very soon I was talking to the Station Engineering Officer and finally to the 'old man' himself.

We were ordered to make further experiments, but when we had tried everything it was finally apparent that we were saddled with a bomber fully laden with bombs which couldn't be released and a damaged undercarriage which would make landing a hazardous affair not to be contemplated when our bombload was enough to blow an aerodrome to pieces!

"Stand by," I was ordered and we circled round, wondering how long it would take them to reach a decision. Tommy Atherton, the navigator, brought me a cup of coffee out of his Thermos flask and we had a quiet crew conference. "What do you think they'll decide, Skip?" – this from Taffy, one of the gunners.

I spoke the thought that had been in my mind since the bomb doors had refused to budge. "How would you like to join the Caterpillar Club?" (This is a Club consisting of airmen who have baled out to save their lives.) There was a bit of joking, but it sounded rather forced and I called up the 'drome to ask them to speed up their decision.

"Reduce height to 5,000 feet and stand by!" I knew then that I had correctly assumed what the order would be – we were coming down to a level where a parachute wouldn't drift too far from the 'drome!

I reported again at 5,000 feet and the next instruction produced a stir of activity. "Fly upwind and order crew to bale out one at a time. Remain at controls and stand by." The crew needed no second bidding. Through they filed – two gunners, wireless operator, navigator and engineer, filling the confined space of the cockpit, their parachutes fixed firmly across their chests. Charlie was already in his compartment in the nose, opening the escape hatch in the floor. As they stepped quietly out of my sight to take their turn at jumping, each one shook my hand vigorously as he passed.

In a very short time I was left alone, and very much alone I felt. The roar of the engines seemed to grow louder, the controls seemed heavier and the aircraft seemed suddenly to be larger, more powerful, more sinister. "All out," I advised control.

"Circle and stand by," I was ordered. Then followed the loneliest few minutes of my life and I was glad to hear 'the voice' again. "Fly across the 'drome on an exact course of 080 degrees. Engage automatic pilot ('George'). When exact height and course being maintained – bale out!"

I welcomed the opportunity of having something to occupy my attention and spent quite a long time adjusting the controls until the aircraft was flying 'hands off' at exactly 5,000 feet on an exact course of 080 degrees.

I engaged the automatic pilot, made a few final adjustments and then, as the 'drome appeared ahead, I hurried down into the bomb aimer's compartment where the escape hatch lay open, almost invitingly.

I was glad that I had taken the precaution of having my parachute hooked on before the crew had gone and, with a final quick check, I crouched beside the hatch, my hand already clutching the steel handle of the ripcord. I sat on the edge of the hole and let my legs dangle. The rush of air immediately forced them against the underside of the aircraft and I allowed myself to roll out into space, head first.

I did four complete somersaults, seeing the four exhaust pipes of the aircraft glowing each time I turned over. I was counting one, two, three, four at each somersault and suddenly thought that I must be near the ground. I pulled the ripcord handle and it came away so easily that I remember gazing at my hand, which was still holding the handle, and thinking, "It hasn't worked!" Before I could feel any panic there was a rush of silk past my face, followed by a not too violent jerk and I found myself dangling comfortably under the silken canopy.

I felt a surge of absolute exhilaration and was grinning like a fool. I wish I could describe the feeling of power, of remoteness, of unreality, of sheer exuberance I felt. No wonder our paratroops are such grand fighters!

There was no rush of air to indicate downward speed and it came as quite a shock, on looking down, to see a field rushing up to meet me out of the darkness and a few scattered houses taking shape around it. I had hardly time to brace myself when I hit the ground, heels first, travelling backwards. I sat down with a bump, rolled over in a backward somersault and pressed the release catch to prevent being hauled along the ground. There was no need: the parachute flopped lazily over me and I lay still for a few moments, not believing that this was reality.

I bundled the parachute under my arm and trudged across the field in unwieldy flying boots towards a large house about fifty yards distant. Fortunately there was a telephone in the house and the old couple, whom I eventually wakened, plied me with questions and cups of tea until the car arrived from the 'drome.

All the crew had reported safe landings and some had already been picked up by the time I returned. There were many theories put forward regarding the part failure of the engines and it was finally decided that they must have been running on 'hot' air, a device used under icing conditions, which reduces the amount of power to each engine.

All this time the aircraft was flying steadily onwards towards enemy territory and we learned later that the Observer Corps had plotted its journey more than halfway across the North Sea, maintaining the height and course I had set.

The Duty Navigator who had given me the course computed that the fuel supply would last until the aircraft was somewhere in the Hamburg area. We can only guess the outcome.

Before abandoning the aircraft I had switched on every available light, and I often wonder what the Luftwaffe and the German AA gunners must have thought when they saw a large bomber approaching from the direction of England, lit up like a Christmas tree, flying steadily on a fixed course and blithely ignoring flak, searchlights and fighter attacks.

I like to think that 'George', guided by his saintly namesake, would point the aircraft in its final dive towards some important military objective, the destruction of which may have contributed in some way to the dramatic collapse of the Reich war machine which was soon to follow.

ALMOST AIRBORNE *The end of the runway looms closer as this heavily-laden Lanc of 419 'Moose' Squadron RCAF pounds along at Middleton St George early in 1944, with 3,000 rpm and +9 inches of boost on the clock. The pilot is already applying coarse right rudder to counteract the swing to port.*

AIRBORNE BY NIGHT *In the gathering darkness, a 467 Squadron RAAF Lanc (above right) thunders away from Waddington as the tower gives a green to the next one already lined up for take-off, for a raid on Bourg-Leopold May 11/12, 1944.*
"Brakes on – Brakes off; Undercarriage up; 2,850 rpm and plus 6."

AIRBORNE BY DAY *"Undercarriage up" and the wheels are already tucking backwards as this 218 'Gold Coast' Squadron Lanc (right) climbs out of Chedburgh for a daylight op on Oberhausen in December 1944 skippered by F/Lt "Wag" Walker. A loss of an engine at this, a critical point of take-off in a heavily-laden kite, could spell disaster.*

BLOW UP *In a mighty mushroom of smoke and debris, a 4,000-pounder goes up at Croft on March 22, 1945, taking a Canadian-built Lanc X, KB832 WL-F of 434 'Bluenose' Squadron with it. Caught by an extraordinarily fierce gust of wind on take-off, the Lanc was lifted sideways and dumped on the right-hand side of the runway, coming to rest, minus undercarriage, in a cloud of earth and flame. F/O Horace Payne, RCAF, and crew escaped unhurt, but the bombload soon began to simmer as the 1,500 4lb incendiaries caught fire. 37 minutes later, at 11.27 hrs, the 'cookie' went off. Eight of 434's Lancasters had already taken off, but this crash prevented the rest of the Squadron from getting airborne for the raid on Hildesheim.*

CLIMB OUT *With: "Undercarriage up, lights out; Safety speed; Flaps up; 2,650 and plus four"; the pilot eases into a climbing turn to port to clear the airfield.*

EN ROUTE

TIME TO SET COURSE SKIPPER – ZERO NINER ZERO MAGNETIC *In the last moments of daylight, a Lanc turns away to set course for enemy territory. Before doing so, it may have circled as far inland as the West Midlands to gain height and to wait for the rest of the main stream to join up. The sky would be full of heavily-laden aircraft, climbing and circling for perhaps an hour, straining upwards. Then suddenly, at a given moment, all* *would turn eastwards, the Merlins would fade, and the sky would be suddenly empty and strangely silent.*

Once airborne, you would be on your own in the dark. Seldom would you see another aircraft save over the target and then perhaps just a fleeting glimpse of some poor chaps caught in a cone of searchlights and being peppered by flak; or a fiery red glow as a night fighter claims another victim.

EN ROUTE – HIGH LEVEL *No
words can adequately describe this scene
as a MkII wends its way towards the
North Sea. What lies in store for the
crew beyond the mountainous cloudscape?*

BOMBER COUNTRY *A 'G-H' radar-equipped 'vic' leader (distinguished by two yellow bars on the fins) from 149 'East India' Squadron, Methwold, just airborne over typical East Anglian countryside, spring 1945, waiting for the remainder of the vic to form up before setting course.*

149, like most 3 Group Lanc Squadrons, consisted of three flights, and this example, a BI, HK793, is from 'C' Flight.

Aft of the enlarged bomb bay is a hatch for a .303in machine gun (some kites had .5in) and many 3 Group Lancs not fitted with H2S had such a feature. The extra gunner was more often than not a 'spare bod' some of whom were Leading Aircraftsmen, even though the lowest rank of aircrew was officially Sergeant.

PLOUGHING A FURROW *This Lanc soon hit trouble. On take-off from Balderton for a raid on Politz, February 8, 1945, BI, PD348 9J-B, lost an engine just as she left the runway. Staggering along, fully laden, at dangerously low level, only a knot or two above stalling speed, F/O George Edge and his 227 Squadron crew were unable to turn back or gain height. Not daring to jettison the bombs for fear of blowing themselves out of the sky with their own 'cookie', they somehow nursed the kite along until a crash landing became inevitable. She was successfully pancaked in a cabbage field at Heath House Farm, near Bircham Newton in Norfolk. Miraculously, the bombs did not go off. Not surprisingly, the crew were in an extremely shocked state and when reached by the rescue party were discovered playing an imaginary game of cricket beside their crashed Lanc, quite oblivious to the seven tons of high explosives simmering nearby.*

OUTWARD BOUND *Climbing steadily away from the coast, this 619 Squadron Lanc heads eastwards, leaving the rear gunner to ponder on the view of Skegness pier below. Will he ever see it again?*

Once out to sea the guns will be tested. The 'can' has already been passed round – just as well to be comfortable.

Late guests

In the spring of 1945, the allied armies were closing for the kill, and Hitler's vaunted Third Reich was crumbling fast.

Those aircrew unlucky enough to be shot down and to fall into civilian or police hands could expect little mercy. The German propaganda ministry had been working overtime inflaming the people against the 'Terror Fliers' and to be caught could mean a beating, stoning or even a lynching.

Those captured by the Wehrmacht often had to join in the retreat, suffering constant strafing by marauding allied fighters. For them it meant a succession of jails, barns or compounds. Many of the PoW camps were being abandoned and the inmates force-marched deep into the Fatherland.

At Mildenhall on Sunday, April 22, 1945, F/Lt Edward Cook and crew were to lead a 3 Group attack on Bremen. The British Second Army were within a few miles of the port, so little trouble was expected. The war seemed almost over. In fact, as they took off for the evening attack – their 28th operation – in Lanc BI, HK770 GI-T, they wondered if the war would end before they could complete their tour. Little did they realise what adventures lay ahead.

The following account is by the skipper, but each of his crew had similar lively experiences.

I was leading the 3 Group attack. At this stage of the war the Germans had become very cunning with their flak. They would throw up a green marker, and visually measure the distance between its bursting point and the leading aircraft. This usually happened in the last three minutes of the GH bombing run, and with minor adjustments they had a bead on the leading aircraft. As the whole principle of the GH radar demanded extremely accurate flying, evasive tactics were out of the question at this point. At 18.28 on that Sunday evening, two minutes short of the target, at 19,500 feet, there was a direct hit on my port outer engine. Fortunately, it hit on the outside of the nacelle away from the fuselage, and blew the engine out of the wing. It also took about six feet off the wing tip. The aircraft went into a steep diving turn to port, with fire in the wreckage where the engine had been. Normal fire drill accomplished nothing, and with the aircraft out of control, things began to look serious. I gave the order to jettison bombload at 18,000, and fortunately the bomb bay was open. With bombs gone, conditions did not improve and at 12,000 I made the decision to bale out the crew.

As my navigator, Mel Parry, went past to exit from the nose hatch, I pointed out to him that he would likely be a little late for church as it was already past 18.30. 'Mac' MacLaren, my flight engineer, inadvertently grabbed his chest-pack parachute by the ripcord instead of the lifting handle, and the only advice I could give him was to go out backwards through the nose hatch and hold as much of the parachute as he could until he was clear of the aircraft. This was apparently successful.

When everyone had gone, I made my first attempt to get out myself, and found it impossible. The moment I let the controls go to get out of the seat, the aircraft went into a screaming dive and started to roll. One good thing that this did was to put out the fire, and I decided that the only thing to do was to crash-land. I was very busy during the next couple of minutes, but fortunately, by a judicious mixing of trimtabs and controls, found that I was able to fly more or less in a straight line, admittedly with left wing low, but maintaining height at approximately 5,000 feet. With fingers crossed, I set course to the west.

I could hold the aircraft fairly steady between 105 and 110 knots without too much vibration. The course I set was as close as possible about 260 degrees true because I remembered that the surface wind was about 340 degrees true. There were heavy clouds to the south and I did not want to steer 270 degrees because of the long sea crossing. I thought the course I was steering would just about clear the Dutch Salient. I had no maps, and it was very annoying to see them floating past me and out of the front hatch, with all sorts of other papers. I had to steer a zigzag course through the cloud lanes and of course it was impossible to leave the controls to fire the Very pistol or switch on the IFF. I called 'Mayday' every three minutes on both UHF and VHF without reply for about 45 minutes before throwing my helmet away.

The clouds ahead thickened up without any lane, and the base looked to be about 2,000 feet. The port inner engine started to splutter; number 2 tank registered empty; number 1 registered about 30 gallons. I hit the balance cock but decided to come below the cloud base. It was now 20.45 hrs. The port inner engine was losing power rapidly. I was using full right rudder to keep straight, but still thought I might make England, as I was maintaining height. I suddenly sighted a forest out to starboard and thought I recognised Appeldoorn, so eased to the south, but 20 millimetre tracers scored hits on the rear of the fuselage. I was in Indian territory! I was soon out of range but three minutes later the 20 millimetres opened up again ahead of me. A Lancaster at 1,800 feet is, of course a sitting duck. I was hit repeatedly and suddenly the starboard outer engine choked. As I got out of the seat the altimeter registered 1,200 feet, and although I went headfirst from the pilot's deck through the escape hatch in the nose, I doubt if my parachute started to open at more than 800 feet.

The aircraft crashed, exploded and burst into flames just before I came down, about two miles ahead of me, at 20.50 hrs. There were two explosions, and I later learned from the Germans that at least one and probably two of my 500lb bombs must have hung up; so it was just as well I never made that belly landing.

I was loose in the dykes for some little time, but unfortunately nightfall came just a shade too late, and I was caught in enfilading fire from each end of a dyke where I had arrived by a zigzag process.

The nearest village of any size to my point of entry into Holland is a place called Culemborg which is about 15 miles north-west of Tiel on the river Wall. The flak batteries which brought me down were at a place called Rijswijk. My plane came down a little south of the midpoint of a line between Maurik and Rijswijk. In 1959 I went back to the area, visited the farm and stood on the spot where the three Merlin engines are still buried, having sunk into the marsh when the Germans blew the dykes in late April. The ancient furrows, three of of them, are still visible, although there is no sign of the cow which I understand was blown to pieces by the exploding bombs. Parts of HK770 may easily be recognised holding up fences in the vicinity.

I touched down about 20.50 hrs on the south-west side of the Amsterdam Bovenrijn Canal, 90 degrees from Zoelmond about 4 kilometres, 330 degrees from Tiel about 8 kilometres, or 100 degrees from Culemborg 11 kilometres. The aircraft came down across the Canal, 075 degrees from my landing point, about 3 kilometres. I was picked up about 21.05 or 21.10 hrs by the Wehrmacht and taken about 6 kilometres west, to a farm at the other side of Zoelmond. There I slept the night in a barn with six German soldiers, had some black bread and cheese for breakfast, and was taken about 10.00 to the Divisional Headquarters of the Wehrmacht which was about two kilometres farther west. I had lunch with a Lieutenant-Colonel and a Major, was taken back to the village, and then, with two guards on bicycles, walked about 10 kilometres in a northwesterly direction, through Culemborg, and across the river, which I think is called the Neder Rijn, by cantilevered bridge.

Walking in flying boots was not exactly my idea of fun, so I took a stand and refused to walk any farther. The guards were rather nonplussed, but finally stopped a farm wagon and I rode in great style for about another nine kilometres to a small town. There I was introduced to a rather nasty SS man and had a little trouble. How-

ever, I maintained my position and refused to walk, and finally, to my great surprise and joy, a captured American jeep was provided to take me to Utrecht. Within another hour I was in the Utrecht jail, and by this time it was 21.00 hrs.

Since lunch time I had been carefully carrying one-quarter of a loaf of black bread, half an ounce of butter and one piece of cheese. From here on I should point out that the daily rations which were handed out, no matter where we were, at 12 noon, were one bowl (a little larger than a cup) of hot water which was called soup, two slices of black bread, two cubic inches of cheese and one cubic inch of meat (I think it was horse meat). Sundays were always feast days when the soup had meat in it.

So I arrived in Utrecht on the night of Monday April 23. There were two American pilots in the jail with me and on the 26th we were moved by truck to Aalsmeer. Moves were always by night. The total officer complement at Aalsmeer was 17. There were seven Americans, three other Englishmen, a Dutchman, a Frenchman, two Poles and two Canadians, mostly pilots. I do not have an accurate record of the dates, but it is my impression that we moved from Aalsmeer about April 30, and travelled through the night to Huisduinen (Den Helder). Here we were handed over to the German Navy, and lived deep in the bowels of the earth adjacent to the submarine pens. I seem to remember that we were here for about five days, living like moles, and coming up for sunshine and air a couple of hours a day.

Then one afternoon, I imagine it was about May 6, 16 of us were put on a boat, leaving our senior officer, Brigadier-General Bartlett, to fate unknown, and headed out to the north-east and what we knew damn well were minefields. Just before dawn we went ashore at what we found later was Terschelling Island. We did learn later that the intention was to take us to Borkum by one or two night stages. Fortunately we never made it, and I say fortunately because we understand that on May 9/10 all the prisoners at Borkum were shot.

I suppose that in the three days we were on the island we made sufficient nuisance of ourselves to exhaust the patience of the German Captain. We were first moved into the hotel, after living on the beach overnight, and finally to cut a long story short, on condition we gave an undertaking as gentlemen to absolve the German Navy of any responsibility, we were supplied with a German E-boat, an Ensign, two crew and put overboard off the Dutch mainland. By devious means and various routes we all eventually found our way back to England.

The report of the Constable of Government Police follows overleaf.

"Report re an Allied plane, crashed in Maurik on Sunday, April 22nd, 1945.

"On a Sun- or Holy-day in the second part of April 1945 – an investigation proved that April 22nd, 1945 was a Sunday – I was in an house between the villages Maurik and Rijswijk, when I was told that a low flying plane was approaching.

"Owing to the fact that we had no more seen any German plane for months and the allied planes were always flying on safer heights, there was a great interest, as well from the public as from the soldiers of the German Wehrmacht, who were quartered in the neighbourhood.

"I then saw that apparently an allied bomber came flying from north-east and I got the impression that the plane had been shot already as it was flying very low. However, I did not understand why the pilot was flying south-west, as by crossing south the plane would have been above allied territory within 10 kilometres distance.

"When the plane, which flied in the produced part of the river the Rhine, had passed me, the anti-aircraft guns of the Germans, placed in Rijswijk near the canal-bridge and in Wijk bij Duurstede near the ferry, opened a violent fire on the plane. Suddenly the plane turned south and thereafter I saw a parachute hanging in the air. In the meantime the plane returned and came in my direction again. Apparently it had been shot by the anti-aircraft guns, the low flying colossus being an easy prey for same.

"The plane lost rapidly height and flied towards me.

Thundering, roaring and raging it made a last turn in southern direction and at a distance of about 400 metres from me it came down in a meadow, where it got fire.

"Weaponed German soldiers and a numerous public ran to that place. While it was then better for me not to draw the public attention to my person, I looked after the parachute. I saw lowering same slowly, drifting away in south-eastern direction, where it disappeared behind an orchard.

"The plane having burnt out after about half an hour, the Germans released the spot and the carbonized wreckage. Later on that evening I was informed that there had been no crew in the plane anymore. It was said that the plane had been shot already above Germany and that the crew had then left the machine, one pilot excepted. This pilot would have landed just over the new canal from Tiel till Wijk bij Duurstede at the frontier of the municipality Maurik, within the municipality Zoelen. The distance between these two 'landing places' is 3 till 4 kilometres.

"Of the plane, the parts of which were spreaded over a distance of more than 100 metres, there is no more remained than some carbonized parts. Everybody tried to get hold of such a part for souvenir, a bolt or another piece of metal being sufficient already.

"The spot where the plane crashed is very well visible, the more so as there are still lying remainders of the plane there.

"Lienden, May 26th, 1947.
"The Constable of Government Police,
(De Wachtmeester der Rijkspolitie)
w.g. Th. W. v. Schaik."

EN ROUTE – LOW LEVEL *Low flying over the sea could be very exacting. On a calm sunny day the surface would shimmer, with a veil of haze on the horizon, while at night it tended to have a mirror effect and the slightest lapse of concentration could send the props churning up the spray. Tail trimmers would be set well back. Part of the 94-strong force (under the appropriate code name Operation 'Robinson') is seen over the Bay of Biscay en route to the Schneider Armament works at Le Creusot near the French-Swiss Border, for the daring dusk attack of October 17, 1942. In the foreground is the 106 Squadron contingent, ZN-P being an old warrior and still having the unfaired mid-upper turret of only the very earliest Lancs delivered.*

ALL EYES PEELED *An unusual view from the astrodome looking forward, with the D/F (direction-finding) loop in the foreground.*

TUCKING WELL IN *Keeping it tight, F/O J. Rosanski, pilot of BI LL807, 'N-Nuts' of 300 'Masovian' Squadron from Faldingworth, tucks in close en route to the target in the spring of 1944 (below).*

Unique in being the only Polish Lancaster squadron, 300 set up a magnificent record despite high losses and left an indelible name in the annals of Bomber Command. A small replica of the Polish Air Force red and white insignia appears on the nose.

THE SKY IS A BIG PLACE
Looking like a stream of black ants over solid 10/10ths cloud, Lancs from 106 Squadron, Metheringham, on their way to a target early in 1945.

The sky may appear empty but the allied fighter umbrella is there, weaving contrails high above the gaggle.

THE SKY WAS FULL OF 'EM
Lancasters on a mass 'daylight' in support of the allied armies in France in the summer of 1944.

OVER ENEMY TERRITORY
Mouths run dry and that 'butterflies' feeling increases as the target draws near.
   The first puffs of flak appear as 75 and 90 Squadrons hold formation over France on a 'daylight' in July 1944.

WINDOW DROPPING *In a sky dotted with flak puffs, a mixed force of Lancs and Halifaxes emerge from a drifting cloud of tinfoil or 'window', used to baffle enemy radar.*

ON TARGET

HAMBURG BY NIGHT *Photography at night was not easy but with the introduction of the photoflash, pictures like these became possible. At 18,000 feet the camera in another kite catches a Lanc over Hamburg on January 30/31, 1943. On this night the weather took a hand, when one of the worst gales for many years raged over the North Sea. This was also the first occasion H2S was used operationally, not by Lancs but by PFF Stirlings and Halifaxes.*

PHOTOFLASH *A confusion of lights, fires, markers, bursting 'cookies', flak and smoke over Pforzheim, February 23/24, 1945. The streets and buildings are briefly revealed as a photoflash lights up the sky and ground. A Lancaster is just visible several thousand feet below.*

BURNING CITY *A Lancaster is silhouetted over Hanover on the night of October 8/9, 1943. The Sallstrasse is clearly highlighted, running diagonally across the picture. A force of 500 Lancasters could drop over 3,000 tons of bombs in a matter of minutes.*

Lightning strike

related by Bill Breckenridge and W. B. ('Biff') Baker

By far the greatest menace on night operations was the enemy night fighter. High in the sub-zero blackness brave young men fought out duels to the death, neither side giving, nor expecting, any quarter. As the RAF fighter pilots had fought so determinedly over Britain in 1940, so did the Luftwaffe night fighter crews fight to save their homeland.

Equipped with only .303 machine guns, our bombers faced the 30mm and 20mm cannon and 7.9mm machine guns of their adversaries – twin-engined Bf110s and Ju88s in the main, but later joined by Do217s, He219s and single-engined Bf109s and Fw190s.

On paper the bomber force stood little chance, but it was argued that, while some would fall to fighters and flak, the sky was a big place and most would get through undetected.

It was a long and bitter struggle, the balance swinging to and fro with constantly changing tactics, ruses and diversions.

Life or death often depended on the keen eyes of the bomber crew, particularly the gunners, who, even in ideal weather conditions, could see no further than 300 yards or so. If visibility was poor, the lurking fighter could suddenly appear, a mere 50 yards away, with all guns blazing, raking the hapless aircraft from stem to stern with devastating effect and giving the crew little chance.

However, by good crew co-ordination, evasive action could be taken and many a crew owed their lives to the famous 'corkscrew' in which the gunners yelled instructions to the pilot, who then threw the kite about the sky, diving and twisting to a set pattern.

Even if the fighter was not seen in time, quick reactions could still save the day. The story below illustrates a grim combat combining superb skill, gallantry and tenacity – plus the necessary element of luck – of a typical well-drilled RAF crew.

As P/O Bill Breckenridge of 626 Squadron and his crew set course for Berlin in Lancaster BI, ME584 UM-Y², in the gathering dusk of January 30, 1944, a life-and-death struggle lay but a few hours ahead.

The crew comprised three Scotsmen, three Canadians and an Englishman. This was their sixth trip together

80

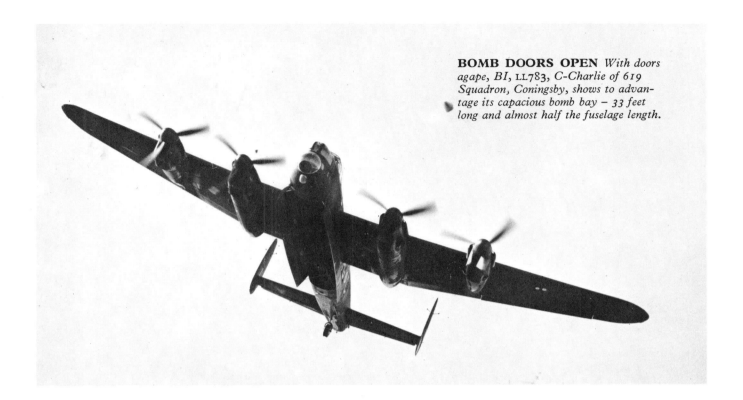

BOMB DOORS OPEN *With doors agape, BI, LL783, C-Charlie of 619 Squadron, Coningsby, shows to advantage its capacious bomb bay – 33 feet long and almost half the fuselage length.*

and already they had been to Berlin three times, besides Brunswick and Magdeburg for variety.

It was a pleasant evening with little cloud, which suited the Canadian navigator, Jack Meek. He was able to get several accurate winds with their direction and strength.

They had no trouble getting to the target. Some combats were seen as they came in from the north and swung in, well on time, at 20,000 feet, with the moon above on the starboard side. There was plenty of flak and the low clouds, with tops to about 8,000 feet, were lit up by searchlights.

They had settled on the bombing run when suddenly an unseen fighter attacked at close range, perhaps 200 yards, on the starboard side. The kite shuddered as shells tore into the metal, making a terrific din, so loud it could be heard above the engines.

The mid-upper turret was smashed and 'Biff' Baker, the Englishman, a keen amateur boxer, was hit on the side of his face, his helmet and oxygen mask torn away. The rear turret was badly holed and the Canadian, Joe Schwartz, severely wounded by a piece of exploding shrapnel in his foot. Both he and 'Biff' Baker soon lapsed into unconsciousness. The intercom to the rear end was u/s so those forward did not know what was happening aft.

Bill, the skipper, took immediate evasive action, diving to starboard. On recovering, he again levelled out on the bombing run and Val Poushinsky, the Canadian bomb aimer, dropped the load on the estimated position of the markers seen before the attack.

A minute later they were again attacked, perhaps by the same fighter, but this time from the port quarter, and at 400 yards. With his two gunners out cold, though he did not know it, the skipper had no warning but dived to port on observing the first tracers coming in.

The kite was pitching around all over the place as the skipper tried everything he knew to shake off the fighter. The navigator, crouched down behind the skipper, was doubled up from hits and instinctively grabbed his chute before passing out.

Things were certainly happening fast. They could not shake off the searchlights or flak, let alone the fighter. It was a madhouse, with the terrific noise of exploding shells and screaming engines.

After a further two minutes, the fighter found them again. He closed in from the starboard quarter, at 400 yards, and let forth yet another devastating barrage. This time the skipper was hit, a passing bullet grazing his legs.

The original course was resumed from the target

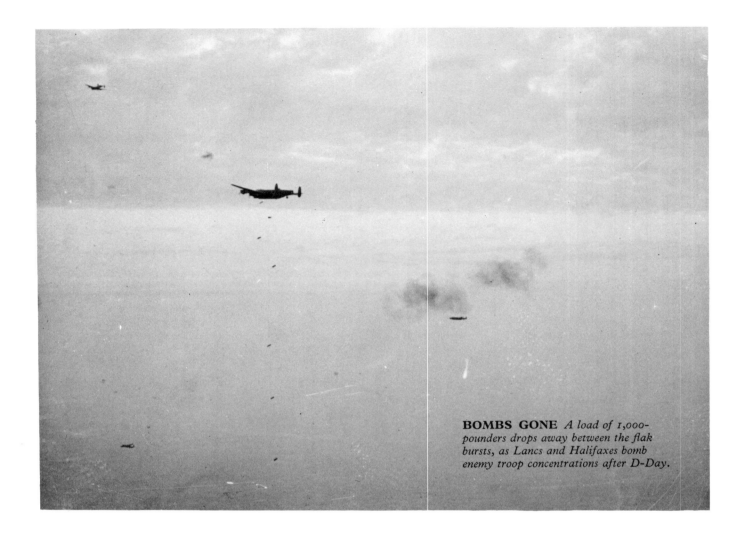

BOMBS GONE *A load of 1,000-pounders drops away between the flak bursts, as Lancs and Halifaxes bomb enemy troop concentrations after D-Day.*

area after further violent manœuvres, but three minutes later came the fourth attack. Again they were hit but the range was now about 500 yards.

By the time the fighter was shaken off, their height was down to 15,000 feet. No further attacks came as the skipper, completely unflurried and flying his battered kite as if on a cross-country trip, got away from the area as fast as possible.

Slowly the crew began to recover. Jimmy, the wireless op, was found slumped over his set. He was warm but unconscious, so he was given first aid. Not until they landed would they know he was past help.

Jack Meek regained consciousness to discover that he had two wounds. One was in his shoulder. The other was caused by shrapnel which went clean through his middle, entering at the right side of his back and emerging at the left front, just below his chest, missing his heart by inches. Though he knew he was badly hit, he would not know the full extent of his injuries until they landed.

'Biff' Baker and Joe Schwartz also revived. The latter extricated himself from his turret, crawled up the fuselage to the rest-bed, but again collapsed. Val Poushinsky rendered first aid to both Schwartz and Meek before taking up a position in the astrodome. Meanwhile, 'Biff' Baker clambered into the still-serviceable rear turret, even though he was injured and without oxygen.

To make matters worse, the rear fuselage began to fill with smoke soon after leaving the target area. Alex Stephenson, the engineer, went aft and put out the fire.

The kite was in a fearful state. The hydraulic system had been shot away. The bomb doors would not close, nor, as they found later, would the wheels lower. One petrol tank was holed, three rev counters and three boost gauges useless, as were the direction finder and gyro-compass. The elevators and rudders were also badly damaged.

Jack Meek's navigational gear was wrecked, but the accurate data on the winds on the route-in now came in handy. All he could do was dead reckon on these, but in reverse. He could not hold up the sextant for his left arm kept dropping down, finally becoming completely useless.

Luckily, his figures were good for they took them right back on track. He also took observation of landmarks he knew. When he saw searchlights or flak over German territory he would say to the skipper, "That's Hanover. Go so many minutes in such a direction then bear so much west." Two hours after leaving Berlin he was able to get a Gee fix despite feeling lightheaded from loss of blood and lack of oxygen. They were now over the Zuider Zee and only three miles off track.

The open bomb doors caused a lot of drag and the skipper could not get much speed, though he did manage to hold altitude. All were chilled through, due to the many gaping holes, while the lack of oxygen was taking its toll.

Over the North Sea the electrical system caught fire, but the mid-upper and flight engineer succeeded in extinguishing the fire after a short, fierce battle.

Thirty miles from the English coast the Gee packed up. A distress signal was sent out and in less than a minute the searchlights were homing them in to Docking, on the Norfolk coast. A crash-landing was inevitable. The wheels would not come down, as the air pressure was blown away, and frantic efforts by the skipper and engineer resisted all attempts to unlock them.

With the crew at crash positions, the skipper brought the kite in, but she was difficult to control and he had to overshoot. On the second attempt he brought her in like a baby, ran forward on the tailwheel, nose well up, then slowed. The open bomb doors hit the ground, snapped shut, and suddenly all was quiet. They were down. There was no fire.

BIRD'S-EYE VIEW *of a Lanc BX, KB745 VR-V, of 419 'Moose' Squadron, RCAF, skippered by F/O A. C. Rokeby, RCAF, gracefully silhouetted over the remains of a flying bomb site in the summer of 1944. In this fine picture, the dinghy stowage is clearly outlined in the starboard wing. This Lanc was almost new at the time, and the glossier finish of the Canadian-built machines is still relatively fresh.*

KRUPPS OF ESSEN *Words which
struck a cold chill when announced at
briefing. No target in Germany was
more vital; none was more heavily
defended. Although frequently pounded
by Bomber Command it was mid-1944
before any real impression began to be
made, so fiercely did the Germans fight
to preserve the country's major arma-
ments-producing complex.*

BOMBS AWAY *"Steady, steady,
left – left, steady, bombs gone, bomb
doors closed." The skipper of this 49
Squadron Lanc from Fulbeck will be
holding her steady for the aiming point
photograph as the 1,000-pounders
hurtle downwards on to an already
doomed V-site in France.*

*Daylight sorties by Lancs on Germany
alone totalled 23,204 for the loss of only
179, such was the allied domination of
the air.*

THE DESOLATION OF WAR
Not a chimney; not a roof; not a building untouched; the destruction almost complete. A tragic scene so typical in the industrial Ruhr which received the constant and unerring attention of Bomber Command. This picture of Wesel was taken soon after the war's close, from the rear turret of a Lancaster carrying ground crew on a 4-hour "Cooks Tour" of places which had hitherto been distant names to them.

PLASTERED *All that remained of the V1 site at Siracourt in the Pas-de-Calais following the Canadian 6 Group attack of July 6, 1944. The Allies waged a massive and prolonged campaign, code-named Noball, against the V1 and V2 sites, which reached its peak in July and August 1944. The brunt of the attacks fell on Bomber Command, the Lancaster squadrons in particular, and in a 53-day period, 179 separate attacks were made, involving well over 10,000 sorties. Such was the intensity of operations in this period that a Lanc crew could complete a tour in three months.*

85

THE WAY BACK

HEADING FOR HOME *Dusk gathers as a G-H leader from 195 Squadron, Wratting Common, nears the English coast on return from an attack on Dortmund, March 12, 1945. This picture was taken by the navigator of another kite in the 'vic'.*

On this raid two Bomber Command records were set: 1,107 aircraft participated, dropping 4,851 tons – the highest number of aircraft and highest tonnage respectively on one target.

THE LAST SECONDS *as flak claims another victim, a kite from 75 'New Zealand' Squadron, Mepal, on the edge of the stream, shudders as she is hit by a direct burst over France in July 1944. A few seconds later she disintegrated.*

The Cathedral and I survived

Fred Smooker

Fate moves in mysterious ways. Many men alive today still wonder why they were singled out for survival while their comrades perished.

Most have no idea how they escaped from their stricken Lancaster and, try as they might, there is an unaccountable gap in their lives, varying from several minutes to an hour or more.

If the aircraft received a direct hit from flak, there was little chance of anyone surviving, save perhaps the pilot if he was wearing a seat-type chute (standard issue by 1944 and later extended to rear gunners). He alone might find himself floating to earth, hanging from a tree, lying in a field or snowdrift, badly shaken but alive, not quite knowing how or why.

Flak or fighters might wreck the bomber or set it on fire, giving the crew some chance of donning their parachutes. However, if the kite went into an uncontrollable dive or spin, none could move, let alone escape, due to terrific centrifugal forces, but one could still be thrown out, perhaps as the aircraft exploded.

Others were thrown clear in crashes, ending up in such unlikely places as haystacks, pigsties, mudflats, or crashing through the roof of a building – sometimes receiving no more than a few scratches and bruises.

When, in the early hours of July 10, 1943, Lancaster BIII, ED720 ZN-R, of 106 Squadron, Syerston, exploded near Cambrai while returning from Cologne, only the bomb aimer was destined to live. As this account reveals, his experiences left an indelible impression on his mind.

Our American pilot, F/O Gene Rosner, was in the RCAF and had returned us safely from some eighteen operations, the last one being on Cologne on June 28, 1943.

After this operation we were due for some leave – aircrew in those days were given nine days' leave every six weeks.

Following interrogation after our Cologne trip and a bacon and egg breakfast, we all tidied up and headed our separate ways to wherever we spent our leave.

On returning a week later, our skipper, who had on numerous occasions been pestering the USAAF authorities to accept him into their ranks, told us he would be returning to London to remuster, and that he would try to get us some more leave while he was away.

On his return from London two days later, he was wearing the olive green outfit of an American First Lieutenant. He had been accepted by his own mob but was to complete his tour of operations with the RAF. Somehow, he was now a stranger to me, and to crown all, operations that night were again on Cologne, and we were to take along a second dickey pilot for experience before he took his own crew on ops. It was his first op.

The met. men told us there would be cumulonimbus clouds up to 20,000 feet over the target. We would not be worried by fighters, because they would be grounded. It was to be an all-Lancaster effort, 'Wanganui' type, bombing through ten-tenths cloud.

There were two types of bombing those days, 'Paramatta' and 'Wanganui'. For 'Paramatta' the Pathfinders laid coloured markers on the ground; red in the middle, surrounded by green, and bomb aimers aimed at the patchwork of red and green markers on the ground. The 'Wanganui' type was used when the target was covered by cloud. The Pathfinders dropped first a white parachute flare which we had to track over and alter course for the target area. Next came a green flare, over which we had to track because it was the run-in to the target which was indicated by a final red flare. Using special settings on the bombsight, bomb aimers had to aim at this red flare. This method was said to be more accurate than visual ground bombing, and that we could obliterate one square mile of target area by such concentration. To me, this type of bombing was also more dangerous, because the Germans knew the height of clouds, and they knew the Lancasters' ceiling, hence all flak was concentrated accordingly.

Our trip over the North Sea was uneventful and, sure enough, over the Belgian coast we were over the clouds, as forecast.

The white flare was dropped at some point north of Cologne where we turned south for the target. Then things began to happen. Searchlights turned the clouds into a dazzling white sea of snow. We began to see that we were not alone on our journey of destruction; in front and to either side could be seen the black silhouettes of our accompanying Lancasters, from whom no help was possible in the event of disaster. The sea of dazzling white was now beginning to be splashed with jagged cherry-red flashes which disintegrated into red-hot coals. The green flare appeared directly ahead. We were right on track and so was the flak. The jagged flashes were now all around us, and I could feel my inside begin its usual churning and my flesh and skin begin to tighten, whilst all my instincts told me to cringe and curl up into a ball.

The red flare appeared ahead; the pilot told me our airspeed and altitude over the intercom, while I busied myself setting the special adjustments to the bombsight.

By now we had ceased our continuous climbing and diving, weaving to port and starboard, and were flying straight and level over a white shiny carpet mottled with an angry red glow. One felt that one could get out and walk on it.

On my instructions, the bomb doors were opened to expose to the hail of red-hot metal being thrown at us, some five tons of high explosive and incendiary bombs. It seemed an eternity before the red flare came into my sights and I literally screamed, "Bombs gone."

Our Lancaster leapt a thousand feet higher on being released from the load in her belly. Within seconds we had the bomb doors closed, and our skipper again started our Lanc doing its jigging and weaving as if our lives depended upon it – which they did.

As we continued south, the worst of the holocaust was beginning to retreat behind us, and my taut nerves began to unwind as my brain told my organs to stop pumping adrenalin into my bloodstream.

"Keep a lookout for fighters," called the skipper to the gunners and myself, who was also front gunner, so I lay on my stomach in the bomb bay, gazing out of my huge Perspex dome.

When we reached a point on our south track, we turned on a westerly course for home, as plotted by our navigator. We were at some 22,000 feet. "Hello, skipper," called Ted Amor, our flight engineer. "The starboard outer is heating up."

"OK, Ted, keep an eye on it."

Minutes later, "Hello, skipper, the starboard outer temperature is worse and still climbing."

"OK, Ted, we'll have to feather the prop. Stop the engine and fly on three." After a while on three engines, the inside temperature of the plane became extremely low, and I found that one of my feet had numbed with the cold. Crouching in my bombing compartment I slipped off my boot and massaged my foot back to life.

"Hey, you guys," called the skipper. "I'm going to fly straight and level to keep up with the concentration." This concentration, although invisible, consisted of 200-odd other Lancs carrying out the same tactics as ourselves and, to prevent the German defences pinpointing on individuals, we all flew more or less at the same height and airspeed, but with our having only three engines our airspeed had dropped.

"Hey, bomb aimer," called our skipper. "Can you get at my feet and give them a massage?" Of course I could if I stood up in my compartment, his feet on the rudders being just at my shoulder height. I pulled on my left boot, and commenced my massaging operation on the skipper's feet. His feet were more important than mine in this position.

However, after five minutes or so, my own left foot was again numb, so I asked Ted Amor if he would come and take over the task of rubbing heat into the skipper's feet while I attended to my own. I think the skipper and I must have had damp socks, because no one else complained.

While Ted was doing his stuff on the skipper's foot, and I had my left boot off, rubbing my own foot, there was a terrific sickening crash. The Perspex dome in the nose disintegrated and a blast of ice-cold air gushed into my compartment where target maps and other sundry items started swirling about the place.

"There's a fighter!" yelled Jim Calder, our Canadian mid-upper gunner. I scrambled up into my front gun-turret but the controls were dead. I was helpless.

"The starboard inner's on fire," yelled Jim Calder.

"OK, Ted," said the skipper to the engineer. "Get back up here."

"Turn tó port," yelled Jim Calder. Ted Amor went back to his position alongside the skipper, when I think they feathered the starboard inner also, but suddenly our two port engines, I assume, started to speed up in an increasing crescendo until they were almost screaming.

Over the intercom came the skipper's voice. "Hey, you guys, we gotta bale out. Somebody get me my parachute. Bale out, bale out, bale out. . . ."

Our two screaming port engines suddenly stopped dead, and then came the most sickening of sensations – falling like a stone out of the sky in a dead aeroplane. I couldn't believe it even as I grabbed my chute and clipped it on. It was impossible! It couldn't be happening! I pulled at the handle of my escape hatch upon which a few minutes ago I had been squatting, massaging my left foot. The square hatch had wedged itself across the hole, and when kicking it free I realised I still had only one boot on.

Even then I was expecting the engines to restart. I didn't want to bale out, but to stay meant death. Gripping my ripcord handle in my right hand, I went feet first into the gaping hole in the floor. My legs were swept under the belly of the Lanc; away went my one remaining boot. My Mae West, which had inflated inadvertently, had me fast in the hole. I wriggled out like a woman wriggles out of a corset; with one hand still on my ripcord handle I was out. I didn't count ten – I pulled. I felt the plane pass over me, then I was whirling in space, cringing as if expecting a sudden violent shock which would jar the life out of me.

The sudden shock came, but I was still alive, although I had a burning pain in my groin. I was hanging in my parachute. Very gingerly I reached up both hands to grasp my shoulder straps and ease the weight off my groin. The chute gave a lurch and my heart almost stopped, then thud, I was on my back on terra firma, looking up at my parachute canopy slowly collapsing on to the ground in front of me.

I stood up, and immediately my legs gave way. My two ankles were lifeless. "God," I thought, "my ankles are broken." Some 500 yards away in the distance there was a terrific fire, crackling like a Browning machine-gun pouring out some 1,200 rounds a minute. My Lancaster, I guessed. Then came the awful doubt that surely no one else could have got out in time.

Overhead, a continuous droning of Lancasters. Come and get me I prayed, then reason returned. Hide your parachute and get away from your aircraft as fast as possible. I got to my feet again and this time stayed upright. Thank God, my ankles can't be broken, only sprained. Hobbling about I bundled up my parachute into a ball, but where to hide it, as I was in a field? Pulling up some long grass, I laid the chute in a hollow and covered it with grass. Not very well hidden, but I was going to have enough to do to walk, without lugging a parachute with me until I found a good hiding place.

Get away from the plane. I hobbled over the fields in my socks, gasping with pain as I went, until all was quiet – no burning Lancaster, no droning Lancasters overhead, only me in a field in France at about 03.30 hrs on July 10, 1943.

I was not caught by the Germans until after mid-September, and did not arrive in a PoW camp until about November 15. For 56 days I was held in solitary confinement in a Paris prison, but that is another story.

On my release from PoW camp in May 1945, the Americans flew us from Halle to Brussels, and for some reason we flew over Cologne. I know it was Cologne I was looking at out of the window of the Dakota because I was astounded to see the huge Cathedral, apparently unscathed, towering up out of a scene of utter devastation.

THREE OF OUR AIRCRAFT FAILED TO RETURN *Bomber Command paid a high price for its sustained offensive. The cost in lives was 47,000 aircrew killed (which represents 67 per cent of the total RAF casualties or 12 per cent of Britain's total service and civilian casualties).*

3,349 Lancasters failed to return from operations. Offset against this, they completed 156,308 sorties, almost half the total sorties of Bomber Command. These are the remains (above left) at NW Sch. Berle in Holland of pathfinder BIII, JB280 LQ-K, of 405 'Vancouver' Squadron RCAF from Gransden Lodge, shot down on a Berlin trip on the night of January 1/2, 1944.

The wreckage (above) of BIII, JB601 ZN-V from 106 Squadron, Metheringham, lying near Laneuville-a-Bayard in the Forêt-du-Val on the Swiss/French border, caught by a Bf109 on the way to Schweinfurt April 26/27, 1944.

First light would find investigation teams scouring the countryside for the twisted wreckage of aircraft brought down during the night.

The morbid task of sifting through the sorry remains would begin, in the hope of gleaning anything useful to German Intelligence.

Often, little was left, and this Lancaster, brought down by flak over the Dutch coast in May 1943, would reveal little of value. To this day it remains unidentified.

DOWN IN THE DRINK *Ditching at night could be a particularly hazardous experience, especially when the aircraft was badly damaged. Often it was a case of a few precious minutes before she sank, calling for a high degree of efficiency and thorough acquaintance with each stage of the ditching procedure and dinghy drill.*

In favourable circumstances, however, some Lancs stayed afloat for many hours and here is a BI, W4318 PM-C, which remained afloat for 33 hours.

On the night of April 13/14, 1943, Sgt Johnny Stoneman and crew of 103 Squadron ran out of petrol over the Channel on the way back from Spezia in Italy. Visibility was clear and the sea calm, apart from a slight swell. Approaching the water at 100 mph, with 20° of flap and all engines serviceable, the skipper ditched in an 85 mph glide, alighting along the crest of the swell.

The first impact was moderate, the second slight and the whole crew immediately took to the dinghy. After 3½ hours they were rescued by a Walrus and Air Sea Rescue launch. Being still afloat at daylight, an attempt at salvage was made and a ship tried to tow her into port. Getting too close, the ship chopped off her tail, when she tipped up on her nose and sank, 50 miles off Falmouth.

Seven more for the Goldfish Club *John Goldsmith*

No crew relished the thought of ditching in the cold, unfriendly sea. It was difficult enough to judge the swell in daylight, but at night it was even more hazardous.

A successful ditching demanded a high degree of skill on the part of the pilot and, once in the water, efficient crew drill was essential if they were to get clear of the sinking plane. It was to prepare crews for such an event that mock 'dry-land' ditchings were practised regularly.

Once in the dinghy their adventures really began. Rescue could be within a few hours in clear weather, but in heavy seas or misty conditions they could drift helplessly for days and quickly become victims of exposure.

If they were unfortunate enough to ditch near the enemy coast, a German rescue launch might reach them first, and the thought of spending the remainder of the war behind barbed wire was a gloomy prospect.

F/Lt Bob Etchells of 156 Squadron brought off a textbook ditching in his Lancaster BIII, PB302 GT-B, in the early hours of August 27, 1944. F/Lt Johnny Goldsmith, his Canadian navigator, wrote the following account a few days later while the event was still fresh in his mind.

In the afternoon of August 26, 1944, I was asked to fly with F Lt Etchells, as his navigator was sick. It was my first bombing operation that month, and I was glad of the opportunity to get in a little action. I was duty navigator that day, and I knew quite early that the target was Kiel, a very heavily defended target; but as most of the route was over water it seemed to be a pretty good trip. Take-off was at 20.00 hrs, so we were well over the North Sea by dusk. We were on track all the way to the target, and on time to within 10 seconds. The bombing run at 22,000 feet was good, although a slight overshoot, so we withheld our target markers but let the bombs go. A split second after the bomb aimer said, "Bombs away," the rear gunner yelled, "Enemy fighter astern. Corkscrew port." The fighter and our gunner opened fire practically simultaneously, opening range being about 300 yards. The rear gunner reported hits scored on the enemy fighter, a Junkers 88, and it was last seen falling away with flames coming from a position between its port engine and fuselage. The rear gunner claimed it as probably destroyed.

Our aircraft was hit in a number of places, and the damage was as follows: starboard outer propeller shot off, starboard inner engine hit and on fire – so the engine was stopped and propeller feathered, and the fire went out. Port tail assembly pretty well shot away.

Front of rear turret smashed, a two-foot square hole in the bottom of the fuselage near the tail turret, caused when one cannon shell exploded inside the fuselage near tail turret. Most of my navigation instruments made unserviceable, so I navigated to the North Sea by dead reckoning. As we still had the target markers, we decided to jettison them in the sea as it would be very dangerous to attempt a landing with them still on board. After jettisoning we found that the bomb doors could not be closed, also the port wheel had come down and could not be retracted. About an hour after leaving the target, the port inner engine caught fire, and we began losing altitude about 150 feet per minute, so 'ditching' was inevitable.

I figured our position at that time to be about 160 miles from England and 50 miles north of the Frisian Islands, held by Germany. This position was given to the wireless operator, but he could not get it off as an SOS because the fixed aerial was shot away and the trailing aerial was earthed on the open bomb doors. We were losing height rapidly, so crash positions were taken. Under the circumstances I doubt if any of the crew expected to live long. I know I didn't. Owing to the darkness and mist, it was almost impossible to see the water. We hit it nose first with a sudden smash, and the aircraft slid along for a short distance on its belly. The racket was terrible, and water was flying everywhere. We came to a stop with the nose under water, which seemed to be coming in everywhere.

Dinghy drill was carried out very well, and we all got out on the wing OK. The dinghy inflated all right, but we had difficulty getting it off the wing and into the water, as the wing was on a slant with the trailing edge in the air. We finally managed to get it into the water but found that it was under the tail, and it appeared that the aircraft would go under at any moment and take us with it. Three of us jumped into the water and started swimming with the dinghy in tow and, together with the aid of the others who were paddling, we finally got it away from the aircraft, which sank in a very short time. The estimated time the aircraft stayed afloat was about four minutes.

Now that we were safely down and into the dinghy, we began to take stock of the situation. It was still hard to believe that after all we'd been through we were still alive; in fact none of us was injured. At the time the sea was fairly calm, and I guess that was the main reason we were still alive. Our dinghy radio had been washed away, so there we were, in the middle of the North Sea and, as far as we knew, not a soul other than ourselves knew it. Things looked pretty black, but we had a good supply of water and emergency rations which we intended to make last for seven days. At the end of that time, if we were not found we figured we never would be. Most important of all we had a Very light pistol and about two dozen red flares. Helmets and boots were thrown overboard since there was some danger of their fittings puncturing the rubber dinghy. We decided to put out the sea anchor and wait until daylight before trying to paddle.

About 02.00 hrs we heard an aircraft approaching very low, and we fired off two red flares when he was overhead. The aircraft turned and circled and dropped a white flare, lighting us up, then proceeded on course. This cheered us up a great deal, and it seemed a wonderful bit of luck that we should be sighted so soon. During the next few hours we heard other aircraft, but none came close. Then, about 05.00 hrs, a Lancaster flew over low, and we fired off more red flares. He circled us four times, flashed OK on his downward identification light and left. By this time we were sure of being picked up soon; it just seemed a matter of time. Occasionally we could see searchlights on the German coast, and we had visions of ending up as prisoners of war.

Daylight finally came, and we started to paddle towards England, steering by small compasses we all carried. After about half an hour we realised how hopeless it was. The dinghy was round, and all we seemed to do was drift around in circles, so we finally gave it up as a bad job.

About 11.00 hrs that morning we heard aircraft, but visibility was very poor, and we were doubtful whether they'd see us. After half an hour we saw three Air Sea Rescue Hudsons patrolling about five miles away. We fired off red flares, but they were too far away to see them and they disappeared in the fog. About ten minutes later they came back, this time closer, and we fired off more red flares; but it looked as though they still hadn't seen us, when suddenly the first one turned and came directly towards us flying very low and followed by the other two. They circled us and dropped smoke floats to get a drift in preparation for dropping an airborne lifeboat. Finally one Hudson flew over at about 800 feet, and we saw the boat fall out and parachute to the sea, the idea being to drop downwind. A sea anchor would shoot out and anchor it, and we were supposed to drift into it. However, the mechanism which was supposed to shoot out the sea anchor didn't work, and the lifeboat drifted away from us, though we paddled furiously. We certainly felt low just sitting there unable to do anything and watching it drift away. Another thing, our dinghy was leaking and we had no bellows to blow it up; so things really looked bad.

A short time later another of the Hudsons flew over and dropped us a Lindholme dinghy which consists of another rubber dinghy and four containers holding emergency rations, water and flares. This was a very good drop, and we drifted on to it about 10 minutes afterwards. For a while it looked as though we were going to miss it, so we fastened a rope to the rear gunner who jumped into the water and tried to swim to it; but after four minutes he was exhausted trying to swim as the water was cold and very rough. He was practically unconscious when we pulled him back into the dinghy and it took quite a while to bring him round. This proved to us that if we fell out of the dinghy and drifted away, there was little chance of survival.

We tied the Lindholme dinghy to our own so that we were about 10 feet apart and, with sea anchors out, lessened the chances of one of the dinghies capsizing. The pilot, engineer and myself transferred to the other dinghy, as it was almost impossible to move with the seven of us in one. During the rest of the day there was at least one Hudson circling us. Towards late afternoon, the sky was overcast and the sea got rougher, and we were all soaked and miserably cold. It was impossible to keep the dinghy dry inside, so we were always sitting in water.

Towards dusk another Hudson appeared with an airborne lifeboat which was dropped fairly close, but it became dark before we could reach it. We stayed awake all the time because the sea was so rough we were afraid we might capsize at any time, and also we had to keep baling the water out of the dinghy.

Shortly after midnight the moon broke through the clouds. It was a beautiful sight and cheered us considerably. We soon saw the lifeboat. This time it was fairly close, and a few hours later we managed to reach it. It certainly felt good to get into it at last. There were seven dry waterproof suits in the lockers of the boat, which is about the same size as a large rowboat. We changed into these and threw our clothes into the sea as there was no room on the boat for them. As I was the only one who knew anything about boats I was elected to run it. I decided to wait until daylight, until the Air Sea Rescue Hudsons came out to us again. At 08.00 hrs the first Hudson appeared. We found out later that about this time a Junkers 88 was circling only a mile away, apparently looking for us, but it disappeared when the Hudsons closed in on it.

We got everything ship-shape on the boat, the two four-horsepower outboard engines were started, and we set course for England. After an hour the sea became so rough that the motors were swamped, and we couldn't get them started again. It was hopeless putting up the sail as a real northerly gale was blowing. It is estimated that the wind had a force of 30 to 40 knots, and the seas were mountainous.

The boat had been damaged when it hit the water and now, under the battering of the heavy seas, it began to break up and leak badly. By about 14.00 hrs the boat was almost completely awash and was held afloat only by the rubber buoyancy chambers lining the sides of the deck and the bow and stern. Practically everything was washed overboard. We had finally given up hope of being saved, and most of us were praying hard. It was decided that, as a last resort when the boat broke up, we would tie ourselves together and with our Mae Wests on would float as long as possible, although we didn't expect to survive long in the heavy seas. Two Hudsons were still circling at this time, but their efforts seemed futile.

About 16.00 hrs, when we had all resigned ourselves to the inevitable, Bob, the pilot, yelled, "A ship!" I didn't believe it at first, but sure enough it was a sailing boat being guided to us by the aircraft. When it got closer we saw that it was a small Danish fishing boat, and I'd say that it was the most beautiful sight I had ever seen or ever will see. It was quite an effort getting us aboard owing to the rough sea, but finally we made it. We were so full of relief we just laid down on the deck for a while trying to realise how lucky we were.

After a while we began to consider the situation. Here we were on a Danish fishing boat heading for where, we didn't know, but even a prisoner of war camp would have looked better to us than remaining in what was left of the lifeboat.

There were four Danes in the crew of the boat, and one fellow had fished out of Grimsby for six years before the war, and he could speak a little English. We asked him where he was going and he replied that he had finished fishing and was on his way to Denmark. Then we asked him to take us to Sweden where we would expect better treatment than from the Germans who would capture us if we went to Denmark, but he said that was impossible. When we said England, he only smiled. About ten minutes later one of the Hudsons flew over and dropped a message container. The message stated, "Steer course 250 degrees for England, good luck." This seemed to worry the Danes and they argued amongst themselves for almost five minutes, then started turning round. One of the boys looked at the compass a while later and saw that we were on a course of 250 degrees, so all looked well. The Danes accepted the situation and took us down to the cabin and lit the stove, and we dried ourselves out and put on dry clothes which they provided. We were told we

could use their bunks, and we were soon fast asleep. I felt better in the morning, but found I was so weak I could hardly stand. The weather was so bad during the night that we had to heave to until daylight.

One of the Danes brought us some food which consisted of canned meat and fish, German bread, which seemed to be half sawdust, and ersatz tea which tasted great to us as it was the first hot drink we'd had, but normally I doubt if I would be able to drink it as it certainly had no resemblance to tea.

During the day we tried to teach the Danes a little English and vice versa. The one fellow who could speak English told us a lot about Denmark and the Germans. They had a very good wireless receiver which they allowed us to use, and we listened to everything from German propaganda broadcasts in English to Bing Crosby. We found it rather amusing watching the Danes shaving off about two weeks' beard and getting all cleaned up for their arrival in England; in fact, when the Air Sea Rescue launch met us they couldn't tell who were Danes and who were English at first.

It was about 17.00 hrs on the 29th that we were met by the rescue launch. They told us they'd been very close to us the day after we'd ditched but lost contact with the aircraft who were circling us. Then one engine broke down, and they had to go back to their base. We were in the Air Sea Rescue launch until after midnight when we were landed in Grimsby, about 80 hours since we had left England. We then went to a Naval hospital where we were given a good meal, and the doctor examined us to see if we were fit. Next night we returned to the squadron, where we were given a great welcome and then went on 14 days' survivors' leave.

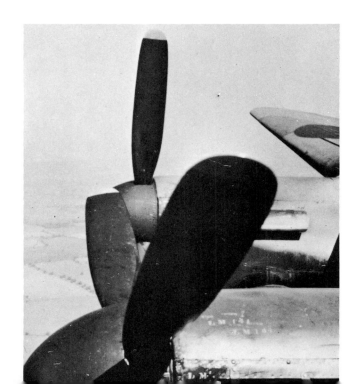

HOME ON TWO *Not an unfamiliar sight to returning crews; with two props feathered, BI LM141 of 460 Squadron makes it back to Binbrook after an argument with German flak in the summer of 1944. Some Lancs are known to have made the last lap on one engine, in a long, shallow descent.*

SAFELY HOME

WELCOME SIGHT *One by one the kites return in the early hours and (left) one enters the circuit at East Kirkby as the sun rises over the Windmill at Old Bolingbroke.*

The local farmers and villagers would count them in and hope. . . . The mill. was the home of the Eleys, regular hosts to crews of Nos. 57 and 630 Squadrons.

MISSION COMPLETED *F/Lt Stuart Anning brings BI, ED763 KC-Z Honor, of 617 Squadron, Woodhall Spa, in to land after the third and successful attack on the battleship Tirpitz, November 12, 1944.*

Flying from Lossiemouth to Bals Fjord, Tromso in Norway, the operation involved a round trip of 13 hours. Load was one 12,000lb tallboy.

We "died" three times

Bill Bennée

Some crews could get through a tour with little or no trouble, their gunners never having to fire a shot in anger. For others, it seemed as if the enemy had taken a personal dislike to them. They would return from trip after trip with graphic tales of duels with searchlights, flak or fighters, their aircraft riddled with holes.

Although a tour normally comprised 30 trips, crews would not always know when they were on their last operation because it could vary either way. It depended on the fortunes of the squadron – who may not have had a crew finish for months, the pressing need for instructors, or revised thinking by Bomber Command chiefs.

F/Lt Bill Bennée and crew, of 101 Squadron, Holme-on-Spalding Moor, were somewhat apprehensive when briefed for Munich – always a tough target – on the night of March 9/10, 1943, for they knew it was to be their last trip in their trusty Lanc BI, ED552 SR-Q *Gremlin Queen*.

Any hopes they may have had of their luck lasting out were shattered even before they left the English coast. The following vivid account was written by the skipper shortly after the war.

It would not be difficult for anyone to imagine that after each sortie, climbing out of the aircraft and standing on terra firma was indeed a wonderful sensation. But never before or since have I experienced a greater thrill or feeling of thankfulness than when I did this selfsame thing after completing the last sortie of my first Operational Tour, having escaped death three times on a trip that took just under nine hours.

On that memorable night we were briefed to attack the famous Beer Cellar town of Munich, and ironically enough our first escape was over this country. Subsequently we learned that our demise was nearly brought about by a member of our own squadron!

Some six hundred aircraft were to rendezvous at 18,000 feet over Dungeness, with navigation lights burning, and were in fact all circling round a searchlight beam which was being shown vertically at that point. On receiving word from the navigator, I had just turned the aircraft on to course and, looking up, saw approaching at great speed what appeared to be red balls of fire. No navigation lights were visible but I realised after a little hesitation that I was looking down the flame traps of the exhausts of another aircraft approaching head on, and immediately commenced a steep turn to starboard. My port wing had barely lifted when the other aircraft passed us; it was so close we actually heard its engines. This is no line – all the

crew heard them. Only one other member of the crew saw what I had seen; he was the bomb aimer on lookout in the nose, and by the time he had opened his mouth to give me warning the danger had passed. This indicates how quickly the whole thing happened. Needless to say, the reaction to this narrowly-averted disaster was sudden and violent and I admit that I could not stop myself from trembling for nearly half an hour. Even then I was still shaken, but although I did not know it at the time, further shocks were awaiting me that night.

Over the target area on the bombing run, with three minutes straight run up to the aiming point, we were coned in searchlights. I am not a brave man but there was a certain amount of friendly rivalry on the squadron as to which crew would get the best picture of the aiming point, and as this was our last trip we were determined to get a good picture. With my crew's consent, we pressed on straight and level, taking no evasive action. Jerry was quick to show his appreciation of the 'clot' above in no uncertain manner and we were subjected to intense heavy flak. Our load comprised 30lb incendiaries and a shell splinter set one off. I shall never forget the sight of the bright red glare of the touched-off incendiary mingling with the intense blue-white of some thirty-odd searchlights reflecting through to the bomb aimer's compartment just beyond my feet. However, we carried on, dropped our bombs, did *not* stop to take a picture and turned back steeply to port. Caught on the turn by a heavy flak burst close to its belly, the aircraft stood on its nose and plummeted vertically.

With the airspeed building up rapidly to fighter aircraft proportions, my trim controls jammed and, blinded by the searchlights, we were extremely fortunate that the Lancaster at last responded to her elevators and we pulled out of our dive at over 400 mph. Suddenly we were in complete blackness; I still could not see my instruments after the glare of the searchlights. When I was able to see them, however, I had a further shock. We were at 5,000 feet and there were hills in the vicinity of over 6,000 feet. This we knew although, of course, we could not see them. The gods were certainly good to us that night; we must have pulled out of our dive into a valley. Soon we were back at a reasonable height of 12,000 feet but still climbing and heading for home.

My next worry was how badly the aircraft had been damaged. The controls did not feel too good and it was therefore common sense in one way not to put too much stress on the airframe by unnecessary manoeuvres. On the other hand, by not carrying out a particular manœuvre we laid ourselves open to attack from underneath by night fighters.

The final episode of my story took place a few miles from the French coast, just when we were beginning to feel that this was not a night meant for our destruction and that we stood a reasonable chance of 'making it'.

Out of the blackness, stabs of tracers flew past our starboard wing and in a moment an ugly orange glare lit the sky only 50 yards away. It was sufficient for us to see that it was one of our own four-engined bombers which would not be returning to base. We all stared, fascinated, as the great and beautiful bird born of the scientific genius of man made its death dive to explode some 16,000 feet below to form the funeral pyre of seven brave lads who had 'had their time'.

Such an end was accepted by all crews as a possibility and I must confess that my feelings towards this scene which I had just witnessed were simply that I was glad it wasn't me.

After this I took a certain amount of evasive action until well clear of the coast. On approaching the shores of England the certainty grew stronger that we were not destined for the 'chop' that night. All the same, we did not really relax until we were once again standing on terra firma at our dispersal.

There was an anti-climax to our night of close shaves. We listened to the German version of the raid and the announcer finished by saying that their defences had accounted for 49 British aircraft, while our own official figures were given as 48. We of our crew of course argued that the one difference must have been our aircraft which the gunners had wrongly claimed as a victim although, in fairness to them, in view of our behaviour over the target, it must have appeared a 'cert' for them. Although we laughed at such 'monstrous lies', we did breathe a sigh of relief when we thought of what might have been.

HOME FOR TEA *A white-tailed formation leader lands back at Waddington, home of 463 and 467 Aussie Squadrons, after a daylight sortie in the summer of 1944.*

From the spring of 1944, the 'softening up' for the invasion began with attacks on communications and oil, etc. With aerial superiority virtually complete, Bomber Command increasingly converted to daylight bombing.

Difficulty was often experienced with identification in the air and Nos. 1 and 5 Groups in particular painted fins and rudders to indicate the base, each base consisting of three stations.

Various combinations of stripes were also applied to wings and fuselage, the paint usually being a washable distemper.

THE HOME FIRE BURNING *as a 576 Squadron Lanc comes in to land (top) at Fiskerton over FIDO towards the close of the war.*

Not only did Bomber Command have to contend with enemy fighters and flak, the weather was a constant problem. Treacherous low-lying fog often greeted the tired crews on their return and, low on fuel, many kites crashed or had to be abandoned.

The answer was FIDO (Fog Investi-gation Dispersal Operation) albeit an expensive one. From the first operational use on the night of November 19/20, 1943, when four Halifaxes of 35 Squadron landed safely at Graveley, some 2,486 allied aircraft landed by it at the fifteen airfields thus equipped (1,200 at Woodbridge alone), at the expenditure of 100,000 tons of petrol.

MINIONS OF THE MOON *Back from Berlin in the moonlit early hours, two Lancs (above) of 106 Squadron taxi back to their dispersals at Syerston in January 1943, using inboard engines only. The usual small clusters of ground crew await their crews' return no matter what the hour or weather.*

This beautiful picture seems to epitomise more than any other the atmosphere of wartime operations by night.

Caterpillars Extraordinaire

'Blue' Rackley

The Caterpillar Club is a unique band of men and women whose lives have been saved with the aid of an Irving parachute. Records of the club contain several thousand reports of parachute descents and among them are to be found many incredible stories of courage, fortitude and amazing luck.

A Bomber Command crew which had its fair share of all three was that of F/O L. N. 'Blue' Rackley, a young red-headed Australian. They joined 630 Squadron at East Kirkby in mid-March 1944 and on their seventh trip had crash-landed on an airstrip in Corsica, after a tough trip to Munich in which they had lost their rear gunner. That Lanc had broken its back; but now, less than two months later, they were doing their ninth trip in their new BI, ME795 LE-G, a map of Corsica resplendent on the nose.

The Caterpillar Club files record the widely differing experiences of F/O Rackley and his Australian bomb aimer, P/O D. S. Morgan. Alas, their sixteenth trip – to attack the hydrogenisation plant at Wesseling in the Ruhr on June 21, 1944 – was fated to be their last together.

Soon after we crossed the Dutch coast we began to see aircraft exploding, so many in fact that I was almost convinced they were spoofs, until suddenly it was our turn. I had just brought the kite to a straight and level attitude after a banking search, when there was a terrific explosion aft, coupled with a muffled cry from one of my gunners.

We were thrown into a steep dive and it took all of 5,000 feet to recover. It was beyond my strength to pull back the control column and I had to call on the aid of Stan Jones, the flight engineer. Together we managed to pull out of the dive.

A Ju88 had attacked from beneath and broken away to port. Jack Jones, the mid-upper, scored some hits and the fighter was last seen on fire in the clouds.

Having righted the aircraft, it was immediately evident that the control surfaces were severely damaged. All aileron control was lost and I was unable to hold back the stick without assistance. She was answering very sloppily to the rudders and the situation looked grim.

The crew reported a large hole in the floor, just forward of the rear turret, but no other damage could be seen in the gloom. I decided to jettison the bombload and attempt to return to base. The engines were not damaged and the noise of four Merlins never sounded sweeter. The radio and intercom were serviceable so at least we had a chance.

Bit by bit we coaxed her through the turn, but it must have been the last straw for, soon after completing the turn, something appeared to snap and the rudder pedals sprang into the 'starboard rudder full on' position. She veered very slowly to starboard and I found that by placing both feet on the port pedal and exerting full pressure, I could bring the pedals to the neutral position and even get a little port rudder on. However, it was beyond my strength to keep this up, so Des Morgan, the bomb aimer, who by this time was up in the cockpit, took it in turns with the engineer to help me hold the stick back. One of them found some rope aboard. Just why it was there no one knew, but it was certainly welcome.

With the rudder pedals in the neutral position, a length of rope was lashed round the starboard pedal while the other end was secured to a part of the framework of the aircraft. This relieved the strain on my legs and kept us near enough to a straight course. What wander there was tended to be to starboard, and I was able to counteract this by exerting pressure with both legs on the port pedal from time to time.

We had no aileron control, but good fortune was with us and the kite did not drop a wing throughout the return trip. More rope was produced and the control column lashed in the neutral position. The bomb aimer stood by with an axe, ready to cut the rope should the need arise. We were now flying straight and level at about 10,000 feet, headed for England, under reasonable control, but with a long way to go.

Over the sea, 'Taffy' Davis, the rear gunner, was assisted from his turret up forward of the gaping hole in the floor. Lifting his chute from the clips on the side of the fuselage, he saw to his horror that it was badly damaged. We did not carry a spare so it was clear we had one helluva problem for there seemed a very slim chance of making England and landing the aircraft in its condition. I announced to the crew that we would have to bale out, and immediately the bomb aimer volunteered to take the rear gunner with him on his chute. Still more rope was produced and a scheme to tie the two men together was discussed. The plan was that as soon as we crossed the English coast, all the crew would leave the aircraft. With the engineer and myself on board, we thought we would stay with the kite, fly straight across England and bale out as she crossed the west coast, hoping she would continue for some distance before crashing into the sea.

It sounded a good plan, but as the journey progressed I realised it was an unlikely one. Gradually, what control I had began to deteriorate.

We crossed the coast somewhere near Ipswich. Immediately the bomb aimer and rear gunner, tied together, baled out through the forward hatch, followed closely by the mid-upper, wireless op and navigator.

Soon afterwards our wander to starboard became more pronounced. To make matters worse, some starboard bank came on, and since we had no aileron control the only method of correction was opposite rudder. However, I could not get enough on, or hold it long enough to be really effective, so it was evident that very soon the kite would be completely uncontrollable.

The original plan, to fly to the west coast before abandoning, was to prevent any loss of life or damage to property which may occur if the aircraft crashed on land. This was now out of the question, and with a doomed Lanc on our hands, it was time for the engineer and myself to leave.

The engineer dropped through the front escape hatch, followed very closely by myself. I went head first through the hatch in the approved manner, started to count as soon as I was clear, turned head-over-heels several times, sighting the wingtip lights of the Lanc at each turn, then at the count of five, I pulled the cord.

The chute opened and all the physical exhilaration of falling free in space ceased. I had lost a flying boot and my left foot was feeling very cold. So I tucked it inside the leg of my right boot for warmth.

Suddenly, I became aware of an aircraft approaching. The noise of engines became louder and louder, and when I saw it pass some distance overhead in a starboard turn I realised it was my Lanc! The engine tone diminished for a minute or so, but then increased once more; my kite was going round in circles, getting nearer the ground on each turn. This time she passed some distance beneath me, still in the starboard turn but the danger of a collision had passed. I heard the engines for some time; then suddenly an orange glow lit up the clouds below, followed by an almighty explosion. I could not help feeling I had lost a faithful friend.

Far below me I could see the tops of the cloud cover, and for some time I did not appear to be getting any closer to it; it appeared I was being carried upwards instead of downwards. In the darkness of early morning, it was difficult to tell.

Eventually I reached the clouds. The base must have been quite low, because no sooner had I passed through than I realised I was being dragged along at a terrific rate and became aware of the distinctive sound made by train wheels rattling beside my ear. I was being bumped about something awful, but it didn't seem to hurt. Neither was I aware of any fear. That came some days later! Looking back, it was a strange few seconds.

Then there is a blank. I remember finding myself beside a railway line. It was still dark and I had no idea where on earth I was. My second flying boot had disappeared, as had my watch. My chute was also gone. I found later that it had got caught up in the train, causing quite a stir on its arrival in London, when a search party was sent back along the line.

I think that while I was being dragged along by the train, the quick-release button of the chute must have been smashed, so that the harness straps were released, ripping the chute from me.

Dazed, I started to walk along the line. My head was bleeding, my shoulder was hurting and I could not move my right arm at all. After walking for some distance I heard a train approaching. When it came into view I could see it was travelling very slowly and was a goods train. Waiting until the engine was almost opposite me, I called to the crew for help. They answered and stopped the train.

The driver and fireman came down from the engine, followed by the guard shortly afterwards. I told them who I was and what had happened, but I think they had some doubt about my story. After some fast talking, the driver pulled the train along and I got into the guard's van. The guard sat outside on the platform and I suspect he thought I was a German and wasn't taking any chances with me.

The train stopped at a signal box to arrange for an ambulance to meet it at Luton and on arrival there, an ambulance and police escort took me to Luton and Dunstable Hospital.

Of the others in my crew, Taffy Davis, the rear gunner, was killed; but Des Morgan, the bomb aimer, landed safely, though badly shaken by his experience. When the chute opened he was unable to hold the gunner and he fell to the ground.

Ian Gow, the navigator, hit his arm against the tailwheel, fracturing his elbow. 'Curly' Carroll, the wireless op, arrived at a farmhouse with his parachute folded over his arm, but was threatened with a rifle by the occupant! He went on his way and found assistance elsewhere.

Stan Jones, the engineer, had an uneventful descent, but Jack Jones, the mid-upper, became entangled in the branches of a tree. In the dark he could not judge his distance from the ground, so decided to remain where he was until daylight. After a while he began to feel cold so kicked his legs to get warm. In doing so he stubbed his foot against a fence post. He was no more than two or three feet from the ground!

BRAKES ON – CUT ENGINES
Skippered by F/Sgt Clive Roantree, RAAF, 49 Squadron's D-Dog BIII, JB362 EA-D, is marshalled into her dispersal at Fiskerton, landing lights still piercing the night, after a trip to 'The Big City', November 18/19, 1943.

Being some 16 feet up, crews could see little of the immediate ground area when taxying, and to assist the pilot, the bomb aimer shines an Aldis lamp from the nose.

A picture taken during the opening rounds of the Battle of Berlin, which began in earnest on November 18/19, 1943, and ended with the 16th attack on March 24/25, 1944. Of Bomber Command's 9,111 sorties against Berlin, 7,256 were by Lancs.

FIRST BACK
All the joy of again being back on terra firma shows in this crew's faces as they gratefully tumble out at dispersal. Here at Waddington in January 1944, P/O Alec Riley, RAAF, and his 467 Squadron crew are first back from Berlin, unshaven dishevelled but happy. After eight hours in a Lanc, ears would be ringing from the noise of the engines for a long time afterwards, making sleep difficult. It would be some time before the feet and legs became accustomed to firm ground again, with no movement or vibration.

BACK FOR BREAKFAST *Despite a tiring nine-hour trip to Genoa in the winter of 1942, a group of 106 Squadron aircrew can still manage a smile for the cameraman at Syerston in the early morning light.*

The Lanc BI, R5573 *named* Admiral – Foo-Banc V, *is one of several specially fitted with bulged bomb doors for the carriage of 8,000lb bombs. The doors, made of wood with rubber hinges, opened by the sheer weight of the bomb dropping on them. Devised at Group level, their shape gave rise to the nickname 'pot belly'.*

ALL SMILES *The elation of this 467 Squadron Aussie crew is obvious as they pile aboard the crew truck at Bottesford in the early morning after the night's operation. Their object now is to get interrogation over as quickly as possible, breakfast on bacon and eggs, then catch up on some sleep.*

AFTER THE RAID

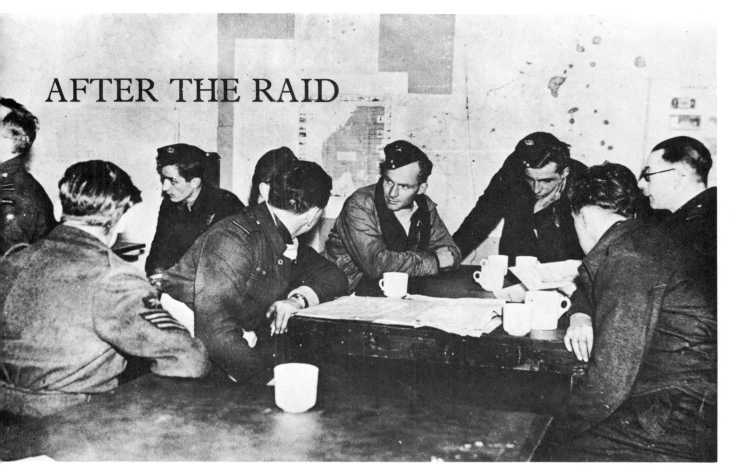

INTERROGATION *The raid is over and the crews – not really in the mood for it – are questioned painstakingly by the Intelligence Officer. "What was the flak like? Any fighters? How many kites did you see go down?"*

This is the scene at Bardney in the early hours of January 6, 1944, as F/Lt Paddy Ervine and his 9 Squadron crew discuss the attack on Stettin, fortified by mugs of tea, well laced with rum.

BEER ALL ROUND *as W/Cdr 'Tubby' Baker, CO of 635 Squadron, Downham Market, returns from his 100th trip (all done on Wimpeys, Stirlings and Lancs), a 'daylight' to Wuppertal, March 13, 1945.*

If you were lucky enough to survive one tour you could be called for a second after a period of 'rest' at a training unit as an instructor, but the chances of completing it were slim indeed.

After two tours you could not be called back; but such was the spirit that some went on and on.

BRINGING BACK THE EMPTIES
Spent cartridge cases indicate a busy night. In general there were few head-on attacks by fighters and normally the only time the bomb aimer would be called upon as a gunner was during daylight attacks by fighters, or on those rare occasions when some strafing of trains was undertaken at low level.

LANCS AT REST 1 *The day's work is done and all is quiet. 149 Squadron's Lancs at rest at Methwold as dusk approaches on a late summer's evening in 1944.*

M.S.I	Letter	No	CREW		Take Off EST	Take Off ACTUAL	EST. TIME OVER TARGET	RETURN EST	RETURN ACTUAL	NOTES
1×4000 8SBCs of 4LBS	V	R 5487	P/o Collier, P/o Hoofy, F/o Ipould	F/o Turner, Sgt Brummitt, Sgt Martin, P/o Jones	0001	0003		0400	0401	CAMERA
1×4000 8SBCs of 4LBS	M	R 5502	P/lt Hallows, P/o Friend, P/o Cutting	P/s Louch, Sgt Jones L., Sgt Broomfield, Sgt Coacher		0007			0345	
1×4000 8SBCs of 4LBS	G	R 5614	P/o Berridge, P/o Long, Sgt Connely	Sgt Fleming, P/o Hellyer, Sgt Buxton, Sgt McPhee		0034			0519	CAMERA
1×4000 8SBCs of 4LBS	H	R 5538	P/lt Miller, P/o Cullinane, Sgt Grossmith	Sgt Robertson, P/o Smith L., Sgt Nickerson, Sgt Westgate		0009			0455	
1×4000 8SBCs of 4LBS	I	L 7577	P/lt Coton, Sgt Kruger, P/o Boddington	Sgt Newell, Sgt Martin P., P/o Robinson, Sgt McMahon		0014			0547	CAMERA
1×4000 8SBCs of 4LBS	W	R 5559	P/o Beverill, Sgt Cooper, P/o Butler	Sgt Irons, Sgt Devine, Sgt Benbow, Sgt Keane		0011			0339	CAMERA
1×4000 8SBCs of 4LBS	Z	R 5497	P/o Hughes, Sgt Lawton, Sgt Isted	P/o Crerar, Sgt Harris, Sgt Mercer, Sgt Overton		0016			0529	CAMERA
1×4000 8SBCs of 4LBS	J	R 5558	P/o McMurchy, Sgt Morgan, P/o Williams	Sgt Richardson, Sgt Girvin, Sgt Hebdon, Sgt Barraclough	/	/	/	/	/	CANCELLED REAR WHEEL BROKE
1×4000 8SBCs of 4LBS	A	R 5571	P/o Davies, P/o Keough, Sgt McMeechan	Sgt Goodwin, Sgt Smith E., Sgt Coone, Sgt Goddard		0030			0513	CAMERA
1×4000 8SBCs of 4LBS	U	R 5496	P/o Adams, P/o Falls, Sgt Creeth	Sgt Stafford, Sgt Dawson, P/o Goldie, Sgt Linnett		0037			0539	CAMERA
1×4000 8SBCs of 4LBS	X	R 5607	P/o Fletcher, Sgt McKenna, P/o Blair	P/o Wilkinson, Sgt Garland, P/o K Mackey, Sgt Bale		0039			0544	CAMERA
1×4000 8SBCs of 4LBS	F	R 5572	P/o Rodley, P/s Colquhoun, P/o Bennett	Sgt Merralls, Sgt Cummings, Sgt Ratcliffe, Sgt Crisp		0031			0416	
1×4000 8SBCs of 4LBS	S	R 5609	P/o Hartley, P/o Briant, W/o Cannam	Sgt Gross, Sgt Mayland, Sgt Suckling, P/o Legace		0044			0526	
1×4000 8SBCs of 4LBS	C	R 5512	P/lt Blakeman, P/o Blease, P/o Shrybman	Sgt Nicholl, Sgt Allen, Sgt Trueman, Sgt McKenzie		0055			0504	
1×4000 8SBCs of 4LBS	P	R 5552	W/o Harrison, Sgt Crouch, Sgt Platten	Sgt Preston, Sgt Farrara, Sgt Townley, Sgt Oates		0042			0541	
1×4000 8SBCs of 4LBS	R	R 5612	P/o Barnes, Sgt Bunt, Sgt Cook	Sgt Kelleher, Sgt Griffiths, Sgt Guy, Sgt Desmond		0046			0302	RETURNED EARLY ENGINE TROUBLE

DUTY INTELLIGENCE OFFICER—COMING IN   F/o STENNING   DUTY INTELLIGENCE OFFICER—RETURNED   F/o BURNABY

ALL BACK SAFELY *The 97 Squadron operations board at Woodhall Spa after the historic 1,000-Bomber Raid on Cologne, May 30/31, 1942 – Operation Millennium. Having only recently been introduced into squadron service, and still in short supply, Lancasters represented only 6.5 per cent of the total force of 1,047 aircraft dispatched, but only one of the 67 failed to return. A Lanc from 61 Squadron's Conversion Flight had the dubious distinction of being the last aircraft over the target. Because of their greater speed, the Lancs took off much later than other types used on the raid.*

A cool welcome

Ken Lane

At take-off conditions could be perfect, yet only a few hours later the bombers could run into vicious storms, with towering cumulo-nimbus clouds tossing them around like straws in the wind.

A cold front could cause ice to build up, often freezing control surfaces, while gale force winds could drive the stream many miles off track.

On the night of March 30/31, 1944, Bomber Command encountered phenomenal weather conditions and suffered as a result its worst single setback of the whole war. Moreover, the target, Nuremberg, was only slightly damaged.

Conditions over the North Sea made it impossible to arrange a large-scale diversion, while the difficulty of predicting changeable March winds led to serious errors in navigation. The high cloud – expected to give concealment – dispersed, leaving the aircraft silhouetted against the lower clouds. Added to this, the aircraft left vapour trails in the intensely cold but clear atmosphere, each taking on a phosphorescent glow in the light of a half moon.

The Luftwaffe correctly deduced the direction of approach from H2S bearings. 'Bomber' Harris and his staff had a shrewd idea of the dangers of using H2S, but they had little choice. On this night some 200 night fighters lay in wait and wreaked fearful havoc. The final toll was to be 95 Lancasters and Halifaxes, besides a further 11 written off after their return.

Thick cloud covered the target and, with the Path Finder Force late, the main force had to mill around, increasing the risk of collision. Impatient crews began to drop their loads anywhere. Even when the markers did go down, 47 minutes late, they could not be seen through the clouds.

W/O Ken Lane and crew of 83 Pathfinder Squadron missed the fighters, but ran into atrocious weather on their return to England. Incredibly, their Lanc BIII, ND333 OL-F, stayed in the air, when by all the laws of aerodynamics she should have crashed.

Some people are able to remember incidents or dates without difficulty, but with me it has to be something really outstanding to maintain a lasting impression in my mind.

The night of March 30, 1944, when I piloted a Lancaster to Nuremberg is a night I cannot forget because my memory is reinforced by three basic points. First, this was the night of the big wind. Second, it was the night when the Lancaster showed qualities which endeared her to all who flew in her. Third, the question is posed, Was this the biggest air defeat of the war?

When Nuremberg was discussed at briefing, there were no exclamations or subdued murmurs such as usually arose when Berlin was mentioned. Not that any target was easy, but Nuremberg did not appear to be worthy of undue comment, and naturally no one could be aware of events to follow.

Wind speed and direction at a given height was of paramount navigational importance to aircraft of the main force, but perhaps for the Pathfinders it was of lesser importance, as special equipment was carried which made it reasonably easy for navigators to find new winds. Using these new winds, appropriate corrections were made and the result was amazing accuracy in navigation which enabled aircraft to be over a given spot at the exact time planned.

I was privileged to be a Pathfinder in 83 Squadron, and although briefing had given us 80-knot winds, we found when proceeding over the enemy coast at 22,000 feet that the wind was now 120–130 knots! Much of the ground was hidden under heavy cloud, making it almost impossible to obtain a 'fix', and as we made the necessary course adjustment, I sympathised with aircraft of the main force who would certainly be experiencing more difficulty.

Flying in darkness can be very lonely, with little or no conversation between crew members, and it was sometimes quite a relief to be almost turned over by the slipstream of an unseen aircraft or to see flames from four belching exhausts spitting at you through the gloom. At least you knew that another aircraft was in front and going in the same direction. However, even this reassurance was lacking on this loneliest of all nights when there was nothing to be seen apart from the occasional glow in the distance. This probably resulted from aircraft being blown off course and drifting over heavily defended areas. Routes were planned with great care to avoid danger spots, and to wander off made for a rough flight.

We were still above broken cloud over the target, where our function was to drop four flares visually to build up those dropped earlier by other Pathfinders, and to add for good measure 8,000lb of high-explosive bombs. This we did with only slight interference from flak, which was rather scattered, and then came the welcome time to turn for home.

The journey was a repetition of the outward flight, without incident of note, but the real problem was to come when we arrived over our base at Wyton. Weather conditions around this part were atrocious with a snowstorm giving nil visibility. All other aircraft had been diverted, but because of a radio fault we were not informed, and now we were in the unenviable position of having to land without assistance from the ground.

Several attempts to approach were made, but each time the runway was lost, and after nearly hitting the water tower, I decided to use Standard Beam Approach procedure which in those days was the popular aid to a blind landing. Picking up the beam, I made my circuit and approach, gradually losing height at the appropriate rate of descent. When only a few seconds from touch-down, I suddenly saw the runway contact lights and, as the colour was red, I realised that I was too far along the runway for a landing. I commenced to carry out my overshoot drill, but when I pushed on the throttles nothing happened; the linkage was probably frozen. As I strained harder, so my seat catch could not stand the backward pressure and, jumping from its locked position, the seat dropped to its lowest point, leaving my head about a foot below vision level. Airspeed literally dropped off the clock, and although well below stalling speed, the amazing Lanc remained airborne. The more I think about this, the more fantastic it appears when one considers a heavy four-engined bomber still flying at little over 65 knots.

As I fought to control the aircraft, I also managed to raise my seat to a higher level, and the return of vision brought full realisation of the extent of the danger. We skimmed across fields and hedgerows which even at this low altitude were not very distinct, but the grim certainty was that we would hit something solid before much longer. Suddenly the throttle levers gave and the engines roared into full life, bringing at least some hope of survival. Even so, height was needed to recover from a near-stall, and we didn't have this luxury; but the wonderful Lanc responded to every touch and gradually reached a safe speed, making it possible for us to climb to comparative safety.

Fuel was running low, but after completing another circuit and approach, a landing was achieved. Conditions on the ground were certainly grim, and the Aerodrome Control Pilot in his caravan claimed later that he had not seen an aircraft actually land, although he had heard some frightening noises.

There was no sign of life on the station, and the duty officer had to be roused to de-brief us, much to his disgust. For us it was a case of 'all's well that ends well', but on the radio next morning we heard the sombre news that 95 aircraft were missing. Others would probably have run out of fuel and crash-landed, but I never heard the final toll.

What a night this had been, with very few aircraft actually reaching the target; but the question as to whether this was Bomber Command's costliest mission remains unanswered.

For me this was the night when the Lancaster bomber performed the impossible.

LANCS AT REST 2 *460 Squadron Binbrook, spring 1944. In the background is the pre-war type of hangar, still in use at Binbrook today.*

BATTLE DAMAGE

FRIENDS OR FOES *Being hit by bombs or incendiaries from a kite above was a constant threat. At night the dangers were not so obvious to the crews, but on the mass day-light raids of 1944 and 1945 it was often difficult to find a safe gap over the target.*

The rear turret of this PFF Lanc was completely sheared off by a falling bomb, leaving the ammunition belts and hydraulic feed pipes hanging. The gunner disappeared with his turret.

Above is 156 Squadron BIII, ND340 GT-S, with a gaping hole left by a 'friendly' bomb over Fort D'Enghos petrol dump August 9, 1944. Mercifully, the bomb did not go off and F/Lt J. A. Wilson and crew all got back safely.

"95 OF OUR AIRCRAFT ARE MISSING . . ." *were the terse words of the communique after the disastrous raid on Nuremberg on the night of March 30/31, 1944. However, the figure did not include the many aircraft wrecked or so badly damaged that they either never flew again or were sent for a rebuild.*

Below is the battered interior of the rear fuselage of a 9 Squadron Lanc BI, DV395 WS-V, caught by fighters from underneath (a favourite attacking position), killing the mid-upper gunner: the dark stains on the floor, doorstep and Elsan tell their own grim story. By a cool-headed piece of flying, F/O Harry Forrest nursed his mount home.

Bomber Command had come a long way since the pioneering days of 1940/1, but even with the sophisticated equipment and techniques available in 1944, things could still go wrong. On this occasion, not only did the Luftwaffe guess the target correctly, but the 'met' boobed: instead of the forecast cloud cover, there was bright moonlight, 150 mph tailwinds and severe icing.

THE FIGHTER MENACE *Steel rods show the angle of penetration from a night fighter's shells in the port wing of this Lanc BIII,* ND356/G *from 100 Squadron, Waltham.*

Attacked over Stuttgart March 15/16, 1944, S/Ldr Hugh Grant-Dalton and crew got away by superb teamwork and full use of the 'corkscrew'.

HOME HAZARD *This 97 (Straits Settlements) Squadron Lanc, BIII, ND495, OF-M, returned safely from a night op in August 1944, but on turning off the peri-track at Coningsby, was struck by another taxying Lancaster with disastrous results. Bad though the damage appears, she had returned to ops within a month as OF-N, complete with new tail section. Although the accident occurred at night, the tail markings distinguish this aircraft as a daylight formation leader.*

108

GROUND ATTACK *Not all Lancs were lost by aerial combats. These two were photographed after a surprise 'last ditch' attack by enemy fighters on Ursel (Belgium) where the Lancs had made emergency landings, taking advantage of airfields captured by the Allies. The foam seems to be taking effect on this kite (left) but there is no hope for the other one (below left).*

ONE WAY OF LOOKING AT IT
F/Lt Ron Gill of 635 Squadron finishes his second tour with a bang! Here at Downham Market he ruefully examines the flak-damaged tailplane of his Lanc BIII, ND735 F2-L, after returning from a night attack on Dusseldorf on November 2/3, 1944. The starboard aileron was also hit and immoveable and it was a near-miracle the Lanc made base at all.

PRANGS

CRASH-LANDED For getting this badly shot-up Lanc home in spite of severe injuries to himself and his crew, F/Lt Bill Reid won the VC. The effects of two night-fighter attacks can be clearly seen. The skipper's own account tells only too graphically how terror could strike:

"3/11/43 BIII, LM360 QR-O 'self and crew Op. No. 10' Dusseldorf. 5h 30m (night) Attacked by Me110 at Dutch Coast. R/G was unable to open fire due to a heating failure, thus his hands were frozen. The I/C was u/s so he was also unable to give avoiding action orders or warning. By supreme effort he did open fire after a brief delay, but not before the N/F had raked us from stem to stern. However, the N/F was driven off. By now the rear turret was almost useless, the compass was u/s, the elevator trim tabs were u/s and the kite kept wallowing. The windscreen was shattered and I was wounded in the head, shoulders and hands. We continued on track but were suddenly attacked by a Fw190 which riddled us all over on two passes. The Nav. was killed instantly and the W/Op badly wounded. The R/G tried hard to hit the fighter but only one gun would function and the turret packed up altogether. The M/U turret was hit, stopped and the oxygen system put u/s. I was hit too and started losing blood fast. The F/E gave me oxygen from the portable supply. The F/E was himself injured.

"We carried on and reached the target bang on track. Had memorised the course luckily. We left the target and set course by the Pole star and moon. I was growing weak now from loss of blood and the oxygen supply was no more. The cold air coming in from the shattered cockpit was freezing. The F/E and B/A between them flew the kite back. On sighting land they looked for the first airfield visible, revived me and we came in to land at what turned out to be Shipdham, a Yank liberator base. There was some ground mist and I could not see the runway lights. Blood kept getting into my eyes and I was almost fainting. The F/E and B/A were both holding myself and the column with all their might. One leg of the undercart collapsed but there was no fire."

ROUGH TRIP *This was how BIII, PB114 GT-N, finished a raid on Hamburg on July 28/29, 1944. It was the last op of the skipper's third tour (S/Ldr H. F. Slade, RAAF) and the account which follows shows just how lucky he and his crew were to get away with it:*

The kite was hit by flak before the run-in to the target. After the bombs had been released she went into a slow spiral dive, completely out of control. The crew stood by ready to bale out but control was regained. With the aid of the nav and flight engineer, the pilot manhandled the stricken kite out of the target area, but with only 10 per cent of aileron control. They had an anxious time over the coastal gun belt because no evading action could be taken for fear of losing control. By intelligent use of petrol from the port tanks only, a better balance was achieved and this eased the flying condition. Once over the North Sea they headed for Woodbridge and though all engines were undamaged height was slowly being lost all the way. *Any momentary loss of power or relaxation in the grim struggle with the controls would have sent them into the sea. Woodbridge was reached at an altitude of only 1,500 ft and a successful emergency wheels-up landing made at 03.15 hrs. All the crew were unharmed but the damage was extensive, the port outer engine being completely wrecked.*

RECOVERY *Very bent, and with engine air intakes filled with earth, an early Lanc, R5845 of 1660 Conversion Unit, Swinderby, is lifted ready for the recovery trolley by a crew of 58 MU.*

Looking rather sorry for itself, the nose is taken away on a 'Queen Mary' for salvage of parts and eventual scrap, the other sections following behind. The scene is somewhat reminiscent of a funeral procession. The camouflage is an unusual pattern for a Lanc, being a leftover from Manchester days.

JUST GOOD FRIENDS *When the movable meets the immovable, the result of a Lanc travelling at over 100 mph colliding with a stationary Fortress.*

On the night of March 24/25, 1944, the 16th and last major attack in the Battle of Berlin – F/Sgt Fred Brownings and crew of 103 Squadron, on their fifth operation, were severely mauled by a Fw190 in a running fight. All turrets were put out of action and the rear gunner killed. With the flaps shot away, tanks holed, both rudders shattered, most of the cockpit instruments smashed, inter-com u/s, the Lanc BIII, ND572

PM-M, was extremely difficult to hold. To make matters worse, they were shot up by flak on the way home.

With no chance of making their home base of Elsham Wolds, the wireless operator got a fix on Dunsfold. By superb flying, the skipper brought her in but, without any brakes, she swung off the runway and suddenly hit something extremely solid in the

early morning gloom.

Dazed but miraculously unhurt, the crew were astonished to see that they had crashed into a parked B-17G Fortress of the USAAF. Both were a sorry sight and had to be written off. Closer inspection revealed a six-foot hole in the port wing and hundreds of flak holes.

THE MORNING AFTER *In the early light of a cold winter's morning, November 28, 1943, Mr T. C. Langton, Avro's assistant repair manager surveys this frost-covered Lanc BIII, JB354 PH-O, of 12 Squadron. Returning to Wickenby damaged after the night's raid on Berlin, P/O R. S. Yell, RAAF, had swung on landing; the port undercarriage leg was ripped off and the kite declared a write-off.*

DITCHING WITH A DIFFERENCE *Some crews came through a tour with little or no trouble while others met nothing but trouble, F/O Peter Todd and crew of 61 Squadron survived this prang without injury but were not so lucky the second time, ending up in the Channel after their 16th trip, to Berlin on March 24/25, 1944, being picked up by a German launch and spending the remainder of the war 'in the bag'.*

On their way to Mannheim, on the night of September 5/6, 1943 – only their second operation – their BIII, DV232 QR-K, lost an engine when the port outer caught fire. The Graviner had some effect and, with the prop feathered, they pressed on, bombed, and headed for home.

Coming in to land at Syerston, with Todd desperately trying to keep the approach at 120 mph she suddenly stalled to port, narrowly missing some station buildings. Staggering over the countryside at zero feet, she finally did a steep turn and literally 'belly-flopped' into the Trent half a mile north of East Stoke, near Newark.

DOWN IN RUSSIA *While some Lancs amassed an impressive number of sorties, others achieved but one or two. F/O Les Keeley's Lanc BI, NF938 WS-H, lies wrecked in a bog in the Talagi area, ten miles from Yagodnik near Archangel in Russia, having done just one op.*

One of the force making up Operation Paravane, the destruction of the Tirpitz once and for all, Keeley and his 9 Squadron crew failed to locate Yagodnik airfield in the early hours of September 12, 1944, due to low cloud.

Having made an 11-hour flight from Lossiemouth, petrol was rapidly running out and after five runs and several square searches, a forced landing became inevitable. After jettisoning the load of 'Johnny Walker' bombs in a river, the crew put down in open marshland (left). No one was injured.

Two other kites from No. 9 and two from No. 617 Squadron were wrecked in similar fashion, and though salvage was not possible, much equipment was recovered.

As is well known, the attack on September 15 by the Russian-based force failed to sink the ship but she was badly damaged and her fate finally sealed.

F/Lt George Camsell's BI, PD211 WS-M, also of 9 Squadron (left), after the undercarriage had collapsed on the rough wooden planking airstrip of Belomorsk.

BURN UP *Some crews hit trouble even before they reached a squadron. F/Sgt J. P. Paddison and crew of 1668 CU Bottesford, had an engine fire on a cross-country training flight but managed to force-land their BIII, JB228, at Fiskerton, where it burns fiercely on March 10, 1945.*

113

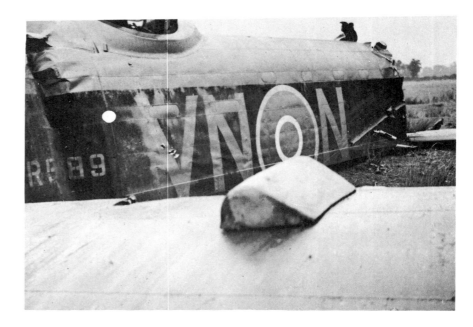

THE FAMOUS FALLEN *The most-photographed Lanc of the war comes to grief; Lanc BI, R5689 VN-N, of 50 Squadron, lies broken in a field at Thurlby (above right). Borrowed by Sgt E. J. Morley and crew for a 'gardening' sortie on September 18/19, 1942, both port engines failed on the approach due to a mechanical fault.*

Though Lancasters had been operating since March 1942, little information had been released to the public except for news of the remarkable low-level daylight op to Augsburg on April 17. On August 28 of that year the free world's press descended on 50 Squadron at Swinderby. S/Ldr Hughie Everitt, a Flight Commander on his second tour,

gave a vivid demonstration of the aircraft's performance and handling qualities in his beloved 'N-Nan' (above left).

For the remainder of the war photos of her appeared in books, periodicals and advertisements and even the Germans used reproductions on propaganda leaflets.

QUEEN ELIZABETH, *Lanc BI R5548 OF-A, ended her days at Wood-hall Spa on December 28, 1942, when her own photoflashes went off inside the fuselage.*

Autographed by HM Queen Elizabeth (now the Queen Mother) on the production line at Yeadon on March 20, 1942, she went to 97 (Straits

Settlements) Squadron and is seen (below left) in her prime with S/Ldr 'Darky' Hallows driving, and who did most of his tour in her.

Irony of fate – he salvaged the nose panel only to have it stolen a year or so later when serving as Chief Instructor at Winthorpe Conversion Unit, and still awaits its return!

UNDER REPAIR

REPAIR SHOP *Damaged aircraft and those lucky enough to survive 500 hours flying were taken for repair or overhaul to a depot such as the LMS railway workshops at Derby, or one of Avro's own repair works, at Bracebridge Heath or Langar. The sections would be divided into nose (D1), mainplane (D2 and F1), fuselage (D3), and tail (D4), each being taken into a different shop. After overhaul, the sections would be reassembled on a 'first off the line' basis, meaning that*

rarely would the same four sections be married up again. Only the nose section would normally keep its original identity, particularly if it bore an emblem. These scenes at Langar in 1943 show (below) 'D1' nose sections being refurbished and (foot of page) the final re-assembly shop. The leading edge of the Lanc in the foreground is lifted to reveal a mass of pipes and wiring. On the inside of the raised panel are the cable cutters. If a balloon cable were hit it should slide along the leading edge

surface intil it became channelled into a 'V' shaped hole. The small detonator would then explode and fire across two hard steel chisels to cut right through the cable – whether the device ever worked in practice is not known. Also in the leading edge is the cabin air intake, and on the side of the cockpit, just below the camouflage line, is the drift sight. The cockpit frame-work is covered in a sealing tape which was painted 'dark earth' before being trimmed.

TEST PILOT *The resident Langar test pilot, S/Ldr Peter J. Field-Richards, signs the Form 700 watched by his Flight Test Observer, Bob Browne. Until the former's permanent attachment, test flights were carried out for Avro by pilots of No. 207 Squadron based at the same airfield. From the time Langar accepted its first Lancaster in September 1942 to the last one in July 1954, 322 were refurbished there.*

PREPARING FOR FLIGHT TEST
In late winter afternoon sunshine at Langar, November 1943, BI, ED430 is made ready after overhaul on a wet, partially completed dispersal. Parts of the aircraft round the tail and fins are still to be repainted.

TAKE 'EM AWAY *The camera angle emphasises the size of the Lanc – big by any standards – as Capt H. A. ('Sam') Brown, an Avro test pilot, gives the thumbs-up to the ground crew before taxying an early machine for a test flight. She is finished in the original 'lamp black' extra-matt, which did not weather well, became powdery and rubbed off easily.*

It was superseded by a smoother paint with a slight sheen. The black finish applied to Lancs became progressively more glossy towards the end of the war, and some Canadian machines were given quite a high gloss final coat. On the starboard chock is Jack Denly.

INSIGNIA

The pawnbroker's sign was a popular feature on many a 'U-Uncle'. Above is BIII, ED480 WS-U of 9 Squadron at Waddington in February 1943, the Lanc in which F/Lt Bill Meyer and crew did a tour

The female form was without doubt the most popular adornment and here is a splendid example on a BX, KB747 NA-X Madam X, of 428 'Ghost' Squadron, RCAF, Middleton St George, in 1945. The bomb symbol presentation is somewhat unusual.

Not all female embellishments were flamboyant and here is one with a difference. F/O Peter Thompson and crew of 12 Squadron, Wickenby, chose Queen of the Chase for their BI, ME788 PH-Q, summer 1944.

A saintly lady is how BIII, PB532 HW-S² of 100 Squadron appeared to her crew. The name stems from the South American origins of her pilot, F/Lt O. Lloyd-Davies, and the style of the bomb symbols suggests there was a musician in the crew. The photograph was taken at Elsham Wolds in April 1945.

Some crews preferred a name instead of insignia and here is a particularly apt one, for aircrews liked their ale!

S/Ldr Dave Robb, RCAF, and his 100 Squadron crew drew many an admiring glance in the air with their BI, PA177 HW-J², Jug & Bottle. *The photo was taken after the Squadron had moved from Waltham, its base since December 1942, to join 103 at Elsham Wolds in April 1945.*

At Linton-on-Ouse in April 1944, a crewman pauses while painting on the insignia devised for a BII, LL725 EQ-Z of 408 'Goose' Squadron RCAF, and already credited with two confirmed fighters. Her usual skipper at this time was F/O E. M. C. Franklin, RCAF.

Many a Disney character emblazoned a kite but rarely more than a single figure on any one Lanc. Here are no less than seven on a BIII, PB480 TC-G² of 170 Squadron, Hemswell, in March 1945, on which F/Lt Bob Chandler and crew did a tour.

Most insignia were painted on the actual metal but some were done on canvas first and then stuck on; the artist in this example was the crew's wireless op, Sgt Ron Woodin.

The Daily Mirror's 'Jane' graced a number of kites and BIII, JB138 QR-J, Just Jane, of 61 Squadron went on to join the elite band of 100-op veterans. Between August 1943 and April 1945 she completed 123 sorties.

With suitable blowsy woman of doubtful virtue is Honky Tonk, *BIII, PB229 LQ-H of 405 'Vancouver' Squadron, RCAF, Gransden Lodge, the mount of F/Lt Lance Burnand, RCAF, and crew for part of their tour in the autumn of 1944.*

405 was No. 6 (Canadian) Group's contribution to Path Finder Force.

Often insignia had no apparent link with the aircraft. S/Ldr Peter Birch (here seen in the cockpit), a Flight Commander with 50 Squadron at Skellingthorpe in the spring of 1943, constantly whistled and hummed the tune The Donkey Serenade, *so his crew had a donkey painted on their Lanc BIII, ED828 VN-S.*

'Old Nick', the devil, was chosen by F/O Ray Hattam, RAAF, and crew of 463 Australian Squadron, Waddington, summer 1944. Each op is denoted by a pronged fork.

A BI, LM130 JO-N, she was one of several of 463's kites adapted to carry cameramen from the RAF's Film Unit. Apart from normal main force operations, they accompanied other squadrons on special raids, such as the Tirpitz attacks.

A caricature of himself featured on all kites flown by W/Cdr Campbell Hopcroft, CO of 57 Squadron at Scampton. This one (below) is his

third, Frederick III, *BIII, ED989 DX-F, in May 1943. Henceforth he became known as 'Freddy' Hopcroft.*

For their emblem S/Ldr Don Rogers, RCAF, and crew of 433 'Porcupine' Squadron, RCAF, had a very young female indeed. The crew's flight engineer Ron Broome proudly poses for a snapshot at Skipton-on-Swale, April 1945 in the cockpit of Little Lulu Mk II, *BI, NG441 BM-L. Note the novel way each sortie is recorded. The crew's first* Little Lulu *was a Halifax, with which the Squadron was equipped until February 1945.*

That well-known symbol of delivery, the stork, was chosen by F/O 'Tony' Davies and crew for their 7 Squadron Lanc BIII, EE129 MG-Y at Oakington, autumn 1943.

No. 7 was 3 Group's contribution to PFF.

Insignia combined with the call letter was the novel idea on BIII, ED539 PO-V, flown by P/O Bill Manifold, RAAF, and crew of 467 Squadron, Bottesford, in the summer of 1943.

A kookaburra dangles the head of Hitler from its beak. Crew decorations appear at the end of the bomb symbols.

Though the nose was the usual place, sometimes other parts came in for treatment. Below is Ropey, a veteran BX, KB772 VR-R, of 419 'Moose' Squadron RCAF, complete with shark's teeth and eyes on all four engine nacelles. Perhaps the skipper had flown Mustangs!

Crew nicknames appear under crew positions, a not uncommon feature.

Air Commodore A. Hesketh, Commander of 53 Base (Bardney, Skellingthorpe and Waddington), watches as the score is chalked on an 8,000lb bomb at Waddington to mark the 100th operation by 467's BI, R5868 PO-S, S-Sugar.

P/O T. N. Scholefield, RAAF, and crew took the old lady on her 100th trip, to Bourg Leopold on the night of May 11/12, 1944, and she went on to reach 137 before retirement.

Mistakenly thought to be Bomber Command's top-scoring 'heavy', and selected for preservation, she exists to this day and stood until recently at the gates of RAF Scampton, from where she first flew in June 1942 with 83 Squadron. She has now been removed to the RAF Museum.

100 NOT OUT

THE 100 OP LANCS There has always been – and, we suppose, always will be – controversy over how many aircraft actually completed 100 operational sorties; and also, whether certain aircraft reputed to have done 100 or more did, in fact, achieve the number of sorties represented on their noses by bomb symbols. Who is one to believe? The ground crews who so faithfully stencilled on another bomb the morning after each op? Or the clerk whose mundane job it was to compile the Operational Record Books? In some cases perhaps we shall never know the true answer however much research is undertaken. For example, there is now some doubt as to whether R5868, 'S-Sugar' did the 137 trips which her bomb motifs would suggest when she was finally withdrawn from service. The ORBs suggest she did only 121 ops, it being possible that the other 16 were added during Operations 'Exodus' and 'Dodge'. Or was she, perhaps, loaned to another squadron for a spell, and recorded in that

unit's ORBs as merely 'S' with no confirmatory serial number?

On some ops the trip would be cut short by recall, battle damage, mechanical trouble, crew illness, etc. At what stage was it counted as an op? Did the aircraft have to cross the enemy coast, or did the hours flown determine the answer? Perhaps the ground crew had their own interpretation of an op completed, which may have differed to that of the ops clerk. Instances have been noted in the ORBs where the clerk has, through habit, continued to quote an aircraft's serial against a code letter for some time after that particular machine is known to have been lost, withdrawn for overhaul, or transferred to another squadron. It could sometimes take several days for changes to be advised due to pressure of war, illness, etc. So, despite a long and exhaustive study of squadron records, it appears likely that some uncertainty will always surround odd aircraft. Unfortunately, aircrew log books, once again, usually compiled

somewhat unwillingly under pressure, contain inaccuracies and do not always provide reliable cross-references.

Whatever the facts and figures may show, let it be said that to achieve something like 1,000 hours of operational flying over an 18-month to two-year period, a Lanc had to possess certain qualities, including luck, durability, good crews (both air and ground), and – above all – a phenomenal standard of mechanical reliability. Apart from the two weeks or so it took to do 500 and 1,000 hour overhauls, a Lanc would rarely see the inside of a hangar. She would be required to stand outside on the most exposed of dispersals throughout most of her life in all weathers.

So far, 28 Lancasters have been traced as having completed the magic 100; other centenarians may turn up in the course of time. In the pages which follow, we show a selection of 100-op kites, some well known, others hitherto unknown.

Mickey the Moocher, *BIII*, EE176 *QR-M* of 61 Squadron, Skellingthorpe, snapped in 1944 after 83 ops. She went on to complete 115 before retiring to become a ground instructional machine; at least, 115 was the number of bomb symbols on the nose, though official records show her as having done 128 ops.

Unofficially adopted by the famous whisky firm, 9 Squadron's *BI*, W4964 *WS-J*, Johnny Walker *began operations in April 1943 and completed her century on September 15, 1944, dropping a 12,000lb tallboy on the Tirpitz in Alten Fjord, Norway.*

On their return to Bardney, F/Lt Doug. Melrose and his crew were presented with a crate of whisky.

After completing 106 trips she was pensioned off, became a ground instructional airframe and survived until scrapped in 1949.

Apart from numerous crew decorations, other symbols adorning the nose include wound stripes, and a searchlight.

Another Lanc whose century was achieved by food drops, represented by tins of spam instead of bomb symbols on the nose, is BIII, PB150 CF-V of 625 Squadron, Scampton.

Lanc *BI*, LM227 *UL-I*, I-Item, of 576 Squadron, Fiskerton, completed the last five of her hundred ops in the hands of F/Lt Stuart B. Simpson and crew on food-dropping sorties over Holland, operation Manna, signified on the side by sacks instead of bombs. The trips were officially credited as ops because of the truce with the Germans being of such a doubtful nature. The insignia include a DFC won by a pilot, a swastika for a confirmed fighter kill by her gunners, and a parachute-mine for a 'gardening' sortie. Removal of the exhaust shrouds dates the photograph as immediately after V-E Day.

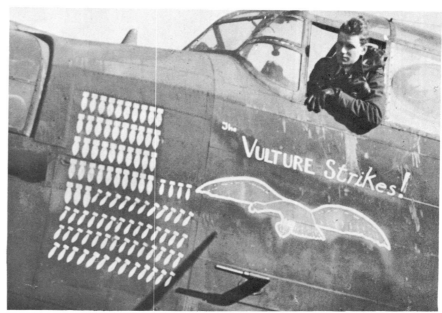

Phantom of the Ruhr, *BIII*, EE139 *BQ-B*, *of 550 Squadron, North Killingholme, completed her century on a daylight trip to Le Havre, September 5, 1944, with F/Lt Joe Hutcheson driving.*

Beginning her career with 100 Squadron (from which 550 formed) at Waltham in May 1943, she ultimately logged 121 trips before being sent to a conversion unit, surviving the war, only to be scrapped in January 1946 without ceremony.

Forward of the insignia is the mustard-coloured gas detection patch as used by 1 Group and which appeared on both sides of the nose.

F/Lt Jack Playford, RCAF, of 100 Squadron, Waltham, in the cockpit of his BIII, ND458 HW-A, Able Mabel, after completing her 121st operation (119 are actually shown here). He had taken Mabel to her century on February 1, 1945, a trip to Ludwigshaven, and on her last bombing op to Berchtesgaden on April 25. With a Manna trip on May 7, flown by W/O Paul S. Tarry and crew, she finally logged 132 ops, before being transferred to the Bomber Command Instructors' School. This worthy veteran was finally laid to rest in 1947.

The 100th bomb goes on ND709 *F2-J* (top right), *a BIII of 635 Squadron, Downham Market after an op on Chemnitz, February 14/15, 1945. Delivered in early 1944, she survived until August 1947, serving at a number of conversion units after withdrawal from squadron use. She is believed to have been Path Finder Force's only century-maker.*

F/O George Blackler of 550 Squadron, North Killingholme, poses (above) *in the cockpit of* The Vulture Strikes, *BIII, PA995 BQ-V, after completing his own tour of 37 ops (27 of them in this machine) and the kite's 100th sortie, with a trip to Chemnitz March 5/6, 1945.*

Beginning operations in May 1944, she failed to return from Dessau, March 11, 1945, only a matter of weeks before the war's end.

There was great rivalry at Skellingthorpe in the summer of 1944 when both squadrons using the base, Nos. 50 and 61, each had an aircraft nearing its 'century'. Which would win, BI, ED588 VN-G or BIII, ED860 QR-N? It was to be a close race between their regular crews, won in the end by F/Lt Basil Turner and crew taking 'N-Nan' to Vitry-la-Francois on the night of June 27/28. 'G-George's' turn came a week later, F/Lt Bill Enoch and crew doing a daylight trip to St Leu D'Esserent on July 4. Unfortunately, 'G-George' failed to return with another crew from Konigsberg on the night of August 29/30, 1944, her 128th op. Almost as if bemoaning the loss of her old friend, 'N-Nan', who had by then done 129, spent the whole of September off ops, presumably on major overhaul. She returned to service in October, doing one more op to bring her total to 130, but on the night of October 28/29, she refused to become airborne on take-off for Bergen, and had to be written off, fortunately without loss of life. Both aircraft achieved over 1,000 hours of flying in a combined total of 36 months of operational use. Not too bad for machines designed for a life expectancy of a mere 40 hours!

A proud bunch of air and ground crew smile for the camera as the 107th bomb is painted on ND578 KM-Y of 44 (Rhodesian) Squadron at Spilsby in January 1945. A BIII, she entered service in February 1944, completed 123 operational trips in the fourteen months to April 1945 and soldiered on until after Operation 'Dodge' in which she took part, being finally retired late in 1945. F/Lt L. W. Hayler and crew did 34 ops in Y-Yorker and had the honour of taking her on her 100th – to Karlsruhe on the night of February 2/3, 1945. The card in the cockpit side-window was a permanent fixture, 'borrowed' by her crew from London Zoo. It read: 'These animals are dangerous.'

'Mother of them all', Bomber Command's top-scoring 'heavy' with 140 trips. G/Capt Sheen, 'Station Master' of Elsham Wolds, paints a DSO on 576 Squadron's veteran BIII, ED888, UL-M² after completing 102 ops. Centre is P/O Jimmy Griffiths who did 30 trips in her and took her up to 99, taking with him on that trip P/O J. B. 'Tinkle' Bell as second dickey and showing not only how she handled but also how to destroy a Ju88 (the crew's second confirmed fighter). The old girl was handed over to Bell and it fell to him and his crew on their first op to take her on her 100th – to Wizernes, July 20, 1944. ED888 started her operational career with 103 Squadron in May 1943, completing 54 sorties before being taken over by 576 Squadron on its formation from a flight of 103 and 101 Squadrons in November. After 77 ops with 576, she returned to 103 for a further nine trips before retirement, her last being to Cologne on Christmas Eve 1944, captained by F/O S. L. Saxe, RCAF. She was tragically scrapped without thought in January 1947 after languishing at an MU for over two years.

WINGS FOR VICTORY

WINGS FOR VICTORY *Lancs played their part in the Wings for Victory savings campaigns and several cities up and down the country had one on display. A new machine cost some £40,000 and many millions of pounds were raised.*

Here are three examples: London (facing page, upper) had 'O-Orange' of 207 Squadron (BI, L7580 EM-O) in Trafalgar Square; Leeds had (facing page, lower) 'P-Peter' of 97 (Straits Settlements) Squadron (BI, R5552 OF-P). *Both were operational veterans, the former having completed 27, the latter 47 sorties.*

It was appropriate that Manchester should have a Lanc for their Wings for Victory effort in March 1943. Above is ED749, *a brand new BI and destined to survive a collision with a German fighter coming back from Stuttgart in the early hours of February 21, 1944, losing six feet of her port wing as well as having the dorsal turret shattered.*

This Lanc, BIII ED930 *(below left), is seen in the Australian outback while on a fund-raising tour of Australasia. For most Aussies, it was their first sight of the aircraft on which so many of their fellow-countrymen were serving, 12,000 miles away. Christened* Queenie, *she flew out from Prestwick in May 1943, in the capable hands of F/Lt Peter Isaacson and his regular crew (the first all-Australian Lanc crew to complete a tour of operations).*

Australia was reached via Canada, the USA, and the Pacific in 72 hours flying. She toured most of Australia and New Zealand and in one day alone helped to raise £17,480. Eventually, she became the pattern aircraft for Lancaster production in Australia, which, as it turned out, was never proceeded with.

In this photograph Queenie *bears South East Asia style roundels. The camouflage later gave way to a natural metal finish and the serial became A-66-1.*

127

MERCY MISSIONS

MERCY MISSIONS *The last bombing operations by Lancs were the destruction by day of Hitler's 'Eagles Nest' at Berchtesgaden on April 25, 1945, and oil storage depots at Vallo (Norway) the same night, but the war was not yet over for the crews. Only four days later they were called in again – to drop, not bombs, but food.*

With communications in Europe at a standstill, and the Germans on the brink of defeat, thousands of Dutch people were left without supplies of food and in a desperate plight. Operation 'Manna' swung into action and, in the space of ten days, Lancasters dropped over 6,500 tons of food from specially designed bomb bay panniers. Although a truce was arranged with the Germans to allow the food-drop to take place, several Lancs were fired on and each aircraft flew fully-crewed and armed 'just in case'.

A 3 Group Squadron, No. 115, carried out the food-dropping trials, the technique being perfected by Major R. P. Martin of the South African Air Force, one of 115's Flight Commanders, and one of several South Africans serving with Bomber Command.

Many air and ground crews contributed their own rations of cigarettes and chocolates for the actual operation, preparations for which went on day and night.

A Mildenhall-based 15 Squadron Lanc unloads its groceries over Holland. NX561, a BI (BVII Interim) flown by F/O C. Hall and crew over The Hague early in May 1945.

ONLY TWO HOURS FROM HOME SWEET HOME *The next and most urgent task was the repatriation of British Prisoners of War, and by V-E Day, May 8, Operation 'Exodus' was well under way. Each Lanc carried 25 passengers, many of whom were a pathetic sight after up to six years in captivity, dressed in any old clothes they could get hold of. In 26 days, 74,000 ex-PoWs were brought home from Brussels and Juvincourt.*

This 149 (East India) Squadron Lanc was, only a few days before, leading a G-H 'vic' on a daylight raid. Now, covered in goodwill messages, she stands at Juvincourt ready to receive her expectant, excited load of passengers, all longing for their first sight of 'Blighty' again and sharing a welcome cigarette with the aircrew before take-off. A lot of the PoWs had themselves been shot down while on Lancs and how they relished their ride!

Included in the repatriation were many Belgian, Dutch and French refugees and this rather bewildered little group waits to board a 514 Squadron Lancaster at Waterbeach on May 17, 1945, some seeing their homeland for the first time in six years.

THE FINAL ACT *for many squadrons before disbanding for good, following Japan's capitulation, was the repatriation of troops from Italy – Operation 'Dodge', in which approximately 100,000 men were ferried home. Many were former 'Desert Rats' of the famous 8th Army who had served throughout the North African campaign, then in the Allied push through Italy, some having been away for nearly five years and who were now only a seven-hour flight from home.*

The scene at Bari in September 1945 as a line of Lancs, now with post-war underwing serials, await their loads of 24 passengers with kit.

FIELD FULL OF LANCS *At one stage of Operation 'Dodge', which lasted from late August until early 1946 over 100 Lancs were stranded in Italy for nearly two months, due to bad weather. Here at Pomigliano they stand stretching almost as far as the eye can see, on roughly-laid metal hardstandings, unable to use the water-logged taxi-tracks or runway.*

Through the summer of 1945 the wartime Squadrons had been maintained in preparation for 'Tiger Force' to carry on the fight against Japan, but following the Atom Bomb and Japan's early surrender, there was a rapid run-down and the end is near for many of the squadrons and the Lancs depicted here.

131

LANCS FROM CANADA

BRAND NEW *Fresh off the Victory Aircraft production line and awaiting delivery to Britain for use by the Canadian squadrons based in the North East. All three turret positions are faired over for the delivery flights via Prestwick, the turrets being fitted on arrival at maintenance units. These Lancs are from an early Canadian production batch, having the 'needle-blade' props. Altogether 430 Lancs were produced in Canada of which 320 were delivered to the UK between September 1943 and August 1945. Clearly visible in this photograph are the bulged bomb doors – a requirement of 6 Group for carrying 8,000lb bombs.*

OFF HOME *With the war in Europe over, the Canadian squadrons soon returned home to prepare for Tiger Force, and the battle against Japan. These scenes are at Middleton St George on the last day of May 1945 as* (left) *the Lancs of 428 'Ghost' Squadron are lined up for a ceremonial send-off and* (below) *the British ground crews wave a sentimental goodbye and good luck to a Canadian crew as the throttles are opened up for the homeward journey via the Azores. Amongst the well-wishers were the C-in-C 'Bomber' Harris and 'Black' McEwen, OC of 6 Group.*

BACK HOME *a Canadian Flying Officer proudly points out his Lanc's part in winning the war – 72 ops! BX* KB760 *NA-P of the 'Ghost' Squadron.*

133

GRAVEYARDS

WAR SURPLUS *The war is over. Almost overnight the squadrons disband and hundreds of Lancs are put out to grass. Some were scrapped almost immediately while others were to languish in fields for several years, awaiting their fate.*

However, many new machines were stored at maintenance units for the Lanc continued in front-line service *with Bomber Command until superseded by the Lincoln in 1947/9, while they were to fly with Coastal Command until October 1956.*

Above is a line-up of veterans at Silloth MU.

THEIR WINGS CLIPPED *Scenes at Malton, Ontario (below and facing page, upper), as brand new Lancs stand cold and unwanted, surplus to requirements, the war in Europe over and Tiger Force disbanded as they were being completed. These are Lancs of a later production batch, with Martin mid-upper turrets and 'paddle-blade' props.*

REPRIEVE *The end of the war did not mean the end of life for the Lancaster. The return of American aircraft under the terms of Lease Lend led to a shortage of reconnaissance and rescue aircraft and it fell to the Lanc to fulfil these roles as a stop-gap measure until newer types were available.*

As the political situation in the early post-war years worsened, Canada in particular had a vast coastline to patrol. Numbers of Mark Xs, new machines and veterans alike, were taken from storage and converted – some remaining in service with the RCAF until 1964.

Rabbit's Stew, still bearing the mementoes of its wartime service, is prepared for conversion at the Malton, Ontario, plant of A. V. Roe, Canada in 1952.

AIRFIELDS – THEN AND NOW

AIRFIELDS – THEN AND NOW
Within a year of the cessation of hostilities, the majority of wartime bomber bases were run down and abandoned. Most reverted to farmland and the farmers from whom the land was requisitioned. Officially, they were classified as 'Agricultural Category 4', which meant they could be ploughed up

and farmed, providing runways, pipes and cables were left intact.

Squatters were quick to move in and farmers also found a ready use for the hangars and numerous Nissen huts for storing farm implements and the like.

Today, a quarter of a century later, even the runways and dispersals on many airfields have disappeared, having

been ripped up for such use as underlays on new motorways. Most of the huts have long since gone and even the black hangars at some bases have been pulled down.

An aerial view of Graveley (above) in 1944 showing the mass of huts and roads. The area occupied by a typical airfield was some 600 acres.

The Watch Office at Graveley (top) as viewed in 1967.
The sole remaining hangar at Gransden Lodge (above) in 1967.
Only seven years after the war, crew huts at Kirmington (left) reduced to rubble.

137

FIDO *demonstration at Fiskerton, 1944 for 49 Squadron crews. This view (above) illustrates to advantage the layout of an airfield built during the war, with black T2 hangars in sharp contrast to the green of the surrounding farmland.*

Painting of a Lanc on the wall of a hut before demolition at Fiskerton in 1961.

By Ermine Street to yesterday

Don Charlwood

Since the end of the war many former Lancaster men have felt a compulsive urge to revisit the airfields from whence they flew on operations.

For those living in Great Britain it is at most no more than a few hours' drive, or a slight detour when on the way to the coast with their families.

However, for the men from the Commonwealth it is more difficult. Some are lucky in being sent to the UK by their company, while others have to save up for years to make the pilgrimage. For all it is a highly emotional experience.

One who returned is Don Charlwood, an Australian from Victoria. His book *No Moon Tonight*, published in 1956, in which he describes his experiences with the RAF, is a classic. The following account was written after a visit to his old haunts in 1958.

Before we began our journey I rang up a number in Cleethorpes. Even after fifteen years, it came easily to my tongue. The voice that had welcomed me then, welcomed me now, nor had the voice changed, although the speaker was past her eighty-sixth year. I remembered going to her home on nights when Bomber Command operations had been cancelled and all Lincolnshire lay under low cloud.

The afternoon was wet and windy, but by five the sky had cleared and down the long, level road I saw Lincoln Cathedral, pale over its city. I remembered it then in cruciform as it appeared to us when we had set course early for Germany, or on days when we had flown low over Lincolnshire for the joy of flying. Soon an odd shock came to me; for the approach to Brigg was upon us long before I had expected it, before I had convinced myself that this was the land of that other life. Insensibly I withdrew from my family. In fifteen years these hills had become places of the spirit to me, so that I saw them now with numb surprise: the windmill outside Brigg, the flesh wasted from its bones; Gallows Wood, now very green, then bare; Barnetby cross-roads above Barnetby village.

I stopped at the cross-roads, the feeling on me that if these hills were real, then hereabouts there must yet be men who had known those days. Signposts pointed east to Grimsby, south to Barnetby, north to Elsham. I felt drawn by the Elsham road, but resolved to come back to it alone. I turned north into the village, descending to the railway that had brought us to squadron life in the autumn of 1942 and had taken us away again. The war had come and the war had gone and there was little change there. We climbed the other side of the valley to a disused Saxon church, sunken in its graveyard, crudely buttressed by men a thousand years dead.

I had once known it well. From its mounded earth it had been possible to see aircraft lift off the Elsham runways, three or four miles away. But now I could see nothing, could only hear the thin whistle of a train in the valley, the train we had caught, no doubt, when departing for leave in London.

Before dark we reached Cleethorpes. When dinner was served I sat again at the head of the table I had known then, the same gracious matriarch before me. I looked at my family with the same faint surprise that had come to me in the wolds two hours before.

"Tomorrow," I said, "I must go to Elsham."

The afternoon was bleak and wet, a day of winter rather than summer. Alone on the Brigg road I passed the gaunt ribs of Kirmington aerodrome, which had once been our satellite. Ahead rose the highest part of the wolds where we had lived.

I had always vowed that if I returned to England, I would walk from Barnetby to Elsham as we had done before. Clearly I would have to break my vow. The rain was steady, my time limited, and the way was incredibly long. As I drove the three miles to the aerodrome, I marvelled that often I had walked this way to Barnetby and back again and then had flown all night. Invariably, it seemed, the weather had been cold, or rain had blown from the North Sea. The trees, the hedges, the fields were miraculously unchanged; I saw a misshapen oak whose arms I had often watched against searchlight beams, a symbol, I had thought then, of the two lives we were living simultaneously.

I turned left to the top of the wolds and came soon to two brick pillars from which the cement was peeling. Here, in 1942, had been our gate. Close by, the guardhouse and the sick-quarters were in ruins, heaps of rubble overgrown with nettles. I kept my eyes turned away still from the aerodrome and the main group of buildings, fearing that all sign of them would be gone. But when I looked, I saw that the main hangar, the watch-office and the water-tower were there still, squat under the rainy sky. Nearer, the dispersal points were empty and the runways were infested with weeds.

I remembered leaving that distant mess one April day in 1943. We had been sitting together as a crew for the last time, our tour over. Our jubilation had drained away, for it seemed incredible that we who had lived so closely should now go our separate ways. I remember nothing of our conversation, but I recall that we were eating bacon and eggs, not by right, but as a last favour to an emeritus crew. Bacon and eggs were the privilege of the men about us. In their white sweaters and their flying-boots they dwelt in a realm far removed from our own. We looked on them with understanding and a degree of envy, but also with relief and not a little benevolent patronage. I left the mess first, for I had a train to catch in Barnetby. We exchanged the usual laconic remarks. Outside there was thick fog. The nearer Lancasters waited, noses to air, but the runways and hangars were invisible. The roads of the camp were busy with cars and bicycles and men on foot, everyone preoccupied with the night's operation.

Now the road was empty. Most of the dispersed Nissen huts had gone, but I had the illusion again that in the intact buildings ahead there must yet be men, or at least a sign left for me. Near the administration block I parked the car. From fifty yards the mess still looked inhabited. I walked through the rain and went in at the open door, all at once anticipating the smell of beer and bacon and wet greatcoats, the sound of voices. But down the long room lay ploughs and harrows and bags of superphosphate. The windows were obscure with dust and cobwebs; the cheap lining of the ceiling hung in tatters. I stood very still. Somewhere hens were clucking and rain gurgled off the roof. There were no other sounds at all. Something in the room eluded me; a deafness shut me from messages on the dusty air. I walked quickly into the rain, groping for understanding of our silenced activity, the purpose of all the courage and devotion I had once seen.

A cracked and puddled road led to the operations block, the bombing-trainer, the barber's shop, the main stores and, finally, the flight office. By a piece of irony amusing and obscene, the long building was now a piggery. Dung was raked into piles where once we had held morning parade – as if the curses of vanished crews had been taken literally by some omnipotent being. The pigs were squealing in conference over the hideous dissolution. I walked slowly to the perimeter track. The wind came clean and free across the last earth touched by our wheels.

I reached the car wet and cold. Rain was still falling steadily, but I stood for a long time, casting about again for some sign of all the comradeship and courage that had ennobled this tattered hill. But the woods and the earth were dumb and the rest was a skull, white in the rain. At the gate I felt an urge to write across the decaying columns: 'Here was the home of 103 Squadron, RAF Bomber Command, 1941–45.'

Under the edge of the aerodrome, at the head of a valley there, I came to Elsham village; a solitary, semi-circular village deserted in the rain. Once it had had a priory, but, like the men of Elsham Wolds, the monks had gone and the priory had gone; only a well, it was said, remained. In the porch of the church I found the names of priors and vicars dating to 1220, and of churchwardens whose family names were repeated over the centuries. I went inside, and on the north wall climbed to a high gallery. I had never been in the church, but once – on the Sunday after El Alamein – we had heard its bells, an unaccustomed, joyful sound, rising from this valley. The war then had seemed almost over.

Close under the roof I could hear rain overtaking the gutters. Except for a tin trunk and a chest of drawers the gallery was empty, but with a start I noticed the bust of a bearded man regarding me fixedly from the shadows. I retreated before his gaze, down to the nave and out of the door.

On the list of churchwardens in the porch the name 'Holmes' was several times repeated, once in 1604, as 'Houlmes'. This had been the name of our mid-upper gunner, a native of these parts and one of the finest poachers on this part of the wolds. His escapades, and the meals he had provided for the crew, and the verve with which he had lived had endeared him to all of us.

THE DAMBUSTERS - FACT AND FILM

THE DAM BUSTERS – FACT

No book on the Lancaster would be complete without mention of its most famous exploit – the breaching of the Ruhr dams by 617 Squadron on the night of May 16/17, 1943. Photographs of the weapon and of the aircraft used on the raid are rare, but (left) is shown a close-up of the special mine designed by Barnes Wallis. The belt drive is to the motor which spun the mine before dropping.

W/Cdr Guy Gibson's aircraft, AJ-G, ED932, is seen (below) at Scampton in January 1947 in use at that time with the Station Flight. After the Dams Raid, it continued on operations with 617 Squadron, being used to drop the 12,000lb tallboys, and was finally scrapped without thought or ceremony in July 1947.

THE DAM BUSTERS – FILM

By the time the decision was taken to make the film in 1953, Lancasters were already in short supply, and four Mk.7s had to be taken out of storage and specially modified. The actual mine was still on the secret list and the mock-up bore little resemblance, though the underhang is thought to have been specially accentuated for filming purposes to make it more obvious.

These photographs were taken by two of the crewmen who did the flying for the film, all crews being on Lincolns based at Hemswell.

Memorial erected at Kelstern in honour of 625 Squadron, with remnants of a once-busy operational station in the background.

The people of the Low Countries have many reasons to be grateful to the boys of Bomber Command. This memorial was erected by the Dutch at Dronten, East Pievoland (formerly the Zuider Zee). The prop is off a 12 Squadron Lanc BI, ED357, brought down by a night fighter on the night of June 11/12 1943, and salvaged by the Royal Netherlands Air Force in 1962. A memorial service is still held here on each V-E Day anniversary.

LANCASTER
PART TWO

Right: **Diverted** Lancasters of No 166 Squadron lined up on the grass at a Midland training airfield on return from a trip and finding their home base Kirmington clamped by weather. Such 'invasions' – often by more than one squadron – on already overburdened OTUs and other second line units, placed great strain on Flying Control, messing and accommodation. The picture was taken late in 1944 and shows BIII ND635 'AS-M' (lost on Nuremberg 2/3 January 1945) in the immediate foreground, still bearing evidence of original ownership! Next in line are BI LM289 'AS-Y', fated to crash in the Kirmington circuit on return from Lutzkendorf 4/5 April 1945, and BIII PB153 'AS-O', lost Nuremberg 16/17 March 1945. /W. V. Francis

1   SECOND PILOT'S SEAT. (FOLDED)
2   WINDSCREEN GLYCOL SPRAY.
3   ENGINE CONTROL LEVERS.
4   FRONT GUN TURRET (2 BROWNING GUNS)
5   EXTRACTOR LOUVER (CABIN HEATING)
6   BOMB AIMER.
7   GLYCOL TANK.
8   AUTO BOMB SIGHT.
9   GLYCOL SPRAY.
10 BOMB AIMER'S WINDOW.
11 AIR TEMPERATURE THERMOMETER.
12 PRESSURE HEAD.
13 PARACHUTE EXIT.
14 PARACHUTE STOWAGE.
15 CAMERA.
16 RUDDER PEDALS.
17 CONTROL COLUMN.
18 NAVIGATOR'S INSTRUMENT PANEL.
19 PILOT'S GLYCOL HAND PUMP
20 FUEL JETTISON CONTROL.
21 AIR INTAKE CONTROL.

22 SEAT ADJUSTING LEVER.
23 BOMB DOOR CONTROL VALVE.
24 PILOT.
25 PILOT'S ARMOUR PLATING.
26 A.R.I. 5033.
27 A.R.I. 5033.
28 NAVIGATOR.
29 T.R.9 F WIRELESS.
30 NAVIGATOR'S D.F. RECEIVER.
31 W.T. OPERATOR'S RECEIVER.
32 TRAILING AERIAL WINCH.
33 T.1154 TRANSMITTER.
34 AMPLIFIER.
35 W.T. OPERATOR.
36 SIGNAL PISTOL.
37 HYDRAULIC RESERVOIR.
38 HYDRAULIC HAND PUMP
39 CABIN HEATING DUCT.
40 CABIN HEATING INLET.
41 B.B.P. PLATE.
42 OIL COOLER.
43 RADIATOR. (COOLANT.)
44 HEADER TANK.
45 MERLIN XX ENGINE.
46 OIL TANK.
47 No. 1 FUEL TANK.
48 UNDERCARRIAGE DOORS.
49 LANDING WHEEL.
50 UNDERCARRIAGE JACK.
51 No. 2 FUEL TANK.
52 FLAME DAMPER.
53 CARBURETTOR AIR INTAKE.
54 No. 3 FUEL TANK.
55 B.B.P. PLATE.
56 B.B. CABLE CUTTER.
57 NAVIGATION LAMP
58 FORMATION KEEPING LAMPS.
59 AILERON.
60 AILERON BALANCE TAB.

61 FLAPS.
62 WHIP AERIAL (BEAM APPROACH.)
63 FLARE CHUTE.
64 MID GUNNER.
65 MID LOWER TURRET (2 BROWNING GUNS)
66 VACUUM FLASKS.
67 ENTRANCE DOOR.
68 DOWNWARD IDENTIFICATION LAMPS.
69 STEP OVER AMMUNITION CHUTES.
70 DIP-STICKS STOWAGE.
71 FIREMANS AXE.
72 FIRST AID STOWAGE.
73 DIPOLE AERIAL.
74 SANITARY PAN.
75 WALKWAY OVER TAIL PLANE.
76 FIXED TAIL WHEEL.
77 AERIAL FOR A.R.I 5000.
78 ELEVATOR.
79 ELEVATOR TRIMMING TAB.
80 ELEVATOR BALANCE TAB.
81 FIN.
82 RUDDER.
83 RUDDER TRIMMING TAB.
84 AERIAL FOR NAVIG. D.F. RECEIVER & T.R.9.F.
85 REAR GUN TURRET. (4 BROWNING GUNS.)

86 DRAUGHT PROOF DOORS.
87 ACCESS LADDER.
88 MID UPPER TURRET
89 AERIAL FOR A.R.I.5000.
90 STEP FOR UPPER TURRET (STOWED)
91 SEA MARKERS AND FLAME FLOATS.
92 AMMUNITION CHUTES.
93 PARACHUTE STOWAGE.
94 PORTABLE OXYGEN STOWAGE.
95 AMMUNITION BOXES.
96 EMERGENCY EXIT.
97 FLARE CHUTE EXTENSION (STOWED)
98 FLAP JACK COVER.
99 RECONNAISANCE FLARES.
100 BACK REST FOR REST SEAT.
101 REST SEAT AND OXYGEN CRATE.
102 DINGHY MANUAL RELEASE.
103 PORTABLE OXYGEN STOWAGE.
104 ARMOUR PLATE DOORS.
105 DINGHY STOWAGE.
106 CONTROL LOCKING GEAR STOWAGE.
107 BOMB WINCH HANDLE STOWAGE.
108 OBSERVATION DOME.
109 WHIP AERIAL A.R.I. 5033.
110 D.F. LOOP AERIAL.
111 VOLTAGE REGULATORS.
112 AERIAL FOR G.P. MARCONI.
113 AILERON TRIMMING TAB.

Contents

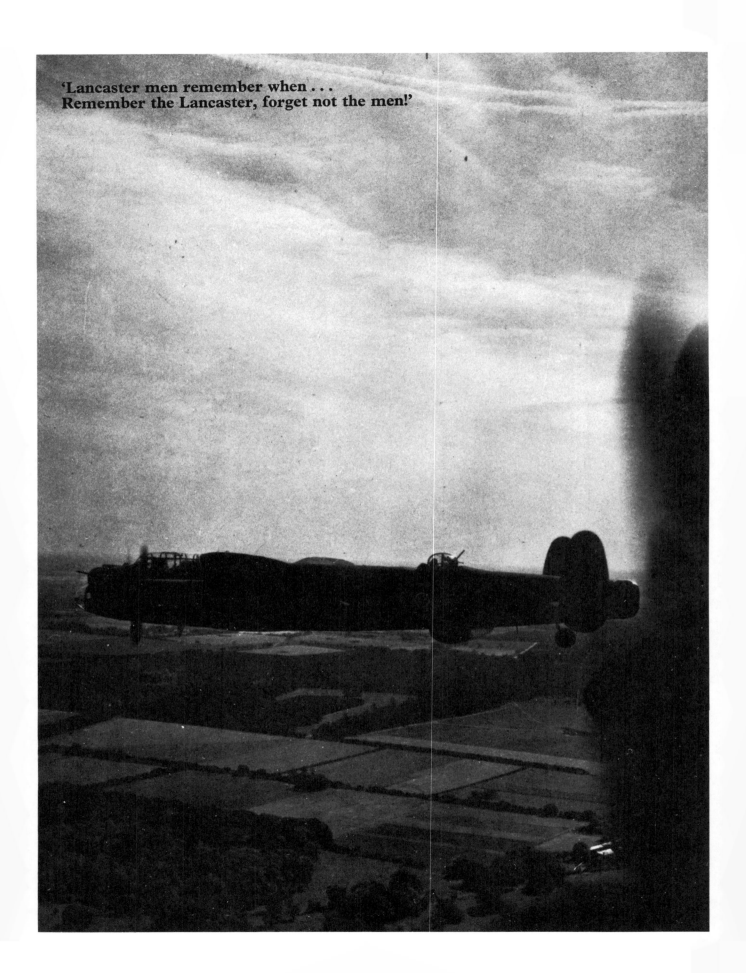

'Lancaster men remember when . . .
Remember the Lancaster, forget not the men!'

Foreword

AIR CHIEF MARSHAL SIR MICHAEL BEETHAM, GCB, CBE, DFC, AFC, ADC, CHIEF OF THE AIR STAFF, ROYAL AIR FORCE

This second volume of Lancaster at War, like the first, is a book about people, people with a difficult, dangerous and unpleasant task to carry out; but it is about a particular group of people, who shared a common bond. The genius and skill of the British Aircraft Industry had put into their hands a quite remarkable tool, the Lancaster, with which to tackle their job.

Each cameo of personal recollection, each incident stands by itself, but in this book they have all been skilfully woven together to produce a recognisable pattern from a kaleidoscope of human experience. Through it the mighty Lancaster, which so many of us still remember with deep affection, stirs, snorts and lives again.

This book is a fitting tribute to a great aircraft, to the aircrew that flew her and to the groundcrew who serviced and supported her. Their contribution to peace in Europe has often gone unsung and has sometimes been denigrated; yet it was a major contribution to that final victory. For the Bomber Offensive had opened up a second front of vast complexity over the skies of Germany, long before the Allies could gather the resources and build up the overwhelming superiority required for the invasion of Europe.

The blood, sweat and tears they shed and the dangers and sacrifices they faced to humble the Nazi war machine must never be forgotten.

Biographical Note:
After pilot training in America, Sir Michael Beetham returned to England for conversion courses, before he joined No 50 Squadron at RAF Skellingthorpe. After a tour of operations

on the Lancaster, during which he won the DFC, he became a Flying Instructor at No 5 Lancaster Finishing School and subsequently, a few months before the end of the War in Europe, he became a Flight Commander on No 57 Squadron at East Kirkby.

His distinguished postwar career has included command of the first RAF air-to-air refuelling squadron, No 214 Squadron at Marham. It was during that tour, flying Valiants, that Sir Michael set up the London to Capetown, Capetown to London non-stop records which still stand. Later he was to command RAF Khormaksar in Aden during the difficult years in the early 1960s.

A variety of senior staff appointments have included a tour as Commandant of the RAF Staff College at Bracknell and the senior Plans and Policy post at the NATO Headquarters at SHAPE. Before becoming Chief of the Air Staff in August 1977, Air Chief Marshal Beetham was first, Deputy Commander-in-Chief of Strike Command and then, Commander-in-Chief RAF Germany and Commander of the Second Allied Tactical Air Force.

Michael Beetham

Left: **Lights Out.** The richly wooded countryside of East Anglia takes on a familiar patchwork of shadowy brown tones as the crews head for the coast and unfriendly skies in the fast gathering darkness. Keeping company with B1 NG361 'OJ-E' from No 149 (East India) Squadron is another Lanc from Methwold. Note rear turret turned to its full port beam position. /*T. W. Simcox*

Introduction

'Not another book on the Lancaster?' One can almost hear the comments. Certainly there has been a wealth of material published on this renowned aircraft, without doubt in the top flight of any list of 'greats', and nudging the Spitfire as the most famous and successful type ever to serve the Royal Air Force and Commonwealth.

This sequel to *The Lancaster At War* is offered in response to continued interest in the Lanc and an inspiring band of mortals through whom she breathed life during three years of war. The original book, published in 1971, broke new ground and was the progenitor of a series of 'At Wars' recalling the life and times of aircraft also in aviation's hall of fame.

We make no apology for following the basic theme of our first volume. Judging from worldwide opinion and comment, veterans, enthusiasts and laymen alike prefer to read about those who flew and maintained Lancasters, rather than study its technical development. For those aviation buffs interested in horsepowers, production figures and the like we cannot recommend too highly *Lancaster – The Story of a Famous Bomber*, an industrious tome compiled by that noted historian and friend of many years, Bruce Robertson.

Through the experiences of men who built, serviced and flew in her, this brilliant jewel in the crown of the British aircraft industry comes alive. Time, in her respect, is relative. She may not, in the end, prove to be absolutely immortal. But certain it is that it only needs the right stimulus to jog not a few memories sharply and bring her past vividly to life.

It is hard to say what the ultimate attraction in her was. She was noisy and uncomfortable, yet those who flew in her loved her. One forgave the cramped conditions for it was clear she was ahead of her time and lifted weights far in excess of what seemed possible in an aircraft her size. One accepted, and ultimately rejoiced in, the shattering roar of her four engines, because they never seemed to fail.

But one does not fall for a raucous harpy, no matter how efficient. There was more to her than that. For one thing, she had a beauty in flight second to none. Then there was her willingness to be thrown about the sky with a great load in her belly, suffer untold damage to her vitals, and still, incredibly, limp back home on a wing and a prayer. It was perhaps this quality of dependability that did it. She inspired affection and that sentiment has not faded with the passing years.

Much has been written about the war in the air, and the role of Bomber Command and its sustained offensive has not always been presented in the rosiest of lights; it is fair to say that its task precluded any possibility of that. A certain magnetic attraction existed for some engaged in it; but the bomber offensive was, in truth, a dark and bloody business. The bloodiness cannot be gainsaid; the dark side has, perhaps, been over-intensified and not always recognised as a necessary precursor of a coming good.

Thirty-odd years on, the majority of those who survived tend to remember the good times; the nightmares and horrors of a bitter, unrelenting conflict have largely receded into memory's limbo. To balance the overriding aura of nostalgia unavoidable in a book of this nature we have included some stories recounting the unpleasant aspects of war.

Inevitably, the accounts represent but a fraction of the outstanding contribution to victory made by Lancaster air and ground crews. Written by men who modestly describe themselves as 'average', they none the less typify the guts and fortitude, skill and devotion to duty to be found throughout Bomber Command. Our thanks to them all.

Selecting the photogrpahs was every bit as difficult as deciding on the stories. Our extensive files date back a quarter of a century and it has again been a case of 'what to leave out'. No attempt has been made to illustrate every squadron; that some are mentioned or illustrated more than others does not indicate any preference on our part. Few of the pictures have been published before and a high proportion were taken illicitly despite an overall ban on cameras and general lack of film. Our thanks to each donor, whose names are recorded at the end of each caption.

Acknowledgements

In the space available it is impossible to name all the people who have been directly or indirectly connected with this book. The majority made their contribution many years ago and have long since dispersed to the four corners of the earth; some are no longer with us; all are remembered in our thoughts.

A number of individuals however deserve special mention for a variety of reasons:

Paula Alexander who, as a young girl lived through the horrors of Hamburg, provided the Aftermath; Cliff Allen who, in addition to writing a story, has guided us on engine matters and the life of ground crews; Trevor Allen for proof reading and constant encouragement; Air Chief Marshal Sir Michael Beetham, GCB, CBE, DFC, AFC, ADC, himself a Lancaster pilot, for his eloquent foreword; Harold ('Barney') Brookes, former fitter, for background on ground crew and forever putting us in touch with fellow erks; Jim Brookbank, one time bomb aimer, for providing the evocative poem, setting the scene so well for the chapter 'We flew Lancasters'; Eric Chapman for performing wonders with old prints; Lilian Chapman, his wife, for so much patient typing; Sqn Ldr Jack Currie, DFC, a Lanc skipper and contributor to our previous book, for his delightful caricature; Tommy Cushing, fellow enthusiast, for many favours; Jim Emmerson, for spreading the word in Canada in addition to penning a story; Stan Hanson provided a story and spent many hours proof reading and offering advice; Charlie Hatton, former Head of the Avro Repair Organisation, for background detail; Harry Holmes for unstinting help over many years; Alex ('Sandy') Jack, C Eng, M IMech E, FSLAET recounted his life with Avro and listened with endless patience to our searching questions; Sqn Ldr J. H. ('Mick') Maguire, MBE, for passing on his peerless knowledge gained as an armament officer; Norman Malayney, an up-and-coming Canadian buff, for sharing the benefit of his labours; The staff of Peter Moss Photography Ltd for difficult copying and printing work; Gerry Murphy, another who spent hours proof reading as well as contributing a story; Joe Nutt, contributor; fellow historian, delighted in spending hours tying up elusive loose ends for us; Captain Jimmy Orrell, OBE, for his memories as an Avro test pilot. Norman Parker, for providing a number of choice items over the years; Cyril Parrish for printing; Bob Roberts for endless copying and printing; Sqn Ldr Jim Starky, DSO, DFC, noted Lancaster driver and test pilot, for the benefit of his sound knowledge; Ron Valentine for endless snippets on the role of the bomb aimer, bombing equipment and techniques; John Walsh, whose emotive verses resulted from an afternoon spent touring abandoned airfields.

153

Abbreviations

AC	Aircraftman	'M' Gear	Medium supercharger gear
acc	Accumulator	NCO	Non-Commissioned Officer
AG	Air gunner	(O)AFU	Observers Advanced Flying Unit
AGS	Air Gunnery School		
ammo	Ammunition	OTU	Operational Training Unit
AP	Armour piercing	PFF	Path Finder Force
API	Air position indicator	Plt Off	Pilot Officer
auw	All weight up	PNB Scheme	Pilot-Navigator-Bomb Aimer scheme
B&GS	Bombing & Gunnery School		
CO	Commanding Officer	POW	Prisoner of war
CU	Conversion Unit	psi	Pounds per square inch
D/F	Direction finding	RAF	Royal Air Force
DI	Daily inspection	RAAF	Royal Australian Air Force
DR	Dead reckoning	RCAF	Royal Canadian Air Force
EFTS	Elementary Flying Training School	revs	Revolutions
		rpm	Revolutions per minute
ETA	Estimated time of arrival	RSJ	Rolled steel joist
Flg Off	Flying Officer	R/T	Radio telephone
Flt Lt	Flight Lieutenant	SABS	Stabilised Automatic Bomb Sight
Flt Sgt	Flight Sergeant		
F700	Aircraft's log book	SBA	Standard beam approach
GCI	Ground controlled interception	SBC	Small bomb container
		Sqn Ldr	Squadron Leader
Gee	Navigation aid	Sgt	Sergeant
G-H	Navigation/bombing aid	'S' Gear	Full supercharger gear
Grp Capt	Group Captain	TAS	True air speed
HC	High capacity	TI	Target indicator
HCU	Heavy Conversion Unit	u/c	Undercarriage
H2S	Navigation/bombing aid	u/s	Unserviceable
IAS	Indicated air speed	u/t	Under training
I/C	In charge	USAAF	United States Army Air Force
IFF	Identification friend or foe	VHF	Very high frequency
ITW	Initial Training Wing	WAAF	Womens Auxiliary Air Force
Kcs	Kilocycles	Window	Strips of tin foil to confuse enemy radar
LAC	Leading Aircraftman		
LFS	Lancaster Finishing School	Wg Cdr	Wing Commander
MC	Medium capacity	WO	Warrant Officer
Met	Meteorology or meteorological	W/T	Wireless telephone
		'4x2'	Linen-like cloth used for cleaning
M/F	Medium frequency		
MT	Motor transport		

The Making of a Legend

SANDY JACK

The technical development of the Lancaster has been well documented and it is not the purpose of this book to repeat a story already well known. However, we present here the personal recollections of a man intimately concerned with the birth and development of this legendary design.

Certainly few men alive today are more qualified to tell the story of this remarkable aircraft than Sandy Jack who, as Chief Inspector of the Lancaster Group, was involved in every aspect of design, production and development. In forthright style he describes some of the trials and tribulations, disappointments and teething troubles which had to be overcome; in addition he provides personal pen pictures of Chief Designer Roy Chadwick and Managing Director Roy Dobson – names forever linked with the Lanc in the hall of fame.

A Scot from Edinburgh, Sandy had moved into the world of aviation in 1932 following 15 years in the marine and automobile industries. A brief spell as Chief Engineer of the Scottish Motor Traction Company's aviation department was followed by a similar post with Midland Scottish Air Ferries, Renfrew, before he moved to A. V. Roe in 1934 as a Field Service Engineer.

Appointed Chief Inspector in February 1935, at the age of 33, he had actively participated in the rapid expansion of the aircraft industry and the Government-sponsored 'Shadow Factory Scheme', and was Avro Group Chief Inspector by the outbreak of war in 1939. The forming of the Lancaster Group in 1942 extended his responsibilities still further, and by the time it disbanded in 1945, the Lincoln and Tudor were on the stocks, Ansons and Yorks continued in production, and the Shackleton was under development.

In a major reorganisation during July 1947 he handed over the Inspection Department to his deputy and moved into a succession of managerial posts until finally retiring in April 1968, when Deputy Product Support Manager. The passing years have not dulled his agile mind, and as a sprightly 76-year old Sandy is still active as a consultant.

' "Although the overall performance of this aircraft design is outstandingly good, the Ministry cannot but deplore the methods employed to achieve this result." These words, or something like them, formed the penultimate paragraph of a letter received at Manchester expressing the almost unanimous opinion that, following official trials at Boscombe Down, the new Lancaster was the most efficient and effective heavy bomber so far produced anywhere. This was but one incident in the stormy passage involved in getting the Lancaster introduced. It is a story of private enterprise at its best; of far sighted men prepared to go to any lengths in order to overcome seemingly insuperable odds.

'We knew we had an urgent problem on witnessing the return of No 207 Squadron's Manchesters on the occasion of the type's operational debut. This was an attack by six aircraft and crews on a German Hipper class cruiser in Brest harbour on the night of 24/25 February 1941. The first operation with a new type of aircraft is always a momentous event and Roy Chadwick and I were there at Waddington to find out at first hand how they had fared. Crews were generally enthusiastic despite a certain amount of hydraulic trouble. More worrying was the flak damage some had suffered. This was not surprising as the designed operational height was only some 15,000ft. Chadwick had flown to Waddington but bad weather the following morning grounded the Anson so he travelled back with me in my car. We naturally discussed the Manchester's performance and prospects and I recall him saying: "Jack, if they are in the flak now, they will be no good a year from now, even if the engines are fully developed."

'Chadwick, Roy Dobson and the rest of the executives had already outlined a scheme using the existing structure and tooling to dramatically improve the machine's performance. Even before the prototype Manchester was through its trials it was clear we would have trouble with the under developed Vulture engines. Consequently, the Avro design team had provisionally prepared two Bristol Centaurus radials, or two Napier Sabre in-lines (both promising engines but

Above: Sandy Jack as a platoon commander in the Woodford Home Guard 1940./*A. C. Jack*

Above: **Problem Child**
General view of the Manchester. The bulky, untidy-looking Vulture installation contrasts sharply with the neat underslung Merlins of the Lancaster; the difference in undercarriages can also be compared. The picture was taken at Coningsby March/April 1942 and features a No 106 Squadron machine being prepared for a test flight. Two of her aircrew can be seen under the bomb bay/*P. Cartwright*

in early stages of development), and designated Mk II; the other to use four Merlins (proven engines equipping the Spitfire and Hurricane), designated Mk III. The latter was the first choice.

'Two factors in the original Manchester specification and design provided the "escape route" which led to persuance of the latter, and thus directly to the Lancaster Mk I. Air Ministry specification P13/36 had called for an airframe structure capable of sustaining the loads arising from catapult launching, amongst which was the high inertia drag loading in the wing structure. This load had been taken care of by using relatively thick skin plating. By the time Chadwick pressed ahead with his four-engined Manchester, catapult launching was no longer a requirement. Increased wing span on the other hand was now an obvious necessity, and could readily be obtained simply and at little tooling cost or delay in production. One simply "stretched" the original wing.

'All existing wing ribs were retained, pitched however some three inches further apart. The spars were stretched to suit by extruding longer booms, which could be machined on the existing Avro designed milling machines, the base of which could easily be adapted to suit. The limiting factor was the ability of the extrusion press at High Duty Alloys to work continuously at maximum capacity without breakdown until a bigger press could be built. I have recollection of a very heated high level meeting at Chadderton where Avro, High Duty Alloys, Air Ministry and Ministry of Aircraft Production representatives hammered out the

risks and benefits involved. Fortunately Avro and HDA were given permission to proceed.

'With no catapult load requirement it was possible to use thinner skin throughout, so the end product was a wing of 102ft span, lighter and stronger. Capable of taking four Merlins, or similar powerplants, it was, moreover, far more aerodynamically efficient, as a result of the improved chord/span ratio. With no dramatic tooling problem involved – the main undercarriage components being adaptable, the engine mountings easy to modify and manufacture – it was possible to have a prototype flying in a remarkably short time. The problem area was the engines.

First Flight
'Air Ministry was adamant that no Merlins could be spared from fighter production. However Dobson and Chadwick, together with Hives of Rolls-Royce, "found" four Merlins and the prototype Manchester III, BT308, took shape in the Ringway Airport hangar. The maiden flight test on 9 January 1941, in the hands of Harry Brown and Bill Thorn, was highly satisfactory and a date for the final design conference was promptly fixed. Little change was required and it was expected that the aircraft would be ready to fly to Boscombe Down for official trials in about one week's time.

'Still MAP was not totally convinced. It had wanted to cancel the whole Manchester programme once development work on the Vulture engine was stopped in 1940. Even when continual pressure from Avro – notably Dobson and Chadwick – resulted in a contract

Origins General views of the Woodford erecting shop (*below*) Rear fuselage sections, brought by road from Chadderton, along with Merlin engines, fuel tanks and other components, ready to be introduced onto the production line. The picture was taken circa September 1943 and the Lancs are from the early 'JB' serial batches. Note the Monica aerials below the rear turrets. (*left*) Frontal view showing cranes positioned in front of each engine bulkhead prior to bolting on and connecting up each Merlin. When in full swing there were four parallel production lines. /*Avro: T. H. Franklin*

for a prototype to the four-engined "stretched" Manchester specification being awarded in November 1940 (1/P1), there was much scepticism in official circles. All this came to a head when MAP gathered together a selection of the latest American types, and asked UK designers to look them over and see what modern bomber aircraft should look like!

'Chadwick returned in a most belligerent mood, snorting: "If that is what these ——— think are super bombers, I'll show them." He promptly brought 20 draughtsmen and their drawing boards out to the hangar and set about modifying the Manchester III to his own satisfaction – regardless of whether or not it agreed with the final design conference decisions. The bomb doors were shorn of the safety locks along their mating edges, along with the hydraulic operating jacks, pipes and valves; the rest bed went out; the radio masts were removed and the aerial run from the tip of each fin to terminal pots on the cockpit canopy; equipment was rearranged internally to improve access and ease of movement by the crew between stations. The flight shed fitters had the Chadwick performance mimicked to the amusement of all and sundry – particularly during meal breaks. It went something like this; "Boy, bring a spanner and a hacksaw. Remove this and that and throw it out to the draughtsmen."

'Meanwhile, No 207 Squadron was working up to operational strength with its newly acquired Manchesters. This was a very busy period for us all and there was much liaison between ourselves, Rolls-Royce and No 5 Group. The relationship between No 5 Group

Above: **Build Up** Woodford circa August 1942, when production was in full swing and the usual crop of teething troubles which beset any new types of aircraft had been ironed out. The rural atmosphere of the airfield – situated on the outskirts of Stockport, itself but a few miles from the city of Manchester – is clearly apparent./*Avro*

Top right: **Personal Glimpse** Poised on the flat roof of Woodford's hangar-mounted Flying Control post, Sandy Jack, facing north, snaps six Lancs on the apron early in 1942. Barely discernible on the horizon are the main assembly sheds./*A. C. Jack*

Bottom right: **Power and Majesty** Posing for company photographs provides the rare opportunity for an Armstrong Whitworth test pilot to put on 60° of bank and show what a Lanc II can do. Delivered to No 408 ('Goose') Squadron RCAF at Linton-on-Ouse, this machine (DS778) was, like so many, destined for an early demise, failing to return from Kassel 22/23 October 1943 – barely two months from the day this picture was taken. /*Hawker Siddeley/AWA*

and Avro was always very close and cordial; so much so that by 1942 the group was often referred to as Avro's Air Force. I have many vivid memories of car journeys over the Pennines, often in the most atrocious weather; or negotiating perilous mountain roads at night by the light of "masked" headlamps. During the winter I carried chains for all four wheels, a spade to dig out drifts, a pinch bar, sledge hammer and rope blocks to recover the car from ditches. Even so I got stuck one night between Chesterfield and Baslow and three hours' strenuous digging was required to reach a friend's house about one mile away.

'In the period following Dunkirk, when we were subjected to the Blitz, I had an amusing encounter with our Civil Defence. It was a Sunday morning and I was en route to 5 Group at Grantham, who had a problem. Near Staveley, police and Civil Defence officials barred my way and told me that I could not proceed as there was an unexploded bomb in the road ahead. Expressing surprise, as there had been no reports of enemy action in the area to my knowledge, I asked how long it had been down, how big the hole was, and added that if there was 6ft clear from hole to edge of road I was going through! They were aghast at this remark and then admitted that it was a practice operation. My reply was none too polite as twice in the previous week I had been driving over real ones in Liverpool docks. However my "emergency pass" (something they did not know even existed), which authorised me to join HM Forces convoys or proceed at my discretion over roads closed to the public, dissolved any further resistance and I proceeded peacefully and happily over their "delayed action bomb".

'About two weeks late, BT308 finally departed for Boscombe Down on 28 February and began intensive flight trials. The first reports were extremely flattering so all the "specialists" who had participated in the final conference went along to see their "brain-child" in final epoch-making form; and to share the glory. Consternation ensued for many or their "pet" items had – far from being modified – been simply eliminated! Shrieks of protest and dismay mingled with the plaudits of the test crews at Boscombe Down. In due course the report of the trials arrived at Manchester, accompanied by the strongly worded letter of diaspproval mentioned earlier. One wonders when, if ever, the changes made could have been carried out through official procedures!

'Due to the basically simple and easy to produce design – plus the fact that tooling was little affected by the redesign – it was possible to start production of the Lancaster (as it was soon renamed), virtually at once. Avro received an initial contract for 450 in June 1941, a number of which had already been ordered as Manchesters and would now be completed as Lancasters. The first production aircraft, numbered L7527, took to the air on 31 October 1941 – just nine months and 22 days after the first prototype's maiden flight. A second prototype, DG595, had meanwhile been flown on 13 May 1941, and joined BT308 at Boscombe Down.

'Barely two months later, L7537 was delivered to No 44 (Rhodesia) Squadron at Waddington on 24 December 1941, a very welcome Christmas gift, and joined by two more (L7538 and L7541) before nightfall. Thus the Lancaster had reached the first RAF squadron only one year and 14 days after No 207 Squadron had accepted the Manchester. As before, an Avro contingent travelled to Waddington for the event and, on 3 March 1942, were on hand when four of No 44 Squadrons' Lancs took off for a mining sortie in the Heligoland Bight. There was quite a celebration when they returned, the crews full of praise for their new mounts. With regret I did not join them at a luncheon party laid on at Chadderton. Seating was limited and those of us who frequently liaised with No 5 Group and the squadrons, gladly stood down so that production staff, normally confined to the factory, could enjoy the crews' company on this historic occasion. Relations between Avro and No 44 Squadron (closely followed by No 97 and others) became very close during this time. Their ground crews, many of whom were Rhodesians, attended courses at the factory in order to know their charges thoroughly, and pass on their knowledge to others. The aircrews, containing a sprinkling of Rhodesians in their number, were frequent visitors as they ferried new or modified machines during the early teething troubles and working-up period.

'By now a sustained campaign by Frederick Handley Page, both at Service and political level, to have the Manchester stopped and Avro's facilities turned over to Halifax production, was finding fewer friends daily. His Merlin-engined Halifax was a superior aircraft to the Manchester with Vultures; of that there was little doubt. Moreover, some 50 Halifaxes were with Bomber Command by January 1942, a time when Manchesters were still giving trouble, and only 14 Lancasters equipped No 44 Squadron. Though the ensuing months would show the Halifax to be a disappointment (unbeknown to us of course), it seems probable the deciding factor in allowing Avro to proceed was a result of the ease with which Lancasters would be produced from existing tooling.

Forceful Partnership
'During these dramatic and unforgettable days, the "presence" of Dobson and Chadwick was undeniable. Individually two quite different personalities, they were complementary to an extraordinary degree, and together formed a most forceful and effective partnership.

'Roy Hardy Dobson – "Dobby" to all in Avro – was born at Horsforth, Yorkshire in 1891. He served an engineering apprenticeship with T. and R. Lees of Hollingwood, Manchester before joining Avro in 1914. Such was his potential that by 1916 he was in charge of the company's Experimental Department. Soon after the end of World War I he became Works Manager; was appointed General

Manager in 1934; became a director in 1936, and Managing Director in 1941. A forceful and often "blunt Yorkshireman", he was always determined to have things done his way – and at once. He suffered neither fools nor delays in any circumstances.

'In my experience, if one was not overawed by him and insisted on stating one's case clearly and concisely, he would give the matter further and fair consideration. He came to quick decisions – in the short term usually good ones – but in my view Roy Chadwick was, in general, more far sighted. Dobby made frequent and unpredictable visits to the factories at all hours of the day or night. Everyone in Avro knew both men by sight and many had spoken with them. Dobby possessed tremendous energy and a personality which inspired the work force. In this respect he reminded me strongly of Winston Churchill. If he decided that certain changes were necessary to keep the Lancaster at maximum efficiency, or to rectify a suddenly disclosed defect, he would authorise immediate action, without waiting for contract action through the Ministry.

'Avro had very close ties with Bomber Command and the groups operating Lancasters. As a result they would always co-operate with Avro by providing facilities on operational units for urgent work to be done. This "short circuiting" of official procedures naturally tended to infuriate many bureaucrats and some interesting and acrimonious correspondence often ensued. If Dobby authorised you to carry out such an operation, he would fully support you in any subsequent upheaval – even to Cabinet level.

'Roy Chadwick was born at Urmston, Manchester in 1893, and on leaving school entered the drawing office of the British Westinghouse Company, Trafford Park, where his father was a departmental head. In 1911 he persuaded A. V. Roe to take him on as a draughtsman, and continued working with Avro for the rest of his life. When J. D. Siddeley bought the Avro company in 1928 Chadwick was appointed Chief Designer. This was followed by his appointment as a director in 1936, in which capacity he continued until his death. During World War I he learned to fly and immediately after the conflict did much flying, notably in the work's "Baby". However, a crash from low altitude in 1919 resulted in serious injury, and probably induced him to devote an unusually high proportion of design time and effort in harmonising flying controls correctly; also ensuring that all aircraft he designed were as safe and easy to fly and land as possible. I feel sure his efforts in this direction undoubtedly saved the lives of many aircrew flying Avro aircraft.

Above left: **Driving Force** For the Lancaster it was the dynamic partnership of Managing Director Sir Roy Dobson (left) and Chief Designer Roy Chadwick./*Avro*

Left: **An Eye for Detail** Chief Test Pilot 'Sam' Brown (in pilot's seat) and his deputy 'Bill' Thorn work their way through the check list before a test flight in one of the early production Lancasters (almost certainly L7577) at Woodford circa February 1942. This clear view shows to advantage the restricted – yet adequate – working space in the cockpit area; emphasis on utility and all-round vision. Note that the armour plate behind the pilot's seat is here shown in its hinged position. Foreground is the navigator's station. /*Popperfoto*

Above: **Production Testing** An early production Lanc about to be put through her paces at Woodford early in 1942. These early batches were virtually hand-built machines and had a slightly superior handling quality. A surprising number survived the war. Note the ventral gun turret, soon discarded in squadron service. Such was the attention to design and ease of production that rarely would each machine require more than two test flights before delivery to the RAF. Each test crew put in upwards of six flights per working day to keep up with demands./*A. C. Jack*

'As a person he was invariably polite and quietly spoken, commanding respect and goodwill from all with whom he worked. He was both an accomplished violinist and artist, and the effect of this training was, I believe, evident in his work and character. Adept at the difficult task of finding the simplest and easiest way to produce mechanisms or structures to meet design requirements, his philosophy was aptly expressed when he said: "We are simple people who design and make simple aeroplanes to be flown by other simple people."

'He was always personally involved with all aspects of design, general and detailed, spending about one or two days each week going around the draughtsmen's boards in company with the leading hand or system designer responsible. A harsh critic of detail design, he would say: "There must be a simpler way to do that"; whereupon he would proceed to sketch out the answer. He also spent much time in the shops watching manufacturing stages and asking pertinent questions of the workmen and supervisors. Workmen could always approach him and he would listen to criticism or complaints, and accept suggestions on how a part could be more easily or simply produced. All would be seriously considered and the appropriate action taken.

'Likewise, Chadwick would discuss handling and aerodynamic problems with the flight test pilots and servicing crews; and when he thought it necessary or helpful, would fly with them to obtain first-hand experience of the problem. Throughout the aircraft industry, government, research and test establishments, and the RAF, his undoubted competence, coupled with unfailing good manners, earned the respect and friendship of all. The success of the Lancaster owed a great deal to Roy Chadwick's foresight in designing from the earliest Manchester project a bomb

bay strong enough and roomy enough to carry the total maximum payload in one piece. This idea was not popular in 1936, when the largest bomb in production was the 2,000lb AP!

Problems, Problems . . .

'The phenomenally rapid introduction of the Lanc was not achieved without incident – in fact many incidents for, like all new aircraft, the Lanc had its fair share of teething troubles. For example, an early production machine (R5539) crashed on 18 April 1942 with loss of the entire crew while engaged on diving trials at A&AEE Boscombe Down. The programme called for a number of dives to be carried out, each to a higher speed, until the maximum diving speed (some 375mph) was reached. Normal procedure was to land after each dive and inspect the structure for signs of damage. Up to the 21st dive – all done by the same crews, with a former Manchester pilot as captain – nothing was found to indicate deformation or incipient failure. The 21st dive – ironically flown by a different crew – proved fatal. Evidently a large section of the top skin had come adrift from the front spar boom on the port wing and caused loss of control; at low altitude and airspeed the Lanc stalled into the ground and was burnt out.

'Fortunately, the evidence identifying the cause of failure survived the fire. A unique method of attaching the wing skin panels to the mass booms had failed due to cumulative tolerance effects in quantity production; this was not foreseen during the development period when only small samples were made and tested. This fastener comprised a solid rivet driven into a blind tapped hole drilled through the skin and into the spar to a controlled depth. For production it had been decided to make a skin lap joint on the boom, but as no adequate tests of production samples had been carried out, the double skin tolerances were such that the rivet could not completely fill the cavity. Another adverse factor was the impossibility of ensuring that the two skins were held closely in contact with each other and the spar boom while the rivets were driven home. By fastening through one skin thickness only, and controlling both hole and rivet tolerances, the problem was completely cured.

'Another incident – fortunately without fatal result – was the coming loose of the detachable centre section leading edge panels designed to facilitate servicing. The problem lay with "toggle" fasteners. These were difficult to inspect and a solution was found by adopting rows of screws with large heads, thus allowing easy checking – even in the dark by feel; and, being more numerous, several could come loose without endangering safety.

'Two major problems occurred in the fuel system. The first arose from the use of immersed fuel pumps (as used in Spitfire overload tanks) in the Lancaster's wing fuel tanks. While the electric pumps performed, all was well; but they did not work for very long. They had been designed for short time runs as Spitfire tanks held only some 50gal; the Lanc tanks held many times this amount so the pumps were required to run continuously for hours at a time. Apart from merely failing they could stop without drawing enough current to blow a fuse: whereupon they would act as electrical fuel heaters and cause complete loss of fuel supply due to vapour locking.

'A typical failure involved a Lanc which force-landed at Balderton with two engines out. In the company of Willis, our drawing office section leader responsible for fuel systems, I dashed to the scene in my car. There we were met by Air Vice-Marshal Sir Alec Coryton, AOC No 5 Group, and he very forcibly said we must provide a remedy forthwith. An obvious engineering solution of fitting continuously rated fuel pumps was not possible at short notice so desperate trouble required desperate solution. Willis and I decided we could weld up from steel tube and plate – available from Anson production – inverted U form suction pipes to replace existing pumps. We telephoned Manchester and by the following morning the works development Lanc was fitted with a set of these simple monstrosities. We flew it with minimum fuel levels in each tank to 25,000ft without incident, and as soon as we landed Roy Dobson authorised the immediate manufacture of enough sets to equip all Lancs extant. These were all made and fitted in about one week.

'Meanwhile, the second made-up set had been issued to Rolls-Royce for tests on their high altitude fuel systems rig. Only two days after delivery they phoned up in a panic, to inform us that the system would not work above 9,000ft. Now and then one is gifted with a blinding flash of the obvious, and fate was kind to me. I asked Rolls-Royce how many hours their rig pumps had run and politely suggested they were "clapped out" and had no suction power left. It was most unlikely at that time that any Lanc engine had run more than 200 hours so I suggested they fit new production engine pumps on their rig. The entire Lancaster "fleet" ran on those pipes for many weeks while the system was modified and no further trouble was experienced.

'Some considerable time later another problem manifested itself. A squadron reported that a fuel cock barrel had remained in the closed position despite the flight engineer turning his cockpit control to "fully open". We rushed over to No 5 Group and obtained the offending cock for examination. Despite being of sound design in allowing easy operation yet preventing plug sticking, it soon became apparent we had another case of tolerance build up on our hands. A taper plug, held in place by a special spring, had a V groove cut across its smaller end, engaging with a like-tapered bar fastened to an operating spindle. If the plug was stiff, the V block, acting as a wedge, pushed the former down against a spring – so moving the plug down the taper and allowing it to turn. On the cock in question, a combination of tolerances had allowed the wedge-bar to rise clear of the plug and move to any position without the actual plug turning.

'The answer was to shape the bar to prevent total disengagement. In addition to new-shaped bars, the plug grooves were milled to suit. The slot was about twice as wide as the spindle tongue, thus permitting a limited amount of wedging in order to clear the plug. This made it impossible for the plug to become clear of the additional tongue on the spindle and a potentially dangerous situation was averted. Despite the Ministry insisting there were not enough cases to justify general modifications, Dobson immediately sanctioned the milling of affected parts. Coryton's No 5 Group set up a unit at Scampton and the whole Lanc force was modified within some three weeks. Identical cocks fitted to Halifaxes were not modified for several months.

Variations on a Theme

'For a short period early in the Lancaster's production life, supplies of Rolls-Royce manufactured Merlin engines became a critical factor. Airframe production was sufficiently ahead of engine supply to the extent that completed aircraft were ferried out to maintenance units, where their powerplants were removed and returned to Woodford so that further machines could be tested and ferried.

'The possibility of an alternative power-plant, already considered by Chadwick during early design studies, now became a matter of some urgency. The only engine of comparable power and weight available in any quantity was the Bristol Hercules – partly due to cutbacks in Short Stirling production. That Lancaster engine mountings were simple welded tubular steel frames and required few modifications to production jigs and tools, also made their use singularly attractive; and so a prototype, DT810 – designated Lanc II – was quickly built and tested.

'Utilising existing engine cowlings, exhaust, and cooling gills, the aerodynamic performance proved to be close to that of the Merlin-powered Lanc I, and the two types were operationally compatible – but for one perplexing aspect. The use of cooling gills produced the effect of considerably increasing drag and under certain conditions the aircraft would climb as fast on cruising power with gills closed as on full power with gills open. In the first case this resulted in a marked reduction in fuel consumption, while the same condition could arise during maximum speed high altitude flight whereby any excess gill opening gave heavy consumption. I fear that a number of Mk IIs were lost due to running out of fuel on operations.

'Thankfully, UK Merlin production was vastly improved as the shadow factory at Trafford Park Manchester came into full

Top and centre left: **Number One** Dressed in Bomber Command's sooty black finish is L7527, the first production Lancaster, here running up before an early test flight from Woodford. Initially painted in 'daylight' colours, she briefly became a 'yellow peril', the colloquial term applied to the two prototypes BT308 and DG595. On at least one occasion all three are known to have flown in formation for some unofficial photography while detached to Boscombe Down. Originally delivered to A&AEE in October 1941, L7527 served as an Avro development aircraft before passing to 1654 Conversion Unit, and ultimately to No. 15 Squadron in March 1944. Her squadron service was however brief, failing to return from Essen 26/27 March 1944. /*Both A. C. Jack*

Bottom left: **Many Parts** The result of marrying some 55,000 separate parts involving around 500,000 manufacturing operations nears finality at Woodford early in 1942. While not a single woman is visible, they represented almost 45% of Avro's payroll by the end of the war. Production was a 24-hour round the clock process and records show that an average working week was a shade under 67 hours! /*Popperfoto*

163

production. As a result, orders for the Mk II – production of which was entrusted to Sir W. G. Armstrong Whitworth & Company at Baginton and Bitteswell – were repeatedly cut back and only 300 were ultimately produced.

'At the same time as the Hercules variant was under development, the American Packard company began delivery of their home produced Mk 28 Merlin, which differed mainly in having a Stromberg fuel injection-type carburettor. When installed in British-built airframes, Lancasters were termed Mk III; while those subsequently produced in Canada by Victory Aircraft at Malton, Ontario, and fitted with the same engines, became Mk Xs.

'The Canadian factory's performance in tooling up and producing their first Lancaster was a remarkable demonstration of the simplicity of the structure and equipment, in addition to the adaptability and economy of the jigging and tooling. Only one set of major jig parts for drilling fuselage and wing main joints was shipped to Canada, together with drawings and specifications; for reference purposes a Mk I Lancaster, fully equipped and latterly operating with No 5 Group, was flown out in August 1942. There were relatively few problems (only one Avro liaison engineer being stationed at Malton during this period), and the first production machine arrived in the UK early in August 1943.

'Structurally, the Canadian Lancs were identical to those produced in England. This included the undercarriage, hydraulics and electrics, but minor items such as switches and gauges were to American or Canadian standards. A practical check was carried out at Woodford whereby a Canadian-built aircraft was dismantled at all main joints. The individual sections were then married up with adjoining units made in Manchester, and all were physically interchangeable.

'Flight testing produced one solitary exception. When Manchester-produced wings were fitted with Canadian-built ailerons there was a noticeably heavier loading on the controls at all speeds. Though dimensionally in line and of the correct aerofoil section, there was never time to discover the reason and the problem was simply resolved by altering the gear ratio of the aileron balance tab.

'The most publicised Lanc operation was, I am sure, the breaching of the Möhne and Eder dams in the Ruhr; moreover, the modifications carried out on each Lancaster to accommodate Barnes Wallis's spinning bomb are now well known and do not warrant repetition. The modification work required on the production line was extensive enough to cause comment in official circles. Some of the Ministry officials wanted the job to be done in a separate screened compound with attendant tight security. The Avro management and myself were completely opposed to this. We wanted to work as usual on one production line and leak information that this was a secret anti-submarine weapon. This was credible as the first trials were carried out over the sea on the south coast. The Avro view prevailed; probably Dobby would not have done otherwise, even if asked.

'Initial trials had not been without incident, the test "bombs" tending to break up on hitting the water. Sam Brown flew the first modified Lanc to Boscombe Down, where it was promptly bombed-up with a missile of the then "latest design". Sam dropped it near Chesil Beach in relatively shallow water, whereupon it broke up on impact and sent up a cloud of spray which enveloped the tail of the Lanc. From then on Sam had problems with longitudinal control and on return to Boscombe Down we found that water containing many pebbles about the size of one's fist had done great damage to the elevators and tail-plane. Many too were trapped in the structure and I still have one to this day.

'The final week before the attack was a very hectic time for me. Although we had no problems involving inspection, we had troubles with accidental damage sustained during practice and I had rushed back from Scampton to Woodford the day before to try and ensure that one aircraft being repaired would be cleared as soon as possible. We got it away from Woodford just in time for it to be bombed-up and take off on the operation without the usual airtest by the crew.

'The Lanc was probably unique in being the only bomber aircraft in the world capable of carrying its maximum disposable load, if required, all in one piece. This ability was no accident for Chadwick was a confirmed advocate of the big bomb. When the Manchester was still an early project I recall an argument with some Ministry and RAF officials. They were very concerned that the bomb gear should release an accurately aimed and evenly spaced row of bombs. Chadwick said: "Gentlemen, if you dropped a stick of bombs spaced within three inches of the pattern you want, and they landed in a field 50 yards from my office, they would probably break the windows. If you dropped one 10,000lb bomb and missed by 500yards, you would at least blow the complete roof off the building."

'The truth of this philosophy quickly became apparent with the build up of German night attacks on targets like London, Coventry and Manchester, when 2,000lb light case bombs were used. Hurried development here produced the 4,000lb "Cookie", a plain cylindrical mild steel welded casing filled with high explosive. These proved effective so two were coupled end to end to produce 8,000lb capacity, followed by a three-can 12,000-pounder as the final development of the type. The only significant changes on the aircraft to accommodate the latter were bulges on the bomb doors to clear the bomb.

'The Germans meanwhile had been very active in building heavily reinforced concrete servicing pens for their submarines, notably in the French ports of Brest, Cherbourg and Lorient; later came launching pads for V1 and V2 and secure underground magazines for the missiles.

'Barnes Wallis of Vickers, a friend of Chadwick's, gave the matter of designing a weapon to attack such targets much thought. He proposed to use very strong hard-case streamlined bombs dropped from a great height and so obtain very high terminal velocity and deep penetration, even in concrete, before detonation. The problems in the production of the cast steel casings were daunting but were eventually solved; and so Tallboy, as the 21ft long bomb was called, became available.

'Carrying it in a Lancaster – the only service aircraft capable of carrying this aerial gargantuan – was no problem. However results on targets appeared to be erratic, particularly so in the submarine pens. Photo reconnaissance showed little external sign that the bombs had done any damage. Later, from Resistance reports coming out of France, we learned that the bombs had penetrated great thicknesses up to 14ft.

'Grand Slam, an enlarged version of similar design and appearance, and weighing 22,000lb, was a natural successor, though trials confirmed Wallis's fears that even the sturdy Lancaster would not have anywhere near the ideal ceiling in order to achieve maximum penetration. Some modification and strengthening of the airframe and undercarriage was required, and lifting this ultimate in conventional bombs resulted in the highest operational take-off weight of any wartime Lancaster. What the Lancs dropping Grand Slams did to certain viaducts among other notable targets has, along with the sinking of the Tirpitz with Tallboys, passed into World War II history.

Tragedy Strikes
'In the late afternoon of Monday, 11 September 1944, there occurred the only fatal accident involving a Lancaster on flight test from any of the factories in the Group. Flown from Woodford, by test pilot Sid Gleave and flight engineer Harry Barnes, Lancaster III PB579 dived at a steep angle into open ground at Siddington, four miles from Macclesfield, and eight miles from the airfield. I happened to be at the Woodford flight sheds when a telephone message came through reporting that a four-

engined aircraft, believed to be a Lancaster, had crashed nearby. As we had an aircraft in that area, Sam Brown and myself left immediately in his car to visit the site.

'On arrival we found, on top of a small hillock in open ground, a large crater complete with four holes wherein were embedded the engines. Small fragments of wreckage were scattered over a wide area, and without doubt it was our Lanc. During the few hours of remaining daylight we examined the local trail of wreckage to see if we could find any clues as to why the aircraft had made no apparent recovery from the dive.

'Every tenth machine was dived once to maximum permissible speed (some 375mph indicated) to verify its control effectiveness and ease of recovery. As this had been a tenth aircraft the initiation of the dive was presumably deliberate. Therefore, some failure or malfunction had occurred. Near the crater I found several small portions of unburnt elevator structure, still with some shreds of fabric covering attached. The raw edges of the fabric were almost completely unravelled and this could only mean one thing; that the fabric covering had been slashed and torn off at an early moment in the dive.

'Nothing further could be done at the site that night so the wreck was left under RAF guard until the following morning. Meantime, Roy Chadwick, Harold Rogerson*, Sam Brown and myself held a hurried meeting to review the known facts and try to determine possible causes; also to discover any clues and decide on the most likely areas of search. In the morning I was joined by an AIB inspector, a Polish engineer named Nowvak. We discussed the results of the previous evening's meeting before further inspecting the wreckage.

'Just beyond the crater, in the direction from which the Lanc had approached, there was a shallow depression about 200yd long, full of gorse bushes and about 4½ft deep. This seemed a likely place to search and, on struggling through the thicket, we recovered sufficient small pieces of elevator and shreds of fabric. These strongly indicated that both elevators had lost their fabric covering,

*Chief Structural Engineer

Above: **First Death** '. . . On arrival we found, on top of a small hillock in open ground, a large crater complete with four holes wherein were embedded the engines . . . ' Resembling a funeral pyre are the remains of BIII PB579 at Siddington. Such was the force of the impact that virtually no trace of pilot Sid Gleave or engineer Harry Barnes could be found./*A. C. Jack* besides some secondary structure before the aircraft hit the ground and disintegrated.

'We now reviewed the Lancaster's structure, all equipment forward of, and in line with the tailplane, and all defect and failure reports originating there. Each inboard main petrol tank had, installed in its base, a fuel jettison valve and discharge hose, which was housed in a small compartment, covered by a sheet metal door in the bottom wing skin. These doors were secured by latches operated by the jettison valve spindle when it commenced to open the valve.

'One or two defect reports had been received, where, under high "G" loads, doors had opened and been torn off. In no case had a tailplane or elevator been reported damaged, which was not surprising as the failures were at high "G" loading and relatively low airspeed. If failure on PB579 had occurred at very high speed and low "G", it seemed probable that either the tailplane or elevators would have been struck by the doors. But where were the doors?

'They could be anywhere within an area of about two square miles of undulating land, with a height variation of about 200ft, and of mixed arable, grazing and heath surface. I took a gamble. It was September; the grain and hay were mostly cleared; the late potatoes and other vegetables were still being harvested. I requested the police to visit all schools in the area and show children a door, about the size of a dinner plate, and ask them to look for anything like it in the fields, gardens – or indeed anywhere.

'Meanwhile, a series of tests and experiments showed that if the fabric covering was seriously torn under high speed flight conditions, there was every probability that all covering would be torn off. What could be done immediately to greatly improve the strength of the covering without grounding all Lancasters for more than one day? Introducing additional metal elevator ribs and strengthening the trailing edge would not be a very quick or easy job.

'Rogerson and Chadwick had spent their lives designing wooden aircraft, so it was natural to consider this type of modification. Wooden ribs that could easily be installed between existing ones, two in each bay, were devised; and the replacement fabric cover was taped and strung to these additional supports. Tests on the first one indicated that this could limit the damage to the one cut panel, while the others would not "balloon" out and fail. The Anson production line at Newton Heath had adequate stocks of material and reserve capacity to produce modified sets and the job was put in hand immediately.

'About a week had now passed since the accident, when the police telephoned to say that a farmer's children had found the two doors, not very far apart in the same field, and on the Lancaster's approach path. Inspection confirmed that both had been torn from their hinges and struck some other structure – probably the elevator. In the long term all elevators were fitted with metal skins; and I am sure this materially contributed to increased safety of the Lancaster thereafter.

'In retrospect I regret that it did not occur to me before the accident just how vulnerable the fabric-covered elevators actually were. All who flew Lancs knew that at high speed in a dive they became progressively heavier to pull out by use of the control column; but they could be controlled easily and positively by the trimmer wheel. This appeared to be the result of the aerodynamic shape of the elevator changing due to "ballooning" of the covering. The phenomena disappeared once the additional ribs were fitted or metal-covered elevators installed.

'This sad and regrettable incident cast a dark shadow over all at Avro for some weeks. Both Sid Gleave and Harry Barnes were popular and known to many.

'Development of the Lancaster was of course a continuous process of improvement in the light of operational experience by the RAF as it strived to keep ahead of a resourceful and technically adept enemy. Fortunately this entailed little by way of major structural change, yet many problems required quick and effective solutions, and we at Avro always enjoyed the closest co-operation with Bomber Command, Farnborough, Boscombe Down, Malvern and Air Ministry.

'With the end of hostilities in Europe the problems changed but did not at first diminish: Operations Manna, Exodus and, later, Dodge all produced their own brand of snags. By then we were heavily committed to the Lincoln, York and Tudor. Production of the Lancaster ceased throughout the group and the last machine, a Mk VII built by Austin Motors, was flight tested on 21 December 1945 at Elmdon.

'On the evening of Thursday, 5 December 1945, a dinner party was held at Claridges Hotel, London to formally "wind up" the Lancaster Group. To me it was a rather sad occasion, marking the end of three years of intensive effort, working closely with a team of first class designers, aerodynamisists, metalurgists, production engineers, assembly and flight test teams widely spread, but intent on a common purpose. Sir Arthur Harris, for three years at the helm of Bomber Command, was prevented by illness from attending the dinner but his message of appreciation for all our efforts was certainly well received. His chapter, too, was at an end.'

Ops are On

Three Cheers for the Man on the Ground
E. Sykes, 1942

Wherever you walk, you will hear people talk,
Of the men who go up in the air.
Of the dare-devil way, they go into the fray;
Facing death without turning a hair.

They'll raise a big cheer and buy lots of beer,
For a pilot who's home on leave;
But they don't give a jigger,
For a flight mech, or rigger
With nothing but 'props' on his sleeve.

They just say 'Nice day' and then turn away,
With never a mention of praise.
And the poor bloody erk who does all the work;
Just orders his own beer,
And pays !

They've never been told, of the hours in the cold
That he spends sealing Germany's fate.
How he works on a kite, till all hours of the night;
And then turns up next morning at eight.

He gets no rake-off for working 'till take-off;
Or helping the aircrew prepare;
But whenever there's trouble, it's 'Qiuck at the double';
The man on the ground must be there.

Each flying crew could tell it to you;
They know what this man's really worth.
They know he's a part of the RAF's heart,
Even though he stays close to the earth.

He doesn't want glory, but please tell his story;
Spread a little of his fame around.
He's one of a few, so give him his due;
Three cheers for the man on the ground.

Left: **Busy Bodies** A case of all hands at Syerston in early November 1942 as No 106 Squadron's BI R5900 'ZN-X' *Admiral Air Goosk* is made ready, watched anxiously by 'Chiefy' and an observer. The reason for the mass of humanity is because R5900 – ostensibly u/s at the time – was hurriedly required for the night's operation, and the press were on hand to record the event. (R5900's career ended in a crash-landing on return from Berlin 17/18 January 1943.) /*Popperfoto*

Right: **Safety First** Another vital task was routine airing and re-packing of the crew dinghy, stowed in the starboard wing root and automatically released when a Lancaster ditched. This one is receiving attention at Faldingworth 1944, home of the Polish-manned No 300 ('Masovian') Squadron. /*Polish Sources*

Right: **Tug of War** A petrol bowser proves a useful tractor for freeing a No 463 Squadron kite from its blocked dispersal following an overnight fall of snow at Waddinton, winter 1943/4. Unless checked, snow could very quickly paralyse all movement and only by the whole station turning out in organised shifts – night and day – could the runways and approaches be kept free. /*D. O. Todd*

Below right: **On Parade** With a low-level strike by the Luftwaffe an ever-present threat, rarely would a squadron line up its aircraft. Here are No 15 Squadron's Lancs being aired at Mildenhall circa December 1943 during the unit's conversion from Stirlings. Nearest machine is BI R5896 'LS-N', a veteran with previous service on No. 97 Squadron and 1660 CU, and typical of the 'cast offs' equipping No 3 Group during its transitional period. /*R. Curling*

Typical Studies of airframe and engine fitters going through their routine checks and servicing. (*below left*) is a Lanc being prepared for the night's operation (probably No 106 Squadron Metheringham circa December 1943), with the usual wheeled trolleys in place. Two of the erks wear 'Donkey' jackets while the others wear 'boiler suits'. Other points of interest are the covers on the main wheel tyre, rough coating of de-icing paste (a dirty yellow colour) on the wing leading edges, and red pitot head cover tied to one of the trolleys. The view (*below*) is of a No 626 Squadron Lanc (BI LL918 'UM-C²') 'surrounded' at Wickenby circa May 1944, with two erks giving the rudder horn balance a periodic check. /*F. E. Harper; R. Hemus*

Top: **Oh My Aching Back!** Snow clearance at Binbrook winter 1943/4. On such occasions the whole station would turn out to man brooms and shovels, working round the clock in order to clear runways, dispersals and roads – an arduous back-breaking task. For the Aussies – many of whom had never even seen snow – it was an ideal opportunity to let off steam and indulge in high-spirited snow fights, which always seemed to end up as Australia versus Great Britain! Perhaps when this particular picture was taken the erks were awaiting the arrival of the NAAFI or YMCA tea van!/*E. D. Evans*

Above: **Four of a Kind** With all the DIs completed it is time to test the engines and so check the Lancaster's services. Canadian Plt Off Jack Sheppard snaps his No 9 Squadron kite (BI LM220 'WS-Y') being run-up at Bardney, summer 1944. On Merlin-engined Lancs the starboard-outer drove the hydraulic pump for the mid-upper turret, and the electric generator from which H2S and Fishpond operated. The starboard-inner powered the hydraulic pump for the front turret, an air compressor feeding the wheel brakes, radiator shutters, supercharger rams and, on Lanc IIIs and Xs, the slow-running cut out. In addition, both inner engines drove a vacuum pump from which the blind flying panel instruments and Mk XIV bombsight operated; an hydraulic pump to power the emergency hand pump, undercarriage, flaps, bomb doors, carburettor air intake shutters and fuel jettisoning; also accumulators to charge engine starter and booster coils, fuel booster pumps, supercharger controls, flap and undercarriage indicators, pitot head heater, wireless equipment, landing lamps, prop feathering and dinghy inflation. The port-inner on its own drove a compressor powering the automatic pilot, and hydraulic pump for the mid-under turret (when fitted). Finally, the port-outer ran the rear turret pump, and generator for Gee and Monica, the latter incorporating a changeover to the starboard-outer. (LM220 survived the war.)/*W. J. Sheppard*

Engine Fitter:
Merlin was a Wizard

CLIFF ALLEN

There was no more vital duty than looking after the engines which powered the Lancaster. Always in demand, engine fitters were an elite band of mortals, ever resourceful and adaptable, whose skills – in common with their fellow airframe riggers, drivers and others – received scant recognition by the outside world.

Whether working on Merlins or Hercules, each day was essentially the same and, through a representative engine fitter of his time, we can measure the problems and frustrations, pride and fulfilment typical of any erk in Bomber Command.

Space regrettably precludes detailed studies of the score or more associate trades that were necessary to keep the squadrons operational; but they are by no means forgotten and evidence of their work can be found throughout this book.

Little more than 21 years old, Yorkshireman Cliff Allen quickly 'came of age' on being posted to the second Australian Lancaster squadron (No 467) in November 1942. He stayed with the Aussies for almost three years, latterly with No 463 Squadron, which formed as an offshoot of No 467 in November 1943, and finished his service on release from No 617 Squadron on its return from India in April 1946, rank LAC.

His postwar life has cetainly been one of variety, beginning with employment in a Scottish ship-breaking yard and including a spell in Canada. He now runs his own driving school but a few miles from the factory where he served his apprenticeship as a machine tool setter.

'My arrival at Scampton one wet November day in 1942 coincided with the forming of a new Lancaster squadron. I'd barely heard of the Lancaster but prospects of working on an operational heavy bomber filled me with mixed feelings. My previous experience since passing out as an engine fitter (FME Group II) from St Athan had been chiefly in servicing Battles, Blenheims, Ansons and Bothas at the navigation school operating from West Freugh. This at least gave me confidence, for

a harder introduction would be difficult to find.

'It was not long before the semblance of our new squadron passed through the gates at Scampton and headed for Bottesford. On arrival we soon saw what a satellite aerodrome looked like, with dispersals somewhere on the horizon. When the planners chose where the living sites should be it must have been done by throwing a dart at a map; it was impossible to arrive for work, meals or leisure without the aid of transport.

'After several days at Bottesford the first Lancs arrived; No 467 Squadron RAAF was taking shape. At first, equipment was lacking and I remember giving the engines of our new "G-George" a check from the steps of a ladder scrounged from the maintenance hangar. Trolley accs were in short supply so in order to start the engines for a test run, the strict rule of not using the aircraft's batteries for starting up was broken (making sure no electricians were about!). At first we were unable to understand why our attempts to start the engines were unsuccessful. Then a reliable source informed us that the first procedure was to switch on the tank immersion pumps for a short spell to get the petrol flowing; we were learning.

'Came the day when the first aircrew arrived for a cross-country flight. They piled aboard and made for their respective positions, the Aussie pilot settling in his seat and doing his checks before sliding open his window and asking we group of erks stood below which engine *we'd* like started first. We thought this very polite of him and quickly told him: "Always the starboard-inner first", as this engine charged the pneumatics and hydraulics operating the brakes, flaps and radiator shutters.

'Those who have never climbed up the wheel of a Lanc to reach the engine priming positions have missed out on life! Port and starboard-inner engines each had their own priming station, while also on the same panel was the connection for the plug to the trolley acc. It required some agility to swing up the wheel and get both feet on the foot rests situated halfway up the oleo legs. Many were the antics performed in the pitch black of night, sometimes during atrocious weather conditions: to get positioned for start-up, rubber boots slipping on greasy untreaded tyres, produced lots of foul language. The ideal situation at start-up was for one man to perch behind each primer, with another seated on the trolley acc. The latter job was usually carried out by our rigger whilst a bod for signalling to the pilot may have been the NCO if available; many would be the occasions when only two men filled this duty.

'Flak in particular was no respecter of engines and to illustrate the work load this could impose I recall "G-George" trundling back to dispersal one night with port-inner feathered and damage to ailerons. On investigation, a sliver of flak had penetrated the coolant radiator from the front, completely missing the rotating prop and making a large hole in the radiator, before finishing up wedged into the bulkhead.

'The following day "George" was towed into the maintenance hangar for a new aileron to be fitted, and the engine rechecked. On removing the offending metal and presenting it to our skipper, who had risen early to view his charge, the only real damage appeared to be to the radiator. This was removed and replaced, during which time the Squadron Engineering Officer paid us a visit, mainly to see if "George" would be ready for ops that night: obviously a maximum effort was in the offing. Repairs completed, the aircraft was towed outside for the vital test run. The port-inner props began to turn, the engine coughed, and at last she was running. Following a short warming up period the throttle was opened wide and then closed: everything seemed in order so cowlings were buttoned on and "George" was towed out to her dispersal.

'Evening came and soon the aircrew were aboard, ready for start-up. All four Merlins turned over sweetly and were run up for mag drops, when a flashing torch casually flicking beneath the port side caught the reflection of liquid running from the port-inner engine, blowing back under the nacelle. By the time we finally got the signal across to our bewildered pilot to cut engines, the rest of the flight were taxying towards the perimeter. With no time for explanations we moved like scalded cats: trestles shot under the leaking port-inner, cowlings were whipped off and torches thrust into the sizzling engine. To our great relief the magic wand was a big screwdriver and it needed but a few turns on a jubilee clip to stop the leak.

'Now the header tank had to be replenished and, whilst this was in progress, flashing lights from approaching cars signalled the arrival of "top brass", coming to a stop with a squeal of brakes and the familiar "What's the trouble?".

Laurie Parker, our Aussie sergeant, assured them the problem was in hand and "George" was soon on her way to join the tail of the queue for take-off. Episodes like this occurred frequently, sometimes for no apparent reason, and it was then put down to gremlins.

'Other than enemy action our biggest headache was naturally the weather. Mother Nature in her many moods could not be taken lightly when working on the flights and anything could be expected. Strong winds and gales howling across the wide-open spaces of an aerodrome did not present ideal conditions for working on aero engines. One memorable day the wind was so strong while doing our DIs that each side cowling could only be removed safely by one fitter holding it securely to the trestle (otherwise it took off), whilst his mate completed the inspection. Somehow the DIs were completed, only to learn later that ops had been scrubbed!

'After dinner we were about to make the trek back to our quarters for some well earned relaxation when the word went round to return to our dispersals. The gale had now reached hurricane proportions and all Lancs had to be turned nose into wind and roped to picketing points. This was the only time I saw Lancasters "dancing" like flimsy scale models.

'Perhaps, by describing the coldest day I ever encountered, I can put on record the conditions we cheerfully tolerated in order to keep the machinery of Bomber Command moving.

Below: **Meet the Gang** Cliff Allen and fellow erks pause for a snapshot at Waddinton June 1944 while working on BIII LM587 'JO:L' of No 463 Squadron RAAF. Identified are, left to right: Eric Offen, engine fitter; Cliff Allen (immediately in front of cockpit); 'Nick' Nixon, airframe fitter (half in, half out of escape hatch): foreground, framed in cockpit window is 'Nobby' Webster, rigger. One of several No 463 Squadron Lancs adapted to carry RAF Film Unit cameramen, LM587 went down on Karlsruhe 26/27 September 1944./M. A. Marsh

Right: **Too Late!** His hat 'gone with the wind', 'Sarg' holds down his curly locks as the starboard-inner Merlin is turned over: a picture taken either at Binbrook or Ludford Magna. This view shows the neat engine installation./E. D. Evans

Below right: **Dab Hands** It was the engine fitter's job to replenish the Lancaster's fuel tanks. A view at Wickenby early in 1944 showing No 12 Squadron's BI ME786 'PH-R' about to receive her allotted quota of 100 octane. On cold days such as this a spanner jammed in the end of the nozzle allowed an unrestricted flow of petrol, and welcome relief for the attendant erks. (ME786 saw the war out with No 12 Squadron and was finally broken up in May 1947. /E. K. Farfan

'The Nissen huts grouped beneath the frost-spangled trees might have been in some far distant outpost in Alaska; but no, this was RAF Station Bottesford one day in February 1943, the mortals beneath those arches of ridged metal safely sealed against the elements under their regulation blankets. The combustion stove in the centre of the hut still showed a red dying glow; the air pollution rate was appalling and ready to be cut with a knife; any mice in there could be pronounced dead.

'The door was opened and standing there holding a pot of tea was early riser LAC Alec Hutton. In his best Scouse accent he announced the time as 7am, and mentioned something about brass monkeys; but this went unheeded. With great difficulty someone eventually stirred and the blackouts were removed, though it was still quite dark outside. The door was left ajar for the contaminated air to escape, and in rushed the biting fresh air; this resulted in a rapid evacuation of beds and quarters.

'We had not yet been issued with bicycles so had to walk over a mile with small kit (soap, towel, etc) to reach the ablutions. The temperature was well below zero and in spite

Left: **Suffolk Punch** A newly arrived No 218 (Gold Coast) Squadron fitter receives instruction in the complexities of the Merlin and its tightly packed attendant pipe runs and wires. The exhaust stubs and shroud appear new, though the Lanc (BIII LM577 'XH-Q') is a veteran of 84 ops and survived The war. This view of Chedburgh provides a splendid panorama of an operational airfield, taking in a ground crew's hut and newly erected hangars, yet to be painted black. Under the nose of *Edith* can be seen a trailer load of oxygen bottles, while beyond are two more Lancs in their dispersals, the nearer machine being 'XH-O' complete with yellow G-H fin stripes./*IWM*

Below: **Air Test** It was general practice for engine fitters and other erks to go aloft on airtests, thus cementing the close relationship between air and ground crews. Shown is a Lanc of the Special Duty Flight returning to Binbrook on an overcast July day in 1944. /*E. D. Evans*

of Balaclavas, scarves and mittens we arrived at the wash house well and truly frozen. The water supply was inevitably solid but help came from the cookhouse in the shape of several buckets of hot water.

'Not far away was the airmens' mess and here we joined the queue for breakfast. The Tannoy blared out music from the BBC and at precisely 7.55, prior to the 8am news, came the familiar march "Into Battle". This boomed out every single morning and became a vital signal to any late comer: if this musical epic had stopped, so had breakfast, and down came the shutters. Many track records were broken during those five minutes! A parade of flight personnel at the MT Section followed breakfast, and then it was all aboard for the dispersals in a fog, thickening fast.

'Lancaster "H-Harry" loomed ahead immobile and inoffensive as the truck drew near and skidded to a halt. Reluctantly her ground crew dropped on to the crackling dispersal pan, the truck moved off and "H-Harry" was swallowed up by the dark curtain swirling behind. The call "G-George" drifted back from the cab and we knew we had arrived at our charge. "George" stood completely covered in white hoar frost; from each airscrew hung a two-inch wide icicle leading to the ground, and tapes holding engine and turret covers were frozen solid. "Dusty"

Coleman, our rigger, found the door into the aircraft welded tight with the frost and disappeared into the fog to report. All the aircraft of No 467 Squadron were enveloped in the deep freeze and, no doubt, so was all 5 Group. However, means were at hand to combat the paralysis created by nature.

'A figure suddenly emerged from the pea-soup in the form of our intrepid sergeant cycling towards our huddled group. Through streaming eyes and clouds of frozen breath he told us a convoy of heater vans was on its way; drums of anti-freeze were also being despatched. The shack provided a welcome haven in times like these and there we took shelter until the anti-freeze arrived within the hour. A stirrup pump of the type used for dowsing incendiaries was brought into use, the de-icing began and soon all covers were removed. Dusty and Laurie gained access to the Lanc but the engine trestles wouldn't budge so they were "given the treatment" and wheeled into position.

'The daily inspections were now under way. A box-shaped van drew near the aircraft door, whereupon the driver released a long, near 12in diameter flexible pipe from the roof and connected one end to the engine; the other was snaked into the Lanc's fuselage. The heater van's engine started up and soon the heat was pouring in to dispel the icy cocoon.

'It was a great relief on days like these to complete the DIs without snags, but this was not always the case. One such day followed a pilot reporting an airscrew which did not respond between coarse and fine pitch. After the DIs, the engine with the faulty prop was test run and shut down. Jack, our Aussie corporal, went through all the possible faults but could find nothing amiss: so, by agreement with Laurie Parker, made the decision to change the prop.

'It was not a long job to fit a new one, but none the less a frustrating task assembling the necessary equipment. Requisitions for replacements were left in our corporal's capable hands, and two of us joined him for a trip back to the maintenance hangar. There he hunted down a new prop whilst we commandeered a portable hand-crane. A large spanner for use on the airscrew hub was booked out and our flight tractor – when we could find it – would be used to tow the gear out to dispersal. The tractor was constantly in use and Jack successfully diverted the WAAF driver to the priorities of our towing job, utilising a bomb trolley as the only available carrier to transport the prop.

'It was now well past our dinner break as we slowly chugged back to dispersal. The petrol bowser was reversing close to the aircraft as we approached and this would mean more

Above: **Down Your Way**
Among the many vital duties performed by WAAFs was that of driving the numerous vehicles required on an operational station. Here, at Linton-on-Ouse summer 1943 a WAAF driver has delivered the oil bowser (its open door revealing the JAP 'donkey' engine) by David Brown tractor to an unusually clear dispersal site (complete with newly mown grass). The Lanc II, 'EQ-D', belongs to No 408 ('Goose') Squadron and bears the inscription 'My Hope is Constant In Thee' on her nose. */Public Archives of Canada*

Above: **Rustic Setting** On a crisp winter's morning at Croft, 13 February 1945, BX KB837 'SE-X' of No 431 ('Iroquois') Squadron RCAF is about to be topped up with oil. One erk works the gauges and controls, while the other is poised precariously atop the bowser, positioning the hose connection to the Lanc. All the usual trestles and step ladders, bikes and oil drums are in evidence, with, in addition, a pair of floodlight stands for working at night./*M. Bachinski*

delay. Eventually, the side we were working on was cleared and we moved in to replace the bowser, already preparing to top up the Lanc's other tanks. The sky had been very grey and overcast, and a slight flurry of snow looked ominous. The spinner was removed, the rope sling attached to the old prop, and the large hub loosened to allow the oil to be drained off: then the hand-crane was brought into use.

'Everything was going smoothly when, just as if someone had turned a switch, down came the snow thick and heavy. Unperturbed, we carried on, swinging the prop away and on to the edge of the dispersal. By the time the new prop was cranked into the air a blizzard was raging and, though only a few yards from the engine, we couldn't see it for the blinding snow. The quick decision to abandon any further attempts was unanimous and on hurriedly applying covers we retreated to our shack. This was one of the rare occasions when we had to submit to the weather and continue the following day.

'Fortunately, winters don't last for ever and working on the flights in hot summers was pleasant in spite of the increasing work load. However, frustrations were plenty and the one never eliminated was the gnawing fact that we were working on a first class aero engine with third class tools. The wooden tool box issued to each mechanic contained a rachet screwdriver; a few open-ended spanners which were too soft and soon useless; a hacksaw; file; engine brush; pliers and hand-vice; a set of BA spanners, also soft; and a feeler gauge. All these looked insignificant in the huge box.

'When Lancasters entered service fitted with American Packard Merlins, highly sophisticated tool kits were supplied with them; but alas only one of these ever reached the flights. This was kept in the Flight Office under the eagle eye of our flight sergeant. NCOs in charge of ground crews were alone authorised to use this tool kit, which contained the very versatile universal box spanner with attachments, and socket-heads precision made to fit aero-engine nuts and bolts. A wide range of open-ended and ring spanners, toughened for the job they had to do, and a host of other useful gadgets completed this masterpiece of engineering. Secrecy kept these labour-saving devices locked away for some time until a hard-pressed ground crew really needed them: then all the flight knew of their existence so the rule "NCOs only" was fixed.

'First on the agenda of every working day came the DIs, and the removal of the side cowlings revealed our first objective – the exhaust stubs and the protective shroud. The 12 stubs on each engine took a terrific pounding from the burning waste gases and a long trip, sometimes 10 hours, created havoc during flight. The six stubs on each side of the Merlin were given a "musical" check by striking each with a screwdriver. Undamaged exhaust stubs gave off the same tone, whilst a lower pitch revealed a cracked stub. This was slight damage, but a common occurrence was to find stubs completely burnt off – even the metal shrouds having disintegrated. Four engines, with a total of 48 exhaust stubs, depending on their condition, could delay an already overburdened crew working against the clock.

'During the DIs, pipes and leads, joints and connections were inspected for leaks and tightness; the lubricating nut on the coolant pump given a turn or replenished with graphite grease; the main oil filter removed and checked for foreign particles and cleaned. To

Above: **Thirsty Horses** Even with the AEC 'Matador' bowser's engine pumping out fuel at 30gal/min, it took up to 30 minutes topping up a Lanc's fuel tanks, usually two at a time. The tanker held 2,600gal; the Lancaster's capacity was 2,154gal. A scene at No 431 ('Iroquois') Squadron RCAF dispersal, Croft 27 October 1944, soon after the unit exchanged Halifaxes for Lancasters.
/*Public Archives of Canada*

Left: **Dizzy Heights** ' . . . First on the agenda of every working day came the DIs, and the removal of the side cowlings revealed our first objective . . . ' Actually a scene at Woodford circa August 1942 with W4129, foreground, destined to go down on Kassel 27/28 August 1942 – barely two weeks after delivery to No 207 Squadron.
/*T. F. Coulson*

do the latter meant removing the bottom cowling – often a two-handed job, and finding help could be difficult. Coolant and oil levels were also checked. If coolant was required, each aircraft had its own drum of glycol so it was a matter of mixing the correct proportions with water.

'The oil bowser, if not on your dispersal, would be somewhere on the flight so this had to be organized. During this period, the petrol tanker could appear on the scene. To refuel efficiently and quickly required three men: one to check fuel contents on the flight engineer's panel, the other two to operate nozzles on port and starboard fuel tanks. In very bad weather, perched on a mainplane, refuelling could be quite an ordeal. Remote control was unknown in those days, so means had to be found to overcome this unwelcome task. Wire wrapped round the nozzle lever was suitable until the tank reached capacity; then much haste had to be used to release it. A screwdriver wedged into the nozzle was the most successful aid and widely used. Dipsticks were provided in the aircraft, one for each tank, and these would be used when a precise petrol load was required.

'On completion of DIs, a test run of the engines would follow. If it was winter, each prop had to be turned two revolutions manually. This was to get the viscous oil moving, which would be more beneficial to the engines on start. "Manually" meant two of us swinging on the prop, and even one revolution took some strength. However, this was a squadron order and had to be obeyed.

'Next to follow was plugging in the trolley acc. The Ki-gas selector was set to the inner engine and its plunger unscrewed. As the prop turned, several pumps with the plunger would get the engine to fire. Engines varied on priming requirements: some gave an instant response, but others were stubborn and had to be coaxed. A hot engine would start without priming: over prime and the engine would refuse to start due to flooding. Familiarity in starting up your own aircraft brought good results and we put this down to the engines knowing their own mechanics.

'When all four engines were running, the usual warming-up period was allowed; each engine was then ready to be checked independently. The throttle of the engine was pushed to maximum take-off revs, and whilst at this speed the starboard magneto was switched off (making this mag dead). Immediately the rev-counter's pointer would fall (the dials were situated on the Lanc's instrument panel), registering the amount on the port-mag which was now the only one functioning on that engine. All engines showed a mag-drop, sometimes very slight, but a maximum 150rpm limit was allowed. After switching

back on, the same procedure for checking the starboard mag was carried out. Care had to be taken not to switch both off together or a resounding back-fire would result.

'During the run-up, temperature and pressure gauges were checked and finally, if satisfied, it was throttle back and all switches off. If, during an engine run-up, a mag-drop registered over the maximum allowed figure, prompt investigation would follow. Perhaps the gaps on the contact breaker points would need re-setting; or the points could be simply sticking. Providing this wasn't the source of the trouble, the next step was a check on the sparking plugs. A drop on the port magneto would indicate inlet plug failure; a fall on the starboard mag meant exhaust plug trouble. Either would have to be replaced, though a final compromise was a change of plugs all round. Having made the latter decision, all would pray for good weather.

'Removing and replacing the exhaust plugs on the outside of the cylinder block presented little problem; to carry this out on the inlet plugs was a different proposition. Positioned down inside the Vee of the engine block allowed minimum access to each plug and the angle of the threads helped to fray the mildest of tempers. Before proceeding it was policy to stuff rag down the Vee, thus preventing anything falling into the depths. Should this calamity occur, a crew member with angling experience was only too willing to try, with the aid of a length of wire – and not a little patience – to hook the offending object and fish it out (some chaps on other squadrons even used small magnets).

'Fitting new plugs would then follow, the inlet side proving the most tedious. A touch of graphite grease on the plug threads and all was ready for some tender coaxing; over-confidence only resulted in crossed and damaged threads, a wave of abuse, and the call for a "rescue" kit in the form of a special insert. One of my most vivid recollections of a plug change was in the black of night before a flight, the flight engineer holding an Aldis lamp at the back of the engine whilst we continued our maximum effort against the clock. On completion of the change the engine would be warmed up to expand the plug seals and the mag-drop re-checked. If this was now within the limit, a final tightening down all round followed to complete the job.

'Thinking back to those Lancaster days and working on an unforgettable aircraft, the satisfactions and frustrations are a nostalgic memory. Never to be forgotten are those four props turning, powered by the healthy growl of the Merlins behind them as they taxied back into dispersal. This must have left an indelible impression in the minds of all flight mechanics who worked on Her; I know it did in mine.'

Armourer: Toil

FRANK HAWKINS

For sheer physical effort there was probably no tougher task than bombing-up. Even allowing for cranes and winches there was a good deal of manhandling to be done, both in the bomb dump and at the aircraft.

Under normal circumstances it would take a team of armourers several hours to load their allotted clutch of aircraft, and they would sometimes still be toiling when the aircrews arrived at dispersal. The pressure was really on following the invasion of Europe when, with tactical targets the order of the day, changes of bomb load were frequent – often several times within 24 hours.

In addition to bombing-up, an armourer's responsibilities embraced the Lancaster's guns, turrets, ammunition, wing balloon cable cutters, flares and photo-flash – all demanding a cool and thorough approach to his work: certainly the term 'all brawn and no brain' often applied to armourers was misplaced and unfair.

Frank Hawkins was a 21-year old corporal when he joined No 9 Squadron in the early spring of 1944: he was still a corporal on leaving the RAF in January 1946, by then redundant from Coningsby as a one-time member of the defunct Tiger Force.

Now, with 44 years in the radio, television and electrical trade behind him, he enjoys life as a buyer merchandiser manager.

'Having worked on the flights at 15 OTU Harwell and suddenly finding myself posted to No 9 Squadron at Bardney certainly opened my eyes; graduating from the small practice bombs to the 4,000lb "Cookie" came as a positive shock!

'My first surprise came on reporting to the Squadron Armament Officer, one Plt Off "Mick" Maguire, whom I'd known and liked three years before as a corporal, later sergeant, on No 88 Squadron in No 2 Group. He was equally pleased to see me and, after bringing me up to date, assigned me to B Flight with responsibility for Lancasters "S", "T", "W", "X" and "Z", and with armourers Dobson, Hayward, Barnaby, Tapper, Salisbury and Jones under my jurisdiction.

'Our day would normally commence with daily inspections, when the armourers would visit their designated kites and go through the procedure of checking guns, turrets, bomb gear, etc. These DIs were very thorough as the squadron – indeed Bomber Command in general – had, during the winter of 1943/1944 in particular, experienced above average trouble with gun stoppages (usually attributed to icing.) While icing may well have been a contributory factor, Maguire was of the opinion that the answer lay in the fact that the armament staff on many stations were overwhelmed; the monumental task of preparing and handling vast quantities of bombs and incendiaries every day meant that other aspects tended to "go to the wall". It was always maximum effort and a month of continuous operations was a shattering experience; and month followed month with only a quick breather in between.

'All the armament staff at Bardney were, during the winter of 1943/1944, either fully or partially employed in the handling and preparation of bombs; no one was immune – except perhaps the WAAF on the ammunition belting section. All armourers could expect to be, and often were, diverted from their normal duties to back up the hard-pressed teams in the bomb dump and under the aircraft.

'Little wonder that other areas of armament servicing suffered: bomb trolleys were for example abused to the point where they became dangerous as well as unreliable. (Skellingthorpe, our near neighbours, had a major accident on the perimeter track which was directly attributable to poorly maintained bomb trolleys.) The situation became so bad that Maguire was forced to set up a section with a corporal and a small team whose sole task was trolley and winch servicing.

'Gun turrets were a different proposition. Badly maintained turrets would show up on ground test and could "scrub" an aircraft from the battle order, or cause it to abort. Thus turrets received the attention they deserved from one of the best teams in the Command, under Chiefy Harrison and his two corporals, Les Delaney and Stan Meadows.

Above: **Much Ado** Once the signal from Group has been received that ops are on, there is feverish activity in the bomb dump. Bomb and incendiary trains forming up at Linton-on-Ouse on a damp and muddy day early in March 1944. Clearly visible on the end face of each 'Cookie' are the three arming pistols, while on top are two outer hoisting lugs, and a central suspension lug for holding the bomb in place inside the Lancaster's bomb bay. Behind the David Brown tractor is a versatile Eagle flat-top trailer. In the distance are Lanc IIs of No 408 ('Goose') or No 426 ('Thunderbird') Squadrons receiving attention from their ground crews.
/*Public Archives of Canada*

Centre right: **Muscle** Muscle was required by these No 300 ('Masovian') Squadron erks at Faldingworth to manhandle a 'Cookie' into position under the bomb bay. The chalked-on message is self evident and clearly dates the picture. Bombing up times depended on the load and weather, but representative averages were 45min to load a 'Cookie' and incendiaries, and 30min for 14 x 1,000 pounders./*Polish Sources*

Bottom right: **Mud** Everywhere muddy, the air cold and damp, Ludford Magna armourers slog to prepare incendiaries for the night's maximum effort. At this stage of the war – 20 January 1944, the height of the Battle of Berlin – virtually every day was the same, the bomb loads a mixture of 4,000lb 'Cookies' and incendiaries./*Popperfoto*

180

'Other badly abused items were the bomb carriers. They looked fragile but must have been robust enough for their failure rate was quite low. On the other hand perhaps I under-estimate the bombing-up teams, who weeded out most of the potential faults before they got on the aircraft. A chafed lead here; a loose junction box there; strips of "Window" blown into the electronics of a small bomb container, where it could do most damage, were typical snags to look for.

'Guns also suffered from all this emphasis on the bombing aids. The difference was that it did not become apparent until they were expected to fire – and no one returned from aircraft missing on ops to say if the guns had worked or not! By this stage of the war the Browning gun was a very reliable weapon; but, like all machinery it required some care and attention – not a lot – but fairly often, and our guns were not getting their share. Firing tests on guns taken straight from Lancs proved that, and with the gunnery leader's co-operation, a large gun room was set up in the

R&I armoury, capable of handling some 30 to 40 guns per day. These comprised all guns which had been fired on the night's operation or on air test; another three or four sets (eight per set) from aircraft, would be selected in rotation for gun change. In many ways this made it easier for armourers out on the flights: all they had to do when their kites were due for a change was to remove the guns and be ready to exchange them for serviced replacements when the armament 15 cwt truck made its round of the dispersals.

'The Bardney gun room was staffed by armament fitter NCOs and armourers, rein-forced by a number of gunners who were not otherwise engaged, or sleeping off the effects of the previous night's operation. Some of the gunners had previously been armourers and they quickly became regular visitors; others came and did a daily stint. The atmosphere was good, the tea "swindle" not bad, and most bods who worked there found it enjoy-able; it also became a regular practice to rotate some of the muscle-bound armourers from the bombing-up teams through the gun room as a break from their labours on the flights.

'We armourers always had our oil can and "4 × 2" handy as the gunners would report such problems as sluggish or leaky turrets, cracked or marked perspex; while the hydraulic rams operating the guns often suffered slight oil leaks and it was generally a question of effecting localised repairs. Once repaired or replaced it was seldom an aircraft was out of commission because of problems on turrets, but we had to constantly see that the guns were clean, the ammo tanks full, and belt alignment correct to avoid stoppages and jams. I wasn't allocated a specific task myself but, as corporal in overall charge, I would be quite prepared to sign for a DI if there wasn't a 700 filled in by one of my armourers.

'All bombs would come from the dump with safety devices intact and would be left on trolleys at each aircraft's dispersal, there to be pushed under the bomb bay and positioned correctly for winching up. The drivers certainly acquired a fair amount of skill to be able to back the bomb trolley accurately into position, but the manhandling was left to the armourers who invariably were helped by the rest of the aircraft's ground crew. The first procedure was to attach the bomb carriers to the bombs and put the fusing links in position, these being safety devices whereby bombs could be dropped from the carriers without them exploding. The latter comprised a clip arrangement in the tail vane, to which was attached a fusing link, and this mated with a solenoid-controlled catch in the carrier fusing unit. It was important for the crutches to be correctly adjusted, as an excessive crutching load could prevent the bomb release unit from operating.

'An armourer would then climb up into the aircraft, position the portable winch by a nozzle which was located in a socket set in the bomb bay roof, and pass a Bowden cable through to the waiting armourers below for anchoring to the bomb rack. Initially, of course, the bombs would start going up quite quickly but as the men on the winch began to tire the process slowed down, and we would take it in turns to operate the winch. The main purpose of the armourers below was to see that the bombs went up steadily, avoiding fouling the bomb doors, and then to position and secure the bomb carriers to the Lancaster's bomb bay attachments.

'There were two main types of winch: the 550lb variety with an aluminium cover, a 20:1 gear ratio and 20ft of free cable; and the sky-blue coloured 2,000lb capacity design with a much thicker cable, some 15ft in length, and a 247:1 gear ratio. Later, in 1944, a hydraulic power unit appeared for trials on

the squadron. This undoubtedly took the hard graft out of bombing-up but some armourers preferred the old manual type, bearing in mind that two long lengths of rubber hose connecting the power unit to the winch made it rather cumbersome. However, once the hydraulic winch was in position it was certainly an armourer's delight – unless the hose burst!

'The "big bogey" to all armourers I consider to be the delay bomb, particularly the type fused with a pistol containing acetone. On the way down the acetone ampoules would be broken by the rotation of the arming vane and crusher, eat through a small acetone disc, and in time allow a striker to move forward to fire the detonator in the bomb. (The time of delay was determined by the number of acetone discs and the strength of the acetone.) Obviously there were times when bombs were brought back from a raid still fused with delays, and we were always a little perturbed as to whether or not any ampoules were broken. I can remember one occasion when, with the delay on each fuse set at 30 minutes, I, as duty corporal, had to check each Lancaster as the squadron arrived back early due to a recall, lobbing down all over the airfield. I couldn't possibly get round all the aircraft in the time available, particularly as it was night time and I had, by torchlight, to look for telltale signs of discoloration on the blotting paper in the bomb pistols.

Above: **Means and Methods**
Manhandling 2,000lb HC bombs into position under the bomb bay of BX KB700 'LQ-Q' *The Ruhr Express* of No 405 ('Vancouver') Squadron RCAF Gransden Lodge, November 1943. Careful study of a picture such as this reveals the identity of the unit from the codes on the bomb trolley (though inter-Group transfers were not uncommon), and capacity and type of bomb. Clearly stencilled on the latter are: capacity (2,000lb); type (Mk 3A High Capacity with Mk 39 tail unit); date of manufacture (October 1943). KB700 was the first of 430 Canadian-built Lanc Xs. Delivered to the Vancouvers on 5 October 1943, she was mainly used for conversion training before transferring to No 419 ('Moose') Squadron in 6 Group. Provisionally scheduled for preservation, she unfortunately overshot on return from Nuremberg at 2338 hours on 2 January 1945 (her 50th sortie), collided with a tractor, and was burnt out.
/Public Archives of Canada

Above left: **To Clean was to Live** Clean and well maintained guns were vital if the crews were to have any chance of survival against fighters; turret perspex free of smudges and scratches was also essential, and responsibility for these actions would generally be shared by gunners and armourers. Here we see 'Titch', an armourer with No 101 Squadron Ludford Magna, cleaning the mid-upper Brownings of BI ME837 'SR-L' circa September 1944 (ME837 survived the war.). */R. T. J. Homes*

Above: **Brain Child** A steady hand is needed by the crane operator as a Tallboy is delicately lowered onto its cradle in the Bardney bomb dump. The picture, taken 9 September 1944, prior to Operation Paravane – the detachment based in Russia in order to attack the Tirpitz – clearly shows the immense size of the near 12,000lb monster. The special trolley, and one of the winches mounted at the base of each corner support (the latter complete with its own wire rope and pulleys) are also noteworthy. The crane in use here is of American design, manufactured by Lorraine and just about at the limit of its capacity (hence angle of jib). Neighbouring No 617 Squadron used an American Bay City crane to handle their grand slams./*F. W. Hawkins*

Left: **Tight Fit** There was little room to spare when a Tallboy was clamped in position inside a Lanc's bomb bay; modified bomb doors, of even more complicated contour than standard, were required to encompass the 38in diameter gargantuan. Body length was 10ft 4in; overall length 21ft; total weight 11,800lb; explosive filling 5,200lb of Torpex. Comparative dimensions and weights for the Grand Slam were: body length 12ft 1in; overall length 25ft 5in; total weight 22,400lb; explosive filling 9,200lb of Torpex; maximum diameter 46in. In the picture Cpl Frank Hawkins and LAC Sid Hodgson (on drum) are seen making final adjustments – if flouting the rules by not taking safety precautions. /*F. W. Hawkins*

183

Above: **Teamwork** LACs Chapman and Lewis provide a steadying hand as a fellow armourer, stationed inside a No 44 (Rhodesia) Squadron Lancaster, slowly winches a 500 pounder into position. This close up, taken at Dunholme Lodge in April 1944, shows well the bomb carrier (a leftover from Hampden days), cable and crutch pads (the latter two appearing surprisingly frail). The presence of nose plugs indicates that this load is set for long delay (the latter were always tail fused), and the Rhodesian sergeant is probably connecting arming wires to fuse links. The bomb release connections (here seen as loops above each carrier) will be plugged into the aircraft's electrical system./*J. I. Hartley*

'Due to a malfunction (usually icing), a bomb could either hang-up on its release unit or become dislodged from one already fired, and drop on to the bomb doors. On landing this was always a dicey moment for the crew – if they were aware of it! When it came to opening the doors – very slowly – we always did a visual inspection, especially at the fusing link. If there was a loose bomb there our usual procedure – one not conforming to Air Ministry instructions – was for us to scout round and collect up as many engine covers as we could, put them under the bomb bay and allow the bomb to come down on to them; if it was a delayed bomb we would use an Eagle trailer and ease it down, sweating profusely.

'In the summer of 1944 the squadron added a new dimension to its arsenal in the shape of the enormous 12,000lb Tallboy. Mounted on special trolleys, these monsters required even more skilful manoeuvring by the drivers to get the bomb positioned as near as possible under the aircraft, helped by an armourer who steered the rear wheels of the trolley. The greater the accuracy in lining up the bomb the speedier the bombing-up process was, for there was little room to spare. It required four (green) winches to lift each Tallboy from its cradle, each armourer cranking at the same time in order to keep an even keel; one armourer working too hard produced all sorts of problems so it was a question of gradually inching up in unison until we were within a foot of the Lanc's bomb bay floor.

'At this stage a fifth armourer would shout instruction – in best bomb aimer tradition – to the men on the winches so that a special recess in the bomb would slot into a spring-loaded dowell attached to the machine's bomb bay floor. The moment of joy came when the two engaged with a distinct "clonk", though it could mean some heaving and pushing before the closely-toleranced dowell went home. Next step was to attach the sling which held the Tallboy in position. This comprised a series of jointed steel bars, slung crab-like around the centre belly of the bomb and secured with an electric release unit. With good teamwork the operation took about 20 eventful minutes.

'To highlight the problems the Tallboy created I recall an incident one winter's morning when, as the bomb being winched up had almost reached the dowel, it began to slip on its platform because of the icy conditions prevailing. Suddenly, to everyone's dismay, there was a violent jerk and the tail of the Tallboy went straight up through the Lanc's bomb bay floor. I dashed over to the armoury on my bike to advise the armament officer what had happened, little realising there would be three similar incidents during the morning.

'Another difficulty was the flapping of the suspension sling in the bomb bay after the Tallboy had been released and one day I found our armament officer in deep conversation with Barnes Wallis himself, discussing the pros and cons of the subject out at dispersal. Soon after his visit we found Bowden cables and toggles running from inside the aircraft to each sling being fitted, enabling the aircrew to pull them up out of the way – a simple but effective means of overcoming what threatened to be a serious problem.

'Eventful days I must say.'

Just an Ordinary Day

IAN CURTIS

Many books and films have recorded the life and times of the aircrews, even if the latter have not always been portrayed with the greatest accuracy. Relatively little has been told of the part played by the long suffering ground crews, whose activities naturally lacked the glamour surrounding their airborne colleagues.

In this splendid story of a typical day in the life of an erk, only the names have been changed to hide the true identities of men as yet untraced. It is hoped this opus will give the reader a deeper understanding of their attitudes and outlook, humility and comradeship.

Under trying conditions their spirit was unfailing; long hours and basic living were, in the main, cheerfully accepted. In a world of colourful characters, drawn from every walk of life, humour was never far away, and the airman's right to 'eff and blind' – fooling no one – hid a fierce sense of purpose and pride.

Born in Singapore, Ian Curtis was 11 years old when he travelled to the UK in order to complete his schooling. A 10-month spell as an office boy preceded his entry into the RAF and by the time he joined 14 Base Major Servicing Section, Ludford Magna, in early 1944 he was an experienced 21-year old armourer with service on Nos 101 and 460 Squadrons. A short spell with No 279 Squadron at Thornaby, before its Lancaster element flew out to Burma in January 1946 to become 1348 Flight, completed his Service career.

Like so many, he found the early postwar years an unsettling period and finally, in 1952, emigrated to New Zealand, where he still leads a contented life as a chartered accountant.

'After rinsing our mugs and cutlery in the hot greasy fluid that passed for washing up water, Roger, Joey and I extracted our bicycles from the heaps stacked along the cookhouse wall and, mounting these, turned out into the lane to join the ever increasing tide of blue-clad humanity flowing towards the aerodrome. The casual observer could have been forgiven if he had come to the conclusion that, on the whole, the RAF had no standard uniform; for the combinations of different types of clothing

and equipment seemed to be endless. Leather jerkins, sea boot socks, gumboots, battledress, oil skins, tunics, scarves, mittens, gloves, jerseys, Balaclavas, all were in evidence. But a more observant onlooker would have noticed that the smart, correctly uniformed types were branching off down towards the administration site, whereas the scruffier specimens were rolling on to the 'drome itself or towards the Base Servicing Section. The three of us were in the latter stream, and on turning off the perimeter track we saw two Lancasters standing outside No 1 hangar.

'As we had only a ground test to do on the kite we had been working on, it was obvious that one of these two would be coming under our hands. We scanned them as we went past. One looked spick, span and new but the other was a battered, tired looking old veteran which caused Joey to remark that he hoped we would get the new one. Roger and I said nothing as we had been long enough in Base Major Servicing to know that an old veteran, well maintained, could be a lot less trouble than a new machine. Joey, on the other hand, had

Above: Ian Curtis warmly dressed for an early flight. /*I. Curtis*

Left: **Chips with Everything** '... After rinsing our mugs and cutlery in the hot greasy fluid that passed for washing up water, Roger, Joey and I extracted our bicycles from the heaps stacked along the cookhouse wall...' No 300 ('Masovian') Squadron Polish Air Force, Faldingworth 1944. /*Polish Sources*

spent a great deal of his service on a training station where it appeared his main job was to make sure the aircraft signal pistols were in good order; a saga which had caused much profane awe that such "cushy numbers" existed.

'We entered the Nissen hut which passed as our armoury, peeled off some of our outer clothing and shrugged ourselves into our overalls which, ripped, torn and generally ill-fitting, did little to protect our clothes. This was only one of the minor irritations of life and was of no account compared with the arrival of Sgt Kells. A darkly handsome man, Kells concealed an incisive efficiency behind a mask of false Irish charm, and proceeded to make our lives miserable by announcing that he had already looked over the two Lancasters outside and, as the old one was in a dreadful condition he was allocating her to his "best" squad. Roger mumbled under his breath, I scowled and Joey looked gratified; all of which caused Kells' expression to brighten till his gaze fell on Cartwright, whereupon it became reflective. Kells did not like Cartwright; but then few did. He was our one and only armourers' assistant and it would have been hard to find a bigger and more useless specimen of humanity. At the moment he was ineffectively trying to light the coke stove with copious quantities of old anti-freeze oil and there was no doubt Kells would soon be finding a harder job than that for him.

'We ambled out to the old veteran. She looked worse close up, and as there was no ladder by the side door we heaved ourselves up into the fuselage. I turned left and crawled over the tail beam and past the flimsy doors, before sitting down on the catwalk to look into the turret. I eyed the four Brownings carefully. They were all set to "safe", a lesson I had learnt the hard way a long time before when, during a turret test, I had shot off a burst of five or six rounds into the ground. The turret did not look too good with some oil on the floor, a cracked perspex panel, drips of oil from the hydraulic firing rams and no modified trigger guards or door quick-release cable. Superficially the guns looked in order, and I flipped up the top covers and disconnected the ammo belts.

'I crawled back into the main part of the fuselage where Roger was pressing the hydraulic spindles near the mid-upper. They went down under his hands – a bad sign – and he grinned wryly when I told him we would probably have to replace the rear turret. He jumped down from the aircraft and I handed out the two Brownings from the mid-upper before turning back towards the rear turret. A flick down on the "Dead man's" lever and I entered the turret, which Roger pushed round to beam. Knocking out the securing pins, I

handed out the four Brownings before dropping down beside him. He looked at the turret and appeared unhappy until he saw the perspex panel. Some time before both he and I had to come to an amicable arrangement with an NCO in the clothing store where, for the gift of a sheet of perspex, we were given to understand that any request for replacement clothing would be favourably considered. Perspex rings and brooches were in vogue at that time!

'Joined by Joey we took the guns back to the armoury, where Roger, being a corporal and boss of our squad, reported to Kells about the veteran's condition, mentioning that we had not removed the ammunition belts. This was cunning of Roger for it was a tedious, heavy task and implied that assistance would be welcomed. Kells took the hint. Roger didn't like Cartwright either.

'In the armoury, we stripped the guns down and went over them meticulously, a job that was interrupted by the arrival of the NAAFI van, which as usual signalled the end of the war for a spell. A milling horde of erks obtained their tea or coffee and two "rock wads", before breaking up into conversational groups. "Magdrop", the base mascot, a dog of uncertain ancestry, hung round looking soulful and, as usual, gobbled "rock wads" unconcernedly without much thought of the havoc to his stomach. A nice dog Magdrop, with only one vice – an incurable habit of leaping up at idling prop blades which, luckily for him, were slightly beyond his reach. Having downed our tea, we strolled back to the armoury, passing our veteran headache, when Cartwright staggered out with the mid-upper ammo boxes. He yelled to Joey to give him a hand, and Joey, reasonable as always, considered the request. On reflection, Joey told Cartwright to assist by carrying the ammo boxes himself.

'Back to the armoury and the guns – an oily job, but one that could be done automatically. Johnson of B Squad, the armoury Lothario, was doing the same chore as us and as usual was recounting some lurid romantic episode; and as usual, nobody listened. Don was concentrating over a flare fuse reel, tunelessly whistling a hymn through his teeth. Don was not religious and the tune fitted a very rude song which had found wide acclaim in the RAF throughout the ages. Gerry had his head inside a nose turret replacing some item or other bolted on by some muscle-bound moron, a fact he declaimed on at great length when his spanner slipped off a bolt with damage to his knuckles. Kells sent him off to get the hand cleaned and covered. Oil had a nasty effect on open cuts.

'The morning wore on and when, at lunch time, Betty the Base driver drove the big

Bedford up to the armoury, we greased out of our overalls and piled on to the truck for a free lift to the cookhouse. We jolted out of the base area on to the perimeter track. A squadron Lanc was being bombed-up, an SBC of incendiaries going up into one of the forward bomb positions. I did not envy the armourer on the winch – he would be contorted under the navigator's table, sweating profusely in a very warm "greenhouse", which would be more than could be said for his lunch when he got away for it. Arriving at the long Nissen hut complex that was the cookhouse, we formed the usual queue snaking down the side of the dining area to the servery, where our rations were slapped on to our plates by WAAFS and airmen who appeared to bear a dislike for their customers. This was deepened by Joey remarking that Mum could cook far better, but as he was hungry . . . . We congregated around a vacant trestle-table, attacked our food hungrily and finished the meal off with the usual pint pot of hot tea, which Johnson insisted was stiff with bromide to dampen our basic instincts. This worried Johnson.

'On our return to the armoury, we noticed that the veteran had been towed into the hangar while our last job had been towed out to dispersal. Roger went over to the engine mechs' bay and asked them to let us know when they would be testing the engines so that we could complete our ground tests on the turrets. Back to the armoury, where time drifted past with the multitude of small jobs which always seemed to accumulate. Outside, the usual noises of an aerodrome echoed around. A metallic clang; pumping noises; the shrill of an electric drill; voices; the muted rumble of a distant running Merlin; the ripping fast rattle of .303in Brownings from the butts; the rising and falling note of a tractor in the field beyond the armoury. Being inured to these noises, we did not pay any attention to the whining noise of a Merlin prop turning over slowly before, with a couple

of explosions, the engine caught and settled into the harsh beat of an idling motor. It was only when Kells came in sardonically saying that he usually thought turret testing could only be carried out when a kite's engines were running, that the penny dropped.

'We raced out of the armoury, over to our Lancaster and dived into the wash from the airscrews. Before we could heave ourselves up into the aircraft, the starboard-outer's prop blades disappeared in a thin filmy haze and the noise climbed to an ear shattering roar, while a gale of fumy, grit-laden wind buffeted us and cut through our clothing. Screwing up our eyes and cursing, we climbed into the aircraft, Roger going to the rear turret, Joey up over the bomb bay on his way to the front turret. He'd make himself popular pushing past the crowd of bods clustered in the "greenhouse", but it was their fault, they should have told us about the run up. I pulled the step down, swung up into the mid-upper and clipped on the canvas seat under me. Guns "safe". Hooking my forage cap over the cocking studs I pulled them back, mentally going through the procedures: depress the triggers; a clang as the breech blocks slam home; no oil from the firing rams; reflector sight bright and dim; spin the turret slow-fast; raise and depress guns; cock the left hand gun; line it up on the tail unit; fire – no action; all in order. Repeat with right hand gun; no action; cut-out working; depress guns over beam; fire guns and spin turret; the rollers lift both guns up and down smoothly over the fairing; no problems. I settled back in the turret.

'The mid-upper was a nice place to be in. The sun beating through the perspex made the inside temperature pleasantly warm and the view of the surrounds was magnificent. The port-outer was being revved up, shaking the aircraft, and I watched the tail unit vibrating in the slipstream. Roger, in the tail turret, would be feeling the rear end of the fuselage bouncing up and down on the tail wheel. Dust swirled in clouds away from the

Above: **Ground Run** ' . . . And I watched the tail unit vibrating in the slipstream. Roger, in the tail turret, would be feeling the rear end of the fuselage bouncing up and down on the tail wheel . . . ' 'AR-U' No 460 Squadron RAAF, Binbrook summer 1944./*E. D. Evans*

Above right: **Erks Domain** Many and varied were the ground crew huts to be found by every dispersal. Knocked-up from oddments of corrugated sheeting, wooden planks and tarpaulins, they were a haven in which the erks could relax when on top of their work. The aircrews considered it an honour to be invited inside for a brew up and a game of cards while awaiting take-off. This example, at Binbrook, even sports its own Standard!/*E. D. Evans*

Centre right: **On the Job** ' . . . Outside, the usual noises of an aerodrome echoed around. A metallic clang; pumping noises; the shrill of an electric drill; voices; the muted rumble of a distant running Merlin . . . ' No 576 Squadron Fiskerton 1945./*L. W. Dorricott*

Bottom right **Prelude** ' . . . The shadows were fast lengthening on the aerodrome, now showing little signs of life, and already that pre-raid air of brooding silence had descended over the place . . . ' No 460 Squadron RAAF, Binbrook summer 1944. /*E. D. Evans*

kite, grass off the dispersal rippled flat in waves and the boundary hedge swayed under the buffeting air. I relaxed peacefully until the four motors cut, then I got down out of the turret, stowed the step and checked the spindles; all clear. I joined Roger outside and, collecting Joey, we walked back to the armoury. On that particular Lanc our job was over and after her air test she would pass out of our lives for ever and we would never know what became of her.

'Towards the end of the working day, the three of us went over to the hangar into which they had towed our veteran, and began the job of preparing the rear turret for removal. Roger, with his customary low cunning, gave Joey the job of undoing the RSJ, which involved him lying on his back and unscrewing the panel under the fuselage and, as we half expected, some oil dribbled out of the half-removed panel down on to Joey's jaw and neck. He reacted vociferously and was in no way consoled when Roger mentioned that usually when the job was done out in the open, the tail was parked over a puddle.

'Finishing some 20 minutes past the official "knock off" time, we collected our bicycles and cycled off the practically deserted site. The shawdows were fast lengthening on the aerodrome, now showing little sign of life, and already that pre-raid air of brooding silence had descended over the place. The blue perimeter track glim-lights were already on, and at their dispersals the Lancasters sat quietly, their bomb doors open to show the stowed loads of incendiaries and "Cookies". Passing a dispersal with a u/s Lancaster, a gentle evening breeze was flicking away at an engine cover, slapping it against the side of the kite and the sound merely served to emphasize the eerie stillness, a spell that would only be broken when they wound up the first Merlin prior to take-off.

'Back in our hut after tea, we collected our toilet gear and walked over to the washhouse. Because we were late finishing, the hot water was tepid but not cold enough to make the decision to boil up some water on the hut's coke stove. This, combined with the gloomy atmosphere of the place – most of the light bulbs had been "borrowed" – did not encourage us to take too much time over our ablutions and we were soon back in the hut, which was already becoming fuggy. I made up my bed and, as always, thought how civilised it would be to have sheets. Lying back on it, I watched and listened to the hut's activities. A card school was operating on Don's bed. Dave and three others were already sitting on the beds adjacent to the coke stove, nattering away about the day's events. Jock and Mac were lying on their beds carrying on their interminable argument about football. Pete

189

and most of the others were either writing letters or reading, while Johnson was dressed up in his best blue, running a comb through his Brylcreamed hair, an action producing the usual crop of rude remarks.

'Johnny was shrugging himself into his greatcoat and slinging on his webbing. A Lee-Enfield stood by his bed. He would have picked this up at the Station Armoury earlier on and Dave was cynically suggesting that if he valued his face and arms, it would be better that he threw it at any intruder he might encounter during his spell of aerodrome guard that night. The chore of aerodrome guard was an infrequent one and a farce at that, for two men walking around the perimeter track in the middle of the night carrying rifles of dubious serviceability did not really have much hope of intercepting anybody who entertained ideas of sabotage. This fact was so evident to even the lowest intelligence amongst us, that nobody took it very seriously, especially as authority never bothered to check up on whether the duty was being carried out properly or not. A drill had been evolved whereby those on their "two hours on" merely made a bee-line to the nearest u/s aircraft and continued their interrupted sleep there. I helpfully told Johnny on which dispersal one of these stood.

'Walking back in the darkness from the NAAFI with Dave later on, we heard the distant sound of a Merlin starting up. It could have been from our 'drome or the one that lay not far over the hill from our billet (this was Kelstern). Shortly, the whole air seemed to be vibrating with the noise of engines and we knew there would be at least 80 of these on our 'drome alone. We stopped and watched navigation lights gliding along that portion of the perimeter track we could see. Another set of lights slid with ever-increasing speed between the runway lights and rose away into the bluey-black night sky. Within no time it was followed by another set, and yet another; and so on until the sky seemed to be full of moving sets of lights. One lot passed over our heads, climbing away into the night. I was struck by the thought that the day which had now passed was just another ordinary day for me, and probably just another "ordinary" night for the seven men up in those lights. But one thing was certain: they would never be able to regard their job in the same detached way I had just done!'

Below: **Nightshift** Throughout the night Methwold ground crews work in a dimly lit hangar to overhaul a No 149 (East India) Squadron Lancaster during the closing months of the war. Next to a windswept dispersal, a draughty hangar would appear to be the coldest place on earth./*A. Pratt*

Distant
Dispersals

Right: **Leafy Lane** The war seems a world away in this pastoral scene showing No 12 Squadron Lancs dispersed at tree-lined Wickenby in 1944. While all roads leading to and bordering operational airfields were cordoned off, there was access for local farmers and known village folk.
/*G. Mastin*

Below: **Merlins in the Dales** The raucous tone of Merlins replaces the whining note of Hercules at Skipton-on-Swale as a freshly delivered No 424 ('Tiger') Squadron Lanc is 'given the gun'. In this beautifully composed picture one can almost hear the 'music' of four Merlins running at full power./*B. P. A. Mose*

Above: **Snowbound** Binbrook during the severe winter of 1943/4, when the station was virtually cut-off for three weeks. With all approach roads blocked, food stocks soon ran out and 'hard tack' became the staple diet until supplies could be dropped by parachute. /E. D. Evans

Right: **Winter's Grip** Frost-adorned barbed wire and hedgerows border a dormant, ice-covered Waddington in January 1945, with No 463 Squadron's 'Y-Yorker' beyond, completely covered in white hoar frost./H. A. Watkins

Centre right: **Clutter** Except for major servicing (generally every 200hr) a Lancaster would rarely see the inside of a hangar. A mass of trestles, oil drums, cowlings and ladders (to say nothing of the inevitable bikes) surround this No 115 Squadron BII undergoing engine maintenance at Little Snoring, autumn 1943. The airfield was still under construction at the time and a contractor's crane can be seen in the background. Rich Norfolk grass has yet to gain a hold around the dispersal pan./K. B. M. Grant

Bottom right: **Exposed** Working on exposed dispersals could be pleasant in summer; authority turned a blind eye as the erks stripped to the waist and baked as they toiled to prepare their charges. Kelstern 1944, with No 625 Squadron's 'CF-X' in foreground. /C. Koder Collection

We Flew Lancasters

The aircrew game was a strange one. It was played out against a backdrop of wine, women and song on the ground, and muck, sweat and fear in the air. Above all, the business end of it was impersonal to a degree bordering on unreality. There were probably few more certain ways of coming to a premature end than by carting those bombs to their targets; and yet, illogically, it was never you who was going to die, but always some other chap. It was a job and one's view remained clinical.

In the following pages typical aircrew of their generation record their duties, fears and impressions.

We shall not see their like again.

Below: **Conflab** Wg Cdr W. Art McKay (facing camera, forage cap), OC No 432 ('Leaside') Squadron RCAF, East Moor, chats with crew before emplaning for Berlin, probably on 26/27 November 1943. /*Public Archives of Canada*

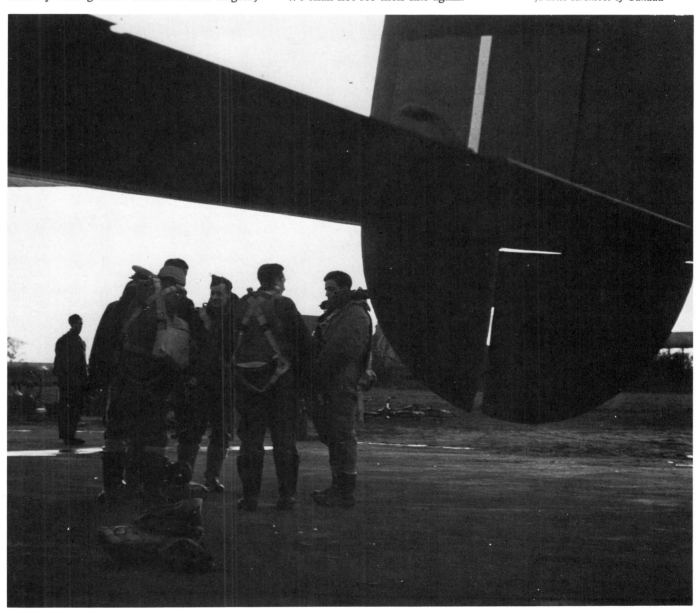

Where Hide the Warriors
J. S. E. Brookbank, 1946

Where hide the warriors, those gay young men,
That once I knew, the chaps who lived and flew
With Death, for Death was ever-present then;
And joked of flak and other things I knew?

Run-ups in the morning, battle orders
And briefing time, the rush and panic in
The Mess, for speed was of the essence then;
The Wingco's voice . . . 'Your target gentlemen . . .'

A soothing cigarette (thank God for those)
Produced and lit, takes grip on nerves much worn
And tried, our hands were never steady then;
And then the kites etched black against the dawn.

Once more the comforting, friendly sound of
Engines revving, and the chaos in the
Crew coach, a jumbled mass of gear and men;
'Have a good trip'; 'Get off my bloody foot then?'

Greens from the caravan, and people there
To wave good luck, wet runways shiny black
And grim – 'Right, twenty six fifty plus ten . . .'
'OK here we go! All set up the back?'

The climbs to bombing height, and the long slow
Monotony, with time to pause and think
Of war, the useless murder of young men;
'Can you get a fix before we cross the drink?'

Those target areas with greens and reds
And fighter flares. Flak on the starboard bow
Ahead. Windspeed two seven zero ten;
A gentle weave – we're on the target now.

The hectic bombing runs: 'Bomb doors open
Left, left, steady' – suspense, and time stands still
Awhile. 'Dummy run, let's go round again . . .'
And fighters there just waiting for the kill.

And then the words 'Bombs gone, get weaving Skip';
The job is done, and yet we may not slack
Or rest, with danger always lurking there;
We'll have a wizard binge when we get back!

The Focke-Wulf One Nineties, silhouetted
Against the fires, and the hang-up in the
Bomb-bay; I thought that one would still be there!
'Prepare to corkscrew starboard' – or anywhere.

A Lancaster in flames and the tracer
Piercing the night. The target burning bright
Below, with the HE bombs exploding there;
Our starboard-outer's not behaving right!

Then the homeward flip with engine feathered
And loss of speed, and the straggle behind
The stream. An easy prey for fighters now;
A hundred little fears flit through the mind.

And the glorious sight of dawn's first rays;
A calm North Sea, the English coast appears
Ahead. 'Smell any petrol up the back?';
And the best cigarette I've had in years!

Panic on the circuit, and natter on
The intercom; then a soft female voice
Is heard (we're back at base without a doubt);
'Rosen Able pancake'. 'Roger out'.

Those interrogations; Martin's Gold Leaf
And cups of char, and the tired and dirty
Faces. 'Flak? No, there really wasn't much';
The usual understatement, and such.

And then again the Mess, the casual
Conversation, the trying hard to keep
Awake. 'That fighter came a bit too near;
Who's coming out tonight to have a beer?'.

The world awakening as we retire
To sleep the while; the Nissen hut that seems
Like home, the cigarettes that glow and fade.
It's just the end of yet another raid.

And all those little things that once were just
Our normal life; a life of coloured scarves
And 'lines', and friends one could rely upon.
Where tread they now, along what varied paths?

Do they remember yet the village pub
And games of darts, and Christmas spent away
From Base, and other things I can recall;
The grim reality of New Year's Day?

Where hide the warriors, in what disguise
Are they concealed; and do their hearts cry out
Again for well-remembered days and nights,
And the old familiar smell of kites?.

Pilot:
How Would You Like to Drive 8,000 Horses?

JIM McINTOSH

A Lancaster pilot in Bomber Command had a dual responsibility. In addition to flying his machine he was, with few exceptions, leader of his crew regardless of rank. While it was the duty of the captain to tell his crew what to do, he was wise to make the fullest use of their specialised knowledge. Failure to heed the advice of his navigator, wireless operator or engineer, or even to consult them, could easily risk his aircraft.

Example was the key to confidence and to secure confidence was the essence of leadership. Whether he had a good or indifferent crew, at times the captain had to drive; on other occasions he had to persuade; but at all times he had to lead. There had to be one person in supreme command who, however well his crew performed, was the one to make decisions in sudden emergencies.

In no other branch of the Service did so great a responsibility devolve on young officers and NCOs as that of being an aircraft captain. Authority and discipline were essential in the air, while even on the ground he had to quietly maintain authority at all times. From the day a Lancaster pilot became a captain he was a man just a little apart.

In the Lancaster, he had under his control a viceless forgiving thoroughbred – often described as the perfect 'heavy' – and in the following story Canadian Jim McIntosh expresses views certain to be echoed by any Lanc skipper.

We have purposely introduced a man who flew the relatively little known Hercules-powered variant, considered by some to be the finest of the breed. His account also embraces the durable Wellington and worthy Halifax – aircraft repeatedly overlooked, yet whose contribution to ultimate victory cannot be ignored.

Born and raised in Revelstoke, British Columbia, Jim McIntosh had been a locomotive fireman with the Canadian Pacific Railway before electing to volunteer for aircrew duties with the RCAF. As a 23-year old flying officer, his active war ended abruptly and he spent the final year of hostilities as an inmate of Stalag Luft 1, Barth before return-ing to Canada for release from the RCAF in August 1945.

Now living in Vancouver, Jim leads an active outdoor life as a forester with the Federal Government of Canada Forestry Service.

'We were new on the station when we were introduced to the Lanc II. Our all-Canadian crew – Alex Small, navigator, from Morris, Manitoba; Bob Elvin, bomb aimer, Clyde Schell, wireless operator, and Len Bandle, rear gunner, all from Toronto; and myself from Revelstoke, British Columbia – had done our operational training on Wimpeys at 22 OTU Gaydon in Warwickshire. After 88 hours flying time, which included a "nickel-ling" trip to Boulogne, we were posted right away to No 432, an RCAF Wimpey squadron at East Moor, seven miles north of York, arriving there at the end of September 1943.

'We felt good about going to a Wimpey squadron. The Mk Xs were fitted with Herc engines as were the OTU Mk IIIs so we wouldn't have any trouble adjusting. Our OTU instructors, all one-tour men, had done a good job convincing us the Wimp was the best kite. They didn't know much about the four-engined types except, from the Wimps, they'd seen the Hallybags and Stirlings catching hell below them on ops. Because of the unique construction of the Wimp it could take an awful beating and still fly. It was a squat, solid looking kite with the high tail being the most distinctive feature. It flew easily and had no bad habits; you just felt safe in it. The feature I remember best was the pilot's seat, the most comfortable of all. The furniture manufacturers would have a winner if they could copy it!

'During our first three weeks at No 432 we made a couple of mining trips and a sea search, and I made my "second dickey" trip. Then we were posted to No 1679 HCF, a Lanc II heavy conversion flight, on the same station. For a couple of weeks we'd seen the Lancs doing circuits and bumps and cruising around, had admired them from afar, but were so green we didn't even know there was a conversion unit on the station. Now we were

Jim McIntosh about the time his DFC was promulgated.
/J. A. McIntosh

joined by our new crew members: Andy Dedauw, mid-upper gunner from Tilbury, Ontario, and Wally King, flight engineer, our only RAF type, from Norwich.

'The "second dickey" trip was my introduction to the real thing, which of course was its purpose. I did mine with a Canadian, WO Erickson, on a trip to Hanover. From the coast to the target area I dropped "Window" from the dark "safe" interior of the Wimp and only the terse comments of the crew indicated the position of flak and searchlights. We were readying for the bomb run when Erickson told me I'd better come up beside him and see what it was all about. God! I moved from the dark "safe" inside of the Wimp to become a spectator at the gates of Hell! All around flak and aircraft, flares, green, yellow, red target markers and scores of probing searchlights, and down below a city writhing in a holocaust of fire. The twisting streets stood outlined in flames and bomb blasts. Whole blocks seemed to instantly disappear in a sheet of flame – "Cookies". I was terrified!

'A stream of fire in the sky showed the path of a burning bomber plunging to earth. I couldn't believe it! About 400yd below on our right, tracers cut into a Hally. I could see it as plain as day against the burning city. Fire flamed out from the base of the starboard wing, return tracers streaked from the top turret. The fighter, a single engine type, swept unscathed over the bomber and headed right for us. I couldn't even yell! He must see us! He can't miss! In a fraction of a second he was gone – passed right over us so close I could see distinctly the black crosses on the wings.

Above and left: **Pillars of Hercules** '. . . The running up and engine testing procedure was the same as the Wimp. Warm up at 1,000rpm; then each engine in turn; check pitch control; at full throttle check revs are 2,800; throttle back to 6lb boost and check mags . . . don't idle the engines below 800 revs or you'll foul the plugs . . .' Graphic studies of No 408 ('Goose') Squadron's BII DS758 'EQ-H' being checked out at Linton-on-Ouse December 1943. Though the picture is said to be dated 23 December 1943, DS758 failed to return from Frankfurt 20/21 December!
/Both Public Archives of Canada

196

Didn't even see us! Flames streamed out from the bomber and in a blast of fire it disappeared.

'The crew continued on the bomb run, unconcerned and unaware of the fighter, the bomb aimer calling directions. "Left, left, steady-y-y, steady-y-y — bombs gone." The Wimp gave a jump as our "Cookie" went and we started the trip back to base. I went back to "Windowing". Below us I'd seen only Hallys, Wimpeys and Stirlings – no Lancasters. They must have been above and safe. If this was what it was all about, I was sure glad we were converting!

'After we had left the enemy coast Erickson asked me to take over for a while. "A few tips for you on ops. I weave all the time over enemy territory, except on the bomb run of course. It makes you a harder target for the fighters. A gentle weave won't take anything from your speed and there is a good chance if a fighter does attack he'll miss on the first pass. This could give the gunner a shot at him and you a chance for evasive action. Also, don't be in a hurry to be first on take-off. Stall around the dispersal if you can, despite the order of take-off. Let the keen ones go ahead. All you do if first off is stooge around up there with a full load using petrol which you may need before you get back."

'Our instructor on 1679 HCF was Flg Off Morton, a Canadian pilot who had completed a tour. First he took us around the Lanc just to show us the aircraft and go over the check list. It really towered over us after the Wimpey. "You'll like the Lanc. It's more powerful for its weight and faster than the Wimpey.

It'll carry a bigger load higher and further. It practically flies itself. The Herc engines are the same as the Wimp and you already know about those."

'We went inside, where he explained the layout. The first instrument inside the door – the Elsan. "You never know when you'll have to use it; only hope you have time to get to it." The ammo trays stretched to the turrets. Then forward over the main spar to the wireless op's and navigator's stations. He showed us the master switch and explained its operation. Then to the cockpit. There was a bewildering array of dials, gauges and levers. "Just remember you've got four engines instead of two so there are twice as many engine dials and levers as the Wimpey. The controls are the same but better arranged. It just looks complicated."

'He went through the cockpit thoroughly, explaining every lever, dial and gauge, then left us to familiarise ourselves with the new aircraft. Sure felt good in the pilot's seat – not as comfortable a seat as the Wimp – but everything was within easy reach and you had excellent visibility. Tomorrow we would be airborne in a four-engined kite.

'Our circuits and bumps started the next morning, 13 November, with Flg Off Morton in DS626. Before starting the engines he went through the pre-starting check. Then the starting – communication with groundcrew, signals for starting and start-up – port to starboard. The running up and engine testing procedure was the same as the Wimp. Warm up at 1,000rpm. Then each engine in turn: check pitch control: at full throttle check revs

The Skipper '. . . Sure felt good in the pilot's seat . . . everything was within easy reach and you had excellent visibility . . .' (*below left*) WO Bill Patterson No 166 Squadron Kirmington, autumn 1943. Foreground is the elevator trimmer wheel. (*below*) Wg Cdr Leonard Slee from No 49 Squadron Fiskerton 1942, suitably attired in Irving jacket and gloves.
/*W. Patterson; L. C. Slee*

are 2,800: throttle back to +6lb boost and check mags.

'Before taxying out he gave me some advice. "You have to take special care when taxying the Lanc. It'll taxi faster than the Wimp if you let it. Start out slow and watch your brake pressure; don't let it get down. Steer with your outers as much as you can and use your brakes to control speed. Stop if necessary to build up brake pressure. Don't idle the engines below 800 revs or you'll foul the plugs. Just take it easy till you get the feel and you'll have no trouble." He waved the chocks away and taxied around the perimeter track for take-off. It looked so easy.

'While taxying, some more advice. "Some pilots have the engineer help with the throttles, wheels and flaps during take-off and landing, but I prefer to do it all myself. If anything happens I know immediately what to do; there is no confusion and less chance of a mistake. The throttles fit perfectly in your hand; the thumb and little finger can control the outers and the inners fit in your palm. Just before take-off tighten the throttle tension so you can just move the throttles; they will hold position at full throttle and won't slip when you let them go. The only bad thing about the Lanc II is that it tends to swing to starboard on take-off. You control this by letting the port-outer back a bit if she starts to swing. You can't leave this to the engineer as you are the one who knows when she starts to swing. When you get some speed you can control swing with the rudders. Lift her off the ground at about 95. Get the wheels up and if there are no trees or obstructions at the end of the runway, hold her down a bit to get speed up faster. Then start climbing. Let the flaps up slowly – 5° at a time – especially when you are fully loaded."

'Before turning onto the runway we stopped. He went through the take-off check: trims; revs; flaps; mags; then called for take-off clearance. We moved onto the runway far enough to get the tail wheel straightened. He applied the brakes, then opened the throttles to about 2,000rpm and DS626 shook in anticipation. The brakes were released, the throttles shoved fully forward and we were off.

'The old Wimp had lumbered down the runway; the Lanc flew! The roar of the engines engulfed you; you couldn't even hear yourself think! In no time the tail was up and she floated free of the ground. Wheels up; back to climbing boost and revs; flaps up slowly, nice and smooth; not even a feeling of any change in attitude. After the Wimpey she seemed to climb like a Spit. "Best climbing speed is 165. You can drop the nose a bit and get your speed up to say 175 but the rate of climb will be less." We climbed out of the circuit to about 6,000ft and levelled off. Morton showed us what the Lanc could do. First turns and banks. The tighter the turn,

Below: **Challenging Moment**
' . . . We moved onto the runway far enough to get the tail wheel straightened. He applied the brakes and opened the throttles to about 2,800rpm and DS626 shook in anticipation. The brakes were released, the throttles shoved fully forward and we were off . . . '
Linton-on-Ouse or East Moor December 1943, featuring Lanc IIs of Nos 408, 426 or 432 Squadrons bound for Berlin.
/Public Archives of Canada

the more rudder was needed to keep the nose up, same as the Wimp. He tried a stall. She sort of stumbled before the nose dropped; no trouble there. He cut one outer; hardly noticed any difference. Both outers and speed had to be reduced, but she still flew alright with a bit more throttle and revs. Both on one side, a bit more difficult; the "dead" wing up and a bit of rudder trim; more throttles and revs on the good ones and she kept going. "She won't go very long on one motor; won't hold height, and at full power on the remaining motor you'll have a problem keeping direction, and of course the motor won't last long."

'He showed me how to get the engines in phase. "You hear them first and adjust the sound with the revs." He flew it with only the trims and she responded quickly. He told me to try it. Just to sit there at the controls, even on the right side, sure gave me a sense of power; just like the recruiting posters back home. "How would you like to drive 8,000 horses? The sweep of the wings and the four discs of the spinning props; the ultimate bomber!" I went through turns, banks, climbing, a stall; she handled so smoothly.

' "Take her back to base and we'll try a couple of circuits." I brought her into the circuit, where he took over and called for permission to land. "Landing is the same procedure as the Wimp; down-wind leg; wheels down and bring the speed back. Cross-wind leg; start the flaps and reduce speed. On the approach, get the speed back to 130 and full flap. You can fly the Lanc on if you have lots of runway, but go for the three-point. Bring her over the end of the runway at about 110, level out, and then cut the motors; she'll settle on at about 90-95. I'll land; you watch straight ahead to get the feeling for the greater height after the Wimp." She touched down like a bird. We did a couple more circuits and landings to give me a better feel for the higher aircraft. Tomorrow I was to take it from the left side.

'The crew were really enthusiastic. Alex had lots of room for his maps and instruments. Clyde's compartment was much better laid out than in the Wimpey and Bob felt he had a much better view, which would be easier for map reading, and he had room to move around. The turrets were turrets; but in the Lanc the gunners just felt better.

'The next day it rained so we had to wait. The following day I was in the left hand seat of DS650, with Flg Off Morton in the right. I went through the start-up checks. "Contact port to starboard." Each engine in turn coughed and then caught. I really felt like something with those four engines going. After the engine temperatures and the brake pressures were up I went through the checks and waved the chocks away. Now the tricky part – taxying. First I used the brakes too much to steer and had to stop to build up pressure; next a couple of wild swings with the outers as I adjusted to the four throttles. Stop again to build up brake pressure. Half way to the end of the runway and I had the feel; from there on nothing to it! The first take-off – just as if I knew what I was doing! The first landing – didn't level out soon enough! Bounce! "I've got her", yelled Morton as he shoved the throttles and control column forward to go around again. I felt stupid! On the next try, a couple of ripples and I had her down; pretty good. The crew gave a cheer. In the afternoon 1hr 55min of circuits and bumps, in DS657. No problems and no difficulty in handling the throttles and controls by myself.

'The next day we were checked out in DS656 by Plt Off McGavock, and then we were on our own. We had forgotten the Wimp now that we were in such a beautiful kite. A few more circuits and bumps and then a cross-country for nav and map reading practice.

'We had yet to do night flying, but before starting this we were called for a sea search. Seems a crew had gone down in the North Sea the night before. The poor bastards! This was November and we had been told that about 10 minutes was all the time you had in the water before the cold got you. Plt Off Boczar, a Canadian instructor from 1679 was the pilot and captain of DS650 and I, as second pilot, was, in this case, another set of eyes. Alex was busy with the search pattern but the rest of us just looked at water for $2\frac{1}{2}$ hours. Sure got monotonous. Nothing but water and one Danish fishboat. Afterwards we were told no one had found the downed crew. We never knew whether they were RCAF, RAF or USAAF.

'Flg Off Morton was still with us for night flying. He took us around for one circuit the first night in DS650 before the rain shut down flying. Two nights later we were out with Plt Off McGavock for 1hr 35min of circuits and bumps in DS650, before he said "It's all yours".

'Taxying at night was supposed to be difficult. I didn't have any problem following the blue lights of the perimeter track. Worst was watching the kite ahead to be sure you didn't run into it. The next night we were checked out by Sqn Ldr Al Avant, the CO of 1679 HCF, in DS632. My landing was the best I'd ever made; hardly knew we were down it was so smooth. Four more hours night flying and we were posted back to B flight No 432 Squadron and ready for ops on Lanc IIs with the grand total of 9hr 20min first pilot time.

'The squadron first blooded the Lanc II on 26/27 November to Berlin with the most

Below: **Profile** The solid lines of the Lancaster II. This profile of No 115 Squadron's LL666 'KO-U' at Witchford early in 1944 reveals the extended bomb bay and double contour doors fitted to the majority of the breed for the carriage of 8,000lb HC bombs. The erk adds scale to the enormous exhaust stacks. Services provided by each Hercules differed from their Merlin equivalents in some respects. On the BII the starboard-inner drove both front and mid-upper turrets via pumps; the port-inner drove the pumps running rear and mid-under turrets. The port-outer fed a compressor from which the automatic pilot, Gee and Monica operated. Cowling gills were controlled from an accumulator charged by an electric generator run off both inner engines. (LL666 was later relegated to use as a ground instruction airframe.) /R. J. Ball

experienced crews. We were waiting when they came back early in the morning to get the gen on the new kites. Despite the long trip the crews were really enthusiastic. "These things go like skinned cats. I bet we could outrun the bloody fighters!" We got our turn on 2 December in our kite, DS843 "O-Oboe", to Berlin, or "Big B", as we called it, with a 4,000lb "Cookie" plus incendiaries. We were green as grass but with a new Lanc of our own, felt confident nothing could touch us! We were out all morning shining perspex and checking everything, again and again.

'Remembering Erickson's advice, we delayed leaving our dispersal as long as seemed possible and were one of the last to take-off. Our first take-off loaded was no problem, only took a bit more runway. There were Merlin Lanc squadrons in the area and in the dusk we seemed to leave them behind in climbing to altitude over Britain. Our Lancs climbed like the clappers with the added power of the Hercs. We were to reach 17,000ft at the enemy coast, yet were already at that altitude when half-way across the North Sea. But from there on, climbing was slower; to 18,000ft

fairly easy, but a struggle to get to 20,000ft which was our bombing altitude. Once the bombs were gone, and with the Herc power, we got out of the target area in a hurry. I'd used too much fuel in trying to reach altitude on the way to the target. Now we were unsure of our position but should be at least near the channel. All at once everything started to come up at us, even the kitchen sink! At that instant Gee started working again and Alex called to say we were over Ostend and gave me a course. A few minutes later we landed at Manston, out of gas. Next trip I'd know better!

'We were on the Lancs till the end of January, with all our trips (seven) to Berlin. To us there was no better aircraft. With the power of the Hercs she was the fastest bomber, with only Merlin Lancs maybe having an advantage in altitude. Certainly the poor Hallys were left way behind and below. The Lanc took us through a couple of "Hairy Dos"; one in particular where it was shot to hell, but got us home although that kite never flew again. Weaving saved us that time and the gunners got the fighter; but that is another

Sturdy Lines '... To us there was no better aircraft. With the power of the Hercs she was the fastest bomber ... We had to concede to the Is and IIIs a bit on the bombing altitude, but on anything else we were better: faster; quicker off the deck; less exhaust glow at night; no glycol and less engine trouble ...' (*top*), DS763 'OW-O' of No 426 ('Thunderbird') Squadron,

Linton-on-Ouse 1944 and among the last Lanc IIs operated by No 426 before it converted to Halifaxes. Written off 10 October 1944 with 1668 HCU. (*above*), No 432 ('Leaside') Squadron erks pose with newly arrived 'QO-B' on a rain-drenched East Moor dispersal, winter 1943/4./*J. McNulty Collection; G. B. Ullett*

201

story. When "O-Oboe" was unserviceable we flew "R-Roger", usually flown by Wg Cdr Art McKay, the CO. But "O-Oboe" got our special attention, with another big "B" going up on the fuselage after every trip. We were debating on our emblem; a nude Piccadilly Special or a Canadian Flying Maple Leaf Express.

'The Lancs flew best, as did the others, in Betty's Bar in York. Although the bull got piled pretty high at times our Lancs were always able to fly over it. We had to concede to the Is and IIIs a bit on bombing altitude, but on anything else we "knew" we were better: faster: quicker off the deck; less exhaust glow at night; no glycol trouble. Some of the guys said they could even outrun the Ju88 fighters. The poor Hallys – and there were a lot in our area – didn't seem to be in it. As far as we were concerned they were bait for the German defences and, while they were being pounded, we in the Lancs could get away free.

'From a pilot's point of view it was the perfect flying machine. All the controls were within easy reach and were designed for use. It flew with an effortless grace, so different from the solid old Wimpey. The Herc engines, in addition to greater power, added distinction to the Mk II in comparison with the Is and IIIs, where, to me, the protruding Merlins appeared as after thoughts.

'Towards the end of January rumours started flying that our Lancs were to be replaced by Hallybags. Couldn't be true! On returning from leave early in February we knew it *was* true. Our Lancs were going.

'There was a lump in all of our throats that day in February as our beloved IIs were flown away. The replacement Hallybags were already there. Our kite "O-Oboe" was one of the last to leave, and as the crew and I watched her pass down the runway and off to Linton-on-Ouse it was as if we were losing one of the crew. In the two months we had flown the Lanc we had become convinced "O-Oboe" would see us through our tour. Others might get the chop but not us. With the heavy losses we needed that confidence. After the Wimpey, a good solid kite which somehow gave you a sense of security, the Lanc was something else. It didn't fly; it soared! Most important, it gave us confidence. The rounded, swept lines, like those of a beautiful woman, gave it "class". No other four-engined kite, RAF or USAAF could compare.

'We *knew* we'd get to the target and once "bombs gone" our Lanc leapt away, and "come hell or high water", would get us back to base. Now out on the field the Hallybag IIIs. After the Lancs, a depressing looking beast, square and squat; no lines at all. A feeling of doom now hung over East Moor when we fully realised that from now on it was to be Hallys. We'd heard nothing good of them, and, on ops, seeing them far below, silhouetted against the fires and lights of the targets, we'd often joked about "those poor bastards" in the Hallys. Now we were to be included!

'The only thing the Hally III had in common with the Lanc II was the same model Herc engines. From the pilot's point of view it was thrown together rather than designed. Compared with the Lanc it looked like a designer's mistake from the outside and was built like one on the inside. It seemed everything was designed to frustrate rather than aid. We often wondered if Hitler had had a hand in the design. The controls and gauges were scattered in such a disarray that both pilot and engineer were in constant communication checking engine temps, and oil pressures and switching fuel tanks. The throttles! I'll always remember them. In the Lanc they were curved, sort of sensually, to fit the hand. In the Hally they were four straight levers with knobs on top, difficult to grasp, and most awkward to manipulate on take-off or landing. No wonder so many Hallys pranged on take-off!

'However everything has its advantages and good points. After we got flying the Hally III we found it did have things going for it. It was fast and could climb like the Lanc, but instead of topping out at 20-21,000ft, it made 24-25,000ft easily. It was the Hally IIs and Vs we'd seen below us! One night we bombed from 29,000ft even though our bombing altitude was supposed to be 24,000ft. No fighters up there! The extra altitude gave an advantage getting home. Another good point was the escape hatch. Without that I wouldn't be here today. In the Lanc an escape hatch was above the pilot's head. I often wondered if I had to use it how I would get out; and if I did, how I would miss getting smashed against the mid-upper turret or cut in half against the tail plane or rudders. The hatch up front was a long way away, and small. In the Hally, just step to the right out of your seat, take one or two steps down and forward and fall out a big hole. However it wasn't quite that easy when the time came and I had to do it!

'Looking back on it all, we had to accept what we got to fly and come to terms with each model's good and bad points. We loved the Lanc and although I can't say that for the Hally, we certainly treated it with respect. It did have its good points, although good looks wasn't one of them. From a pilot's point of view I guess you could say we "flew" the Lanc but "drove" the Halifax.

'My brief, but hetcic, tour ended abruptly on yet another Berlin trip, 24/25 March 1944, but that's another tale; a Halifax tale. I wonder if any historian will remember the Hally; it, too, was a good kite.'

Navigator:
No Flying Suppers O'er the Styx

STAN HANSON

Next to the pilot the navigator was undoubtedly the key man of the crew. His was an exacting role demanding a nimble, adaptable mind for, in addition to the prime aim of getting to and from the target, he had to know his aircraft's position at any time regardless of adverse weather or enemy action.

Constantly working, he would rarely have the time – or inclination – to venture outside his curtained-off compartment and his view of an operation would generally be restricted to the occasional terse comments and instructions passed between the crew on the intercom.

By 1945 he had at his command a complex array of scientific aids – far removed from the observer of 1942, who doubled as bomb aimer and was limited to visual aids and dead-reckoning until the introduction of Gee.

The Path Finders of No 8 Group went one stage further and instituted a dual role, whereby the actual route plotting was done by the true navigator (Nav I), with the bomb aimer (retitled Nav II) operating the radar – a pattern which set the standard for the postwar Lincoln and beyond.

A clerk before joining the RAF, Stan Hanson – a typical product of the Empire Air Training Scheme – was still only 23 on leaving the Service in December 1946, by then a warrant officer in Pay Accounts at Hednesford. He is today a qualified company secretary/accountant and recently saw published the story of his evasion in Holland under the title *Underground Out Of Holland* (Ian Allan Ltd, 1976)

Stan has never forgotten the help he was given by the Dutch people; numerous trips to Holland and return visits to the UK have forged lasting friendships. Fittingly, an edition of his book, translated into Dutch and retitled *A Leap In The Dark*, has enjoyed success and created much interest throughout Holland.

'First effective scene was the Initial Training Wing at Paignton. For there, far removed from aeroplanes and airfields, the basic groundwork was provided. Many subjects were taught, but principal among these was navigation.

'I aspired to be a pilot, and was sent to RAF Booker to try my hand at a 12-hour flying course on Tiger Moths. Landings were the problem. Mine tended somehow to have a detrimental effect on the kites' undercarts. So for the greater good of His Majesty's aircraft I was promptly remustered to u/t navigator.

'Having in due course crossed the wide Atlantic, a party of us headed for the Canadian mid-west in August 1943. We were posted to No 1 Central Navigation School, Rivers, Manitoba. RCAF Rivers lay out in the wide open spaces, and at that season resembled an island set in a sea of golden grain. The five-month course was intensive, the week consisting of seven working days. Flying training was done in pairs: the duties alternating between 1st and 2nd navigator. The 1st nav did the dead-reckoning and passed courses and airspeeds to the staff pilot on message pads. His colleague occupied the co-pilot's seat, wound the Anson's undercarriage up after take-off, down for landing, and in between times indulged in map reading for three to four hours.

'We flew the prairie from Winnipeg in the east to Regina in the west, and between the 49th and 52nd parallels. Quickly we discovered that the classroom concept of the triangle of velocities was in reality always bedevilled by the wind. The art of air navigation consists principally in being able to calculate a compass course and airspeed which, together with the wind's effect, will cause the aircraft to move along a required track at a desired groundspeed. A great boon in this respect was the Dalton computer – a sort of circular slide-rule with a perspex centre – on which one did all sorts of classy little sums. But even with this invaluable instrument at hand the job was not easy. For there was always the wind, the lousy wind! And that was fickle and blew precisely where it listed. There was only one way to find the velocity of the ever fluctuating wind: you had to know your ground position reasonably frequently. Which was where the chap who sat in the co-pilot's seat came in.

Above: **Navigator's Eye**
Looking forward from the nav's station in a typical Lancaster operating in 1944 (in this case No 619 Squadron Dunholme Lodge July 1944). In the immediate left hand foreground is the nav's working table, with the H2S indicator and receiver hinge-mounted beyond. Depending on the production batch, the radar gear could be shelf-mounted directly facing the operator. On the extreme right foreground can be seen the flight engineer's panel, next to which is his 'dickey' seat, shown in stowed position. Also visible are the yellow-painted guide rails leading down into the bomb aimer's compartment. /*F. G. Secker*

'The 2nd navigator observed the territory over which he flew. The great prairie, though flat, was by no means featureless. It contained lakes, rivers, railway lines and towns. Even in the remoter parts there was always something distinguishable (usually it was lakes) on which you took a bearing, estimated the distance and passed the gen back to the sweating labourer at the plotting table.

'Late in the course came the astro trips. Each navigator was required to go round two 400-mile night cross-countries, reliant only on his sextant for position fixing. Learning the navigational stars in their constellations, the intriguing idea of sub-stellar points and so on had seemed, at ITW, to imbue astro-navigation with a certain charisma. Actually to stand on a small lurching dais, peering through an astrodome at the dead of a Canadian winter night, and trying desperately, with numbed hands to hold in the bubble of a sextant whichever star you'd managed to locate, was hardly anybody's idea of fun. For various technical reasons astro proved a slow, cumbersome and inaccurate way of going on. But man was not lost! There was always the 2nd nav doing his stuff up front!

'Flying at between 5,000 and 10,000ft over that part of the world was always interesting in the changing seasons. But it could be exhilarating: particularly on those deep midwinter nights after the snows had transformed the prairie into a white wilderness, above whose vast solitude the ephemeral, multi-hued yet sinister Aurora flickered and glowed and danced with icy vibrancy from the horizon to the zenith in the northern sky.

'A couple of days after one of those northern spectaculars my colleague, Peter Hayes, and I went on leave to Winnipeg. In typical Canadian fashion, the Skagfeld family had on previous occasions offered us marvellous hospitality. But the Christmas they gave us in that fair city was unforgettable. Three weeks later we mustered with the rest of the course on the parade ground at Rivers where, after 120 amiable flying hours together, our navigator's brevets were awarded. Most of us came back to England and Bomber Command.

'We had first to accustom ourselves to British conditions. Cloud, rain and mist, rather than the sparklingly clear skies of central Canada, was the normal weather pattern now. There was also the blackout. The 30 flying hour course, still on Ansons, at 10(0) AFU, Dumfries, aimed to bring the difference home to us. It did! Due to the atrocious elements, we managed only 20 of the allotted flying hours before moving on.

'The vitally important matter of crewing-up was done informally. In fact, the entire intake of airmen of the various flying trades arriving at 29 OTU, Bruntingthorpe, in June 1944, was simply put into a large room and left to sort themselves out. I never had cause to regret such wisdom, for I landed among as agreeable a set of bods as one could ever meet; two of us from now on being Australians.

'Vickers Wellingtons, battered but unbowed, were the aircraft flown, their ageing sinews being daily further stretched by rounds of circuits and bumps for the pilots and fighter affiliations requiring vicious "corkscrews" for the gunners. Less taxing on them was the spattering of countless smoke bombs on the local ranges to keep the bomb aimers happy; but navigational cross-countries now extended to trips of about five hours, involving some 800 miles of flying.

'The new thing for navigators was Gee. This radar system used groups of three synchronised stations which transmitted electronic pulses to a Master and two Slaves pattern. In the aircraft, a cathode-ray receiver displayed these pulses visually on its screen. What the set was really doing was to measure the infinitesimal differences in time it took the pulses to reach the plane, so that as it flew towards or away from the ground stations the Slave pulses moved along an upper and a lower horizontal calibration scale. Thus at any desired moment a reading could be taken, and translated via a special Gee lattice-chart into a two-position-line fix.

'Effectively, western Europe up to a maximum unjammed range of about 400 miles was covered by an unseen radar grid of intersecting position lines depicted on these charts with great accuracy. It was also possible, by using an enlarged time-base, to "home" successfully on to an objective of which co-ordinates were known. All in all, it was a cornucopia, by comparison with which astro was imprecise and very pedestrian. The snag was that the Germans had long since discovered how to jam it well before its maximum range was reached.

'During the three-month course I clocked up 60 hours flying, including one "flight" of less than a miunte when a Wimpey's port motor failed at the very moment of take-off and we finished up wrecked in the overshoot area. However, I much enjoyed crew life: especially the nights spent in the back rooms of Leicestershire village pubs where many RAF ballads were rendered to the accompaniment of a piano-playing Aussie pilot until throwing out time.

'The next stage consisted of a tilt with the Stirlings of Swinderby. According to the pilots, the word "heavy" in Swinderby's designation as No 1660 Heavy Conversion Unit was singularly appropriate. For the four-engined bombers there flew with all the lithesome manoeuvrability of housebricks and also, being clapped-out by heavy usage, were prone to all the ills known to aviators. The 40-hour flying course was similar in style to that at the OTU but navigators were now initiated into the mysteries of H2S. Fundamentally, this entirely airborne piece of radar made it possible for a navigator to mapread in any weather without leaving his cabin. The terrain below the aircraft was scanned by a high-speed underslung unit, the echoes of the pulses from which being displayed on a cathode-ray tube. The result was an echo map, calibrated for bearing and distance. Coastlines stood out particularly well: the strong echo from vertical cliffs contrasting markedly with the nil returns from the flat surface of the sea. With practice, lakes and major rivers came up recognisably and towns at least as a considerable blur.

'Last scene of all before the operational squadron was the short course at No 5 LFS, Syerston. Primarily designed to convert pilots and flight engineers on to the incomparable Lanc, this involved but a few hours flying. Nevertheless, they were enough to convince us that we had a dream of an aircraft in which to go to war.

'RAF Spilsby lay in fen-like country near the Wash. Within its bleak confines were housed, in December 1944, two of No 5 Group's precision night bombing squadrons: Nos 44 and 207. The group's attacks at this time were aimed largely at German oil and transportation targets, and in the ultimate were invariably controlled by a master bomber who in the closing moments directed the show, and particularly the bomb aimers, over the VHF system. Before that climax came, however, the entire force had individually to reach the target via a carefully worked out route and to a rigid timetable. No route marking was employed, and for purposes of concentration the bomber stream was required to stay within a rectangle approximately 30 miles long by not more than 10 wide from rendezvous to finish. Navigational standards were therefore stringent: one minute only being allowed either side of a fixed time at tactical turning-points, including the target. In furtherance, it was a group requirement to calculate a "wind" and check your groundspeed every 10 minutes while Gee lasted. And since logs and charts were collected at debriefing for clinical assessment later, you got a large flea in your ear if you failed to comply.

'In practical terms this meant continuous work, particularly at the outset, with pencil, ruler, protractor and dividers, building up the airplot on the navigation chart. Gradually, with the help of Gee and the Dalton computer, the wind pattern for the night emerged: so

Below: **Trying His Hand**
'... In practical terms this meant continuous work, particularly at the outset, with pencil, ruler, protractor and dividers, building up the airplot on the navigation chart ...'
No 50 Squadron engineer Flt Sgt Tom Peacock, all set to do a spot of navigation, checks his figures before a local flight. The captain of a well-drilled crew would ensure that each crew member had a rudimentary knowledge of each other's duties. The Lanc pictured has the later type radar console.
/T. C. W. Peacock

that later, when radar faded, you had reasonable data on which to base the dead-reckoning. Wind shifts – and they were not infrequent – meant alterations of course and adjustments of airspeed, for there was no such thing as a revised ETA. Times were fixed; it paid dividends to stay in the stream; you were often on the intercom informing the pilot of a need to change direction a fraction, or battling it out with the engineer, whose precious petrol you proposed rapidly to diminish in a spurt for the next turning point. In spare moments you kept the navigational and met' logs of the flight.

'On the nights of 13, 14, and 16 January 1945, there occurred a group of three raids, each involving some 10 hours flying, against the oil refineries at Pölitz, on the Baltic; Leuna-Merseburg, near Leipzig; and Brüx in Czechoslovakia. It was the one against Merseburg that bugged us. Not only because of the reputation that huge oil complex had acquired, but also by virtue of the dramatic way in which things initially went wrong.

'The last Lanc but two in the line got the green light, turned sharply on to the runway and thundered off in the winter twilight. Its speed picked up normally for quite a way until, inexplicably, it was observed to lose momentum. Progressively its headway declined. Off the concrete she went, bumped heavily for a short distance across the grass of the overshoot area, and finally stood, a dark blur, directly in the path of her successor. Her load included a highly sensitive 4,000lb "Cookie". The Control caravan at the opposite end of the runway flashed emergency red. The two Lancasters remaining on the perimeter track were curtly told to stand by.

'Then came silence. Time ticked relentlessly away. Suddenly, 23 minutes after last time of take-off, the caravan signalled a steady green. We were incredulous. But off we went, scraped over the stranded bomber in the overshoot and up into the gathering dusk. We circled on to course. As Spilsby faded from view the rear gunner reported that the sole remaining viable Lanc still stood motionless on the ground.

'There was no possible way in which our heavily laden Lancaster could chase after and overhaul the long-since vanished bomber stream: the fuel considerations of a lengthy flight precluded that. And yet, as "Y-Yoke" of No 207 Squadron heaved herself up the sky en route for the rendezvous point in southern England, her crew was acutely aware of the need to arrive over the target for that particular night on schedule. Leuna-Merseburg was reckoned a bitch of the first water at the best of times. The thought of flying into the teeth of its fighter defences and 600 heavy guns well in the wake of everyone else defini-

Above: **Basic Aids** '... Facing me were repeats of the altimeter, airspeed indicator, and compass – the latter being one of three such run from the main gyro compass slung near the entrance door. Adjacent to these was the API which indicated the latitudes and longitudes of the air position...' No 619 Squadron Dunholme Lodge July 1944./*F. G. Secker*

Left: **Night Exposure**
'... you were often on the intercom informing the pilot of a need to change direction a fraction...' In this case No 106 Squadron skipper Plt Off Jim L. Cooper, before a trip from Syerston November 1942, receives an additional 'thumbs up' from navigator Sgt Frank H. Drew. Beyond the latter's left shoulder is the electrical services panel./*Popperfoto*

tely lacked charm. "Yoke's" pilot, navigator and engineer held brief conclave over the intercom. The consensus was that the navigator had some improvising to do.

'Just north of London the bomber diverged from its appointed track and flew on a course a fraction south of east. The easterly leg was a long one. During it "Yoke" crossed the static winter front line, where a flak gun or two took a desultory bang at the lone raider. At present altitude that did not much signify. What seriously did was the aircraft's groundspeed. Our bee-line for the third tactical turning-point was going fine in terms of direction. But, Gee lasting well, it became increasingly obvious that our impromptu, corner-cutting plan had brought about a problem opposite to the one which had originally beset us. I began, therefore, to call for successive cuts in airspeed. Slower and slower went the Lanc, but still not slowly enough until, in reply to yet another shout, the pilot demurred: "Can't do that, mate. Because if I did we should fall out of the bloody sky!", he said.

'Too soon we reached the turning-point and headed in a direction hopefully construable by some as a move towards the targets of northern Germany. Well over that country and bang on track we now were. But an uncomfortable

distance ahead of the field. Doglegging was a time-wasting stratagem not beloved of Bomber Command aircrew. On dark nights, with other unseen aircraft around, the implications of first moving sharply away from and then abruptly returning to the line of flight had decided disadvantages. However, the time now seemed ripe. It was towards the conclusion of the second six-minute dogleg that the intercom crackled: "There's some Lancs coming up fast and we're right across their track", said the rear gunner urgently. "Not to worry, sport! They'll be the markers arriving", the pilot replied, as he swung on to the true heading pronto.

'The target markers where they should always have been, just ahead, I gave routine attention to the port wall of the aircraft. Facing me were repeats of the altimeter, airspeed indicator and compass – the latter being one of three such run from the main gyro compass slung near the entrance door. Adjacent to these was the API which indicated the latitudes and longitudes of the air position as the aircraft flew and, given occasional resetting, acted as a useful check on the airplot. Next I gave an ETA for the final outward turning-point and calculated a subsequent course and airspeed. Momentarily my gaze fixed on the flask of coffee, the glucose sweets and chocolate which reposed on the extreme right-hand corner of my table, near the wall. Being forgetful, I preferred to have my personal impedimenta in set places. Thus the most important item, D-ring of the rip-cord uppermost, reposed between the stout wooden case of my sextant and the bottom of the table leg. All seeming in order, I rose, passed through the blackout curtain on to the flight deck, and took a met' observation.

'We approached the target from the west-ward. From a short way off it looked impressive. The ensuing sea of flame had not then engulfed it, and the combination of glittering red and green markers, the wispy white smoke tinged with yellow from the first incendiaries, and the incessant flickering of countless guns whose muzzle flashes pulsated over a wide area of the ground below seemed, in the incandescent light of descending flares, as unreal as a glimpse of fairyland.

'Then came the reality of being over those guns. The interminable moments straight and level amid the bursting flak as the bomb aimer sang out his seemingly endless chant. And climactically, in quick succession, the upward heave as the bombs fell away and the down-ward lurch as "Yoke" stood on her wingtip, then dived like a bat out of hell for the south. Down she went until almost all the four miles of laboriously won height was lost. Finally she levelled out and went skimming at predeter-mined altitude, just above the uplands of southern Germany and just below the enemy radar screen.

'I reached for my thermos. It was becoming ritualistic neither to eat nor drink until we were well established on the way home. Indeed, after the sumptuous meal of bacon, fried potatoes and real eggs, commonly known as the flying supper, with which aircrew were regaled before each operation, it seemed near sacrilege to tinker about with glucose sweets and chocolate for a long time. Now, the moment to break fast appeared to have arrived. The tactics seemed to have worked perfectly. The holocaust high over Merseburg was a thing of the past. By contrast we were cruising steadily over snow-clad Bavaria, and no doubt shattering the eardrums of sleep-craving Krauts in the isolated villages which passed a few hundred feet below our wings. At low altitude we continued to fly.

'At a point on the western leg I became concerned by the relative nearness of heavily defended Stuttgart to the authorised route home. Gee had long since been defunct; H2S, because its transmissions could be "homed on" by the enemy, was as usual prohibited; the bomb aimer unable to provide a visual pinpoint. I therefore turned, without great expectation, to the Long Range Navigation set. "Loran", almost as a Christmas Box, had been installed in the kites at Spilsby. It worked in much the same way as Gee, but had potentially much greater range. Unfortuna-tely, it was still at an experimental stage and some navigators' language concerning it unprintable.

'It stood now perched on a sort of trestle over the navigation table, as blank and useless as ever. Nevertheless, I commenced to twiddle hopefully with the projecting screws round its base. The result was astonishing. The rough tuning worked for once. Suddenly, like the fairy queen in the pantomime, a perfect picture appeared before my eues. Rapidly I noted the co-ordinates from the first pair of stations, and one minute later took a plotting line from the second pair. Techically there was an element of the "running fix" about Loran and some averaging to be done. But what matter? We had a first-class ground position, comfortably near to track, at a crucial moment when no such thing had seemed remotely likely.

'After a slice of luck like that, nothing could go wrong. And neither did it. That Cook's Tour of a trip ended peacefully on an English runway a little over nine and a half hours after it had begun.

'My flying career ended abruptly one winter's night, but fortune was kind and that is another story. Looking back I am certain that, while many things helped, two aids were indispensable to independent night navigation carried out to tight schedules over wartime Europe: the faithful old Gee-box, without which accurate position fixing would largely have been impossible; and the home-spun Dalton computer, in whose absence the calculations necessary to do the job could never have been made in the time available.

'Bomber Command never lacked for hum-orists, some of whom managed to combine wisdom with wit. Like the canny navigation leader in Lincolnshire, for instance, who via a fixed board in his section (more the writing on the wall than graffiti) permanently conveyed a wry, yet telling message to his flock. During a recent holiday in Greece I was sharply reminded of that message. On a lonely hilltop in Epirus, on the far side of that river with a ferryman whose crossing was referred to in aircrew parlance as "going for a Burton" or "gone for the chop", stands the Necroman-tion, or Oracle of the Dead. Having now visi-ted that desolate spot and communed with the Oracle, I'm more than ever convinced the nav leader was right. Boldly emblazoned, his maxim ran:

"Check your groundspeed at each fix,
No flying suppers o'er the Styx!" '

Bomb Aimer: A Glimpse of Hell

GERRY MURPHY

In the early days of World War II, bomb aimers as a separate aircrew entity were unknown in the RAF. This function was previously carried out by the observer who, along with his many other duties, had somehow to get himself into the right frame of mind for the bombing run over the target. Moreover, there was the problem of protecting his night vision after working over charts under dim cabin lighting.

The new pressures thrust upon the observer by the increasing variety of radar and other navigation aids, saw the creation of two new specialists – bomb aimer (officially termed air bomber) and navigator.

Whilst initially, aircrew of both roles continued to carry the winged 'O' brevet, from 1943 onwards 'B' and 'N' rapidly took over; those few observers remaining by 1944 later survived a misguided – and promptly withdrawn – Air Ministry order to remove their treasured 'badge of office'.

The call of the sea was somehow inevitable for Liverpudlian Gerry Murphy, and as an apprentice marine engineer he began his working life. Already in an occupation certain to see him as an active participant in the war, he succeeded in joining the RAF in April 1942.

Transferring to intelligence duties following his tour, Gerry was discharged as a flying officer in 1946 and entered the teaching profession.

Now holding the satisfying, if demanding post of headmaster at a school for physically handicapped children in Coventry, he is daily reminded of his good fortune.

'Like the majority of bomb aimers I joined the RAF to be a pilot. However, during my sojourn at No 13 ITW, Torquay, in the summer of 1942, the introduction of the PNB Scheme was announced. With the advent of the four-engined bomber, the post of second pilot was abolished and the duties of the observer divided between two new aircrew categories – the navigator and the air bomber. This provoked a great deal of discussion among cadets and we realised that for some of us the writing was on the wall and that we would become bomb aimers and not pilots.

'After 14 hours pilot instruction at No 9 EFTS, Anstey, near Coventry, in order to grade us, we were posted to the Aircrew Distribution Centre at Manchester. There, much to my regret, I found that I had been regraded to air bomber. I swallowed my disappointment and followed the Duke of Wellington's dictum that if you could not change things – make the best of them.

'Training in my new category was carried out at No 41 Navigation and Bombing School at East London, South Africa. Practical training consisted of high level and low level bombing, dropping 11½lb practice bombs, and gunnery using the Vickers gas-operated machine gun, carried out in Oxfords. For map reading and reconnaissance Ansons were used.

'On returning home about 14-15 hours of night familiarisation flying in the blacked out conditions of wartime Britain took place at No 3(0) AFU, Halfpenny Green. The next step was to join a crew at 30 OTU Hixon and Seighford where we learned to work as a team flying in clapped out Wellingtons.

'We picked up our flight engineer at No 1667 HCU, Sandtoft (nicknamed Prangtoft because of the number of accidents), where we converted to Halifaxes. After a short spell at No 1 Lancaster Finishing School at Hemswell we joined No 101 Squadron based at Ludford Magna in July 1944.

'After three or four operations we were given our own Lanc, "S-Sugar", known as "The Saint", an old kite which had completed over 60 ops at that date. Our feelings towards this were mixed. On the one hand, we thought, she could be a lucky aircraft; on the other, her luck could be due to run out.

'On our squadron the bomb aimer's preparation for an op began when he reported to the bombing section after the pre-op meal. The bombing leader usually had some advice and warnings to deliver, the one most frequently quoted being the danger of the attack on the target creeping back, through the temptation to some crews to release the bombs a little too soon.

'After collecting our green canvas navigation bags in which to store topographical maps, target map, flak and searchlight-belt map, pencils, etc, we made our way to the map section. As we walked to the section one thought was always uppermost in my mind, and I am sure it must have been the same with the others: "What is the target for the night – easy or tough?" Usually I had some inkling from the skipper's remark made earlier in the day: "From the petrol load it looks like the Third and bloody last Reich tonight!" The maps I was given at the map section generally confirmed his prediction. Then we headed for the briefing room.

'As we entered the room all eyes focused on the huge map of western Europe spread across the far wall, with the coloured tapes stretching out from base like malevolent fingers indicating the way to the turning points and the target. I joined my navigator at one of the tables where he was already busy with his plotting charts and instruments. Then I would set to work drawing in the tracks on my maps, discussing navigational points with the navigator and studying the target map.

'Later we were joined by the other crew members, and as they saw the nature of the target we listened to their comments. One could sense the feelings of the crews: excitement; anticipation; tension; fear – all covered over by a veneer of ribald remarks and jocular comments.

'Presently the briefing team arrived. The proceedings were always opened by the squadron commander, followed by the intelligence and met officers and section leaders who added their contributions. The bombing leader would inform his section of the composition of the bomb load, types of fuses fitted and the method of target marking: "Newhaven" (target marked visually); "Parramatta" (target marked using H2S) or "Wanganui" (where target was obscured by cloud and bomb aimers used a sky-marker as the aiming point). The danger of creep back was stressed again. The bombing leader was not going to tolerate any "fringe merchants", as Bennett contemptuously called them, in his section.

'The closing comments were always made by the station commander and usually terminated with a reminder to bomb aimers to drop "Window" exactly at the intervals given. Window dropping was a chore allocated to

Right: **Prone and Clear** '. . . The next step was to check the equipment inside the aircraft, and while the skipper ran up the engines it gave me the opportunity to check if the bombsight was functioning correctly . . . ' Flt Sgt Ray Osborne RNZAF, hand on release 'tit', demonstrates the excellent view from the bomb aimer's position. This No 101 Squadron machine has the familiar 'Z Equipment' mountings on the front of the one-piece nose dome for 'friend or foe' identification by aircraft fitted with Village Inn (AGLT) radar-controlled rear turrets./*C. J. W. Barton*

bomb aimers on our squadron and it was generally disliked. The station commander was well aware of our feelings on this score and now and again he would hint that a machine was being developed to drop Window automatically. We never believed him and suspected that he was trying to con us.

'Briefing over, we emptied our pockets of items which could be helpful to the enemy if we were shot down and captured, and placed them in a bag, marked with our names, until, we hoped, we returned. After being issued with escape kits, containing among other useful items silk maps and currency of the territories over which we would fly, we dispersed to the crew room. Having changed into flying kit and collected parachutes, Mae Wests, coffee and sandwiches, the crew 'bus delivered us to our dispersals.

'On arrival the bomb aimer's first task was to check the bomb load. Then he was presented with a form to sign for receipt of the bombs. I found some amusement in this ritual of signing as I could never imagine a bomb aimer wanting to flog the bombs, even if he could have found the means of carrying them away!

'On at least one occasion propaganda leaflets were packed in among the bomb load. It gave me a mental picture of a German, after a heavy raid, standing outside the smoking ruins of what had been his home, reading a leaflet informing him not to blame the bomber crews but to blame his own leaders. I knew what my comments would have been if I had been in his shoes! I agreed with the view, that with the exception of leaflets carrying news to the occupied countries, the only purpose of dropping propaganda sheets was to supply the enemy with toilet paper!

'The next step was to check the equipment inside the aircraft, and while the skipper ran up the engines it gave me the opportunity to check if the bomb sight was functioning correctly. Checks completed, there followed the tense period of waiting generally disliked by aircrew, and if news came through that the op was scrubbed it was rather like condemned men being given a "stay of execution".

'It was a great relief when the clock crawled round to the time for starting up engines and taxying round to the end of the runway. Although some bomb aimers sat up in front during take-off my skipper would never allow me to do so. Take-off was always an anxious time, because with Lancs loaded beyond peacetime safety standards there was always the possibility that the aricraft would not unstick before running out of runway.

'Once airborne I crawled through the hole into the bomb aimer's compartment. This area was very restricted in our squadron's Lancs because of the bulky packages of Window stacked inside. At night there was not much

for the bomb aimer to do until the aircraft entered the range of enemy radar, except to act as a look-out.

'With the sound of four Merlin engines drumming in one's ears some aircrew said that at times they could hear music. This was an experience I shared and it was always the same composition I heard – The Warsaw Concerto. I never mentioned it to the crew at the time in case they thought "Spud" had gone off his rocker or was trying to work his ticket.

'When the aircraft entered radar range I began the monotonous task of dropping bundles of Window, at pre-determined intervals, down a small chute located at the starboard side of the compartment. Monotonous the work may have been but at least it gave some comfort to know that it was helping

Above: **Two Steps Down**
'. . . Once airborne I crawled through the hole into the bomb aimer's compartment . . . at night there was not much for the bomb aimer to do until the aircraft entered the range of enemy radar, except to act as a look-out . . . ' Checking flak positions on his map.
/Paul Popper

to form a screen between the bomber stream and the eyes of the enemy.

'On my first night op in "The Saint" I had some unopened packages left on return to base. In the morning one of the ground crew found the surplus packages and promptly voiced his disapproval in no uncertain terms. Apparently it was his duty to load the Window into the aircraft and he would have to remove the surplus packages, check them, record the details and replace them with additional packages for the next operation. He advised me that in future I should get rid of any surplus before return. From then on, when "Windowing" was completed, I dumped unopened packages overboard, hoping that at least some of them on landing would reduce the Wehrmacht by one.

'It was when the target was reached that the bomb aimer's main task began. If one's aircraft was well back in the stream then the target was usually well alight on arrival. The sight of a city in flames was an awesome spectacle. The sky above erupted with bursts of flak, with the occasional "Scarecrow", a device we thought was used by the Germans to simulate a bomber blowing up. Since the war we have been told Scarecrows did not exist and that what we saw in fact were bombers blowing up over the target. I wonder! Downwards through the flak floated target indicators, known as Christmas trees to the Germans because of their shape, splashing the target with patches of brilliant red and green when they landed. Winking among the fires below were the bursts of exploding "Cookies". As one crew member remarked, it was like looking into the mouth of Hell when Old Nick was celebrating Guy Fawkes Night. Since those days firework displays on Bonfire Night festivities have had no attraction for me! One wondered how an aircraft could plough across it and remain unscathed. However, such thoughts had to be suppressed and concentration firmly fixed upon the task of delivering the bombs on the right place.

Below: **Climax** 'Crews usually felt most vulnerable during the bombing run. At least things were a little better for the bomb aimer as he was fully occupied in trying to get the target in his sights.'
/Portsmouth and Sunderland Newspapers

Above: **A Closer Look** Inside the bomb aimer's compartment of a No 619 Squadron Lancaster (whose nose dome has been covered by a tarpaulin). Centre is the Mk XIV bomb sight (or XIVA, the version designed for operations above 20,000ft) mounted from a fabricated bracket fixed to the left hand side of the nose. Left foreground almost out of view is the computer box, from which run two cables to the bomb sight's gyro unit. Right foreground is the bomb aimer's control panel, complete with 16 bomb release switches along the top left hand edge, and timing selector below.
/*F. G. Secker*

Right: **Big Bomb, Big Bang** Remarkable still from a film shot during No 617 Squadron's attack on the Catroux factory of the Michelin rubber plant at Clermont-Ferrand, France on the night of 16/17 March 1944. A huge column of smoke is illuminated by the flash of a 12,000lb HC bomb as it explodes in the target area. Note the marking flare visible at the left hand edge of the picture.
/*British Official via A. C. Jones*

'Crews usually felt most vulnerable during the bombing run. At least things were a little better for the bomb aimer as he was fully occupied in trying to get the target in his sights. A number of bomb aimers did feel very vulnerable as they were in the prone position and, as one put it, he was afraid of being hit in a vital part of his anatomy and being ruined for life! It was not unknown for some bomb aimers to take tin helmets aloft and slip them under their crotches as protection over the target!

'The bomb aimer's instructions: "Bomb doors open – master switch on – bombs fused and selected" were always repeated by the pilot. At the time I was operating there was usually a master bomber over the target issuing instructions as to which group of TIs should be ignored, and which group should be used as the aiming point. Getting the sight on the target so that the TIs appeared exactly on the intersection of the arms of the graticule was a matter of co-operation between bomb aimer and pilot. The responses of the pilot in following the bomb aimer's instructions of "Right – Left, Left – Steady" could make or mar a bombing run. In training, most bomb aimers had experienced the odd ham-footed pilot who could ruin their efforts by slow or exaggerated corrections. I could not complain about my skipper's corrections as I think he appreciated the problems involved as a result of trying his hand at bomb aiming while we were at Heavy Conversion Unit.

'If the target was not in the sight at the time for bomb release one could be tempted to follow the routine of training and call "Dummy run". This was a dicey thing to do as the pilot would have to take the aircraft round again for a second run. On one occasion when I called a dummy run the skipper complied while the rest of the crew cast doubts on my parentage, one even advising me to perform an impossible physical feat!

'When the bombs were released the aircraft lifted and with the announcement: "Bombs gone – bomb doors closed – let's get to hell out of here"; the crew sighed with relief. If there was a hang-up, the wireless operator had to release it manually. Hang-ups fitted with delay fuses had to be jettisoned in case the fuse became activated.

'On one op a hang-up occured on "The Saint". The night before had been the occasion of my 21st birthday, and as I had celebrated it a little too well with the crew I was rather under the weather. Consequently, I confused the properties of the fuse fitted with those of the delay fuse and told the w/op to jettison it. As he was unable to release it manually I told him to jettison the bomb carrier as well. The following morning an irate armament officer telephoned the bomb-ing leader demanding to know what had happened to one of the bomb carriers on "The Saint". I received a rude awakening and a right rollicking from the bombing leader, who finished philosophically with the following comment: "Let us hope that the carrier did some good at least by wrapping itself around the head of some SS thug."

'The return run to base always seemed much longer than the trip in. Relieved of the tension over the target one would experience tiredness, and there would be a strong desire to relax. For the smokers among us there would be a longing to light one up, but this was not allowed. The temptation of relaxing had to be resisted and vigilance maintained because of the danger of prowling night fighters.

'During the trip back at least one of us would want to relieve himself, and for this purpose we carried a can. On one occasion we took a milk bottle instead – with dire results. On the way back one of the crew called for the use of the bottle, and it was duly passed to him. However, he ran into trouble when he got struck in it and only managed to free himself after much painful struggling!

'With his main task completed, the bomb aimer reverted again to acting as look-out. Vigilance had to be maintained even when the aircraft arrived over base, as there was always a possibility of a night intruder getting into the circuit.

'Landing, even in an undamaged aircraft, could be hazardous sometimes. On our last op another crew from the squadron were also completing their tour. To mark the occasion it had been agreed that the other crew would take a gramophone with them, and when they arrived over the base on return their wireless operator would place the spare R/T microphone in the sound box and play a record.

'When our aircraft arrived over base the skipper called Flying Control. The pilot of the other Lanc followed suit, the gramophone was brought into use and a chorus of "Jingle Bells" was broadcast far and wide. There was a cross wind that evening and so either runway could be used. At this point the high spirits of youth took over and there was a race between the two crews to be the first to land.

'As we came in over the chimney stacks of Ludford village and the "Black Horse" pub, towards the short runway, the other Lanc was making its descent on the long runway. The ground crews could see both aircraft on converging courses and there was much nail biting, accompanied by comments such as: "What a hell of a way to go at the end of a tour!" At the intersection of the runways our skipper and flight engineer were shaken when the wheels of the other Lanc just cleared the top of ours. A slightly hair-raising way to finish one's tour!'

214

Flight Engineer: The Practical Type

JOE NUTT

Apart from the wireless operator the flight engineer was probably the most unsung member of a Lancaster crew. Yet, in many ways he was the most knowledgeable for he had to know his aircraft inside out and be prepared for any emergency caused either through enemy action or mechanical/electrical malfunction.

While in general he tended to come from the ranks of re-mustered ground crew, or had an engineering background as a civilian, he had to possess a practical mind and be capable of instant diagnosis and remedial action.

A Lancaster crew would already be an established, closely-knit team when he was 'introduced' to them at Heavy Conversion Unit, but once over the initial barrier of suspicion he would quickly prove his value. Often he would be the oldest man in the crew, with a family and responsibilities, looked upon as a 'counsellor' and one to whom his colleagues could take their troubles.

Joe Nutt, a 25-year old former capstan-setter operator, who had been 'scrubbed' as a pilot at OTU due to 'night flying deficiencies', graduated from St Athan and met his crew at 1661 CU Winthorpe, before joining No 207 Squadron. Moving to No 97 (Straits Settlements) Squadron, he ended his Service days as a link trainer instructor at Coningsby, followed by a spell as Aircrew Discip Warrant Officer at Hemswell.

Leaving the RAF in May 1947, he then joined the first of several civil charter companies as a flight engineer, and finally retired from British Airways in 1977.

'With the coming of the four-engined bomber the aircraft's auxiliary equipment became almost quadrupled, and somewhat more complicated. The four engines, with a total of some 20 gauges, propeller and throttle controls, plus fuel and electrical systems, required full-time monitoring, so a technical man was introduced into the crew. In addition to being an airborne trouble-shooter or "Mr Fixit" he was also the pilot's mate, handling fuel management, undercarriage, flaps, throttles and props, etc, and capable of flying the aircraft at least straight and level. Two hours link

trainer per month and "poling" on cross-countries ensured this. On our PFF squadron (No 97) the engineer did the visual bomb aiming, whilst the bomb aimer became the set operator and helped the navigator. Also, in order to obtain his PFF badge, the engineer had to be able to use the bubble sextant, know the astro-stars ("Beetlejuice", Riga, Polaris, etc) and operate the turrets. The other crew members had to do the same with each other's jobs.

'After a six-month course at St Athan (shorter for re-mustered fitters and riggers) the engineer joined the crew at Heavy Conversion Unit (HCU). Here we flew Stirlings, an aircraft whose 14 tanks, some of which held only 40/50gal, plus its liability to "coring", initiated one rapidly into the attributes of a flight engineer. A "crash" course at Lancaster Finishing School (LFS) followed, and then posting to a squadron. By then the engineer had moulded into the crew (who had teamed up at OTU) and, by handling the ancillaries, allowed the skipper to concentrate on flying the Lanc and lead his men.

'Like most trades there were wrinkles. Fortunately coring on Lancs was non-existent, as the oil cooler was behind the coolant radiator. Coring occurred in exposed oil coolers in icing conditions and can briefly be described as oil congealing as it passed through the cooler, thus restricting the return flow into the engine. If not rectified by throttling back, and putting the revs up, the engine could seize through oil starvation. Another piece of vital knowledge concerned Lancs fitted with Packard Merlins, where the idle cut-off (ICO), which shut off the fuel to the Bendix-Stromberg carburettors, was spring-loaded to the "on" position, and pneumatically held off. Thus, if one did a faulty pre-start check, and did not put the ICOs on, *and* if the pneumatic pressure was low enough, the engines could be started with the switches off, but held open by spring pressure. Should the pneumatic pressure be slow in building up, due to a faulty compressor or a clogged oil and water trap, all four engines could cut as one was belting down the runway.

Below: **Mr Fixit** ' . . . From an engineer's point of view the Lanc was a good aircraft . . . engine gauges, fuel system controls and gauges, plus ammeters, were on the starboard side of the cockpit . . . ' A still from an official film shot at Scampton 1942 to demonstrate a typical crew's preparations for a raid. Here Sgt Fred Blocksidge shouts out the gauge readings to his No 49 Squadron skipper Plt Off Neil Green. From top to bottom the rows of circular gauges are: for oil temperature; coolant temperature; then two rows to reflect fuel content. Above the top line of dials are the oil pressure gauges arranged in vertical paired banks. A hinged glimmer light projects from the top of the panel while beyond can be seen the engineer's 'dickey seat' in stowed position. /*British Official via N. C. Green*

'Apart from the normal hazards of ops, icing was the biggest problem. The super-cooled water-droplets in a cumulo-nimbus cloud retained their liquid form in temperatures below freezing. One theory was that the droplets being carried up and down in the vertical currents obtained latent heat through friction. On being struck by an aircraft this heat was released and the water froze, resulting in increased wing loading, disrupting overwing airflows, forcing carbs and props to ice up, and sometimes the loss of such vital instruments as the airspeed indicator and altimeter. The Lancs' protection against ice was anti-ice paste on the leading edges, warm and hot air for the engines, plus a glycol spray for the bomb aimer's clear vision panel (some later Lancs had glycol slingers for the props). Icing on the carburettor ice guard meant about ½lb of boost being lost if above full throttle height. One dodge to get out of the worst icing range was to put the power on, nose down, and at a goodly indicated airspeed pull back and climb quickly at a very high rate, through the worst freezing range.

'From an engineer's point of view the Lanc was a good aircraft. Throttles and prop controls were on a central pedestal, with boost and rev gauges above, and flaps, trim tabs and undercarriage controls about a yard aft. The remainder of the engine gauges, fuel system controls and gauges, plus ammeters, were on the starboard side of the cockpit. Everything could be handled without stretching and the automatic boost control relieved one of constant throttle pushing. At sea level, with 2,850 +9 on, the throttle butterflies were only a third open, but as the aircraft climbed, the boost capsule, reacting to the drop in atmospheric pressure, progressively opened the butterflies, maintaining the boost until full throttle height. Automatic radiator shutters eliminated constant switch toggling to keep coolant temperatures within limits, and with the prop constant speed unit maintaining the selected revs, more time could be spent in looking out for the opposition.

'Operations began for the engineer with main briefing. Any particular flight engineering aspects, such as the need for fuel economy if target was a long haul, was stressed by the engineer leader. Good fuel economy was shown in air miles per gallon (AMPG), and at least 1.0 was the aim. This was nearly always achieved by keeping the throttles at the gate, and bringing the revs down when the indicated airspeed built up a knot or two.

'Before climbing into the Lanc some 40 external items were checked by the engineer, covering flying controls, undercarriage, tyres, pitot and static vents, etc: and once inside, another 90 items were checked in co-operation with the skipper. Engines were started from No 1 tanks, with No 2's selected for run up, take-off and first hour of the flight. All systems were checked during warm-up by the individual crew members and if all was well the engines were run up when oil temperatures were +15°C and coolant +40°C. Each engine in turn was opened up to zero boost; props exercised; supercharger gears checked; and finally, magnetos for a maximum 150rpm drop. With maximum revs and zero boost the rpm had to be within 50 of static and generator charger rates were checked on the inboard engines.

'Run up complete, chocks were signalled away, and the Lanc moved onto the perimeter track. During the taxi out, take-off checks were carried out, the engineer setting manually and the skipper checking visually: trim tabs; throttle friction; "M" gear; cold air; maximum rpm; flaps 20°; No 2 tanks on crossfeed off; all booster pumps on; tit pulled; radiators auto. Pulling the tit on Merlin 24s bled 4psi from the boost capsule chamber, and upped the boost from +14 to +18. Lined up, the skipper opened the throttles while the engineer watched the boost and rev needles swing round, the nav ready to call out the air speeds. At the same time, the engineer's left hand was following the skippers' right on the throttles: with all engines pulling, the engineer took over the throttles when about ¾ open, pushed them to, then through the gate, the gauges showing 3,000rpm, speed approaching 90kts. Boost gauges generally gave the first sign of engine trouble and they were watched like a hawk until airborne safety speed was reached.

'With a positive rate of climb established, the engineer raised the undercarriage on command, and set climb power to 2,850 +9. Throttles were moved first to prevent overboosting and detonation, followed by the flaps coming in by 5° snatches at 145kts safety speed, height 400ft. Once "clean" the Lanc climbed well, and with the increase in speed, coupled with the power reductions, oil and coolant temperatures came down. Once satisfied that all was well, the engineer began to keep a lookout: the sky was pretty full and midair collisions were not unknown.

'Climbing at 155kts, with booster pumps off, radiators auto, the first tank and engine instrument readings were logged by the

Below: **Close Liaison** Liaison with the ground crew was an essential part of the flight engineer's duties and here we see No 101 Squadron's Sgt 'Curly' Ormerod (second left) in deep discussion with the engine fitters working on the starboard-inner Merlin of BI ME565 'SR-W' at Ludford Magna in the spring of 1944. Noteworthy are the tool kit spread out on the wing, the exhaust stub box spanner on the engine armour plating, and the partially completed hangar in the background. (ME565 failed to return from Foret-de-Cerisy 8/9 June 1944). /R. R. Waughman

engineer – the first of many. When sufficient fuel had been used from No 2 tanks, both No 1 tanks were selected, and the contents of No 3 tanks pumped into No 2: No 1 tanks were used until they equalled the fuel in No 2. Thereafter, tanks were changed about every 20 minutes, limiting the loss of only a quarter from any one tank if one was holed. Petrol could be used from a leaking tank if one was quick enough with the crossfeed. When the boost had dropped off to +6 the engineer pulled back the throttles to zero boost and selected "S" gear, accompanied by a slight thump, a cough and a spit before the throttles were pushed up to give +9 boost again, until full throttle height was reached. With the constant speed units controlling the props, engine handling on the Lanc was almost automatic.

'Flying at night, there wasn't much light about. Pilot and engineer, forward of the blackout curtain, were in a little world of their own; only the luminosity of the instruments, and a faint blue glow from the inboard exhaust shrouds broke the darkness. To maintain his log the engineer used a torch, its light diminished by three thicknesses of white paper. Reaching cruise level, power was set for 155kts, and the accent was on keeping a look-

Man Friday '. . . Pilot and engineer, forward of the blackout curtain, were in a little world of their own . . . ' (*left*) Sgt C. H. ('Dossy') Doswell seated by his No 9 Squadron skipper, Plt Off Jim Cowan RNZAF, Waddington late 1942; (*above*) Sgt Jeff Collier stands by driver Sgt Dave Tribe RCAF, No 12 Squadron Wickenby 1943. /*L. J. Brown; D. F. Tribe*

Right: **Vigilance was the Key** '. . . About 95% of the engineer's airborne time in a Lanc was spent with his eyes out of the cockpit . . . ' Wg Cdr Leonard Slee and his No 49 Squadron crew airborne from Fiskerton late 1942./*L. C. Slee*

219

out, not only for fighters, but aircraft dog-legging in the stream. Gauges and instruments were scanned periodically, fuel readings taken, and then watch was resumed. About 95% of the engineer's airborne time in a Lanc was spent with his eyes out of the cockpit.

'Windowing was done by the engineer. This meant going into the nose and, squatting amongst umpteen brown paper parcels, pushing out a bundle every two minutes. Watch was kept through the nose, interrupted by quick nips up for fuel checks and engine readings. A lookout was kept for route markers. These stood out against the enemy's blackout, and gave a good track check, in addition to being a boost for the nav if we passed right over one. Approaching the target, the engineer on a Flare Force aircraft began preparations for flare dropping. As the centre flare of a stick of 12/14 had to drop over the Primary Blind Markers (PBMs) to give a wide area of illumination, the bombsight cross was projected forward by means of a height/distance scale. The basic settings were set at base, sea level pressure at target, target height above sea level; aircraft's weight; terminal velocity of flares. Only the broadcast wind remained to be set, when known. As the PBMs went down the engineer, holding the quadrant on the datum, would direct the skipper over the markers and, when the cross was on the markers, "call now" to the set-op. From his duplicate bomb panel in the nav compartment, the set-op released the first flare, and then, timed by the navigator, one every 10 seconds. During the flare run the engineer would resume Windowing.

'With the last flare gone and bomb doors closed, power was increased to clear the target area, and hang-ups, tank leaks, and damage checked for. The photo-flash was checked by the w/op, a most important task, for if the flash was primed but not dropped, its barometric fuse would operate when the aircraft passed through its firing height. In order to fool the enemy controllers, the route home was not always a reciprocal of the outbound. Usually, it resulted in a longer way back, so fuel economy was always in the engineer's mind. With a Lanc lightened of its flare load, and a fair amount of fuel, cruise IAS could be held with relatively low revs and consumption: 2,000rpm +2 boost gave a total fuel flow of around 165gal/hr. Remembering the cruise rule "don't fly in the sky with your revs too high or your boost too low", the engineer would inch the revs down when the IAS needle went a hairsbreath over 155kts. Flying for range, the engineer, nav and skipper liaised to get the best out of the aircraft and its remaining fuel. The engineer with his fuel calculations, the nav with his estimated times

of arrival, and the skipper trimming so that it flew true, with no deflection showing on the turn and slip, squeezed the last drop of aerodynamic efficiency from the Lanc.

'Sometimes a warm or cold front would have to be flown through, producing icing and turbulence. If severe, the icing would coat the Lanc thickly in about five minutes. Boost would drop off as the carburettor ice guard was blocked, and lift would be lost as the ice distorted the wing air flow. With the use of warm or hot air to de-ice the carburettors, revs would go up to maintain height; this, coupled with the higher wing loading and low IAS, would force oil and coolant temperatures up to near their limits. Not having to worry about coring was a blessing, but even so it was a busy time for the engineer. Fuel economy took a knock, for with an iced-up aircraft, fuel flow was generally higher than true airspeed (TAS). Best thing to do was to get out of it, either up or down; it was usually up, as freezing level in the German winter was on the deck.

'Nearing home, the flight pattern continued; monitoring and logging instrument readings, plus tank changes and look out. As Gee and W/T met came in, plus a firm ETA obtained, the Lanc was allowed to roll, If, however, met was bad it was back to range flying until overhead base, then endurance flying, circling about 10 knots above minimum handling speed. Diverting meant the engineer diving into his fuel consumption chart to find a power setting which would give about a half hour hold over the airfield. Advantage was taken of the best winds: going up a few thousand feet could put another 20kts on the tail, and boost track miles per gallon – the real proof of range flying. Base being clear, the descent was commenced: IFF was switched on and "M" gear selected at the right height. Revs were brought down – not right down – as the charge temperature would drop and lead the plugs up. A final fuel check was made, and the last instrument readings taken. From a full instrument log, a good idea of engine performance could be taken; any on the blink showed up with high temperatures and low oil pressures. The rest of the crew were noting their snags, all to go into the F700.

'Crossing the coast, VHF contact gave landing information, and as the Lanc joined the circuit the engineer became the skipper's third hand; throttle handling, flap and under-carriage setting kept him busy. With full flap selected at 500ft, undercarriage down, and 2,850rpm, the aircraft well in the glide path green, he waited for his last airborne command as the fence was crossed at 95 knots – cut! Then, closing the throttles and with the Merlin crackle in his ears, there was another op for his log book.'

Wireless Operator: Plenty of Time to Find Out

TED BROOKS

Arguably having the most unglamorous role in the crew, the wireless operator, w/op or 'sparks' was, like his colleague the engineer, a virtual jack of all trades.

In addition to his official duties he was expected to have a working knowledge of the navigator's equipment, understand the aircraft's electrical and intercom services, and administer first aid as necessary.

In most crews he was required to act as fire controller, perched in the astrodome, directing the pilot and gunners in the event of visual combats with enemy fighters. With vigilance the key to survival, he would rarely leave the astrodome when in the target area.

There were a number of wrinkles to the job, such as switching on the IFF or firing off the enemy colours of the day to douse searchlights and attendant flak barrages, or deterring fighter attacks. Other vital functions included checking for hang-ups in the bomb bay by lifting a small cover behind the main spar immediately above the bomb bay, and inspecting the flare chute to ensure release of the photographic flare.

Ted Brooks packed a lifetime of experience into his two tours with No 1 Group and saw the introduction of most of the technical developments, including Monica, Fishpond and Village Inn fighter-warning devices.

He returned to civilian life in July 1946 a doubly decorated 23-year old flight lieutenant, none too keen to resume his pre-RAF job as a purchasing clerk in the motor trade.

Still 'flying a desk' he is currently employed as an administrative manager in the consumer industry.

'Following an initial three-month training course at Blackpool, where I attained the required standard of transmitting and receiving 12 words per minute, I was posted to No 2 Radio School at Yatesbury for further technical training.

'Passing out as a qualified ground wireless operator awaiting aircrew training, I was sent to a fighter training station at Heston near London and spent a month or so servicing the R/T sets on various aircraft. The unit was subsequently transferred to a new airfield near Shrewsbury, where conditions were very primitive and signals personnel were responsible for erecting telephone lines and many other forms of communications. After a few months I had an individual posting to Northern Ireland and served on a small aircraft observation unit in Co Antrim. To say that conditions here were primitive would be a studied understatement.

'Since joining the RAF I had not in fact left the ground. All the radio training I had received was to all practical purposes wasted. I seriously considered applying for a transfer to the Army – and then it suddenly happened! I received a signal to report for aircrew training at No 4 Radio School at Madley.

'The course at Madley was very concentrated and differed from Yatesbury in as much as the emphasis was more on operational procedure, such as the use of degrees of priority, how to obtain M/F fixes, the use of the D/F loop, etc, rather than the pure theory of radio. And of course we flew. My first flight was in a Rapide (not something I would recommend) and, along with five or six other trainees, I carried out simple air-to-ground exercises at about eight words per minute using the awful T1082/R1083 sets. After a few exercises in the Rapide I flew in Proctors, the crew consisting of a pilot and radio operator. Although we never flew very far from base the wireless operator felt a certain sense of importance; after all, if we did get lost who would bring the aircraft home?

'The Madley course lasted about 10 weeks and included probably 12 hours flying. The pass/failure rate was about 60/40 and those who passed were posted immediately to Gunnery School. I was sent to 3 AGS at Castle Kennedy. It was a diabolical place, staffed by Instructors who would make the Yatesbury people appear angelic. We were required to qualify as air gunners, the course lasting about six weeks and including flying training in Bothas, a very uncomfortable aircraft, reputed to be under-powered and highly dangerous, later taken out of service. I spent about eight hours in the air firing at air-to-ground targets, and of course at drogues towed by light aircraft. The ammunition was marked with a dye so that hits on the drogue could be registered.

'I left Gunnery School complete with air gunner's brevet and sergeant's stripes and was posted to 27 OTU at Lichfield. There I met the RAAF! All the wireless operators were RAF men but the vast majority of other trades were Australian and consequently there was a rush to crew up with the isolated British. Mine were all Australian, a fact which I subsequently had good cause never to regret. I did hardly any gunnery training at OTU and received very little ground radio instruction except to be introduced to the so-called miracle of the age, the Marconi T1154/R1155. Compared with the old T1082/R1083 it obviously was a tremendous improvement, but it was manually tuned and a lot of practice was necessary. Most practice was done in the air, mainly on cross-country flights or tactical exercises, flying Wellingtons. I flew about 60 hours at OTU over a period of 10/12 weeks and the course ended with a leaflet raid on Rouen, this being intended as a gentle introduction to the real war. I listened out but did not transmit as no emergency arose.

'The next stage was 1662 Heavy Conversion Unit at Blyton. Here we were joined by a flight engineer and mid-upper gunner. We started the course on Halifaxes and completed it on Lancasters, and as far as I was concerned, it did not differ greatly from OTU. There was very little ground training and the flying was really an extension of that which I had already experienced, only excepting a fair amount of ditching practice, which included tuition on the dinghy radio and some practice with the Aldis Lamp. Very cartridges were of course carried, but I had been instructed in the use of these at Gunnery School.

'After completing the conversion course of some 40 hours, my crew, being Australian, opted for posting to No 460 Squadron but in the event we were sent to No 12 Squadron at Wickenby. I was introduced to the signals leader, Flg Off Leslie Gray who had served in France with the squadron and was now completing a second tour. He was a very considerate and helpful person and explained the mysteries of the coding system. In those days the codes for the night were printed on rice paper and quite seriously the operator was expected to literally eat them in the event of baling out or in a forced landing in enemy territory. This system was changed as the war progressed and we finally carried stiff-backed code books. Les Gray particularly emphasised the need for radio silence at take-off and especially cutting R/T down to a minimum, it being possible for the enemy to listen-in and so form some estimate of the strength of the attack.

'In addition to gathering information from the signals leader I spent a fair amount of time in the navigation section learning how to operate the Gee navigational aid apparatus and plot the results on the charts. After about a week on the squadron our pilot went on a "second dickey" trip with the wing commander and the day following we were on the Battle Order for Bochum. Battle orders were usually displayed mid-morning, following which the allocated aircraft was taken up (time and conditions permitting) for an air test, during which each crew member tested his equipment. I tuned the W/T, checked the R/T, D/F Loop and all the equipment for which I was responsible. I wound out and wound in the trailing aerial, which had to be done by hand as it was not mechanical. Like most Service equipment it was situated in the most awkward of places and was, of course, difficult to handle. It was at the side of the aircraft and so near the floor that the operator was on his stomach with the oxygen hose compressed almost to the point of cutting off

Below: **Sweat Shop** The w/op's station in a Canadian-built BX of No 431 ('Iroquois') Squadron, revealing a number of variations compared with its British equivalent. Included in the mass of equipment shown is the Fishpond console, next to a shortened working table complete with Morse key. Immediately beyond the w/op's seat (bottom left) can be seen the doors hiding the trailing aerial./*J. W. Madill*

his supply. The whole procedure was undignified and very exhausting.

'After the air test there was nothing more to do until the main briefing. Following this the wireless operators had a short, separate briefing by the signals leader who distributed the codes for the night, also the English colours of the day, confirming the times these would change. Just before we entered the aircraft an intelligence officer handed me the enemy colours of the day and verbally quoted the times they would be in use.

'We took off, I opened the watch and recorded this in the operator's log book. I wound out the trailing aerial, tuned the W/T receiver, switched on the IFF and commenced a listening watch. My first operation over Germany had begun. As we circled over the rendezvous point the navigator several times asked me to check the DR compass. This was situated near the rear turret, so it was something of an effort to journey back and forth at oxygen height. I continued to listen out and was constantly tuning the receiver as the frequency kept drifting more than I had previously experienced. The main purpose of listening out was in case of recall or change of route and that night I was particularly nervous of missing such a vital message, a fear I never altogether lost even after many operations.

'I found that I really had to concentrate, for the wireless operator's station in the aircraft was particularly noisy and the signal strength of base was fairly low and deteriorated with interference and static. Another problem was the heat. The supply was controlled from a turn cock in the wireless operator's position near the trailing aerial. The other crew members wanted the heat on – I did not. They won (they subsequently always won) so even though I was flying in an open-necked shirt and battledress I was steaming. Even to this day I do not like heat! If, of course, the heating broke down then the position would be very serious indeed. The cold could be so

Below: **Sparks** '... each crew member tested his equipment. I tuned the W/T, checked the R/T, D/F Loop and all the equipment for which I was responsible ...'
Checking the electrical services panel before an operation. Looking forward, the navigator can be seen standing by his table, while in the immediate foreground is the Lancaster's main spar./*Paul Popper*

intense that to remove gloves would almost be inviting immediate frostbite.

'During the sea crossing I spent a fair amount of time in the astrodome, the maximum observation being a necessary precaution against collisions. On approaching the enemy coast I switched off the IFF and loaded the Very pistol with the enemy colours of the day. Having crossed the coast I assisted the navigator with Gee fixes and then listened out.

'It is almost impossible to describe what happened next but I was suddenly aware of a sound rather like hail on a tin roof, a loud thud and the aircraft losing height. I switched off the W/T, connected my R/T plug so that I was in contact with the crew, and as I did so I saw that a starboard engine was on fire. The flames appeared to be sweeping right across the wing and the whole aspect was fairly disturbing. I heard the pilot and engineer discussing the situation and it seemed that the extinguisher had failed to operate and the propeller feathering mechanism had also failed. By this time the pilot had changed course and was heading out of enemy territory. He called up each member of the crew, explained the position and said there were two alternatives; we either abandoned the aircraft and parachuted, hopefully over Holland, or took a chance and attempted a ditching, always assuming the fire did not get any worse. We all opted to attempt a ditching.

'The fire remained fairly constant as we approached the sea and a further problem was of course the propeller, which continued to windmill. There was apparently little I could do so I tuned into the international distress frequency of 500 KCs just in case. Whilst engaged on the set the navigator passed me a written note which read: "Our position is —— send SOS."

'It would be pointless to describe my feelings. I'm quite sure I was very frightened, almost totally unable to grasp that this was really happening on my first trip. However I reacted quickly, probably mechanically, and with the set already tuned in, sent the SOS fairly slowly, and I suppose calmly. The receiving station came back immediately at an equally slow speed. It was an incredible feeling – the system worked! I felt we were already saved.

'The receiving station wished to take fixes from us to check our position. This meant that the transmitter key was depressed for some 30 seconds or so whilst they took a bearing on the continuous signal. Meanwhile we were now well out to sea and still losing height when the pilot decided to try a dangerous tactic by putting the aircraft into a dive, thus hoping the fire would be extinguished. He did this and the fire went out; but the propeller continued to windmill. I transferred my frequency to my base station and we got home, albeit very low, very late, but safely. So ended our first attack which was, in fact, abortive and did not count as part of our tour.

'Then followed a dozen or so attacks on the Ruhr towns during which we sustained a certain amount of damage. Looking at the aircraft the morning after an attack I always marvelled that it continued to fly having sustained such damage, and if there were holes near my own station I reflected on my good luck as, of course, there was no armour plate in the wireless operator's position.

'Shortly after the series of Ruhr raids, wind speed reporting was introduced. This meant that the wireless operator was required to listen out on the group frequency for wind changes, and in fact selected crews would transmit wind speeds back to group for them to re-transmit to the main force. This was a time-consuming operation as the frequency was constantly drifting and it was not easy to tune the transmitter to the receiver.

'After several visits to southern Germany we took part in two of the Battle of Hamburg raids, the last being in atrocious weather conditions. Sufficient to say that we did reach the target area but in so doing had two engines out of action and all navigational aids gone. Survivors of this attack will confirm that it was impossible to identify visually any landmark or use astro as the cumulo-nimbus cloud was impenetrable and the electric storm impossible to describe. My trailing aerial had vanished, presumably because I did not have time to reel it in when the bomb doors were opened prior to jettisoning. I was therefore unable to transmit on the correct frequency for an M/F fix. The weather conditions were so bad that it was a near impossibility any fighters would be sent up. Therefore the need for radio silence was not so vital and if broken would not endanger the bomber stream (if such existed in those conditions).

'Since we had only a rough idea of our position the pilot ordered me to try to obtain M/F fixes. We were probably somewhere over the Elbe and since I could only use the fixed aerial I thought the chances were somewhat remote at that range. However I did as ordered. The static and noise was awful but after two or three attempts and using a priority second only to an SOS, I finally heard the ground station acknowledge. They requested me to carry out the normal fix procedure which meant that I depressed the key for 30-40 seconds whilst three or more ground stations took a bearing on the transmission. The aircraft's position was then calculated on a map and re-transmitted back. The M/F station told me to repeat this procedure every 15 minutes and this took us safely back home. We were the last aircraft to return, very, very late.

'I half expected some sort of reprimand for breaking radio silence but in fact I was congratulated by the CO and I understand our action that night became standard procedure in the group if similar emergencies arose. I have never forgotten Hamburg and even today I am less than happy in a storm.

'Peenemünde, Munich, Italy all followed until I finally finished this tour. I spent a few months instructing at 1656 HCU based at Lindholme and during this time there were several new technical developments. The H2S navigational aid was introduced and also the practice of jamming the German fighter controllers. In the case of the latter the wireless operator would search the frequencies listening for the German controllers who were vectoring their fighters into the bomber stream. On hearing such instructions the transmitter was tuned into the German frequency, the Morse key depressed and a microphone situated in one engine switched into the circuit. By such means the fighters' instructions were hopefully drowned by engine noises. To hear the voices of the controllers on operations was somewhat disturbing but I always felt the jamming was fairly effective.

'My second tour, with No 460 Squadron RAAF, followed much the same pattern as previously except for the alarms and excursions at the beginning. The signals leader was an Australian, Reg White, a nice enough fellow, but in fact we hardly ever met. His attitude apperared to be that I knew as much about matters as himself so he left me alone. In fact he frequently left me to take the signals briefing.

'For a short while I operated an experimental fighter detection device called Village Inn, which in simple language consisted of an audio signal (bleep bleep) which sounded when an aircraft entered the radar field, and also a blip appeared on the screen; an additional device indicated the range, speed and direction. As the range closed the audio signal increased in speed and volume. When the fighter was apparently in range of the bomber's guns, the wireless operator would instruct the gunners to open fire at a specific range and direction, etc. Theoretically the gunners fired blind, but since the equipment could not differentiate between friend or foe, the gunners visually identified before firing. As I recall this equipment was later abandoned.

'On my very last attack, which was on the night of the Arnhem drop, our crew were selected to remain behind and carry out a fairly low level reconnaissance, reporting back by W/T from the target details of weather conditions, strength of defences, etc. At briefing we were told this special duty was so important that the radio equipment would be modified to take quartz crystals, thus ensuring that the tuning would be spot on. I had no previous experience of crystal tuning so was somewhat concerned. However no one appeared to be particularly interested. Just as I was about to enter the aircraft the station signals officer drove up and thrust two small objects into my hand. "These are your crystals", he said. "I don't know how to use them", I replied. "Neither do I", said he, "but you've got plenty of time to find out." So ended my operational career.'

Air Gunner:
I'll be Riding a Cloud in the Morning

DOUG TRIGG

No other member of a Lancaster crew experienced the same sense of detachment as did the two gunners. Suspended in space, the rear gunner could certainly claim the most remote station; but it is debatable who had the most uncomfortable. Whilst the rear gunner suffered mainly from lack of leg room, his colleague in the mid-upper had the disadvantage of sitting on a canvas sling, his head and shoulders within the turret dome, his nether regions within the confines of the draughty fuselage.

In general the rear gunner would already be established when the mid-upper was introduced to the crew at Conversion Unit. Rarely would they exchange positions for operations though each would be fully conversant with the other's turret and responsibilities.

By the time the Lancaster entered service the air gunner was recognised as a specialist. No longer was he recruited from the ranks of armourers or riggers, paid an extra shilling a day as an AC or corporal. Now he graduated at least a sergeant, often an officer and Australian Doug Trigg from Morwell, Victoria, representative of the latter, relates life in the tail turret, experiences typical of the average gunner, mid-upper or rear.

An engineering student before enlisting in the RAAF, Doug Trigg's outlook on life had somewhat changed by the time he returned home. Newly married to a Yorkshire lass, he saw the war out as a fighter-controller at Air Defence HQ in Melbourne before taking a course in pharmacy soon after discharge.

At the time of writing Doug and his wife run a health food shop in Cranbourne and he still acts as a 'locum' in two pharmacies he once owned.

'I think of myself as just an average air gunner because I can't think of any way in which I distinguished myself. I didn't have any confirmed "kills", didn't get a "gong", didn't bale out and wasn't shot down. And yet in some ways I was not average. Gunners were generally looked upon as less intelligent and not as well educated as the rest, so the fact that I had a public school education was not average, But the thing that made me even

less average was that I am just over six feet tall!

'When I arrived at 2 B&GS Port Pirie, in South Australia, I was just over 19 years old and had never seen a Fairey Battle. Here I found my height a decided advantage. When we had completed our ground lectures on the theories of air gunnery, bullet trajectory, deflection, the Vickers gas-operated machine gun and aircraft recognition, we were allowed to put the theories into practice.

'It was then, in the rear cockpit of a Battle standing to operate the Vickers and firing at a drogue towed by another Battle, that I found being the tallest gunner on the course was good for something other than being "marker" on parade! Several gunners would fly on each detail, and we would each take our own drum or drums of ammo, each containing 200 rounds, dipped in a distinctive paint so that each gunner's hits could be counted.

'At the end of the course we had all managed to hit the drogue a few times, and with a total of about 12 hours of this flying we had our AG wings pinned on, together with our three stripes and were passed out as qualified air gunners. Most of us knew so little we didn't even realise this was just the beginning of learning our trade. I had to wait some time and travel quite a few miles before I could continue my education in air gunnery and survival.

'The next step was at 84 OTU Desborough in Northamptonshire where I met the other members of my aircrew for the first time, the Vickers Wellington or Wimpey, and the Fraser Nash rear turret. First came more lectures from gunners who had completed a tour of operations. The things we learned here seemed more to the point than the lectures at B&GS. However the real problem was about to present itself in the shape, or perhaps more particularly, the size, of the Fraser Nash turret!

'Because we were approaching our first English winter the actual start to our flying training was delayed; but finally the day came when I dressed myself in all the cold weather gear, flying suit, parachute harness, etc, clambered aboard the Wimpey and found my way to the rear turret. The turret was locked in

Above: **Gubbins** '... I was sitting on a rather firm pad or cushion, about 15in by about 9in, the locked metal doors forming my back rest, while between my legs was the control column, topped by the hand grips and triggers. Immediately in front of my face, if I stooped a little, was the gun sight ...' The standard Fraser-Nash FN20 rear turret with doors removed for clarity and tarpaulin cover draped over its exterior for the benefit of the photographer. Note that only one ammo feed is in place on this No 619 Squadron Lanc at time of the photograph. (July 1944). */F. G. Secker*

Right: **Night Watch** '... By reaching behind I was able to slide the doors together so they locked ... dropping my right hand down to the turret locking lever I unlocked the turret on its rotating ring ...' */Paul Popper*

position facing astern with its doors open into the aircraft. All I had to do after placing my 'chute in the stowage near to, but not in, the turret, was to grab the two hand grips in the roof of the airframe and hoist my legs up and into the turret, followed by the rest of me, remembering to duck my head.

'By reaching behind I was able to slide the doors together so they locked. I was sitting on a rather firm pad or cushion, about 15in by about 9in, the locked metal doors forming my back rest, while between my legs was the control column, topped by the hand grips and triggers. Immediately in front of my face, if I stooped a little, was the gunsight. Switching on the illumination I could see the red circle, with a dot in the middle superimposed on the fields beyond the dispersal bay. Then the intercom jack, oxygen tube and lead of my electrically heated inner suit were plugged in.

'Dropping my right hand down to the turret locking lever I unlocked the turret on its rotating ring, by which time the pilot had both motors running so that I was able to rotate the turret with the hand controls. Twisting the hand grips raised or lowered the guns and sight. As soon as we had made sufficient height and reached the designated area, we were joined by a Miles Martinet, which proceeded to carry out simulated attacks from both quarters, while I gave a running commentary to our pilot, directing him through corkscrews, and at the same time trying to aim-off ahead of the "fighter's" apparent motion through my sight.

'My total flying time at OTU was 90 hours. I had shot 400ft of film at the Martinet, 100ft at a Tomahawk, 2,000 rounds air-to-air, cleaned 24 guns, carried out 11 daily inspections and harmonisations. I had at least reached the stage of realising there was still much to learn. Final instruction in my trade came on our last flight at OTU by doing a night "nickel" run to Orleans in France dropping leaflets. I crossed the enemy coast for the first time and began to learn what my function would be from now on – vigilance.

'The next step was conversion to four-engined aircraft and the addition of two new members, the flight engineer and mid-upper gunner. We were fortunate that with the change of seasons, the weather was better when we reached 1651 Conversion Unit at Wratting Common, Cambridgeshire. Here we were introduced to the Short Stirling – not an aircraft we came to love – and I finally came to terms with the rear turret.

Above: **To See was to Live**
From late 1943 gunners began removing some of the perspex from their rear turrets to aid visibility. Narrow elongated cut-outs running vertically down the turret centre line had given way to virtually no perspex at all by mid-1944, as illustrated on this No 186 Squadron Lancaster at Stradishall in 1945 (Sgt 'Geordie' Beer).
/K. G. Orman

Right: **Lifeline** Despite the approaching take-off deadline mid-upper Des Hughes insists on checking both guns now his crew (skipper Flt Sgt Jack Taggart RAAF) has been forced to switch to the reserve aircraft; No 460 Squadron RAAF Binbrook before Munich 2/3 October or Berlin 22/23 November 1943. The Taggart crew subsequently transferred to No 156 Squadron PFF and completed a double tour.
/D. J. Hughes

Above: **All Round Vision**
The standard Fraser-Nash FN50 provided a wide angle of vision for the gunner. Inside this 6 Group No 424 ('Tiger') Squadron Lanc mid-upper is Canadian Flt Sgt Ken Hawdon with right arm hiding his firing triggers. In line with his hand is the breech casing to the left hand Browning, while the ammunition feed can be seen immediately behind the vertical outer turret band: the machine-gun is complete with flash eliminator and heat dissipating fins on the vented outer sleeve surrounding the actual barrel. The perspex dome was manufactured in separate panels. /S. D. Sanders

'Fighter affiliation in a four-engined aircraft was different, and I had to get used to the idea of another gunner being there to help me. During the ground lectures there was a certain amount of inter-crew rivalry between the gunners and we felt we had done fairly well when we attained second and fourth places at the end of the ground lectures.

'By the end of this period of training I had another 47 hours in my log book, including several hours cine-camera gun fighter affiliation with Hawker Hurricanes, and our work as a crew was settling down to the "no worries, no fuss" inter-reliance that would eventually carry us through a tour of operations.

'When we left Wratting Common we had only one brief interlude before we were posted to a squadron, and that would be to convert to the Lancaster. I have always regretted that the Lanc proved such an easy aircraft to "learn". The station to which we were posted was Feltwell, one of the permanent bases offering a decided improvement in living accommodation, and the time spent in learning all about the Lanc was so enjoyable we could have done with a lot more of it; but for one thing. By now we were all eager to put all the "gen" into practice. In fact we did not have long to wait. Total flying time at 3 LFS was 7hr 55min and the additional instruction in air gunnery was minimal, just four days of lectures prior to the brief flying familiarisation programme.

'Of course, as much as the sense of excitement at the prospect of going to a squadron was the eagerness to know which one it would be. In our case it was to be No 75 (New Zealand) Squadron stationed at Mepal in Cambridgeshire, not far from Ely. The squadron was so busy it was not long before we were operating regularly. In fact, our crew set something of a record by doing our first nine operations in 12 days! Then we went on leave.

'As I remember, there were no hard and fast rules, though firm "do nots" were established in my mind from training: talking to tour expired gunners; and from my early ops experience, do not fire unless seen; do not stare at fires or bright lights; question in your mind any unusual movement by another aircraft. I did not clean my own guns on No 75. This, together with loading bins, harmonising, etc, was done by our own armourer, although I assisted with harmonisation, checked the actual load of the ammo, and often decided on the proportion of armour-piercing, incendiary and tracer. My tracer was usually 1 in 8. The other thing to be watched was switching to night trace after doing a "daylight". This was overlooked on one occasion because of the frequency of our ops, and as it happened we had an attack. When I opened fire I just about blinded myself, and gave the Jerry such a fright he never did open fire!

'My 'chute was left in a stowage outside my turret, and so was my flask. I did not take sandwiches, only gum. The lack of heat, or the extremes caused by the "all on – all off" nature of my suit heating could be hell at times. A rheostat would have made so much difference. I always sat in the turret during take-off; in fact, on ops, never left it at all. Strangely enough there was no real bladder problem. Even on some of the longer trips of eight or nine hours, I can't recall having any trouble, but do remember there was just one thing I needed more than a cigarette when we landed!

'There were moments of loneliness, although I never felt alone or cut-off. I never heard music as some gunners swear they did, but believe the thing that prevented either that or any feeling of remoteness, was my never ceasing wonder at the extent of my vision in

231

the so-called darkness. Far from feeling there was nothing to see, the other aircraft, near or far, the changing light and shade of the sky and clouds, the sometimes amazing detail of the ground below, filled my time and sense to such a degree that I had no time for music.

'The only exceptions, and they were thankfully rare, were on one or two very long trips when the combination of cold, extreme cramp and discomfort, and utter tiredness to the point of exhaustion, made the final stages of the trip home sheer hell. Apart from these rare occasions I loved flying, particularly at night. Not only could I not stretch my legs, I could barely move them, having to maintain a slight but permanent stoop, which became second nature after a while, and the small and very firm seat cushion (pad would be a better description) made some movement of the buttocks imperative. Unfortunately, my size made any attempt to ease the ache and numbness almost impossible, but I went on squirming. After all these years my greatest discomfort is to be trapped in a lecture or theatre where the seats are small and firm and my old discomfort returns so that I have no peace until I can stand.

'During our very busy early phase of operational activity all of our trips were to France except for one, and that was to lay mines off Flushing. The rest were either railroad targets before the invasion, or targets in support of the Army immediately after D-day. It was during one of these early operations, in fact the date was 7 June 1944, the day after D-day, that we met our first Jerry.

'As we left the ground I switched off the white tail light to let the crew behind us know we were clear. Having reported "Rear light off!", I immediately started my search pattern, to accustom my eyes to the night sky, and to warn the skipper of any other aircraft movement near to us. We would expect all of these to be friendly at this stage, but even they could sometimes come too close; and of course, night intruders had to be watched for, although the danger from these was greater on the return flight.

'As we climbed away, in company with a growing stream of Lancs it was about 0045 hours and the target was some railway yards south of Paris. The trip out was quiet and uneventful and as usual our navigator had us right on track so we didn't stray over unexpected flak areas. Coming into the target, however, it was apparent from comments by the skipper and bomb aimer that flak over the target area was very dense, and I could soon see the effect of this, with other aircraft around us reflecting the orange and pink glow from the light of the target ahead of us.

'As we got nearer still and began our bomb run, we could feel the bumps caused by the explosions around us and as it got worse, with our skipper fighting to keep to the minor alterations given by the bomb aimer, an aircraft near us was hit and flames appeared as it began to lose height. Even though I was aware of the dangers of watching too long I did see one parachute open behind the plunging Lanc. We had been warned about the dangers of reducing our night vision by staring at fires, either on the ground or in the air, and of course there was the obvious danger of being jumped by a fighter from the other quarter while engrossed in watching something like this. So back to the continual search of the night sky as we flew through the target and heard the call "bombs gone" with the usual sigh of relief.

'We had bombed just under a heavy cloud cover which had kept things very dark, and now, as we turned for home we climbed up through this into clear moonlight. We had not long settled onto our course for home when I saw an aircraft well away on our port quarter and at about the same height. As I watched, it grew larger but could still not be identified. I reported this to the skipper and watched as it grew rapidly nearer until just before it passed across our stern.

'As he passed our stern I got a full plan view of an Me210 because he banked away sharply to our starboard quarter, where he turned again to take up station. I knew it would only be for a moment while he prepared to attack. As soon as he banked again to come in I gave the order to skipper: "dive starboard – Go!"; and down we went! I immediately began firing, as did the mid-upper. The Jerry kept to his curve of attack, but our skipper's tight diving turn meant he could not get enough deflection for accurate shooting, and while my tracers were curving toward him, and getting some hits, I was having some difficulty in aiming-off. Just after deciding to allow a bit more, and let him fly through my pattern, he entered the cloud. The last we saw of Jerry was a slight glow through the cloud. We did not leave the cloud for some time and nothing further was seen in spite of vigilance, sharpened considerably by the recent encounter.

'This was the first time I had used my guns in combat and although we could not claim a kill, we had returned unscathed, which was a gunner's main duty. As I said at the beginning, I got no gongs, but at least the navigator stopped describing me as ballast, and there were no more remarks about my being there "just to keep the tail down on landing".

'Later we were to do German targets, daylights, and have other fighter attacks, but this trip remains in my memory as the one on which I earned my AG wing.'

Prelude

Right: **Getting the Griff** In the dimly lit fuggy atmosphere of the Witchford briefing room, No 115 Squadron crews are taken through the impending operation. The building is of basic Nissen pattern with concrete base, brick end walls and curved corrugated sheeting lined with composite plasterboard-type interior covering forming combined sidewalls and roof. Official charts and diagrams abound, in addition to the inevitable Station Routine Orders. The aircrew, generally one crew per row, sit at simple trestle tables and benches./*J. N. M. Heffer*

Left: **Collecting the Brollies** The briefing is over and now it is time to don all the clobber. Here we see No 103 Squadron crew members collecting their parachutes at Elsham Wolds prior to a raid in the spring of 1943. At the counter is Sgt Pat ('Iron Cross') Oliver a rear gunner who drew many a raised eyebrow by wearing an Iron Cross taken from a German soldier by his father in World War I. Luck was certainly on Pat's side for he missed the fateful Berlin trip on which his crew met their end (1/2 March 1943; skipper: Flt Sgt W. F. 'Bunny' Austin) and he completed most of his remaining ops as a 'spare bod'. The ladies shown here serve as a reminder of the admirable work done by WAAFs on Bomber Command stations, and this fine picture was later chosen to aid their recruitment./*D. P. Oliver*

Bottom left: **Check Now, Pay Later** While awaiting the crew trucks there is time for a final check of gear, including the flying rations (note orange). Three of Plt Off J. M. Desmond's crew pictured at Bottesford before Berlin early in 1943, watched intently by Jock the Scottie, well known to No 467 Squadron RAAF crews. Less than three months later they did not return from Essen 27/28 May 1943 and became yet another statistic./*G. E. Fitt*

Right: **A Helping Hand** No 467 Squadron RAAF crews pile aboard the covered trucks outside the locker rooms: Bottesford before Berlin early in 1943. Two of the aircrew have yet to don their parachute harnesses. /*Mrs M. Claridge Collection*

Below: **Tension** Tension shows in the crew's faces as the time draws near to clamber aboard. All is in order and there is just time for a last fag and a final chat with the ground crew. No 300 ('Masovian') Squadron Faldingworth June/July 1944, almost certainly picturing WO J. Zoltanski and crew who went down in BIII PB171 'BH-K' on Scholven 18/19 July 1944. /*Polish Sources*

Bottom: **Moonlight Sonata** Under the bright canopy of a full moon a No 150 Squadron crew runs through the checks on a cold winter's night at Hemswell in November 1944. Bright moonlight will make their coming camisade ever more alive with danger. /*D. D. Winston*

The Off

Below: **Time to Go** The air is charged with expectancy and the airfield echoes to the rhythmic throb of some three score Merlins as, one by one the aircraft start up and move out of their dispersals. A scene at Metheringham on 22 March 1944 as No 106 Squadron Lancs, each well down on its oleos, tyres appearing flat under the load, head for the peri-track. The night's operation was to Frankfurt and 106 lost one crew from the 33 who did not return. /IWM

Above: **On the Move** From the cockpit of 'X-XRAY' Canadian engineer Mike Bachinski – an avid photographer despite a ban on cameras – snaps the remainder of No 431 ('Iroquois') Squadron waddling round the peri-track. The airfield is Croft set in the rich farmland of the Yorkshire Dales./*M. Bachinski*

Right: **Awaiting the Green** The cockpit of a pranged Lancaster provides an ideal vantage point for an enterprising Canadian photographer as he captures the recently formed No 582 Squadron PFF preparing for a dusk take-off at Little Staughton in April 1944. /*P. B. Browning*

Centre right: **Top Gear** The runway is lined with well wishers (surprisingly lacking any WAAFs) as No 622 Squadron's BI LL885 'GI-J' (Flg Off H. P. Peck RAAF and crew) begins her take-off run at Mildenhall 25 October 1944, bound for a daylight on Essen. This Lancaster was to tot up 113 ops by the end of the war in Europe, and by coincidence 'J-Jig' (BI LL806) of No 15 Squadron, sharing Mildenhall with No 622, topped the century mark./*R. V. James*

Bottom right: **Bellowing Power** Fine action shot of No 149 (East India) Squadron's 'OJ-N' (BI PD284) thundering down the Methwold runway at 1218 hours, 29 March 1945, with Flt Lt Dick Schuster and crew bound for Hallendorf, their 14th trip. The skipper will now be guiding her on the rudders, leaving his engineer thrusting the throttles through the 'gate' and preventing them falling back./*E. Rosier*

236

Below: **Evening Pageantry** A mackerel sky, breaking up as dusk rapidly approaches, forms an imposing backcloth to a No 35 (Madras Presidency) Squadron PFF Lanc taking off from Graveley autumn 1944. On warm clammy nights, with no wind, a Lancaster would require virtually the full length of the runway, and many pilots preferred to hold the nose down until the very last moment./*K. C. Gooch*

Bottom: **Night Errand** A heavily laden No 166 Squadron Lanc presents a purposeful silhouette as she climbs out of Kirmington in the fast gathering dusk. A few more feet and the engineer will pull up the undercart, set climbing power and retract the flaps in 5° snatches once safety speed reads on the clock. Eyes are beginning to scan the sky (the rear gunner's turret is already turned to port) for soon the air will be full of milling aircraft, all circling and climbing for height./*J. T. Lambourne*

Above: **Clean Sweep** With port-outer covered in foam, one u/c leg ripped off, BIII ND936 'TL-C' is a sorry sight at Graveley 22 July 1944. Flt Sgt Ted Hislop and crew, only recently arrived on No 35 (Madras Presidency) Squadron straight from a Halifax Conversion Unit, developed a swing on the take-off run (the target was a VI site at L'Hay), forcing them to the left hand side of the runway. On correcting they veered voilently to starboard and tore across the grass at an angle of 30°, running over the FIDO pipes and bursting a tyre (though they did not know it). Undaunted, the skipper called for full power and they 'sped' across the grass on a highly individual take-off heading. However, acceleration was comparatively sluggish, and with the Mossie dispersals of No 692 Squadron looming up, the throttles were slammed shut. The kite promptly ground looped but all aboard escaped unhurt. Though ND936 would be repaired, the incident ended the crew's spell in PFF and they were posted to No 4 Group on Halifaxes after just six ops. Poor Hislop was fated to go down with another crew, having survived another take-off prang. ND936, usually flown by Flt Lt H. C. Hoover RCAF and crew, bore a vacuum cleaner emblem and the motto 'We Sweep Clean' on her nose: she survived the war. /*G. Acklam*

Right: **In Open Skies** Rear gunner's view of outward bound No 405 ('Vancouver') Squadron PFF Lancs from Gransden Lodge pictured high above the clouds. Though constantly scanning for enemy fighters few aircrew failed to appreciate such magnificent cloudscapes. /H. W. Lees

Below: **Forming Up** Flying low over the wooded landscape of southern England, the Lancasters of No 5 Group present an impressive sight as they head for Milan, Saturday 24 October 1942. Despite the costly daylight to Augsburg on 17 April 1942, the group (at that time the first and only one equipped with Lancs) made several long distance daylight/ dusk attacks later in the year, heralded by Le Creusot on 17 October. Three crews failed to return from the 88 despatched to Milan./C. W. Gray

Clap Hands for the Walking Dead

FRED SIM

Flak or fighters – it was an evil choice. Both could mean death in its least pleasant form; each could strike without warning and obliterate the most alert and skilful of crews. While flak was the cause of a goodly proportion of Lancasters failing to return, German night fighters undoubtedly accounted for around 70% of those lost over enemy territory.

At best it meant a prisoner of war camp for those crew members lucky enough to survive. Flying an aircraft without peer, in a class of its own, inevitably meant that Lanc crews bore the brunt of Bomber Command's offensive against the toughest targets, near and far. Even so, the crew survival rate of Lancasters shot down was unfavourable by comparison with its contemporaries.

Good crew discipline was vital in the event of an attack as the following story by Canadian bomb aimer Fred Sim clearly reveals. As events turned out Leipzig 19/20 February 1944 proved to be the crew's 22nd and last trip with No 166 Squadron Kirmington (they had begun the tour by doing three ops with No 103 operating from Elsham Wolds). In view of the mauling they received, coupled with the severe losses suffered by the Command during the winter of 1943/1944, it was deemed prudent to tour expire them.

All seven were decorated. Engineer Sgt Barry Wright received an immediate CGM; skipper Plt Off Jim Catlin, bomb aimer Plt Off Fred Sim, and navigator Plt Off Tony Pragnell collected DFCs; wireless operator Sgt Tommy Hall, rear gunner Sgt Billy Birch and mid-upper Sgt Tom Powers were awarded DFMs. Their Lancaster, BIII LM382 'AS:Q', was broken up where she lay.

Barely 23 at the time of the experience described, Fred hailed from Tisdale, Saskatchewan. Growing up in a farming community, he worked on his parents' farm for two years until deciding to 'spread his wings'. Employed first in the construction industry, he then moved to a Manitoba mining company engaged on zinc production before signing on in the RCAF at Regina.

His service followed the usual pattern and by the time he was rotated back to Canada in March 1945, taking with him his Welsh bride

(a former WAAF) of eight months, he was a qualified bombing leader, having latterly 'done a stint' at 82 OTU Ossington.

On transferring to the RCAF Reserve he immediately enrolled at the University of Saskatchewan in 1946, to begin a postwar career in agricultural and industrial equipment. Since 1956 Fred has been with the Ford Motor Company, and is currently the Zone Manager for the Province of Saskatchewan.

'The weather was fairly good and the visibility generally better than average as we took off, climbed to height and headed as if making yet another massive attack on Berlin; at the last moment we would alter course and fly south to hit Leipzig.

'About the time we crossed the enemy coast, we found ourselves running ahead of schedule. Immediately throttling back, we started flying "doglegs" to lose time. We had been advised at briefing that we could expect a headwind of 50kts: we actually had a tailwind of 50kts! At this time there was no provision made for altering zero hour and some 800 or so bombers were in the same bind and dog-legging like us to lose time.

'In short order, all phases of the raid were mixed together and all doing their utmost to lose time and get back to their schedule. The concentration of our aircraft was multiplied immensely and the zig-zagging on track presented a singular situation for sightings and interceptions of one another. This situation of delaying forward progress and resultant high concentration I'm sure accounted for several collisions that night; it also enabled the enemy to get many more fighter aircraft than usual up to our stream. I personally saw some 17 or 18 enemy aircraft that night before we were attacked – more than in the balance of the tour put together.

'It was a very interesting situation and we were certainly at the peak of alertness to keep out of trouble. The flight engineer, gunners and myself were concentrating on our outlook areas and all reported several sightings of our own aircraft and enemy fighters. The Bf110 which attacked us first was reported and upon

Left: **Baptism** On only their second outing Sgt Ken S. Knott and crew of No 103 Squadron were coned for four minutes and severely mauled by at least six Bf109s (operating in pairs) in three coordinated attacks while on the photo-flash run over Berlin 23/24 August 1943. The port-outer was stopped but would not feather; oil pipes to the mid-upper turret were shot away; the port wing opened up to the main spar, holing one petrol tank; flaps jammed. Thankfully the home flight was uneventful and Knott made a flapless landing back at Elsham Wolds. Picture of BIII JA868 'PM-U' was taken following day. After seven ops crew transferred to No 166 Squadron but did not complete their 10th trip, falling to a brace of Ju88s on Hanover 27/28 September 1943. JA868 was scrapped at 45 MU in August 1947. /*R. J. Franklin*

Right: **Men of Action** The Catlin crew lined up in front of BIII ED905 'PM-X' shortly before they left No 103 Squadron in September 1943. Left to right: Sgt Tommy Hall, w/op; Sgt Billy Birch, rear gunner; Flt Sgt Fred Sim, bomb aimer; Flt Sgt Jim Catlin, pilot; Sgt Barry Wright, flight engineer; Sgt Tom Powers, mid-upper; Sgt Tony Pragnell, navigator. /*W. Birch*

Below right: **Scarecrow?** This No 50 Squadron Lancaster (BIII DV227 'VN-F') came back from Mannheim 23/24 September 1943 minus her starboard fin, rudder and elevator, and with the port rudder and elevator trimmers u/s. Her crew (pilot: Plt Off H. A. Litherland) reported a direct hit from a scarecrow at 19,000ft and the skipper had a difficult time nursing his mount back to Skellingthorpe. Neither crew nor aircraft were fated to survive the war, the Litherland crew going down on Berlin 15/16 February 1944, DV227 failing to return from St Leu D'Esserent 7/8 July 1944. /*E. T. McCabe*

Above: **A Near Thing** Flak almost brought disaster to Flg Off 'Mo' Croker RNZAF and his No 227 Squadron crew on a Bohlen stooge 5/6 March 1945. Despite penetration of lethal enemy hardware, the fuel tanks of BI NN802 '9J-K' held and they made it back to Balderton. This was the second occasion on which the Croker crew were shot up by flak (to say nothing of fighter attacks) during an eventful tour. /*M. R. Croker*

Right: **Close** In the cold light of day, Plt Off 'Jock' Torrance RAAF (left) and his Canadian bomb aimer, Flg Off Bill Fox, of No 626 Squadron Wickenby inspect the shattered starboard fin taken from BIII JB646 'UM-R²'. Letting down over the Zuider Zee on return from Dortmund 22/23 May 1944, their Lanc was caught in light flak, peppering the fuselage and tearing a huge chunk off the starboard fin and rudder. Feeling he must retaliate, the bomb aimer threw out an empty milk bottle (carried for obvious reasons) from the nose vent. The firing stopped – perhaps by coincidence – but maybe the scream of an empty bottle hurtling down from 12,000ft did the trick. The Torrance crew went on to complete an eventful tour early the following month; JB646 later passed to the Poles at Faldingworth – the last squadron in No 1 Group to convert to Lancs. She was 'reduced to produce' at 45 MU in August 1947./*G. W. Fox*

us almost immediately. Rear gunner Billy Birch was firing before he finished his alert call but we were raked from rear to front with cannon fire. In this burst the mid-upper, w/op, navigator and engineer were all wounded. A cannon shell exploded in the area of the rear turret servo feed ammunition tank on the port side of the aircraft, scattering .303in ammo from the bulkhead to the turret. This shell also blew a hole in the port side of the Lanc, roughly $3\frac{1}{2}$ft square

'At the same moment most of the perspex was blown out of the mid-upper turret and Tom Powers was out cold. A shell ripped through the large electrical panel on the starboard side of the aircraft and fused every light on "bright" from front to back (like Crystal Palace). Jim Catlin, our pilot, selected bomb doors open and ordered the bomb load to be jettisoned. This I did on to a built-up area below.

'The second Bf110 closed about then and Billy Birch was on to him immediately. This was one he shot down in flames. The first Bf110 then attacked again and was hit and driven off by fire from Billy Birch.

'During this period, Jim Catlin was putting to use all his training and experience in flying our disabled Lancaster, and because of his difficulties he requested that we "prepare to abandon aircraft". I snapped on my 'chute pack and got rid of the nose escape hatch cover. The intercom went dead and I stepped forward ahead of the hatch to watch for signals and direction. After a pause of possibly 20 seconds I stepped back over the

Left: **Scars** Rather the worse for wear in Witchford's 54 MU hangar stands BI NG205. Flg Off G. E. Gibson RAAF and his No 115 Squadron crew were caught by a flak barrage over the outer Ruhr defences while on a Duisburg daylight 8 December 1944. In addition to peppering the bomb doors and fuselage mid-section (wounding mid-upper Sgt A. J. Kingham's face and hands), the port wing and fin, DR compass and H2S were also hit. Complete with new sections, NG205 returned to the fray and was still active (with No 115's C Flight) when the European war ended./*D. Humphery*

Below left: **Human Ordeal** 'Diving out of control for more than two minutes . . . losing 14,000ft . . . her controls jammed . . . her ASI needle travelling twice round the clock until it registered 410mph . . . her rear gunner injured . . . a lively fire in her "innards" . . . and a persistent Jerry fighter still on her tail' – that, in a nutshell, is the story of Plt Off J. D. Mortimer and crew's ordeal on the way home from a gardening sortie in the Baltic on the night of 9/10 April 1944. BIII JB557 'HW-U' of No 100 Squadron had crossed the Dutch coast at 21,000ft when an Me410 attacked from astern, wounding the rear gunner and rendering his turret u/s. With port-outer stopped, a Verey cartridge in the dinghy pack, and hydraulic oil ablaze, the kite descended in a near vertical dive, and it took the combined efforts of the skipper's 15 stone weight, plus the pulling power of the engineer to ease her out at 7,000ft. All was not over however and the fighter, which must have followed them down, came in again. Despite intercom trouble (to say nothing of the crew's ears being affected by the dive), the pilot was able to nip into some cloud cover and escape. The stick was still virtually impossible to hold back so cords from the nav's Mae West were slung round and held by the bomb aimer for the remaining flight home. For the actual landing, Mortimer had to use his weight unaided (flaps and u/c having been lowered by emergency air) to bring her in at home base Waltham. Despite 15 cannon shell splinters in an arm and leg,

rear gunner Sgt S. Rudman quickly recovered and the crew went on to complete tour. (JB557 later passed to second line duties and survived the war on the strength of a Conversion Unit.)/*L. F. Lampitt*

Below: **Gutted** Close up of No 156 Squadron BIII ME378 'GT-Q' at Manston, revealing extensive damage to her bomb bay as a result of the close attentions of a flak barrage when approaching Harpenerweg at 17,000ft in daylight, 24 March 1945. With his kite on fire, the cockpit full of smoke, driver Flg Off Gil Hampson lost control and went into a dive, and ordered his crew to abandon, besides jettisoning the load. Engineer Sgt Denis R. Bowers was badly wounded in the left thigh by shrapnel, which splintered the bone, but despite profuse bleeding, had until the dive, continued 'Windowing'. At 13,000ft Hampson regained control and headed out of the target area, minus the nav and w/op, in addition to the mid-upper who, though his 'chute was still in the aircraft, must have fallen through the gaping bomb bay floor. Taking evasive action from predicted flak did not prevent further damage and they were hit again, the engineer, half in, half out of the nose escape hatch at the time, having his left leg all but severed. From the time of his first wound Bowers showed great fortitude and continued to 'Window' until completely disabled. Even while lying on the cockpit floor he advised his captain of the fuel state, and generally offered advice. With Gee and H2S u/s, the set operator, Flt Sgt 'Doc' Reynolds produced courses enabling the skipper to follow the bomber stream to the coast of Holland. Hampson then map read to Ostend before the set op, using the nav's last found wind, gave him a course for Manston. For his courage and devotion to duty that day, Denis Bowers was awarded the highly prized CGM; but surgeons were unable to save his leg. Gil Hampson was awarded an immediate DFC; F. G. ('Doc') Reynolds and rear gunner Flt Sgt John R. Mann each received DFMs. They were among the last gongs of the war awarded to Upwood crews./*G. B. Hampson*

hole and up into the pilot's compartment, to receive a smile and a pat on the head for not having jumped.

'I saw the predicament Barry Wright our flight engineer was in and immediately attempted to get him to sit or lie down – with no success. It was conveyed by signs that we would stay with the aircraft as long as possible. W/op Tommy Hall was desperately working on getting the lights out and finally succeeded.

'Acting as a messenger for the pilot, I obtained a course to steer for getting us out of the area and back home. I grabbed an emergency oxygen bottle and walked back to check our damage, and assess the mid-upper's condition. Tom Powers was a big lad and, with the aircraft flying erratically there was no way Billy Birch and I could lift him sufficiently to release his seat. There was no evidence of extensive bleeding and we were compelled to leave him and handle other problems.

'The Lanc was proving difficult for Jim Catlin to control. The bomb doors were open and could not be closed because of the hydraulics being shot away. The trim controls were locked-up as set for the full bomb load and the skipper had to constantly apply forward pressure to his control column to keep us from climbing. The aircraft maintained a more or less straight course when the pilot held one rudder fully on. However, on two occasions when he attempted to change position in his seat the Lancaster veered off course and could only be brought back by completing a 360° turn.

'Tony Pragnell, our navigator, was working by means of a flashlight and our aids and radio equipment were dead. When I was not running errands and assisting the flight engineer I was down in the nose watching for landmarks. A gap came up in the cloud and I identified a large river junction north west of Hanover. We were on track as per Pragnell's DR navigation. He was as cool as a cucumber and right on.

'We encountered predicted heavy flak on approaching the coast and it is true we could smell the explosive as we flew through some of these puffs. The enemy started working his searchlights on us, and in desperation we fired our colours of the day; the action stopped! Needless to say we then became concerned that possibly they were sending up fighter aircraft, but this did not happen. We assumed our colours of the period coincided with theirs and we were lucky.

'Our w/op continued working on our wireless equipment and partially restored the intercom. We used up our supply of "Window" throughout the return trip. Tom Powers continued to regain consciousness from time to time but could not be freed from his turret.

'After altering course at the enemy coast we were met by a real hot searchlight group on approaching the English coast. With no IFF, no radar, far ahead of the returning main bomber stream, and way off course, it looked for a moment as if we were in for yet another hot reception. Momentarily we were coned and had to fire the colours of the day for the second time that night. I flashed the letters of the period with a flashlight from the nose, as well as SOS several times.

'We were homed on by searchlights to our aerodrome, which turned out to be shut down due to weather. We again sent out a distress signal with the torch and were forwarded to Manston. Barry Wright and I got the undercarriage down via emergency means and at this point Jim Catlin realised the port tyre was flat. He reared up in his seat and saw that the starboard tyre was also flat so we assumed crash positions at the last moment and came in for a beautiful three-point landing in a shower of sparks. As we pulled off the runway another – unannounced – aircraft followed us in.

'Transport arrived and we called for an ambulance before proceeding to get our mid-upper gunner out of his turret with the aid of the fire axe. We cut his flying suit off and fragments of metal clinked to the aircraft's floor like a handful of nails. He was conscious and cheerful as he was taken off to hospital.

'Barry Wright, our flight engineer, was helped to a stretcher and also taken to hospital. His wounds were such that he could not stand up straight, and moved about only with assistance. Navigator Tony Pragnell had shrapnel in the top of his shoulder near his neck. W/op Tom Hall had a piece lodged in the back of his upper arm. The latter two were released to return with us to the squadron the next day.

'Our aircraft was fit only for scrap. We had even brought back two cannisters of incendiaries which had hung-up due to wiring damage. After de-briefing we were fed and bedded down at Manston before returning to Kirmington by train the next day – to be screened forthwith.

'The night of 19/20 February 1944 was a rough one on our force – 78 aircraft were lost. As a result of our experience with unexpected windspeed and direction changes, a new policy was adopted whereby Command could move up the zero hour during a raid, thus avoiding the doddling and dogleg flying.

'My thanks go out to a fabulous aircraft, powered with tremendously good engines serviced by the most dedicated people in the world – our ground crew. Also the automatic teamwork of our aircrew (whose average age was 22 years) ensured that we completed this trip.'

Harbinger of Hell

PHIL MARTIN

No other aircraft of comparable size could take the ever increasing loads progressively introduced on the Lancaster. Even so, the design was stretched to the limit to accommodate the 22,000lb Grand Slam monster, the ultimate in conventional bombs, and some strengthening and lightening was necessary. It is staggering to reflect that the Lancaster began life in 1941 at an auw of 55,000lb and ended the war weighing in at 72,000lb, an increase of almost 31%.

With removal of front and mid-upper turrets, a certain amount of interior stripping, and the fitment of Merlin 24s with their superior take-off performance, these machines – officially termed BI(Special) – were extremely fast when not carrying the bomb and became known to the crews as 'Clapper Kites'.

In this feature, Phil Martin, an Aussie skipper on 617 Squardon, gives an illuminating account of flying PB996 'YZ-C' (subject of a well known RAF Film Unit sequence) on the Arnsberg viaduct daylight raid of 19 March 1945.

A native of Gosnells, Western Australia, he had worked as a clerk in the state Government Mines Department at Kelmscott before volunteering for aircraft duties. It was as a twice decorated, two-tour (No 61 and 617 Squadrons), 22-year old flight lieutenant that he returned to his homeland in mid-1945.

Whilst still on extended leave prior to demobilisation (effective January 1946) he began civilian employment as a press photographer. Phil is still in the same line of business, 32 years later, though these days more behind a desk than a camera.

' "Remember", said the Groupie (Grp Capt "Johnny" Fauquier), "If you have to bring the bomb back you can't drop the aircraft more than six inches on to the runway. If you do, the tyres will burst." If anyone among us sitting in that Nissen hut had had a pin and dropped it, it would have sounded like an unexploded Tallboy hitting a steel plate floor.

'Fauquier went on with his briefing. His previous comment was just one in a string of pearls of wisdom we mentally fingered as we came out of the briefing room, knowing we were to fly the op to obliterate the Arnsberg viaduct with one of the biggest iron bombs ever made – the awesome Grand Slam.

'The first doubts had tip-toed into our minds when we saw the mother and father of all trucks wheel onto the airfield at Woodhall Spa, all big wheels and thick tyres. This was the beginning of our brief encounter with Barnes Wallis's 10-ton brainchild. On that truck was the business section of a monstrous bomb. Another truck followed, loaded with the Grand Slam's tail section. All this lethal ironmongery was eventually to be bolted together and hung under one Lancaster. Ours.

' "No worries", said Chiefy, watching our faces as that incredible cavalcade inched past. "We've fitted stronger tyres on the Lanc." "Fine", said the aircrew, "but we've only got two wheels." "Well, don't corner too fast on the perimeter track", replied the flight sergeant.

'We could think of no suitable retort but knew no normal aircraft could ever get off the deck with that weight hanging under it. The only kite which could even make a brave stab at the job, pregnant with this enormous bombload, had to be the Lancaster. And the Lancaster I was to fly was no ordinary Lanc. It didn't even look like a complete aircraft.

'Flown in from some other establishment, this machine had an orphan, unfinished look about it, as though it had been pushed out of the nest before it had properly hatched. The mid-upper turret had gone and the hole faired over. The front turret was minus one gun, the rear turret minus a brace of the comforting Browning foursome. There was ammunition for a two-second burst per gun. After that it was a case of disassemble the Brownings and hurl them at the enemy in an airman-like manner, no doubt.

'We would carry no wireless operator or W/T sets this trip. The navigator had been de-seated from his normal alloy and leather throne, and was to ensconce himself in a cane chair as part of the fight against a 10-ton weight penalty. The pilot – me – was to feel rather exposed about his *derriere* with the armour-plate taken out from under the

Right: **Leading Lights** Phil Martin and his boys pose for a crew snapshot at Woodhall Spa. Back row, left to right: Plt Off George Lovatt, w/op; Flt Sgt Tom Trebilcock, mid-upper; Flt Lt Phil Martin, pilot; Flt Sgt Don Day, bomb aimer. Front row, left to right: Flt Sgt 'Tosh' Mayoh, rear gunner; WO Alf Jackson, navigator; Flt Sgt 'Curly' Blagborough, flight engineer./*P. H. Martin*

driver's seat. I cannot recall if we were deprived of the Elsan's weight.

'The Lancaster's fuselage had been scooped out along the under belly from about the pilot's position, 33ft rearwards to make a great gouge into which to fit the Grand Slam. Fuelling was a case of metering enough fuel for the flight out and back with no frills. Not even an extra 100gal for the gremlins. When the bomb was hoisted into position and clutched in a pair of crane-grab arms secured with an electro-mechanical release unit, it looked lonely, almost appealing in its solitude, but also unbelievably lethal.

'I looked at the loaded Lanc. All I could think of was: "It looks as though we're carting a Spitfire fuselage. But it's probably the best armour-plating we've ever had – no flak from below would ever get through to the cockpit."

'The day was fine as we started engines and began leaving dispersal. As we tried to move, we forgot the weather and wondered how much power we would have to apply to overcome the inertia and reach a satisfactory break-out force merely to move this massive load of nuts, bolts and high explosive.

'We got under way – a loose term for a slow waddle; oleos bottoming at the slightest hint of surface undulation; flat-footed; incredibly lifeless and spongy. I knew – we all knew – that take-off would be a time of trying to coax a hopelessly overloaded aircraft off the runway in the face of logical impossibility.

'It was. Full bore on the brakes after we had lined-up. Release the binders, and begin lumbering forward like a tired carthorse pulling a loaded coal cart. Those four Rolls-Royce Merlins were building up to their superb crackling best as the throttle levers went forward like life members of the "Throttle-Benders" Club.

'Speed. More speed. And it came so slowly. The temptation to shove those throttle levers through the gate into emergency boost, but knowing we still had a long journey ahead of us. The runway's end at Woodhall Spa getting closer, literally looming ahead like the end of the world, and still no lightening feeling of wings taking over from the battering wheels.

'This can't be flying. "Wheels up!", as we trundled alarmingly slowly over the bitumen's end. We staggered. We wallowed. But the Lancaster was airborne, somehow and against all the rules of aerodynamics. Then came that sinking feeling as the wheels began retracting

Left: **One Lanc, One Bomb** ' . . . And there she stayed, governed by the law of gravity and that dam' great bomb hanging there like an overgrown pilot fish under a whale's belly . . . ' Second of the BI (Special) Lancs, PB995 is here seen carrying a Grand Slam while on trials from Boscombe Down, in the experienced hands of Grp Capt H. A. ('Bruin') Purvis, DFC, AFC. At this stage she mounted all three turrets, but on passing to No 617 Squadron the FN50 mid-upper was removed, and her front and rear turret armament was reduced by one gun and two guns respectively. However, in a further effort to reduce weight (and thus increase ceiling and range), she was soon modified to a revised BI (Special) standard and lost the FN5 front turret completely, while retaining the FN20 rear turret (the latter again complete with four guns). /*British Official via Mrs M. Purvis*

Left: **Mixed Bag** ' . . . Anyone looking down from above would have been justified in thinking this force was composed of mother taking the chicks for a flight . . . ' A near standard BI, NG494 'KC-B', in company with two BI (Special) Lancs, PD114 'YZ-B' and PD119 'YZ-J', aloft from Woodhall Spa 1945. Note the mixture of 'day' and 'night' camouflage schemes, 'YZ-J' even having a replacement port fin and rudder in 'night' finish./*S. J. Venton*

Below left: **Clapper Kite** ' . . . An immense feeling of lightness and power flowed through the stick as the Lancaster drew breath, delivered of its mammoth babe . . . ' PD119 'YZ-J' No 617 Squadron, spring 1945./*S. J. Venton*

Right: **Going Down** ' . . . That Grand Slam, spinning impeccably, went down . . . ' Dramatic view of the one 'live' Grand Slam to be dropped on British soil, falling away from PB592/G at 18,000ft over Godshill on the extreme edge of Ashley Walk bombing range in Hants. The local people – already accustomed to regular 'noises' emanating from the range – were not informed of the drop; did not see it; but certainly felt it! Observe black and white markings for monitoring bomb's behaviour in flight by cine-cameras./*British Official via W. Shawney*

and wings were asked to promote an airflow which would somehow get this thing flying.

'Wonder of wonders, it flew; if staggering through the English air in this fashion could even loosely be called flying. Then came the battle to actually gain a few feet of altitude. It was a fine day – most of us remember that. But we don't recall how many buildings, chimney pots, hayricks and what-have-you we flew round on that crazy departure from Woodie Spa, en route to the coast.

'We were proceeding at less than 100ft. In retrospect, I feel our climb pattern must have looked rather like the trace of a mad temperature chart graph, of a patient *in extremis* from triple influenza. Gain a few precious feet and try to stop counting grass blades. Milk up a few degrees of flap and lose that height gain. Fly round a church, a building, Merlins howling, knowing full well that it we met a 'bus on the road we'd have to fly through the damned thing. This went on, sweat oozing into my battledress, until we had retracted flap and fed more fuel to the engines, thus lightening the load by a scant few pounds.

'The Lancaster crossed the British coast at about 1,000ft, the Tallboy Lancasters in our force beginning to form up loosely astern. Anyone looking down from above would have been justified in thinking this force was composed of mother taking the chicks for a flight. From memory, we crossed the enemy coast at about 6,000ft, thanks to constant fuel consumption and precious little else apart from sheer hand-flying, feeling for each foot of height. But it still felt low enough to be clobbered by a rock thrown up by some stray German soldier or flak-gunner.

'All through, I remembered the bombing leader's warning. "Don't drop under 14,000ft or you'll get the benefit of shock waves." This was perhaps the funniest part of the whole operation. He might just as well have told us not to drop this bomb until we reached the black side of the moon.

'We managed to coax this flying bomb up to about 12,700ft. And there she stayed, governed by the law of gravity and that dam' great bomb hanging there like an overgrown pilot fish under a whale's belly. We began attracting predictor-guided flak as the viaduct neared, and the bomb aimer set up his SABS sight. This was where the fun really began.

'We were committed to a five-minute straight and level bombing run after the sight had been set up, win, lose or draw, I concentrated on flying the Lancaster to the tolerances demanded by the SABS sight – within half a mile an hour of airspeed, and plus or minus 10ft of height – during those five minutes. Everything had to be forgotten if the bomb was to go down on target. Everything but flying.

'I had dropped Tallboys and knew what the upward spring was on release. But this Grand Slam was a beauty. I heard the release unit "fire" with its usual sharp retort, and the slam of those great arms hitting the fuselage as they swung free. That Grand Slam, spinning impeccably, went down. And we went UP. Lord, how we ascended. Most of us made it 600ft upwards, the Lancaster's wings flexing and reflexing like an overstrung bow – and we were the human arrow.

'Strange noises emanated from the bomb aimer's compartment down in the nose, as my bomb aimer, Don Day, and the man crouching by his shoulder – bombing leader Sqn Ldr Jim Moody – became entangled like a pair of Saturday night stadium all-in wrestlers. I couldn't see our Grand Slam descending. Regulations demanded that I fly the Lancaster straight and level until the bomb hit. As it struck the viaduct, I banked to port to see for myself what I had unleashed. In actual fact, no human thumb pushed the button – it had all been done by clockwork after the SABS sight was set on the target.

'Down below, a magnificent pattern of concentric shockwave circles were shuddering out, the apex being where the viaduct had once arched. Tallboys were already slamming into the circles, creating cross-circle patterns. All the other bombs were released, in the air and curling wonderfully downward when the Grand Slam struck. An immense feeling of lightness and power flowed through the stick as the Lancaster drew breath, delivered of its mammoth babe. The aircraft felt light, responsive, full of bellowing power – in fact, like a Lancaster again.

'Losing height on the way back, we broke out the thermos. We had had no time or inclination to do so on the outward flight. And all the time, that Lanc was feeling more and more like a Spitfire on a fighter affiliation exercise – no weight, all urge and a dream to handle.

'And so we came home, back to Woodhall Spa. A time of calling, "funnel", remembering the five other aircraft in the circuit as we touched, feather-light, on the bitumen with no need to recall the group captain's doleful warning about not dropping more than six inches to the deck. It was one of the lightest landings I ever made. It felt rather as one does after having carried a heavy load – as if one was some inches off the ground, all hollow and indescribably airy.

'We were back in time for tea. And I never flew that particular Lancaster again. Ours was a brief encounter, and I think she forgave us for the bawdy, curious looks we shot her way when we saw her standing there, incomplete as if put together by someone who didn't care.'

Target

Below: **Mind Your Heads** Unique view of the stream massing near a target in France during the summer of 1944 – occasions when it paid crews to keep a look out to avoid 'friendly' bombs. The picture was taken from the cockpit of No 617 Squadron Lanc III JB139 'KC:V' *Dark Victor* flown by Flg Off Don Cheney RCAF and crew, destined to go down (in this very aircraft) on a Brest daylight 5 August 1944./*A. Curtis*

Left: **The Crowded Sky** To witness the aerial might of Bomber Command was an unforgettable experience: Lancasters en masse approaching a daylight target, as viewed by a No 35 (Madras Presidency) Squadron crew from Graveley. /*K. C. Gooch*

Below: **Death** The end is near for a No 195 Squadron crew trapped by centrifugal force as their Lancaster, a victim of flak, hurtles upside down over Solingen 4 November 1944. The picture was taken automatically by the camera on HK679 'A4-A' flown by No 195 Squadron Flight Commander, Sqn Ldr Bill Farquharson and crew, and depicts one of three kites lost by the unit that day. /*K. B. M. Grant*

Right: **Pitching In** Lancs bombing and orbiting a French target on 2 July 1944, illustrating the vastness of the sky, an obvious lack of flak and fighters, and Bomber Command's loose gaggle approach on daylights over France and the Low Countries where there was total Allied air superiority in the months following D-Day./*IWM*

Right: **Grandstand** The camera of a sister aircraft catches No 12 Squadron Lancaster III LM509 'PH-M' (Plt Off H. S. S. Trotter and crew) poised over the burning V1 site of Siracourt on 29 June 1944. Note the weather-worn camouflage, uneven exhaust stains and dinghy hatch in starboard wing root; also evident are a number of repaired areas, including a replacement wingtip. (LM509 survived the war, having latterly served with a number of training units, and was finally struck off charge in May 1947.)/*P. Leonard*

Left: **Ambush** Photoflash released by a No 49 Squadron Lancaster reveals a Ju88 stalking the bomber stream over Pommereval 24/25 June 1944. A second aircraft visible at the right hand edge of the picture is either another Ju88 or, as is more likely, a Lancaster. /*W. F. Jordan*

Below left: **Doomed** This No 7 Squadron Lancaster burning like a blow torch in the inky blackness on the run-in to a German target one unrecorded night in 1943 is finished. Such a glow would be visible for many miles and when a PFF kite loaded with flares blew up, the result would be a horrific spectacle of dripping colours and flame. This remarkable picture was taken from a No 156 Squadron machine a few seconds before a fellow PFF crew met the Reaper. /*P. B. Browning*

More Deaths than One

'MICK' SMITH

As the Allied armies swept relentlessly forward to the Rhine and very heart of Germany, so Bomber Command increasingly turned to daylight bombing. However, as the early daylights quickly showed, the forming up and controlling of large formations or gaggles required new tactics, already learned the hard way by the Americans.

A number of experiments were undertaken to improve identification and visual order procedures. While Nos 1 and 5 Groups favoured combinations of coloured wingtips, fuselage and tail bands, No 3 Group, who specialised in precision G-H bombing, went one better and introduced such inventive concoctions as streamers and rockets.

'Mick' Smith, a 20-year old rear gunner with No 90 Squadron Tuddenham, has vivid memories of the first trials with rockets, and from the two Lancaster crews involved, he alone survived to tell the tale. His story also illustrates the added dangers of meeting enraged German civilians on being shot down, and lynchings were not uncommon.

As a 17½-year old apprentice with Handley Page Limited at Cricklewood, Mick had his first attempt to volunteer for aircrew turned down on the grounds that he was in the aircraft industry and therefore a reserved occupation. Undeterred, he was informed by his company's General Manager that he would only be released for dishonesty or rudeness (said with a wry smile). Mick immediately chose the latter, was fired on the spot and joined the RAF six months later as soon as he was 18!

On return from captivity he was employed on ground radar duties until demobbed, his briefly held rank of warrant officer by now reduced to sergeant. Believing he was entitled to his old civilian job, he found himself confronted by the very General Manager with whom he had crossed swords before, and was promptly turned down!

So he became a sales representative out in the open air, and steadily progressed to his present position of District Manager with one of the country's largest television rental companies.

'We, Flt Lt B J Aldhous and crew, were detailed to fly on air operations to Wesel, Germany in daylight, 19 February 1945. At briefing we were told the operation had been requested by the Army, who would appreciate the town being flattened.

'The CO (Wg Cdr Peter F Dunham) stated that No 90 Squadron would be leading the stream and he would be leading the Squadron as a new technique in area bombing would be tried out. He then went into details as to how it would work.

'At the rear of his aircraft (Lancaster 1 PD336 "WP-P"), aft of the rear turret, a framework had been built, fitted with two huge Roman candles. We would be bombing on radar and at a precise time the rear gunner would electronically fire one of the candles from inside his turret. This was to notify the stream that we were to formate closer together; no more evasive action was to be taken, or any weaving.

'The second Roman candle would be fired four minutes from the target on the run up, with bomb doors opened at the same time. As he was bombing strictly on radar his bombs would be aimed at the furthest end of the target, and all aircraft would drop their bombs simultaneously. His final words to us were: "So gentlemen, when you see me batting across the sky with yellow flames coming out of my arse end, do not worry." So ended briefing.

'The trip up to the target was uneventful. The first candle was fired, and as we were leading the second box directly behind the CO's Lancaster, I watched the stream creep in towards each other until it was a tight column stretching neatly backwards. I knew the second candle had been fired by the opening of bomb doors. As far back as I could see the flak was heavy and very accurate, but relentlessly we pressed on.

'As the bomb aimer started to say "Bombs gone", I heard and felt one almighty bang and we were bucking through a filthy black stench. My first reaction was that it was us who had been hit and I mentally prepared to bale out, when we came out into clear skies again, not flying too smoothly. "The CO's blown up", said the skipper, "And it's bloody cold up here", when asked what had happened. Flying backwards as I always did, I never witnessed exactly what did happen, but the skipper, flight engineer and bomb aimer confirmed it at de-briefing.

'The CO's candles burned as promised. His bomb doors opened, and as his bombs started to fall we pressed our tit. The flak was very intense and accurate and, as his 4,000lb bomb was just underneath his bomb doors, in free flight, everything just blew up. The whole lot disintegrated into a black cloud and we can only assume the bomb received a direct flak hit.

'It was all over in a matter of seconds; no one had a chance to get out. We just flew through the debris minus a lot of paintwork and perspex.

'We had to go back to Wesel a few days later.

'It was strange that the next time the Roman candles system was used turned out to be my own crew's last trip. I awoke on 9 March 1945, convinced I would not be returning from air operations that day. For the first time during our tour I made my bed, packed all my kit, wrote a letter to my girl friend, ate a hearty breakfast and reported to the briefing room. When I saw the skipper I knew that he also had a premonition, for, with a grin he just said: "This is it Mick."

'At briefing Wg Cdr Scott informed us that once again we would be using the Roman candles, adding that, as this was the final operation of Flt Lt Aldhous's crew, we would have the honour of not only leading the squadron, but the stream. The candles had been fitted to our aircraft, PA254 "WP:A", a new Lanc delivered in February after our old aircraft had been damaged on the Wesel trip.

'Staying behind after briefing, the CO, navigation leader and gunnery leader then gave us very strict instructions on the use of the candles, timing, and the fact that the turret must be locked in the fore and aft position whilst the candles were in process of burning. Then we were introduced to Flg Off J C Paton, an Australian coming along as second navigator before promotion to a navigation leader.

'We then got kitted up, picked up our Mae Wests and parachutes. I always wore a pilot-type 'chute since the time my chest-type 'chute had shot out of its storage place in a severe dive. We then clambered into the crew 'bus and went out to dispersal to view the conglomeration of angle iron, wires and rockets fitted aft of the rear turret, and panel fitted on to the turret control, with red and green buttons wired to each of those darned rockets.

'We took off at 1037 hours and slowly the whole squadron in their various boxes formated on us. We set course to the predetermined assembly point over Southwold, and as the rest of the stream arrived, headed for Germany. We crossed the coast of England at Point Clear south of Clacton-on-Sea, a strange coincidence as two weeks before this I had spent part of my last leave there; again I had that strange feeling.

'As we crossed the Continental coast and on into Germany, hundreds of Lancasters in semi-formation over 10/10ths cloud (about 10,000ft below us) produced a sight never to be forgotten. We were at 21,000ft in glorious sunlight. "Eight minutes to target coming up", said the navigator (Plt Off C. D. Palmer). I locked the turret in fore and aft position. "Press green button, 5-4-3-2-1 – now!", said nav, and on doing so a sheet of yellow flame shot 20-30ft behind us. The rest of the stream crept together, closer and closer and I could see the two Lancasters of our own vic formating about 20ft away slightly behind and either side of us.

'The yellow flame died out and I reported the fact to the skipper and nav. The flak had opened up, moderately heavy but very accurate, as the two navs were talking about how clear reception was on the tube, and how nicely the blips were lining up. "Four minutes to target", said the nav. "5-4-3-2-1 – press red button Mick."

"Bomb doors open skip, keep her straight and level", voiced bomb aimer (Plt Off C. Foy). "Roger", said the skipper, "no talking crew; how's it looking Mick?" I reported that the formation was very close and could see bomb doors open all the way back. I looked right into both Lancasters either side of us and could see their bomb aimers holding their release tits, staring at our bomb bay, ready to discharge as soon as our bombs began to move.

'The yellow flame died out, the flak grew in intensity and seemed to be bursting in bunches of twos or threes. As the navigators started on "Bombs gone", all hell broke loose, and we were shrouded in flak bursts all around us. "We're on fire, I'll dive port", said the skipper, "Away from the stream."

255

Right and below: **Daylight Paint – 1** Nos 57 and 630 Squadrons at East Kirkby, part of 55 Base, used several marking combinations. Illustrated are No 57 Squadron BIII LM624 'DX-A' (Plt Off A. E. 'Nick' Nicklin RNZAF and crew) and 'LE-C' of No 630 Squadron displaying the more commonly used dull red fins and rudders and black bands. Note yellow-outlined code letters, standard in No 5 Group from autumn 1944; also that black band on 'LE-C' does not extend over the rudder – perhaps indicating a replacement yet to be painted. BI LM216 'LE-K' (Sqn Ldr Roy E. Millichap and crew) in foreground bears her nose identity letter in a square, common to No 630 Squadron kites at the time. Evidently there was an interchange of bomb trolleys. (LM216 was struck off charge at Lindholme March 1946; LM624 failed to return from Gravenhorst 6/7 November 1944.) /F. Foster; W. L. Goodwin

'They were the last words I ever heard from any of my crew, as with more great explosions we were again in the middle of flak. I felt severe, hot pain in my legs and bottom. Looking port and starboard all I could see was great sheets of flame shooting backwards. I unlocked the turret but had no hydraulics, no intercom or electrics. Rotating the turret by hand to full port beam I leaned out over my controls as far as possible but could only see flames shooting back from the port wing.

'I tried both my intercom and communication light again. They were completely dead, so I peered through the side of the turret, but could not see further than the Elsan because of the smoke and flames in the fuselage. This confirmed what I had heard: the Lancaster burned well. The feeling came back to my legs and bottom and the pain started again. But I felt no panic or fear, only the feeling of well-being, and looking down between my legs was surprised to find the turret full of holes. My oxygen tube was slashed through and I

256

realised why I felt so stupid and drunk – lack of oxygen!

'I took off my helmet, opened the turret doors and pulled myself upright; then stood balanced on the rim, glad that I had always worn a pilot-type 'chute as I would never have made it to the storage place of the chest-type 'chute. Looking forward I could see the two starboard propellers slowly rotating, with flames steadily coming out of the manifold covers, the two port engines a mass of flames, and the fuselage just aft of the entrance door melting away.

'The Lanc was diving and turning to port and I could see the stream up above. Another Lancaster was following us down, all the crew staring, so I just waved at them and let go. Counting to 10, I pulled the rip cord and with a comforting jerk stopped falling, to hear the whoosh, whoosh of falling bombs. Looking up I saw not only the tail end of the stream flying above me, but also heard their bombs plunging earthwards. It was then I realised that these events, which seemed to have taken hours, had in fact happened in a few moments.

'The canopy of my parachute was full of holes, pitted like a colander. I looked around me but could see no other 'chutes in the sky and felt very lonely. All I could see was the trail of smoke going down where our Lancaster had passed, and the black column of smoke coming up where I hoped the target, Datteln, had been. Passing through cloud I started to oscillate and swing from side to side. A cock crowed as I came out of the cloud and there stretched below me was a fair-sized town. In the distance a huge black column rose up to the clouds.

'As I neared the ground I could see the remains of a railway siding, a crowd of people rushing towards my expected landing place, and the two great black exits of factory chimneys directly beneath me. I'll never know how I missed these, but did notice I only had one flying boot on, and that my left foot was a peculiar red colour.

'With a thump I arrived in Germany. A crowd of men, women and children were running towards me, armed with shovels, broomsticks and lengths of timber. Then I saw German authority at its very best as over the rubble came one solitary man in uniform, pistol drawn, and shouting at the hostile crowd. He informed me in perfect English: "You are my prisoner." I did not argue, and was urged to pick up my parachute, whereupon I discovered, embedded into the thick sorbo cushion, five pieces of flak which had come through the canopy pack. That parachute saved my life twice for, if I had not been sitting on it I would have been the opposite of decapitated.

'So, with the occasional kick and thump from the crowd I was marched into captivity. It was obvious to me as I descended into Germany, and saw the welcoming committee assembling, that the Air Force motto of trying to evade the enemy and get back home was going to be difficult. I was marched, harassed, spat at, cursed and shouted at, in a language I'd never heard before, guarded by one "proud as a peacock" German policeman, who was having his day until we reached the local police station.

Above: **Daylight Paint – 2**
No 1 Group extended high visibility markings to wingtips and, on occasions, fuselages. Here we see No 166 Squadron's BIII ME499 'AS-D' (Flt Lt Doug E. Batten and crew) airborne from Kirmington sporting yellow wingtips, fins and rudders spring 1945. It was all very experimental, apparently devised at Base/Group level and no two aircraft seemed to be the same. Some machines had only their outer fin and rudder surfaces painted; others had complete tailplanes daubed. No 166 Squadron formed part of 13 Base, with No 103 Squadron at Elsham Wolds using blue, No 550 Squadron at North Killingholme (one of whose Lancs is pictured (*above*) bearing a fuselage band) using white. The paint was a form of distemper and easily rubbed off. /*D. Batten; IWM*

'This I discovered was on the outskirts of Dortmund. I was placed in a kind of rest room for tired policemen, as they kept tramping in and out. After about two hours an officer type came in and started interrogating me, first informing me that all my crew were dead. I refused to answer any questions until my wounds had been seen to, but was left alone for another two or three hours, before being dragged out, put in the back of a horse-drawn cart and packed off to the local hospital. My wounds were wrapped up in paper bandages and I was taken back to the police station.

'This time I was put in a 10ft by 10ft cell without a bed, already occupied by nine RAF and one American aircrew. My arrival was not really appreciated. After three days in this cramped style of living the 11 of us were paraded and surrounded by 20 or so elderly World War I soldiers, and we set off for Dulag Luft. This took about three days of shunting backwards and forwards, often marching when no trains were available. We eventually arrived in the middle of a great air raid on Frankfurt.

'At Dulag Luft I spent four days solitary in a 6ft by 4ft cell with one bed and chair, a very good "central heating" system, and a window high up in the wall. Three times I was interrogated, the first time by a smooth-talking officer who knew all about the squadron and its history, but just wanted the latest gen. He was very free with his Players, even leaving them on the desk when he left the room, yet took the three back I'd slipped in my pocket with a "naughty boy" expression.

'What really shook me was that he knew all about the new CO, who had only been with us for a couple of weeks. Two hours later I was interrogated by a medical man, who told me I was sure to die because of my wounds, so would I fill in his Red Cross form! I told him I'd rather die anonymously so the following day it was back to the posh office, but a different officer. This fellow had long legs which could shoot out under the desk my side, but no Players. He insisted I'd been flying in an aircraft called a Lincoln. I'd never heard of this aircraft, so he said he would prove it by showing me a lot of photographs. I could not stop laughing at this idiot so back to the cell I went.

'On the fourth day I was pulled out of my cell, and together with a party of about 20 RAF and 10 Americans, was surrounded by some 50 elderly German guards, and marched away to the local station to entrain for Wetzlor. We boarded at about 06.00 hours and eventually, after much huffing and puffing, the engine got up steam and we pulled out of the station. After only 200yds of efficient movement the engine gave up the ghost and we were left standing.

'Presently we heard the sound of aircraft engines and saw circling above, three Mustangs. One of our party, who must have been good at aircraft recognition, said, "It's OK, they're ours", and started to resume his sleep. At the same time the Mustangs came into attack and strafed the station. Out went the guards, out went the prisoners, who hotly pursued the former across the track, picking up their discarded rifles.

'I dived into a coal bunker built up with railway sleepers, hotly pursued by one Yank and a pompous German officer. We crouched down as time and again those Mustangs came in strafing the area. I saw the puffs of dirt and dust as the line of cannon shells and bullets shot along and through our bunker, saw the opposite wall disintegrate into splinters and a nine-inch sliver of wood slice into the little German's thigh. The Yank and I willingly offered to pull it out, but one look at our eyes was enough for pompous fatty, who, with a yell of "Nein, nein", crawled away.

'The Mustangs departed and all was quiet again, except for the screams of the wounded. The guards decided it would be best if we got out of the area and began walking. We did not disagree, and so a depleted party set off, minus one German officer and three guards (two dead and one injured), three RAF and one Yank unfortunately killed in the attack, besides one Canadian who was last seen going like a bat out of hell as fast as his legs would carry him up the lines westerly.

'So, for us the war was over, mercifully with only a short period of imprisonment, slightly battered and dented, but still able to breathe.

'I always wondered why my skipper was buried at Venray, Holland, and the rest of the crew in the Reichwald Forest. It was not until 1973 that I got the solution. When the Germans captured me they had only six more to find to make up the usual crew of a Lancaster. Scattered around the rear end of the Lanc, which had broken up in midair, they found six bodies with partly opened parachutes, so assumed they had the whole crew, not knowing about Flg Off Paton.

'The nose of the aircraft had crashed on Waltrop railway station, so the six bodies were buried in Waltrop cemetery, and moved to Reichwald Forest war graves plot later. Meanwhile, when the Americans advanced through Waltrop, two GIs inspecting the nose section of the Lancaster on the station, came across the body of the skipper still in his seat. His remains were taken to Worgrattin or Margratten in the Netherlands, to be re-interred at Venray.

'So by a quirk of fate Flg Off Paton died with my crew and inadvertently stopped the skipper being buried with his boys.'

Second Dickey

WALTER THOMPSON

Though often a costly exercise, the practice of sending a freshly trained pilot on his first operation with a seasoned crew was, in the main, an unqualified success.

A 'second dickey' outing was, in many ways, a frustrating affair for all concerned. No crew liked an extra man aboard, disrupting their close-knit harmony; added to which there was so little room in the cockpit, and he would be forced to man the front turret or stand for the whole trip, making life particularly difficult for the engineer.

There was little he could do but look and observe, though captains would usually allow him to take over while they used the Elsan, or perhaps when stretching their legs on nearing the English coast on the return leg.

Meanwhile, the sprog pilot's own crew would spend several uneasy hours awaiting his return, eager to learn about the 'shooting war'. If his aircraft failed to return the dejected, headless crew would depart for a conversion unit, pick up a spare pilot, and repeat the process. At one time navigators also did 'second dickey' trips, but so many were lost the exercise was abandoned.

Here, Canadian Walter Thompson describes his own maiden operational flight, with no lesser person than his squadron commander, the later legendary Guy Gibson, and provides a fascinating insight to Gibson the man.

Born in New Westminster, British Columbia, Walter Thompson was a student in civil engineering at Washington State College, USA when World War II commenced.

Five years later, in July 1944, he went home as a flight lieutenant with two DFCs, to find an inflexible official Canadian ruling which did not 'encourage' its returning sons to continue operations for fear of bad publicity in the event of them being killed.

Totally disillusioned, Walter resigned his commission in January 1945 and returned to England. The ensuing months saw him undertake numerous odd jobs, including washing dishes in a holiday resort hotel, stunt work in the movies, and a spell on a farm.

Then, in September 1945 he enrolled at Cambridge in the Moral Science Tripos, there

to receive his Master of Arts degree (he had earlier spent a few weeks at Oxford but did not settle) before completing his studies at the University of British Columbia with his Bachelor of Laws degree.

He is currently a partner in a New Westminster firm of barristers and solicitors.

'On the 11th day of March 1943 Flg Off Walter R. "Punch" Thompson, J10506 RCAF, 22 years of age and freshly converted to Lancasters, arrived at RAF Station Syerston, Notts. I remember the young man with amusement and affection. He was me!

'Kit bags in hand, I lumbered into the mess in the mid-afternoon of an overcast day. There were but two officers in the mass. The wing commander with the DSO, DFC and Bar must, I thought, be CO of No 106 Squadron. The other, the flight lieutenant, must be his adjutant. He seemed the friendliest wing commander I ever met. In retrospect he was probably the only friendly wing commander I ever met. Not a tall man, but firmly and squarely made, his smile lit up the day.

' "You must be Thompson", he said, walking across the room and extending a strong hand. Before I could acknowledge he said: "My name is Gibson, will you have a drink?" "Thank you sir, a half of bitter would be fine." The barman drew a glass as Gibson turned to the adjutant and I heard him say: "Maybe he'll be another Joe McCarthy." I had of course heard of McCarthy. He was an American from New York. They once had to pry him from a Hampden with a winch! I forgave Gibson for blurring the distinction between Canadians and Americans. He said: "You're just in time, you'll be flying tonight." I hoped he hadn't seen me gulp as I asked: "With my own crew, sir?"

' "No, you'll be coming with me, so get yourself settled in and I'll see you at briefing." I had only a sip of the beer.

'The target that night turned out to be Stuttgart. Gibson introduced me, in the Nissen hut which served as Intelligence office and briefing room, to Scrivener his navigator and, strangely I thought, to a naval officer who was to be our bomb aimer. I also met for the first time the overgrown menace that was Gibson's dog. He was a huge, black mutt with a white chest and appeared part Labrador and part Great Dane. He was reputed to deflate bicycle tires with one bite and I was warned by one of the gunners to treat him with respect.

'It occurred to me at briefing that, notwithstanding the expensive training which His Majesty had lavished on me, no one had told me, or anyone else as far as I knew, the duties of a second pilot. I knew that they'd have very little to do with the success of the operation because there was but one set of controls in the Lanc, and when I enquired what those duties were, Gibson too seemed a little puzzled. Fishing in a brief case however, he soon found a form called a fuel log. "Here, you keep this", he said. It seemed to me he'd written that job description on the spur of the moment. He went on: "You keep a log of fuel consumption. Take readings from the gauges and write them down every half hour. And change the fuel tanks when I ask you to." I put the form in the pocket of my battle dress.

'We took off and climbed "X-RAY" (ED649) into the night without event. The visibility was good above the clouds and I felt secure in the company of experts as we approached the French coast. For a few moments we witnessed a phenomenon which was new to me. Twinkling little lights were appearing some distance ahead on the starboard bow.

Left: **Hero Figure** A rare study of Wg Cdr Guy Gibson wearing an 'operational' moustache when commanding No 106 Squadron Coningsby. The picture, taken by his rear gunner, Plt Off Johnny Wickins, was posed by Lanc R5551 'ZN-V' following a rough trip to Saarbrucken 1/2 September 1942. This was the first time an 8,000lb bomb had been carried successfully by a Lancaster. For their pains the crew, bombing at a mere 8,000ft collected a number of flak holes. (R5551 failed to return from Oberhausen 14/15 June 1943.)/*J. F. Wickins*

Below: **Marking Time** The briefing and meal over, the crews – each man with his own thoughts – line up outside the locker rooms to await transport to take them out to the dispersals. No 106 Squadron Syerston winter 1942/3, with the CO, Wg Cdr Guy Gibson, clad in Irving jacket, standing back to camera, hands on hips in characteristic manner. /*J. F. Wickins*

Left: **Fires of Hell** '... It appeared a lively, well-lit but smoky place to this neophyte and I was intrigued at the sight of my first target ...' Actually a still from a film taken over Essen in 1943 at the height of the Battle of the Ruhr, showing a Lancaster and falling bombs clearly silhouetted above a bizarre pattern of fires and billowing smoke clouds.
/*British Official via H. Vikholt*

Below: **Farewell** The CO, Wg Cdr Guy Gibson, poses with some of his No 106 Squadron boys at Syerston before departing to form the special unit which was to earn undying fame as No 617 Squadron, the Dam Busters. The signature was added as a result of a special request by Thompson's mother (unbeknown to her son in England) when Gibson was in Canada following the Dam Raids. Among those present in this historic picture are: adjutant Flt Lt Martin (on Gibson's immediate left); his two flight commanders, Sqn Ldrs Peter Ward-Hunt (on Martin's immediate left) and John Searby (on Gibson's immediate right). Walter Thompson is in the back row, behind the naval officer's left shoulder), while the dog is Dinny (not Nigger as might be expected), whose master, Flt Lt Eric Hayward, stands next to Searby. The Lancaster is BIII ED593 'ZN-Y' *Admiral Prune II*, which was finally pensioned off after at least 72 ops, and survived the war as a ground instruction airframe./*W. R. Thompson*

261

'I wondered what they were. Gibson, sensing my naiveté, said: "Flak – probably Cherbourg." How could anything so deadly look so pretty, I wondered? It was like Halloween in Canada. A few moments later we crossed the enemy coast and I saw one of those twinkles at closer range. It hit our starboard-outer engine with a thump.

'My immediate reaction as Gibson throttled the engine back was: "Well, I suppose we'll be heading for home now. It does seem a pity but c'est la guerre." But he didn't feather the engine and, to my surprise, said to the bomb aimer: "We'll probably have to attack from below 15,000ft bomb aimer. Any problems?" "No problem, sir", was the Royal Navy's answer.

"Well, let's have a course, Scriv". The good visibility we had enjoyed changed abruptly as we lost altitude. I didn't have to ask Gibson, I knew that if we were going to be isolated we should seek cloud cover – even though it was pitch black outside.

'This we did, gradually dropping to 12,000ft as, after some time, we passed over Lake Constance in Switzerland. The Swiss let off a few rounds just to show us that they were there but made no effort to hit us, so far as I could see. We soon entered upon the bomb run over Stuttgart. It appeared a lively, well-lit but smoky place to this neophyte and I was intrigued at the sight of my first target. Vastly different from the old bombing range I thought. Although we'd lost altitude we had managed to keep our speed. I could see Gibson applying left rudder as the starboard-outer was now virtually useless. The Navy, after some chit-chat, got the bombs away nicely. Or as I put it to myself, "It's nice that he got the bombs away." Then, as I examined for the first time what I was told were target indicators, we were hit again. This time it was the starboard-inner. And a good blow it received because Gibson asked me to feather the propeller. This I quickly did. By now I was convinced that if this sort of thing happened every time out I should have tried very much harder to be a night fighter pilot.

'With our load diminished by loss of the bombs we seemed to be making reasonable speed, though with only two engines on the return journey. Gibson, even with full rudder trim, was working very hard with left rudder to keep a straight course. He leaned over and said: "Thompson, how much fuel do we have?" I looked at the gauges and blurted out: "600 gallons, sir." "Hm", he said, "barely enough to make the Channel. Are you sure? What does your log show?"

'I was appalled. How could I tell him? "I put the log in my pocket with a chocolate bar sir. I can't read it, it's got chocolate all over it." I thought: "My God, if we go down in the Channel it's all my fault. And if we don't I'll probably be shot." I could hardly bring myself to look at him but when I did I could see the twinkle in his near eye. I quickly read the fuel gauges again. I'd only told him the quantity of the tanks on one side – 600 gallons. That was the starboard side which had been consuming the least. Gibson had seen my mistake before I had. I thought to myself: "Really, I'm not this incompetent, I won't do these stupid things when I am flying with my own crew." With a few hair raising exceptions it later turned out that I was right.

'Gibson by this time was having leg strain from holding on rudder with his left leg. He asked me to fly "X-RAY" for a while. This I did as we changed seats and I bent my good left leg to the task of keeping her straight with rudder. We hared back over France at low level. Light was beginning to show in the east.

'Gibson took control again over the Channel and we soon came in for the landing at Syerston. I noted somewhat smugly that even the squadron commander did not invariably land his aircraft like a feather. In fact our landing was more in the nature of a controlled crash. Gibson's grin was sheepish as he taxied to the dispersal area. His faithful black hound was there waiting impatiently for him to deplane. Intelligence officers were waiting for the rest of us to interrogate.

'The next day we had a No 106 Squadron photo taken and shortly thereafter Gibson let it be known that he had been asked to form a "special duties" squadron, the details of which were still secret. I understand that the Bar to his DSO was awarded to him for the Stuttgart trip, among others.

'I of course asked him if I could join his new squadron and the answer was that I hadn't acquired enough experience. I knew he was right but I was disappointed. Much to the chagrin of my crew I then volunteered all of us for Pathfinders. We stayed with No 106 Squadron for about 13 operations, during which time we managed to get to and hit the target a few times – twice in spite of the Pathfinders rather than because of them. Eventually therefore, our offer to point out the target to uncertain but disbelieving crews was accepted by the Group Commander and we were sent to No 5 Group's Pathfinder participant, No 83 Squadron, based at Wyton, Hunts.

'We had almost completed our first tour of operations at Wyton when we heard the great news of Gibson's "Dam Busters" having breached the Möhne and Eder dams, and heard also with delight that he had been awarded the Victoria Cross. Perhaps Gibson had been right, I thought, in selecting pilots for his squadron who could read fuel gauges!'

Homeward Bound

Below: **Home and Away** With North African bases secure by the summer of 1943 it was possible to arrange occasional 'shuttle' raids. Here we see No 617 Squadron Lancs churning up the dust at Blida 24 July 1943, bound for Leghorn before landing back in the UK. They had taken off from Scampton as a force of 18 crews to immobilise the San Pola d'Enza, Arquata Scrivia, Reggio Emilla and Bologna electricity plants in Northern Italy on the night of 15/16 July before landing at Blida. They were joined in the baking North African sunshine by fellow No 5 Group crews, who had hit the transformer station at Cislago on 16/17 July, and the combined force of 33 crews all bombed Leghorn on the night of 24/25 July on their way home. No crews were lost on any of the sorties. *W. Howarth*

Bottom: **Good Turn** Nearing the English coastline, the crew of this No 90 Squadron Lanc from Tuddenham, keeping station with another of the breed, heads south over the North Sea at low level on a fine autumn evening in 1944. They are probably enjoying a welcome flask of coffee and cigarette to ease the tension of the past few hours. They will nonetheless be watchful and alert, ever mindful of the dangers of a surprise attack from marauding fighters, despite general Allied air superiority by this time. The baking sun would make the inside of the Lanc unbearably hot, forcing the crews to wear a minimum of clothing./*A. T. Coles*

Above: **Two's Company**
Snapped from another Lanc is
BI PA264 'P4-O' from No 153
Squadron Scampton droning
along in clear skies heading for
home. A near-new machine with
red trestle markings clearly
visible, her engine cowlings and
underwing surfaces are already
liberally discoloured with
exhaust stains./K. C. Gooch

Left: **Racing for Home** With
all the taps wide open, a No
622 Squadron G-H leader roars
low over the flat Suffolk
landscape heading for
Mildenhall, the race on to see
who will be first back.
/E. D. Williams

Some Returned

Right: **Under Cover** Near Ringsted, Denmark, locally based Germans sift through the remains of BIII PA988 'LQ-P' from 8 Group's No 405 ('Vancouver') Squadron RCAF, Gransden Lodge, unaware the onlooking hunter is in fact a member of the Danish Underground movement. On the return leg from Stettin 16/17 August 1944, Plt Off 'Bud' Walter and his all-Canadian crew were caught by a night fighter which hit the port-inner engine and set fire to the wing petrol tanks. All except the mid-upper gunner (killed by the fighter) baled out successfully and no less than four (pilot, nav 1, w/op and rear gunner) evaded capture. Though only the crew's fourth trip with No 405, they had completed seven ops with No 428 ('Ghost') Squadron RCAF flying Halifaxes in No 4 Group before graduating to PFF./*J. L. Umscheid*

Far left: **Home in Style** The Kiwis of No 75 Squadron arrive over Mepal in immaculate formation following another successful daylight operation – Le Havre 11 September 1944 – and . . .

Left: **Peel Off** One by one in a left hand circuit for a stream landing the Lancasters peel off. The close proximity of neighbouring Witchford and Wratting Common forced strict obeyance of circuit procedure – something common to virtually all bases in 'Bomber Country'. /*Both S. H. Richmond*

Right: **Double Take** Typical scenes showing No 49 Squadron Lancs landing at Fiskerton 1943/4, one devoid of the usual small gathering by the Control caravan and probably a crew's return from a cross-country exercise. The mobile caravan is painted in the standard red and white chequerboard finish and is complete with windsock mast. In the second view can be seen the Chance light, mounted on its own mobile stand, the black-painted corrugated steel construction Type T2 hangars, and adjacent buildings. Keen eyes will also detect the presence of a Lancaster or Manchester fuselage (still bearing the code 'TV' of 1660 HCU) used for crew crash/ditching drills./*Both D. T. Weston*

Left: **Fortune was Kind** The wreck of BI HK767 'XY-A' following an eventful trip to Merseburg 4/5 April 1945. Hit by flak on the run-in, Flt Lt Eddie Field and his No 186 Squadron crew lost the port-outer and suffered damage to the port aileron. Pressing on, pulses again ran high when, soon after dropping their bombs they almost collided with another, unidentified aircraft. The remainder of the home flight was uneventful until turning onto the final approach at Stradishall. Before aligning with the runway, the port-inner suddenly cut, causing the Lanc to yaw viciously to port. Opening up the starboard engines to try and maintain height and speed had no effect, and with the port aileron useless a turn to starboard by use of rudder only, and so line up with the runway, was not possible. The skipper took overshoot action but was unable to maintain height and heading, and they crash-landed heavily in a field adjoining the airfield. Amazingly, the only serious injuries were a broken arm for Jack Enwright the engineer and a broken leg for rear gunner Chick Turner. It was the crew's 32nd completed trip and, with the end of the war in sight, they were tour-expired. Eddie Field collected an immediate bar to his DFC; navigator Peter Upson a DFC. /*P. A. Upson*

Bottom left: **Unlucky for Some** Adding to the mounting pressures on a crew during their tour was the stress imposed by continual 'scrubbed' operations. This reached its peak in the months following D-Day and we illustrate here a typical casualty of the period: BIII PB761 'AA-Y' from No 75 (New Zealand) Squadron Mepal, wrecked at Wood Ditton near Newmarket on return from Wanne Eickel 16/17 January 1945. The crash occurred 21 hours after Flt Lt T. D. Blewett RNZAF and crew were originally alerted for operations, including three separate briefings. The mental and physical strain, coupled with a lack of night flying experience proved too much. /*I. H. Nicolson*

Jamie

ANON

Away from the aura of glamour and nostalgia surrounding Bomber Command lie countless stories of tragedy and grief. Death in the skies did not always come quickly and men often died horribly, burned to death in flaming coffins or torn apart by cannon and machine gun fire.

We present here without apology one such horror story, written by a former air gunner stricken with terminal cancer and sentenced to die, aged but 53. His wife Margaret had written begging us to visit her now bedridden husband. It was an unforgettable meeting for he was a pathetic sight, no longer able to speak, his eyes sunken and haunting, his once stocky frame no more than seven stone.

His dying wish was for the world to share his burden, to understand, and to spare a thought now and then for his kind who gave their all.

Anonymity does not detract from a very moving story for names and squadrons, dates and targets do not really matter.

'For 34 years I had dreamt of this wild hillside, vowed to come back and pay homage to Jamie. For all those years this quiet and peaceful corner of France had been a place of the spirit, the horrors of that hot, clammy night in 1943 still haunting me.

'I looked about me trying desperately to orientate myself. All those years ago there had been no time for sightseeing: we were at war. Where had I buried Jamie? Somewhere in these overgrown gorse bushes and ferns, beneath a majestic fir was an unknown tomb to as gallant a lad as these isles ever gave birth.

'Late afternoon when Margaret left me alone to climb this hill and search for Jamie, it was now almost sunset and still the little wooden cross would not show itself. Another hour and it would be too dark to continue and I did so want to complete my pilgrimage on the actual anniversary. Cumbersome crutches biting into my arm pits did not help, more so on uneven ground. Time and time again I fell heavily into the prickly bushes, yet somehow found the strength to struggle to my feet. One call would bring Margaret

running to my side, but this was something I had to do myself.

'Suddenly, there it was. Turning a bend on the far side of the hill there stood facing me the very misshapen fir on which I had carved a small arrow to indicate the burial site. Through sheer exertion my heart was already pounding, but now, so near to journey's end, it felt as if it would burst. With sweat oozing from me I staggered forward and fell again, the wind knocked from me, only to see, not two yards from my face a little weathered cross.

'There I sat, alone with my thoughts on this hallowed ground, not a sound of life about me. The memories flooded back, the tears flowed. Jamie's broken body had long been at rest but never would I forget those piercing screams as he lay crumpled before me, begging me to end his life.

'We had been mauled by a Ju88 which none of us saw. Despite our constant weaving he had come from a particularly black patch of sky, cannons blazing, the first evidence of danger when the kite shook violently, accompanied by tremendous thumps. Almost immediately Jamie yelled "corkscrew starboard go" and the skipper threw the Lanc into a vicious bank, down into the black void. The noise was ear-shattering and it seemed an age before the screaming engines resumed a normal tone.

'The R/T was dead and obviously we were in bad shape. Jamie (if he was still alive) and I were completely cut off from the boys up front, yet dare not leave our turrets. Acrid smoke began to drift down the fuselage, followed by the blackened figure of the w/op, torch in hand. He passed a pencilled note to me which told of the skipper, engineer and bomb aimer being killed on the fighter's first pass. The navigator was flying the Lanc as best he could.

'Speech was impossible due to the wind howling through the shattered nose and cockpit area. The nav's maps and instruments had been sucked out and petrol was pouring from a ruptured tank. The nav had his hands full but luckily for us our skipper had insisted he learn to fly straight and level, so we had a fighting chance of making it back home – or had we?

'The w/op came back from the rear turret and by signs made it clear that Jamie was in trouble. My heart sank. Evidently the fighter's shells had raked us from stem to stern, opening up the fuselage like a can opener, yet, ironically, unbelievably, missing my own and the w/op's stations.

'Crouched there in the darkness, the w/op scribbled another note. It said that Jamie's right leg had been severed just below the knee, and he was covered in burning oil and in terrible pain. Despite using the axe the turret could not be un-jammed.

'There was nothing for it, I would have to leave my turret and chance not having another fighter attack. The Lanc, already lurching and wallowing, seemed to stop dead in her tracks. The w/op and I ended up in a heap with a

Above: **Death Trap** Ringed numbers indicate telling hits registered by a fighter on No 57 Squadron BI NN701 'DX-K' during a night attack on Stuttgart 28/29 July 1944. With two of his turrets out of action, and rear gunner Sgt L. West dying, skipper Flg Off D. M. Watt elected to press on, and ultimately made a forced landing at Woodbridge before returning to East Kirkby and a resulting immediate award of the DFC. Sadly for poor West there was no tomorrow, but his crew, and aircraft, survived the war./*N. Westby*

Left: **The Spirit of Bomber Command** Here symbolised in this intimate study of two No 9 Squadron air gunners enjoying a joke while awaiting the crew 'bus. Canadian, Sgt Jack Dickinson would return to his homeland: Sgt 'Darky' Gilkes from Trinidad would make the ultimate sacrifice. A picture taken at Bardney prior to one of the Hamburg fire raids mounted during the last week of July 1943 and ending 2/3 August./*W. Woollard*

Right and below: **Raw Deal** Ground crew demonstrate the damage done to No 619 Squadron's BI PA180 'PG-G' on a 7½-hour gardening stooge to Stettin Bay on the night of 8/9 February 1945, killing the rear gunner Sgt V. Pascoe in addition to wounding mid-upper Sgt J. Cracknell and w/op Flt Sgt A. Horne. An attack could come at any time and no crew could ever relax. This was the 30th completed operation for Flg Off 'Dicky' Dickinson and crew's previously trouble-free tour and they finally left Strubby with a total of 35 to their credit. (PA180 passed to No 9 Squadron in July 1945 and was scrapped at 38 MU in May 1947.).
/*Both R. Dickinson*

Bottom left: **Three Came Home** Flt Lt H. M. Johnston of No 635 Squadron, together with his rear gunner Flt Sgt J. K. Ledgerwood (here on pilot's right) and w/op Plt Off R. T. Padden, pose at the rear of BIII ND965 'F2-K' on return to Downham Market following their eventful trip to Nantes 11/12 June 1944. Acting as Deputy Master Bomber, he was called down to 3,500ft to help mark the target. On breaking cloud he was soon coned by searchlights and hit by flak, a direct burst setting fire to the rear turret oil reservoir, spreading burning oil the length of the fuselage. The explosion forced the Lanc into a dive and Johnston applied maximum trim in order to recover, though fire had burned control wires so that he could not keep her straight. With the intercom u/s the order to 'abandon aircraft' was passed verbally. By the time the bomb aimer, mid-upper and flight engineer had baled out he had throttled back and selected 30° of flap to bring the aircraft to a level attitude, with an IAS of 90mph. Using both feet and arms he could barely hold the stricken Lanc horizontal while the crew jumped, and was about to follow them when Ledgerwood appeared holding the quick release buckle – all that was left of his parachute. The rear gunner just stopped the w/op before he jumped and together they went aft to put out the fire. By now the rear turret had fallen off, which had the effect of creating a vortex inside the fuselage, making it extremely difficult to extinguish the fire. Eventually the gutted kite was brought home to Warmwell on the south coast. All three received immediate awards: the skipper a DSO; the r/g a DFM; the w/op a DFC. ND965 was repaired and put back into service (with 1660 HCU), to survive the war./*R. Nash*

tremendous jolt, knocking the wind out of us for a minute or two. We staggered to our feet, still unable to talk in the howling gale.

'We hacked and tugged at the turret doors, seeming to find Herculean strength in this aerial madhouse, quite oblivious to what was happening up front. Perhaps the nav had abandoned the kite believing us all dead in the rear? However the old girl was still in the air so there was a chance.

'After what seemed an eternity we wrenched off the doors and dragged Jamie out. In the glow of the torch the full horror hit me. Where his leg should have been there was a jagged, blood-soaked stump. His bright yellow Taylor suit was almost burned off him as a result of burning oil, and his face was twisted in pain. Clearly he was in agony and needed immediate attention. I administered morphine where he lay, while the w/op went forward to tell the nav.

'Reluctantly I climbed back into my turret and again began scanning the sky. Nothing was to be seen and it was impossible to determine height or position. We were alone, lost and virtually defenceless.

'A tug at my legs told me the w/op had returned. Again by a note he informed me that two motors had packed up, we were losing height rapidly and would have to throw overboard as much equipment as possible. The nav estimated we were down to 3,000ft and would try to put the Lanc down at the first opportunity.

'The w/op and I worked like beavers throwing out guns and ammunition, oxygen bottles and parachutes. We even hacked out the Elsan and ammo racks, each of us taking it in turns to wield the axe, while the other did the heaving. Soon our gloves were in tatters, our fingers torn and bleeding.

'Suddenly – oblivion. Surely I must be dead? Slowly, realising I was still alive, I became aware of intense heat and a loud crackling about me. Feeling myself all over, no bones seemed to be broken, though I ached from countless cuts and bruises.

'Tottering to my feet an appalling scene surrounded me. Countless burning fragments of wreckage signified the end of our dear old Lancaster. Evidently we had flown into a wooded hill and the kite had broken into a dozen pieces. Apart from the crackling of the flames and exploding bullets, all seemed silent to my dulled brain, yet, could I not hear a human voice in pain? I listened, and sure enough, faintly heard the cry again.

'Searching through the burning wreckage, stumbling rather than walking, produced five charred bodies of the boys and a shudder of despair passed through me. Identification was impossible other than by their tags. Half an hour later I stumbled across the inert body of Jamie, face down in some ferns among pine trees. He was a pitiful sight with his clothing almost completely burned from his back, and with one remaining leg. There was I with but scratches, cuts and bruises, yet five of my crew were dead and dear Jamie surely dying.

'Jamie was drifting in and out of consciousness and I felt helpless. What could I do? Dare I turn him over? Sitting there, my tired brain desperately recalling basic first aid lectures, Jamie came round and began alternately moaning and screaming with pain, begging me to end his life.

'There seemed no other way, yet I was no butcher. How could I kill in cold blood? Further cries of agony stirred me into action, looking for something with which to end Jamie's life. Frantic searching produced only a large stone so, with some hesitation, I crept up behind him, prayed to the Almighty, and brought the stone down on the back of his head, two-handed with all the force I could muster. There was a sickening thud and I knew it was all over. Then I slumped down by Jamie's side and retched until exhausted.

'The sound of high revving engines brought me to my senses. Soldiers, looking for the crew had spotted the burning remains of our kite and were now approaching. By the light of torches could be seen a number of soldiers walking through the undergrowth at the base of the hill. Surely they must find me? Luckily they did not have any dogs and never searched beyond the main group of wreckage. They seemed satisfied finding the five bodies and after about half an hour returned to their trucks.

'As they disappeared into the night I set about digging a shallow grave with bare hands, an exhausting task which must have taken me at least an hour. The first grey patches of dawn were already showing as I marked the site with a hand-cut wooden cross and said goodbye to a dear friend.

'Looking back I realise I should have removed his tags and ultimately reported the details of this ghastly night, but Jamie was an orphan and unknown to the outside world. It seemed appropriate to share his passing with no one.

'The next few hours are a blur for I recall little of my subsequent tramp through the French countryside, mostly soaked to the skin as the heavens opened. When captured I had a stinking cold and was hurriedly transported to a POW camp in Poland via Dulag luft at Frankfurt. Being a lowly NCO the Germans did not seem to be interested in me – maybe because of my cold.

'The war ended, I returned to Blighty and kept my secret. Jamie was, and still is, listed as "missing presumed killed" and I shall take his identity to the grave.'

Black Thursday

JOE NORTHROP

Facing fog, icing and thunderstorms, crews often wondered who their real enemy was. Whether battling their way through towering cumulo-nimbus clouds, invisible barriers of black ice, or swirling banks of fog, they cheerfully took all in their stride. However, periodically, even *their* mantle of youth and confidence could not hide a temporary drop in morale.

Such an occasion followed the night of 16/17 December 1943, forever labelled 'Black Thursday' by those who survived. As events turned out the fact that Berlin was again the target proved to be of secondary importance. Treacherous ground fog greeted their return and the resultant toll in crashes as tired crews attempted to land or abandoned their aircraft, exceeded by five the 25 lost over enemy territory.

The PFF squadrons based in the low-lying counties of Cambridge, Huntingdon and Bedford were particularly hard-hit; No 97 (Straits Settlements) Squadron based at Bourn alone lost five Lancs and crews, while the Canadians of No 405 ('Vancouver') Squadron at Gransden Lodge lost two.

Then a seasoned 31-year old, Joe Northrop needed all his skill and experience, aided by a well-drilled crew, to survive, and remembers the event as though it were yesterday.

Now a retired wing commander, Joe began his RAF career as a Halton 'Brat' in 1929. A tour of flying on radio-countermeasures against the German beam systems with 1473 Flight / No 109 Squadron, culminating in special bombing operations against the 'pocket' battleships in Brest, flying Stirlings of Nos 7 and 15 Squadrons, preceded his spell with No 83 Squadron; then, in July 1944 came a posting to command No 692 Squadron flying PFF Mosquitoes, with whom he collected a DSO to add to the DFC and AFC won earlier.

When Head of Commander-in-Chief RAF Germany Joint Secretariat, 31 years of continuous service ended in November 1959. A new life as a civilian began with five years in industrial security, followed by 13 as a Higher Scientific Officer with the Road Research Laboratory before retiring for the second time in November 1977.

Now an energetic 66, Joe wonders how he ever found the time to work!

'The night of 16/17 December 1943 is still referred to 35 years afterwards as "Black Thursday". It was the occasion when the weather blanketed the airfields in the British Isles with fog earlier than was expected and created havoc amongst the returning bomber crews, many of whom were unable to land safely under such conditions.

'I flew with Bomber Command that night as captain and pilot of Lancaster JB453, "F – Freddie", an aircraft of No 83 Squadron Path Finder Force based at RAF Wyton, Huntingdonshire. Mine was about the last aircraft in the PFF Group, if not in the whole of the Command, to land safely in one piece, but not before I had experienced the most frightening moment of my flying career.

'As the crews trooped yet again into the operational briefing room at Wyton on the afternoon of the 16th, already it was evident we were in for another foggy night and odds were already being laid against take-off by the squadron bookmaker. This time however, he was in for a surprise!

'As the curtains covering the wall target map and route were drawn aside, the usual noisy outburst from the assembled crews confirmed that Berlin was once again the target. The hubbub died down as the squadron commander (Grp Capt John H. Searby DSO, DFC) called for order and waved a signal form in the air. "I've just received this signal from the Commander-in-Chief", he said; "Butch wants you all to know that the only reason you haven't been going to the Big City of late is that he's been waiting for a night when the weather is so bad that all the German fighters are grounded and so give you all an easy trip. Tonight's the night for sure, so you'll soon be on your way. However, he wants to assure you all that you won't always have it this easy."

'The crews' tense expressions dissolved amid roars of laughter at the very thought of the tough C in C sending such a message, and in a more relaxed atmosphere we settled down

Above: Joe Northrop briefing his No 692 Squadron crews at Graveley November 1944: a still from a de Havilland film recording the history of the Mosquito.
/de Havilland via J. Northrop

to the more serious business of briefing. All, that is, except for the station commander (Grp Capt L. E. Jarman DFC) seated in the front row, who was a stickler for Service procedure and hardly noted for his sense of humour. For the rest of the briefing he sat deep in thought, no doubt wondering why he had not been the first to get a copy of the mythical signal. Such "jollying" of the crews certainly helped to relieve tension, particularly at this period as the squadron was going through a bad patch.

'Briefing was soon over. The met officer had painted a gloomy picture of fog obscuring the country, and with no diversion airfields available by the time of our return, the general attitude was one of "If we're going let's get on with it – we might even get back then before the fog really clamps down." Indeed, by now little enough time remained to hastily swallow operational meals in the messes and get along to the aircrew changing rooms to don flying kit and draw out personal parachutes.

The short December day was rapidly drawing to a close and already the chill in the air and the clear skies indicated that radiation fog would be forming only too quickly after dark.

'By the time we had carried our heavy parachutes and dinghy packs out of the building the aircrew 'buses were waiting to take us out to the dispersal area, and we piled on board the first one complete as a crew. Our 'bus was soon filled to capacity and it then trundled off around the peri-track dropping off each crew close to the aircraft they were flying, the aircraft letter being announced at each dispersal pan. The crews waddled out of the 'bus looking like overgrown teddy bears in a weird and wonderful assortment of flying kit to the accompaniment of a chorus of well wishes from those remaining. The superstitious ones clutched or wore their personal good luck charms while others, particularly the Canadian contingents, affected the tougher "Wild West" style with .38 Smith and Wesson

FIXES 1ST CLASS   2ND CLASS   3RD

Nº 49 SQUADRON
BERLIN   18/19 Nov 1943.

A/C & LETTER	CAPTAIN	BOMB LOAD	CALL SIGN	FIXES ETC	ATO	ETR	ATR	CLOUD	BASE	A/C Nº & LETTER	CAPTAI
1st Wave O	W/C ADAMS	NMY	LANDED WARBOYS	1657	0131		**LOCAL WEATHER**				
" A	S/L DAY	"	" TANGMERE	1658	0140		**TIME:-**				
" G	F/O COTTINGHAM	"	" DUNSFOLD	1700	0115		STATION VIS QFE WIND				
" N	F/SGT EDY	"	"	1702	0112		SCAMPTON				
" C	P/O HALES	"	"	1704	0135		FISKERTON				
" T	P/O BLACKMORE	"	"	1705	0121						
" M	W/O JUPP	"	"	1706½	0116						
" H	P/O HIDDERLEY	"	"	1710	0147		**AERODROME STATE**				
2nd Wave F	F/O REYNOLDS	"	"	1708	0129						
" V	F/LT TANCRED	"	"	1707	0137		FIXES QDM'S ETC				
" S	F/O PALMER	"	"	1706	0138		A/C L^r A/C L^r A/C L^r				
" R	F/O FOSTER	"	LANDED CRANWELL	1711	0135		FIX TIME FIX TIME FIX TIME				
" J	F/O BACON	"	" WOODHALL	1714	0159						
" U	W/O WEBB	"	" GRANSDEN	1715	0229						
" K	W/O JONES	"	"	1716	0142						
" Q	P/O BARNES	"	"	1719	0148						
3rd Wave E	P/O SIMPSON	"	LANDED MANSTON	1717½	0100						
" B	P/O GEORGE	"	" W. MALLING	1720	0139						
" D	F/SGT ROANTREE	"	"	1713	0143						

OFFICER I.C   G/C GRINDELL DFC AFC.

revolvers or murderous looking Bowie knives tucked in the tops of their flying boots.

'Soon the driver called out "F – Freddie" and we bundled out of the 'bus giving the thumbs-up sign to start pre-flight checks on our aircraft; this was standing on the pan well down on its undercarriage legs with the weight of the high octane fuel and the 5 x 2,000lb HC bomb load pressing down on them. From now on there was no time to think of anything other than our respective jobs as part of the crew and the prime necessity of getting Freddie airborne on time. Fortunately there were no snags and the crew soon settled down in their stations and checked-out on the intercom, The engines were started and, maintaining radio silence, the chocks were taken away from the wheels and we moved out to take our place in the line of aircraft taxying towards the runway holding point. Each aircraft took off in turn on receiving a steady green from the runway controller in his caravan, and in a very short time we were at the head of the queue. I flashed the aircraft letter in Morse on the downward ident lights and got a steady green in reply. Then turning smartly on to the runway, I lined up the compass and set the directional indicator, opened up the Merlin engines against the brakes until they were running evenly, then released the control and started the take-off. After some juggling with the throttles to keep in a straight path the aircraft began to gather speed, the tail came up and the controls began to respond. I eased the control column back as we began to run out of runway and we were on our way.

'We headed towards the North Sea on our first course, climbing to reach our operational height of 20,000ft before the Dutch coast. Aircraft could be seen all around us in the still-light skies above the now dark ground of East Anglia, all with the same purpose in mind. Looking down at the patches of grey mist and fog already forming above the dark earth I could not help wondering what it

Below: **Berlin Season**
'. . . The usual noisy outburst from the assembled crews confirmed that Berlin was once again the target. The hubbub died down as the Squadron Commander called for order . . .' Wg Cdr R. H. Shaw briefing his No 115 Squadron crews at Witchford 1944. */J. N. M. Heffer*

Right: **Nightfall** A No 97 (Straits Settlements) Squadron Lanc climbs out of Bourn on a beautiful June evening in 1943, conditions far removed from those met by PFF squadrons on the disastrous night of 16/17 December that year. The picture was taken only a few weeks after No 97 joined the ranks of No 8 Group for pathfinding duties, when the fitment of H2S radar was still some way off./*P. B. Browning*

Below: **And So To Bed** A No 83 Squadron freshman crew, back from a training flight, cross the boundary fence at Wyton as the autumn sun sets, casting gigantic shadows over the now quiet airfield. Note the illusion of anhedral on each tailplane. /*P. B. Browning*

would be like in seven or eight hours time if and when we came back. By the time the Dutch coast was reached we were cruising at operational height above a thick woolly blanket of greyness stretching as far as the eye could see. Although a sharp lookout was kept for fighters none were seen as they were undoubtedly grounded by the weather at the airfields in the Low Countries controlled by the GCI centres. We pressed on over Germany, checking the route markers as they were placed by earlier PFF aircraft, as though on a navigational exercise; and still no sign of the enemy other than sporadic bursts of flak and occasional glows from searchlights appearing in the murk below as the odd aircraft strayed off course and passed too close to a defended area. Time began to drag a little until, with 30 minutes to go to H-hour on target, H2S set operator Frank Foster came forward to switch on the bombsight and so ensure that the gyros would stabilise in good time before the bombing run.

'Tonight, at least, we were to be spared the blinding searchlights criss-crossing the path of our aircraft on the approaches to Berlin and the sudden cessation of flak indicating fighters moving into the area. All we had to face was the heaviest barrage of exploding shells surrounding any city in Europe, and to bomb Berlin we had to plough through it straight and level following the bomb aimer's corrections.

From now on the run-in seemed endless sitting on top of the 5 x 2,000lb HC bombs and TIs nestling in the bomb bay, the greasy black puffs of exploding shells all around – any one of which could well deliver us to Kingdom Come in a single flash. For what seemed an eternity we stuck rigidly to the heading, correcting as necessary on Frank Foster's instructions, until at last the welcome "Bombs gone" came over the earphones, accompanied by the familiar lurch upwards of the aircraft now free of its five-ton load of high explosive.

'I held the aircraft on its last heading to make sure of a photo flash picture of the aiming point on the ground, then dived to port out of the target area to get away from the forest of greasy black puffs of smoke that still came up all around us. After a while we were clear of the defences. Now silhouetted against a sky lit up blood-red from the reflected glow of the fires raging in Berlin, I headed for home on Charlie Burdett's course. Feeling naked and exposed in the clear night at altitude, and apprehensive of what was yet in store for us on return, I ordered boost and revs reduced to a minimum and trimmed the aircraft to fly for maximum endurance and thereby conserve fuel.

'As it turned out the trip back proved as uneventful and devoid of enemy action as the outward flight; although some reflected searchlight glow and bursts of heavy flak

Above: **Tempting Fate** Berlin was the graveyard of many fine crews. With their superior performances and weight carrying capability, Lancasters bore the brunt of the onslaught against the German capital during the so-called Battle of Berlin. Pictured is a victim of an earlier Berlin raid – BIII JA678 'MG-S' (Sqn Ldr Chas Lofthouse and crew) from No 7 Squadron Oakington, brought down by a fighter on the night of 23/24 August 1943, only hours after this snapshot was taken. She bears the small code presentation unique to No 7 Squadron and begun on its Stirlings in 1941. Note also the non-standard identity letter./*C. J. Lofthouse*

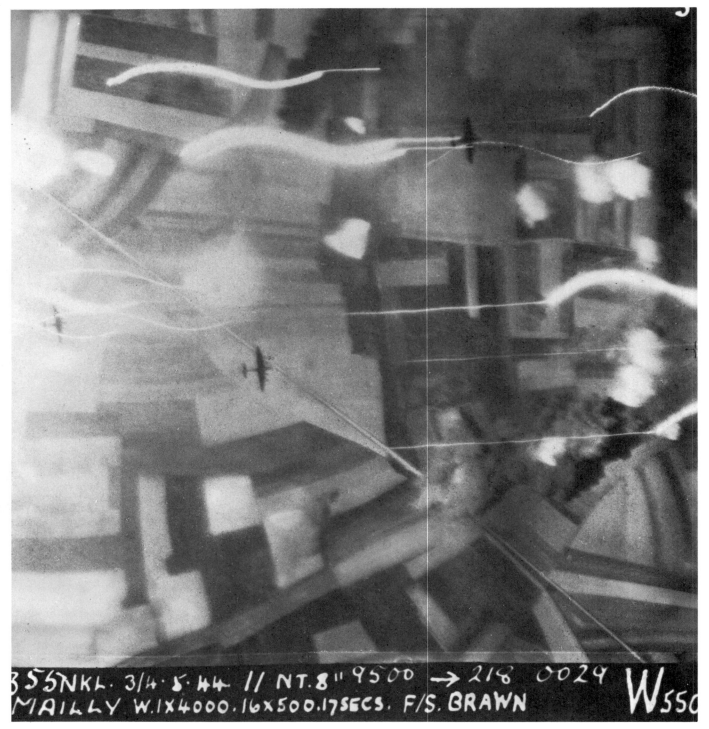

355NKL. 3/4.5.44 // NT.8"9500 → 218 0029 W
MAILLY W.IX4000.16X500.17SECS. F/S. BRAWN W55C

Above: **As Light As Day** Soon after the so-called Battle of Berlin ended, Bomber Command turned its attention to bombing military targets as part of the softening up process prior to D-Day. On these some spectacular – if often costly – successes were achieved, typified by the attack on the Panzer training and re-inforcement battalions housed at Mailly-Le-Camp some 160km east of Paris, mounted on the night of 3/4 May 1944. From 9,500ft – somewhat higher than most of the attackers – the camera on a No 550 Squadron kite (Flt Sgt W. N. H. Brawn and crew) captures three Lancs in the target area, in conditions of bright moonlight, time 0029 hours – 10 minutes past H-Hour. Due to an unfortunate breakdown in communications, German fighters enjoyed a 'field day' and hacked down 42 of the 346 heavies. Brawn and crew survived this night and subsequently finished their tour.
/K. Bowen-Bravery

Right: **War Booty**
'*And those of them who died,*
No cenotaph we need erect,
To assist us to recall,
How many of those gallant crews did fall.'

So penned an unknown South African who felt moved to record his tribute to the dead of Bomber Command. These pictures help to convey the grim reality of war. (*top right*), the twisted hulk of a Lanc downed at Beckhansen, south of Varel (dated 17 December 1942; (*bottom right*), a German officer inspecting pitiful remains of a Lancaster which evidently nose-dived into the ground and broke up near Bockhorn (dated 1 March 1943).
/German Sources via IWM

appeared at intervals through the grey cotton wool mass below us, there was still no sign of any Luftwaffe night fighters as we ploughed westwards. Once over the North Sea I brought the aircraft down below oxygen level and navigator Charlie Burdett passed me the last of the coffee from the crew thermos and lit me an illegal cigarette; it tasted good. We crossed the English coast seen on the H2S scope and wireless operator Gerry Hoey identified. We shook off more height as we headed over home territory for base and I switched on the beam approach set to check that it was functioning. It was a relief to hear the old familiar Morse signals coming through loud and clear as there was no sign of a break in the grey mass below in any direction, and the beam was our only let-down aid.

'Nowadays people take it for granted that all aircraft carry efficient landing aids and· most airfields have a diversity of installations to enable them to land in all but the worst conditions of weather. In 1943 the only facilities available to bomber crews in really bad weather, apart from a few homing and navigational aids, were the standard Beam approach installations used at base airfields separately or in emergency, in conjunction with the FIDO (Fog Intensive Dispersal Of) equipment installed on the emergency landing strips on the coast at Woodbridge, Manston and Carnaby. Many of the wartime bomber pilots had little more than a few hundred flying hours experience; on operations they had to fly long distances at night and in bad weather, much further than most pilots ever flew before the war, and also suffer enemy attacks, cold and discomfort, fatigue and fear as a matter of routine. For example, after one of the earlier attacks on Berlin in November half the squadron air gunners were out of action with frost-bitten faces, fingers and toes; the next night we had to borrow half-trained gunners from the training units to make up the crews. Later on, electrically-heated flying kit became available for gunners.

'Pilots too had their problems. Although every opportunity was taken to practise SBA approaches during air tests or practises in Oxfords, or in simulation on the Link trainer, the lengthy process of homing on the "cone of silence" over the transmitter and flying accurate procedure patterns required a high standard of skill and no little experience. Nor only that, but as many as twenty or thirty aircraft might have to get down using the beam in the space of an hour or so before they ran out of fuel. On such a night, a single pilot unable to cope could play havoc with the stacking and positioning of other aircraft in the circuit. These thoughts ran through my mind as we approached Wyton airfield, at which stage Flying Control passed routine landing information and instructed us to join the stack of Lancasters already milling around above the overcast. Due to the economies in fuel consumption achieved on the return flight we had a fair amount of fuel in reserve and a plan for landing. I intended to start my approach on SBA well above the fog layer, the top of which was around 1,200ft; then, with all cockpit checks done except for final flap, I would be able to concentrate on flying the aircraft accurately on a straight approach and let-down.

'The stack of aircraft dwindled slowly until at last I was given No 1 to land. At this time Control warned me to watch out for an unidentified aircraft in the circuit attempting to land visually. I acknowledged and alerted the crew to keep their eyes peeled as I flew the aircraft well out from the outer marker beacon, carrying out landing checks on the way and started a procedure turn to bring the aircraft on a straight approach to the main runway. When lined up in the centre of the beam I let down the aircraft into the rather turbulent upper layer of fog and mist at a constant rate of descent until the altimeter read 600ft: at which stage I applied power to maintain height until the outer marker signal was heard. I then continued to descend keeping in the centre of the beam and listening for the inner marker signal. At this moment, with the altimeter showing around 200ft, we received the full impact of the slip-stream of another aircraft which suddenly crossed our path from the port side in a steep turn, its port wingtip almost scraping the mid-upper turret and nearly causing the gunner to throw a fit.

'Our aircraft plunged madly and lost height (we found afterwards that it had actually ploughed through the upper branches of some trees in the area) and I slammed the throttles fully open to emergency boost to keep us from hitting the ground. For what seemed ages "Freddie" literally hung on its props: then, as the engineer retracted the undercarriage and the speed began to build up, it started to climb through the murk to temporary safety, bearing one very shattered crew aloft.

'Once above the fog I called Control and let them know in no uncertain terms what had happened. They replied that an unidentified aircraft had just crashed near the funnel and was on fire. It was later found to be an aircraft of my flight, flown by an Australian Plt Off (Plt Off F. E. McLean, fated to be killed on a trip to Brest on 14 August 1944, still with No 83 Squadron) who, after sustaining flak damage over the target that had put all his communications equipment out of action, had been trying to land visually. During what must have been his final desparing attempt he had flown the aircraft into the ground and almost taken us along with him. Safe for the moment at least, I turned back on the beam to take us on a reciprocal course over Wyton. The airfield was now identifiable by the flickering red glow of an aircraft burning on the ground seen through the murk.

'At this moment, hearing my engines no doubt, Control called me up again to ask for my fuel state. I replied that although I had a good hour's endurance in hand, in the light of what had happened I hadn't the least intention of attempting another landing until all other aircraft were out of the way and the circuit was clear of hazards. With that I broke off contact and stayed in the clear atmosphere around 5,000ft to practise simulated let-downs on the beam for a while. After half an hour or so, having simmered down to some extent, I called up Control again, much to the relief of the controller. He then informed me that I was the only pilot in the group still airborne and gave me No 1 to land. I looked at my watch and calculated that we had been in the air for just on eight hours as against our estimated time of flight of around seven; it was obviously time to land.

'Once again we repeated the landing procedure up to the point over the inner marker which had almost proved fatal for us, and carried on with the descent from there, still entirely on instruments and keeping our fingers crossed. The engineer and the navigator, who were both standing up and peering ahead, saw the first of the runway lights flash under the port wheel simultaneously and yelled out. I pulled everything back, prayed, and "Freddie" sank gently down through the last few feet, to touch down with one wheel on the runway and one off. What matter – we were down in one piece.'

In a Tiny Moment of Time they were Gone

CLIFF BEADLE

Ask any man who flew with Bomber Command what he feared most next to being shot down and he will say 'collisions'.

The risk of collision was an ever-present threat in the unlit skies over Europe. Statistically the chances were small for the sky is a vast place; yet, many did occur and few lived to tell the tale. Who did not hit the slipstream of another aircraft (a comforting experience in many ways for at least you knew you were on track and in the stream); or suffer a near miss as a black shape suddenly flashed across your Lanc, taking away an aerial, a fin or rudder?

With so many airfields clustered together, their circuits often overlapping, you still could not relax back at base. Related here is an eyewitness account of one such incident on the night of 7/8 November 1942, when two No 9 Squadron crews perished in the Waddington circuit – 14 men gone in an instant.

Cliff Beadle had been a transport and shipping clerk in the oil refining and chemical industry before enlisting in the RAF during January 1940. Trained at Cosford as a fitter, he joined No 9 Squadron (then based at Honington flying Wellingtons) in November 1940. Promoted to sergeant when the unit moved to Waddington and converted to Lancasters, he was a seasoned veteran of 27 at the time of the incident described. He finally left the squadron in August 1944, posted to 1668 HCU Bottesford, which had moved to Cottesmore by the time he was demobbed in October 1945.

Rejoining his old firm, he elected to transfer to engineering maintenance and is still with them 33 years later, a welding specialist, and due to retire in 1980.

'I walked out of A Flight office, outside and along the front of E hangar, until I came to the crew room. It was very quiet, the crew room was empty now and there was a stillness all around. The greyness of the dawn was just beginning to show itself as I stood there looking across the airfield. It was very cold and a typical November morning. I could just see across towards the Sleaford road.

'In the thin ribbon of the skyline I could see the fire tenders and the "blood wagons". The crews were still searching the wreckage of the two Lancasters. It all seemed so unreal and wrong. Somewhere under that mass over there were 14 aircrew lads who were dead. That was real. That, but for a split second of time, they need not be dead was very wrong. A couple of hours ago the two Lancs, "R-Roger" and "L-Leather", had collided over base. (Lancaster I R5916 'WS-R': Flg Off K. A. Mackenzie RCAF & crew; Lancaster I W4256 'WS-L': Flt Sgt A. J. McDonald RCAF & crew.)

'I walked back to the office and wished that Chiefy would hurry and relieve me from duty so that I could get away. I wanted to get away and bury my head under the blankets and, at least for a while, forget this terrible night.

'The squadron had been here at Waddington for some months now and shared the base with No 44 (Rhodesia) Squadron. We had left Honington in Suffolk and our wonderful Wellingtons to join 5 Group and convert to Lancasters. We converted via Manchesters in record time and were very quickly back into the war again.

'During these past few months Bomber Command had stepped up the attack on enemy territory, and extended it to Italy. Last night the squadron had been back to Genoa for the second time. Everything had gone like clockwork during standby and take-off and now the ground crew on night duty could relax for a few hours. I was NCO I/C night flying for tonight and settled myself in Chiefy's office to prepare the night's programme: snag sheets to be made out for each aircraft, all to be ready for tomorrow. Chiefy, Flt Sgt Tavener, was a quiet type to work under. An ex-apprentice and a very good fitter, he was a quietly spoken chap and probably the most unflappable type anywhere in the RAF. He wore a small "Charlie Chaplin" – type moustache which made it almost impossible to guess his age. He was young enough to play football but looked much older than any of us. His organising ability was second to none and he had a flight of NCOs and men who grew with him to be part of a very efficient flight.

Right: **Cropped** Keeping well in the stream on return from Ludwigshaven 1/2 February 1945, BI NG202 'TC-T' from No 170 Squadron Hemswell was struck by another aircraft at 2002 hours. Rear gunner Flt Sgt V. J. Fernquist died instantly and, with both rudders partly torn off and elevators damaged, Canadian skipper Flg Off J. P. Dixie had a struggle to reach base. Though it can never be proved, it seems certain the other machine was a No 550 Squadron Lancaster. New Zealander Flg Off A. W. L. Lohrey and four of his crew were forced to abandon BI RA502 over France following a violent collision with an unidentified aircraft in the target area. Lohrey's Lancaster got the worst of this encounter and, in addition to extensive wing and fuselage damage, had three engines put out of action. Dixie (who subsequently earned himself a well merited DFC) and crew went on to complete their tour, while NG202 was put back into service./*C. J. Hatton*

Below: **Friend or Foe?** Despite moonlight conditions on the night of 10/11 April 1944, the crew of BIII ND333 (captain Plt Off N. McConnell of No 83 Squadron) did not see the aircraft which chopped out a huge chunk of their starboard wing at 16,000ft over Lille. The damage made little difference to the Lanc's handling and the crew landed at home base Wyton after a total flight time of only 2hr 5min. ND333 returned to No 83 Squadron from repair by the end of the month and later passed to No 106 Squadron, totting up 90 ops by the end of the war. McConnell and crew did not return from Aachen 11/12 April 1944, their very next trip! /*T. Warmby*

'Our flight commander, Sqn Ldr "Tubby" Fry, was operating tonight, flying in "D-Dog", which was "my" particular Lancaster. He had an uncanny knack of always being first back from operations. I finished with the paperwork and switched on the radio. This radio had a very short wave band and was useful for picking up the watch office and aircraft. We could pick up each aircraft as the pilot called up and as we identified our own so everyone was in the right place at the right time.

'Now, everything was completed up to ETA and, for a while, there was nothing to do but wait. I sat there thinking of some of the weird tricks some of our aircrew bods got up to. We had one air gunner who never allowed his flying boots to touch the ground. He would come down to dispersal with them under his arm and sit in the aircraft to put them on. He then reversed the proceedings on returning.

'Then there was McDonald, pilot of "L". He was a Canadian and looked it. He was half way there with an RAF-type moustache and very proud of it. A stocky, powerfully built chap, he had a little ritual he performed just before climbing in – one of nature's duties at the very last minute. The NCO I/C "L-Leather", corporal Frankie Watts, thought the world of Mac and his crew. Another chap always took with him a complete change of underclothes just in case he might be taken POW.

Home Reaper Returning from Berlin 1/2 March 1943, Flt Lt Jim V. Verran and his No 9 Squadron crew were forced to complete a circuit just below an 800ft cloud base before landing back at Waddington. Given priority to land, the skipper had squarely lined up BIII ED490 'WS-J' with the barely visible runway lights when suddenly, he saw navigation lights coming straight at him. Reacting instantly, he pulled back on the stick before oblivion. Though they would not immediately know it, those who still lived had miraculously survived a near head on collision with a No 57 Squadron Lanc (R5894 'DX-T') from Scampton. Just why Canadian Flg Off J. F. Greenan and crew were on a collision course will never be known as they perished when their kite hit high tension cables at nearby Riseholme. Thus ended the Verran crew's tour – just 6 ops; pilot Jim Verran (a New Zealander in the RAF) collected a broken left leg, paralysed right arm, broken jaw and severe skull wounds; bomb aimer Plt Off Frank T. Johnson RAAF suffered an internal haemorrhage and severe burns; w/op Flg Off John H. Moutray (a Canadian in the RAF) was paralysed on his right side; mid-upper Sgt K. W. Chalk escaped with cuts and bruises; but for nav Plt Off L. H. Leach, engineer Sgt A. D. Smithson and rear gunner Sgt K. E. W. Matthews it was the end of life./J. H. Moutray

Left: **Ground Hazard** Not all collisions occurred in the air. This smashed turret on a No 405 ('Vancouver') Squadron Lancaster is said to be the result of being struck by a skidding 3-ton lorry. Though few details of the incident have come to light, it seems that the rear gunner was not in his turret at the time. Had he been so, it is doubtful if he would have had time to evacuate – assuming he even saw the offending vehicle./S. E.Kanka

Above: **Hidden Danger** Just how many aircraft were lost through 'friendly' bombs will never be known. While at night the dangers were rarely visible, and to some extent diminished by the relative looseness of the bomber stream, it was a different story on the daylight gaggles. Illustrated here is the extensive damage done to the starboard-outer of No 49 Squadron's BI LM190 'EA-R' by a 1,000 pounder over Sequeville on the night of 7/8 July 1944. Flg Off Geoff Poole and crew made it back to Fiskerton and subsequently finished their tour. LM190 survived the war, by then flogging the circuit with 1654 CU./*J. A. Edwards*

'I looked at the clock on the wall and it showed that it was 02.30 hours. I got up from the office chair, put on my leather jacket, and went outside. It was a black night, there wasn't a star to be seen in the sky. A stiff breeze was blowing and it was very cold. Behind the watch office and over to the left of it stood the duty fire tenders and "blood-wagons". The drivers had started up their engines in readiness.

'At the end of the hangar the crew 'bus stood with engine warming up, with Gladys, our WAAF driver, behind the wheel. She was a good, steady type and could be relied upon to do her job of bringing in the crews. These girls did a great job for it called for a special type of driver to drive around the track in absolute darkness. Life could become quite dicey when the squadron returned. Everything happened in a very short time and four-engined Lancs belting along at 30-odd mph could be a hair-raising experience for anyone.

'Chiefy's small runabout gharry was outside the office, parked on the grass. I went across to it, climbed in, and started the engine to warm it up ready for action. I should want it in a few minutes' time because we always afforded a small privilege to our flight commander by collecting him personally and bringing him to his office. I switched off the engine, satisfied that all was well, and went back into the office. Almost as I entered the radio started up and the first call was "S-Sugar", followed instantly by "D-Dog"; Sqn Ldr Fry was back.

'At the door I watched for the landing. The aircraft were calling up fast now; several more from B Flight, two more of ours. McDonald called up, then Mackenzie. One by one they arrived and each was told to fly at different altitudes to await landing instructions. This was the worst part, being stacked up, circling around the base. No one enjoyed these situations and it was always a relief when it was all over.

'By now "D-Dog" was just taxying past so I ran out, jumped into the gharry, and tagged on behind, following the Lanc to dispersal. We were about halfway there when it happened. There was, above the roar of scores of engines, a crunching explosion, followed instantly by a tremendous flash. In a second the whole sky was illuminated. I braked hard and jumped out of the gharry. "D-Dog" had also stopped.

'There, in the sky above me was a Lancaster completely silhouetted in flames, turning, slowly at first, then spinning, dripping and trailing fire. It spun faster and dived steeply into the ground on the south side of the airfield with a great belch of flame as it exploded. As I watched there was another great flash of flame and an explosion, slightly to one side of the first Lanc. Obviously there had been a midair collision over base.

'I could see in the glow of the fires the fire tenders and ambulances screaming their way round the track. Theirs would be a futile effort for no one could hope to survive a crash of this sort. "D-Dog" had started moving again so I started up and followed to dispersal. On reaching there the crew climbed out and wanted to know who it was had crashed. I didn't know but could think of possibilities because I knew a few of the squadron who had called up before I left the office.

'The flight commander climbed in and we set off back to the hangar. On arrival there it didn't take long to check up. A Flight had one missing and B Flight had one missing: McDonald in "L", Mackenzie in "R": two Canadians and their crews. In a tiny moment of time they were gone. Sqn Ldr Fry departed to report for de-briefing and soon the ground crews arrived from dispersal. The night's operation was over.

'I heard later of two events which had taken place during the crash. It had been too much for Gladys our driver; she had collapsed and been sent to her quarters. One Lanc had landed first and reached B Flight dispersals. The crew had left in the crew 'bus but before doing so the mid-upper gunner reported a jammed gun. The duty armourer climbed up into the turret and had just started to dismantle the gun when an engine fell out of the sky, crashing through the fuselage, cutting the Lanc in two. He was completely unhurt.'

One More Op Chalked Up

Below: **Time to Unwind** Witchford 12 March 1945 as No 115 Squadron crews, back from a daylight attack on Dortmund, enjoy a welcome 'cuppa', served up by a pretty WAAF officer, before their turn to pass on impressions and observations to the intelligence officer. The press are on hand to gather first-hand accounts for tomorrow's newspapers./*R. T. Robson*

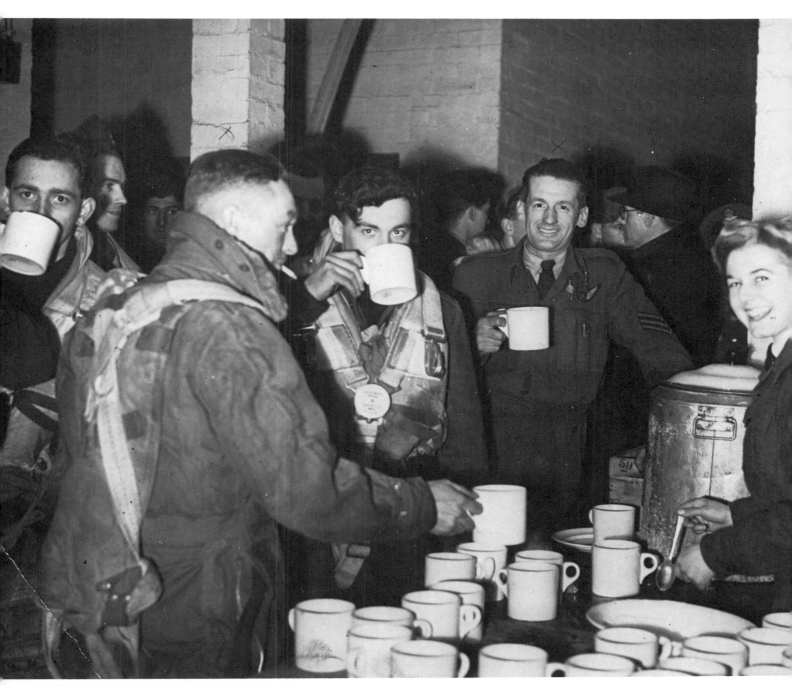

15 SQDN. LS — ARLEY

A/C	CAPTAIN	OFF	INFORMATION	LAND
A	F/O COLLING	18.51	JETTISON BOMBS	00.11½
B	F/S SELLWOOD	18.54		23.22
D	F/L BUCHANAN	18.49		23.16½
E	F/S PAYNE	18.47½		23.14
F	F/O MORRISSEY	18.49½		23.30
G	F/S BARFORD	18.55½		23.15½
H	F/O SLEEMAN	18.48		23.31½
J	F/S JENNINGS	18.52		23.24½
K	F/O MARSH	18.54½		23.18½
L	F/O LESLIE	18.55		23.37½
Z	F/O WILLIAMSON	18.50	CRASHED ON RUNWAY	23.05
N	F/O SYLVESTRE	18.59½		23.33½
O	F/S PERRY	18.57½		23.27½
P	F/S JONES	19.00	S/I FEATHERED BRAKE NO PRES LANDED WOODBRIDGE	00.20
R	F/S HOBBS	19.01½		23.36½
S	F/O MARRIOTT	18.58½		23.29
T	F/O HALL	18.56		23.49½
U	F/O CAPEL	19.01		23.35
W	F/O MARSHALL	19.03	HANG UP	23.55
V	F/O HASTINGS	19.02½		23.39
Y	F/O COULTER	18.57		00.21½

ETD 18.48 / 23.17 ARLEY

622 SQDN GI — MAPLIN

A/C	CAPTAIN	OFF	INFORMATION	LAND
A	F/L THOMPSON	19.15		00.02
B	F/L JONES	19.17		00.10
C	F/L STEPHENS	19.20		00.18
D	F/S STRATTON BRIGNAL	19.14		00.03½
E	F/O BOURNE	19.13		00.05
F	F/S BARNETT	19.18		00.28
G	F/O NEILSON	19.19		00.13½
H	F/O ARMITSTED	19.21½		00.19½
J	F/S PECK	19.21		00.15½
K	F/O HANSEN	19.22		00.23
L	F/O RICHARDS	19.06½		23.43½
O	F/S ORTON THOMAS	19.08		23.45
R	F/O CAMPBELL	19.11		00.07½
T	F/S RICHARDS CLARK	19.10½		23.53½
U	F/S NICHOLLS	19.12		23.59½
V	F/O MYLES BENSON	19.10		23.51½
Y	F/O MITCHELL	19.07		23.49
Z	F/O BONNER	19.09	S/O ENGINE U/S FIX 6100 N-0238 E-22-27 (LANDED NEWMARKET)	00.02

ETD 19.05 / ETA 23.45 MAPLIN

BMD SQDN — APPLA

AVERAGES

TAKE OFF 48 SECS 39 A/C (RUNWAY 29)

LANDING 1.48 SECS 37 A/C (RUNWAY 29)

RUNWAY CHANGED TO 22.

VISITING A/C

A F/L HOFKIN 00.46 TUDDENHAM 23.44 (LANCASTER)

SEPTEMBER 23rd/24 1944

ETD ETA APPLA

Top left: **Maximum Effort** A typical operations board to be found on a two-squadron Lancaster station, in this case Mildenhall, recording a raid on Neuss by Nos 15 and 622 Squadrons. Evident in the display are the station and squadron call signs, runways in use and average take-off and landing times. The inclusion of two names against No 622 Squadron's 'D', 'O', 'T' and 'V' indicates the presence of 'second dickey' pilots doing a freshman trip for experience./*I. C. K. Swales*

Left: **When Day is Done** The day's operation and hectic activity is over. A Lancaster of No 424 ('Tiger') Squadron RCAF silhouetted against a pale winter sunset at a now dormant Skipton-on-Swale. /*L. H. Williams*

Above: **The Boss** Seeing for himself; though not officially 'encouraged' to fly operations, Air Vice Marshal 'Black Mike' McEwen, AOC No 9 Group, was not a man to shrink from danger. He chose to fly with No 426 ('Thunderbird') Squadron RCAF crew (skipper Wg Cdr Bill Swetman) to Berlin and so learn at first hand the realities of the Big City. He is seen here (right) posing with fellow Canadian Bill Swetman at Linton-on-Ouse the following day, the event already recorded on the nose of BII 'OW-A'./*H. J. Thomas*

Right: **Relief** Relief is reflected in the faces of Canadian Flt Lt Don Maclean (fourth left, peaked cap) and his No 419 ('Moose') Squadron crew as they celebrate the end of their tour at 'The Oak Tree' in Middleton village. Well in evidence are the ground crew who looked after their kite. When they took off from Middleton St George at 2158 hours on 1 May 1944, bound for St Ghislain in KB719 'VR-T', the Maclean crew became the first to operate in a No 6 Group Lancaster X./*D. H. Maclean*

Above: **Paperwork** Looking somewhat drawn and disinterested – their minds intent on breakfast and sleep – Flg Off Eddy Jones RCAF and his No 103 Squadron crew are interrogated at Elsham Wolds on return from Magdeburg 21/22 January 1944. Visible are, left to right: navigator Flg Off E. N. (Ted) Hooke RCAF; rear gunner Sgt Sid Willis; w/op Sgt Frank Smith; mid-upper Flg Off J. R. ('Bob') Boys, an American in the RCAF; bomb aimer Sgt J. G. ('Johnnie') Johnson. They went on to complete a hectic tour./*Public Archives of Canada*

Bits and Pieces

Below: **Behind the Scenes** A general view of the LMS railway sheds at Derby crowded with crashed and damaged Lancasters undergoing repair, a large part of the labour force being women. The leading edges of the mainplanes in the foreground reveal some of the many miles of wiring required by each machine. Units represented include No 44 (Rhodesia) Squadron (KM), No 50 Squadron (VN) and 1661 Conversion Unit (GP), the latter a veteran still without a dorsal turret fairing./*British Rail*

Above: **Hybrid** This No 207 Squadron Lanc from Bottesford may carry the serial number R5509 but she is in reality two aircraft (note the different paint partition lines.) Though few details of the 'marriage' are available, it seems the main fuselage at least (original identity unknown) was from a crashed machine, the rear portion from a battle-damaged R5509. The 'new' R5509 did not however survive long, failing to return from a 'Willows' gardening sortie 16/17 August 1942, by then coded 'EM-N'. Such hybrids – sometimes with mixed British-built and American Packard Merlins – were not uncommon as the Avro Repair Organisation was constantly under pressure to return crashed and damaged Lancasters back into service.
/Mrs M. Claridge Collection

Right: **What to Do?** The salvage crew receive their instructions before dismantling BIII EE190 'QR-M' at Blida following an overshoot in a dust storm by Flt Lt Tommy Stewart RNZAF and crew of No 61 Squadron Syerston on return from Reggio Nelle Emilla/Cislago 15/16 July 1943. Though close inspection revealed extensive damage to the front fuselage and engine nacelles, it is probable a lack of heavy lifting gear and facilities forced the decision to write her off. This was the second Lancaster belly landing by Tommy Stewart during his two tours with No 61 Squadron, and he was fated to ultimately end the war 'in the bag' on being shot down during the Peenemünde raid, 17/18 August 1943.
/Both W. Howarth

Above: **Surprise Visitor** Sgt Charlie Medland and crew had an inauspicious start to their operational career. They had only been with their squadron (No 514 Waterbeach) for around 10 days, and had yet to do a trip, when they set off in BII LL669 'JI-K' for another cross-country exercise on 17 March 1944. Attempting to land at Leiston (an American 8th Army Air Force fighter station), with the navigator acting as engineer – the intention to do a 'touch and go' on the grass-covered 'drome – the skipper realised he would not make it. Forced to do a 'wheels-up', they arrived in a swirling cloud of grass and dust before skidding to a halt, shaken but unhurt, the Lanc later declared a write-off. The Medland crew went on to distinguish themselves before going down on Duisburg 21/22 May 1944./*C. J. Medland*

Below: **Where Do We Start?** This seems to be the talking point as this No 460 Squadron RAAF Lanc is inspected following a wheels-up landing on the runway at Binbrook. While no details of this particular prang are known, it is probable the Lanc would be declared a total loss for, apart from the nose section (easily replaced), virtually the entire belly has been crushed, and her back broken: much would however be salvaged for future use. This view clearly shows the vulnerability of the bomb aimer's position in crashes./*E. D. Evans*

Right and below: **To the Rescue**
While the Binbrook fire fighters
quench a wing fire by pumping
foam through a hole hacked in
the port wing of No 460
Squadron's 'AR-N', the crash
crew discuss the situation before
attempting salvage. Though no
details of the episode are to
hand, it seems likely the Lanc –
her back unbroken – would be
repaired and put back into
service./*Both E. D. Evans*

Final Curtain

JOHN MacBEAN

Inevitably, despite the utmost care and attention accidents happened, not least when handling temperamental bombs, incendiaries and ammunition. Of several large scale explosions on Lancaster stations we have singled out East Kirkby 17/18 April 1945 – only three weeks from the end of the war in Europe – to represent at least one part of the sterling work done by hard pressed, largely unsung armament elements of Bomber Command stations and squadrons.

In a remarkable sequence of events six of No 57 Squadron's Lancs were blown up or wrecked: BIs PD347, NN765 and RF195, BIIIs LM673, ND472 and PB360. It began with the explosion of a number of 1,000lb MC bombs at 1740 hours on 17 April, leaving a smoking pit and scene of devastation where once PB360 'DX-U' had stood.

Next to go was LM673, amidst hectic activity to put out dozens of fires and remove bomb trolleys; and so it went on, the final explosion not taking place until 09.30 on the 18th. The final human toll was three servicemen killed and 14 injured, while in addition there were two civilian casualties – one fatal.

Recollections of those traumatic hours were – and still are – naturally somewhat confused, and this story by John MacBean, East Kirkby's Armament Officer, is a combination of his own experiences, and those of other participants and survivors.

A Scottish Highlander, 'Mac' had joined the RAF in December 1937, and by the time he moved to East Kirkby in September 1943 he was an experienced armament specialist, aged but 22. In August 1945 came a posting to HQ BAFO Germany to begin a series of postwar appointments until his retirement in July 1975, by then a wing commander with responsibility for all explosive regulations in the RAF and Bomb Disposal Organisation.

It was retirement in name only for his knowledge and experience was widely recognised and he immediately took charge of a NATO Explosive Ordnance Disposal Centre, where he is still gainfully employed at the time of writing.

'The scene is East Kirkby 17 April 1945, a beautiful spring day with the end of the war in sight. Most of the aircraft were bombed-up from the previous day but had not taken off. About 09.30 hours a change of load was called for. This caused a large workload and much frantic activity for an early evening take-off for marshalling yards in Germany (Cham).

'Many of the Lancasters were already fully loaded with 1,000 or 500lb bombs but the new requirement was to change the fusing from direct impact to long delay on some 30 plus machines belonging to Nos 57 and 630 Squadrons. Because of the large number of No 53 long delay chemical pistols required, quite a few had to be obtained from neighbouring Spilsby.

'In the main, bombs already on aircraft had to be down-loaded, either for a change of fusing, or return to the bomb dump. Because of the large number of bomb trolleys which would be required to cope with the change of load, it was decided that a cetain amount of the new fusing could be done at the aircraft dispersals. Normally, this would all be done in a fusing shed in the bomb dump. This decision did add to the problems later on because some surplus bombs and detonators were still at dispersals awaiting return to the bomb dump when the explosion happened.

'No 57 Squadron was bombed-up with a mixture of 500 and 1,000lb bombs, all with No 53 pistols, some with a half-hour delay and others with one-hour delay. By about 17.00 hours work was still going on at No 630 Squadron, though the majority of its aircraft were bombed-up ready. Work was in hand to clear the dispersals of excess weapons at No 57 Squadron and the crews were due out to the aircraft between 17.30 and 18.00 hours.

'At 17.40 the first explosion took place – which, to the Station Armament Officer, Flt Lt John MacBean, did not sound quite like a bomb; a photoflash maybe? At that moment he was on his way to the mess for tea but turned at the East Kirkby village war memorail, "put his foot down" on the motorbike, took the turn at the guardroom too fast and came off. Gravel rash was the worst he would have over the next two traumatic days!

Top: **Fire Leaves its Mark** The battered East Kirkby incendiary hangar pictured on 23 April, with the unrecognisable remains of a Lancaster in the foreground. Note the earth and brick banks lining each hangar side wall; also a lone incendiary propped against a can. /*T. L. Redding*

Above: **Regrettable** Frontal view of the incendiary hangar and the twisted and burnt remnants of at least two Lancs and attendant servicing gear: one bomb door is clearly identified; the tree right foreground has suffered badly but two Lancs visible in the distance have escaped damage. 'DX-Y' behind the hangar is a BI (BVII Interim). /*T. L. Redding*

'No one was sure if the "bang" came from the bomb dump or the dispersals, but as MacBean headed down the peri-track he saw a black smoke cloud over No 57 Squadron dispersals. Other people were heading quickly for the scene but both then, and later, there was little time or opportunity to recognise or speak to them. Perhaps three or four minutes had elapsed since the first explosion.

'There was already considerable destruction just beyond the incendiary storage hangar. People were moving about but there was an air of confusion. One badly burnt armourer was lying near the hangar, his shirt either blown or burnt off, his burns extensive.

'MacBean decided ir would be safer to approach the actual scene by going through the incendiary hangar, knowing only too well the fickleness of 53 chemical long delay pistols; they would not stand too much shock and heat. Just as he entered the hangar the fire tender arrived and Flg Off Grebby and some of his fire staff made their way into the danger area.

'The hangar contained some 300 tons of 4lb and 30lb incendiary bombs, the former made up of solid thermite, a form of magnesium alloy, the latter having a methane/petrol mixture. The outer doors were somewhat buckled and holed, and to make matters worse, one or two of the 4lb bomb clusters had been blown out of their stacks and were alight.

'If something was not done quickly there would soon be a real conflagration. John MacBean remembered his own instruction to the staff: "Unless there is great danger to life and limb or vital property, don't try to extinguish any four pounders which function inadvertently." The reason for this was that a certain percentage were fitted with an explosive scatter charge to discourage enemy firemen and could be lethal at close range.

'As he ran back down the hangar with a five-gallon drum filled with sand, all hell was let loose. There was a tremendous explosion, which a corrugated hangar did nothing to lessen. He found himself sitting on the floor, his cap "gone with the wind", and being by-passed by incendiary bomb clusters, roller conveyors and other bric-a-brac. At the same time things were dropping on the hangar roof, just like a gigantic hailstorm. Of all the wonders, this explosion and blast from outside the hangar extinguished the incendiary fires and no more occurred.

292

Above: **Beyond Repair** The strange effects of blast are apparent on BI PD347 'DX-P': a largely undamaged rear fuselage contrasts with completely peppered front fuselage and engine nacelles. Virtually all cockpit perspex has gone, the nose dome is askew, and both mainwheel tyres are flat. She was broken up where she stood. Beyond the starboard fin and rudder can be seen a Lanc tailwheel assembly./*T. L. Redding*

Left: **Laid Waste** Distant shot of BI PD347 'DX-P', taking in a burnt out fire engine next to a Merlin and prop still attached to an engine bearer. The house at the edge of the airfield – probably abandoned for the duration – has suffered badly, and everywhere are craters and clods of disturbed earth. /*T. L. Redding*

Bottom left: **Debris** An electrical short circuit apparently caused the entire bomb and incendiary load on BIII DV172 to drop to the ground at Binbrook on the evening of 3 July 1943. Most of No 460 Squadron's Lancs had been bombed up and many of the ground crews were tucking into their evening meal when the alarm sounded around 1800 hours. Within minutes the 'Cookie' and two 500 pounders exploded, scattering incendiaries far and wide, and leaving little trace of DV172. Soon, R5745 was on fire, and others affected included ED774 and W4783. The squadron CO, Wg Cdr Chad E. Martin was quickly on the scene to direct operations and many heroic deeds were performed before the area was cleared and 17 crews were able to take off for Cologne. /*A. E. Mardell*

'Although it seemed like hours, no more than perhaps seven or eight minutes had passed since the first explosion. At the seat of the explosion more casualties were being attended to; among these were the fire officer, Flg Off Grebby, who was badly wounded in the upper leg, and a fire corporal who appeared to be dead. A number of people were helping to get the injured clear of the immediate danger area and fires were raging among the other Lancasters.

'By then it looked as if three, if not four aircraft had exploded. One or two bombs were lying about and posed a considerable threat. Their tails had been torn off so it was possible to check and see if the blotting papers on the 53 pistols were stained. Such stains indicated that the chemical acetone capsules had ruptured and the bombs would, in all likelihood, go off after the appropriate delay period. However, none appeared to be stained and there was no smell of acetone when sniffing the head of the bomb pistols.

'At this stage it was fairly obvious little or nothing could be done to contain the fires without loss of life. Those present had done all that could be done; some more than enough. One No 57 Squadron navigator, Flg Off John Gott (well known as a broadcaster and chief constable postwar) was very active and did sterling work getting the injured away. A former policeman, he already had a George Medal for some previous episode. In the immediate chaos there was no time to determine who was doing what but, among others, Flg Off Grebby and his firemen did some admirable work before some of them were cut down.

'The armament officer let it be known quite forcibly that some of the bombs scattered around the area might go off at any time; so by common consent those few remaining evacuated the site. There were other dangers too. A patch of grass on fire near some detonators was stamped out and averted more trouble.

'Almost immediately afterwards there were two more violent explosions in quick succession. The air was full of flying debris – engines, undercarriages, and one bomb, which fortunately did not explode. This was the last aircraft of that particular clutch to explode. The remaining No 57 Squadron aircraft and the nearest No 630 Squadron dispersals appeared to be in no danger from fire, but one could not be certain if blast or fragments had affected the loads and perhaps set the bomb pistols in operation.

'Apart from the crackling of aircraft fires and sporadic sound of .303in ammunition exploding, the area was now quiet and completely deserted. However, because of the uncertain state of the aircraft bomb loads and loose bomb status, the situation was still full of menace. Here and there was evidence of the human carnage: an armourer corporal from the bomb dump lay dead near his bicycle, while on the lip of another crater was a soldier's leg, neatly chopped off at the knee, the trousers beautifully creased and the boot shining. It was later learned that some soldiers who happened to be on the spot at the wrong time quite inadvertently were among the injured and missing.

'Later on that evening the station commander, Grp Capt B. A. Casey, accompanied by Flt Lt MacBean, inspected the considerable scene of desolation. No more bombs had gone off and everyone began to feel more confident because, in theory at least, the maximum delay period had passed. Events the following day proved how wrong they could be.

'It was decided that apart from moving the dead no more clearance work should be done on the site that night. Sample checks were made late in the evening on the loaded No 630 Squadron Lancasters, and on the bomb loads standing on their dispersals. This indicated there was unlikely to be any danger from that source.

'Early the next morning the armament team set out to review, and clear if possible, the bombs lying around the devastated area. They dealt with something like 15 bombs without too much difficulty. One crater just where an aircraft had been standing had at least three unexploded bombs in it so a Coles crane was sent for, but not before the men sat down to enjoy a welcome flask of tea.

'Meanwhile, the rest of the team went over to inspect a broken-backed Lanc with its bomb load still on, and almost immediately the bombs in the vacated crater detonated. It could only be assumed that the acetone had been taken up to the celluloid delay discs by capilliary action of the cotton wool wick ever since the explosions of the previous day. This held up further clearance of the area but fortunately that was the last of the detonations at East Kirkby during World War II.

'The actual incident apart, there was an air of considerable foreboding regarding the implications of the ensuing court of enquiry. Right from the start, Flt Lt MacBean couldn't help but worry that his armament staff had failed somewhere along the line, while personally convinced that the first explosion was not caused by a bomb detonation. One civilian witness said he saw petrol overspilling when Lancaster PB360 was being refuelled and it is believed a spark did the rest. If indeed so, the first explosion was caused by a petrol tank blowing up.

'As a result of this and some previous incidents, a number of MBEs and BEMs were later awarded, among them Flg Off Grebby, Flg Off Gott, and Flt Lt MacBean.'

The Hundred Club

A further selection of Lancs which topped the 100 mark on operations. While space regrettably precludes illustrating them all, we have, including 13 shown in the original *Lancaster at War*, thus pictured 24 of the 30 identified centenarians. Others, known to have existed, may be recognised in the fullness of time.

Above: **Uncle Joe** BIII ED611 'JO-U' of No 463 Squadron RAAF, seen taxying out for her 100th operation (date and target unknown) from Waddington – the occasion clearly chalked on her nose by the ground crew. Beginning life with No 44 (Rhodesia) Squadron in April 1943, she totted up 43 ops before transfer to No 463 Squadron RAAF in February 1944. The portrait of Stalin and name *Uncle Joe* originated on her former unit, but her original ops score, recorded forward of the motif, was later replaced by stars to match the 463 sorties. Finishing the war with at least 115 trips to her credit, ED611 later passed to the Bombing Trials Unit as a general hack before being struck off the active list in January 1947. /*N. Sharman*

Centre Left: **King of the Air** The name applied to No 106 Squadron's BIII JB663 'ZN-A', which completed her 100th trip on the Dortmund-Ems canal 4/5 November 1944. Here Flt Sgt A. V. ('Tubby') Hallett (second left front row), I/C A Flight ground crews, is grouped with those of his charges responsible for keeping JB663 flying. Brand-new when delivered in November 1943, a day or so after No 106 moved to Metheringham, her total was at least 111 before being pensioned off and ultimately broken up at 15 MU Wroughton in October 1946./*A. V. Hallett*

Bottom left: **The Fair Fighters Revenge** Already a veteran when inherited by No 153 Squadron on its reforming at Kirmington in October 1944, BI ME812 'P4-F' was originally on the strength of No 166 Squadron from May 1944 and ended squadron life when No 153 disbanded at the end of September 1945. Surplus to requirements, she was flown to 20 MU Aston Down and scrapped a year later. The picture was taken at Scampton in May 1945 when in the hands of Sqn Ldr F. R. 'Paddy' Flynn (seen in cockpit) and crew. /*Mrs M. Flynn*

Right: **Take it Easy** No 100 Squadron operating from Waltham had no less than three Lancs which topped 100 operations: BIIIs ND458, ND644 and JB603. Pictured in the latter when 15 short of her century and in the hands of New Zealander Flg Off D. W. Lee (here in cockpit) and crew. Under the cockpit is a blue duck – to represent the skipper's home area of Kaikoura – and the legend 'Take It Easy'. Shortly after leaving the squadron having done 20 ops (beginning Revigny-Sur-Odon 14/15 July 1944, ending Saarbrucken 5/6 October 1944) in the old warrior, Dick Lee (by then instructing at Westcott) travelled back to Waltham in order to witness the occasion of her century and toast the crew concerned. Sadly, JB603 'HW-E' (which had been with the squadron from new in November 1943) did not return from Hanover 5/6 January 1945, her 112th trip./*L. F. Lampitt*

Left: **The Captain's Fancy** BIII NE181 'AA-M' which survived 101 trips with No 75 (New Zealand) Squadron from May 1944 to operational retirement early February 1945. The 'ton' came on 29 January 1945 and here at Mepal we see the skipper who took her to Krefeld that day, Sqn Ldr Jim M. Bailey (second right foreground), on hand to witness the ground crew record the 101st bomb symbol on the kite's nose. NE181 passed to neighbouring No 514 Squadron Waterbeach in July 1945, there to do little flying until the unit disbanded a month later. The end came in the huge Lancaster graveyard at 5 MU Kemble during September 1947./*IWM*

Above: **On Tap** No 166 Squadron's BIII LM550 'AS-B', Kirmington circa August 1944 sporting 30 beer mugs to represent operations completed since joining the unit from new in May 1944. Transferred to No 153 Squadron, which re-formed at Kirmington in October 1944, she finished the war with 118 beer mugs recorded and survived until broken up in May 1947. Her original nose adornment comprises a brown barrel complete with black hoops; a yellow scroll with 'Let's Have Another' in red; yellow beer mugs for night ops, white for daylights./*W. I. Warmington*

296

Top left: **Big Day** Only two PFF Lancasters are known to have achieved 100 operations: ND709 of No 635 Squadron and ND875 of No 156 Squadron. Here is BIII ND875 'GT-N' on return from Dortmund-Hapenerweg 24 March 1945, her 100th sortie. Her proud ground staff pose with the aircrew – skipper Sqn Ldr Peter Clayton (squatting far right front row) – who flew the old girl that day. On the strength of No 156 Squadron from new in April 1944, ND875 (with a total of at least 108 ops to her credit) later passed to a succession of Conversion Units before being dumped at 15 MU Wroughton and scrapped in August 1947. /*P. F. Clayton*

Centre left: **Dressing Up** At Wickenby in 1945, Wg Cdr Mike Stockdale, OC No 12 Squadron, awards BI ME758 'PH-N' a DSO and DFC on completion of her 106th op. Both flight commanders (Sqn Ldr Peter Huggins, B Flight stands with arms folded at base of ladder; Sdn Ldr K. W. 'Pop' Hinds, A Flight is fourth left) pose with members of the squadron's ground services echelon). Flown into Wickenby at the end of April 1944, she completed 108 ops (all with No 12 Squadron) and was finally struck off charge in October 1945./*P. S. Huggins*

Below: **Check List** Fiskerton 24 March 1945 – the day the Allies crossed the Rhine – and Flg Off Don Graham and crew are about to open up the taps of BI ME801 'UL-N^2' and head for Dortmund-Harpenerweg – the kite's 102nd trip. Delivered in May 1944, ME801 served her total operational life with No 576 Squadron (completing 113 sorties) and was ultimately written off in a crash 16 October 1945, a month after the unit disbanded./*H. Allen*

Above and right: **Spirit of Russia** Shown here in her heyday with No 189 Squadron Fulbeck circa December 1944 (coded 'CA-R'); and – to show how most centenarians ended up – a comparison picture taken at the RAF Fire School Sutton-on-Hull in January 1954. A BIII, EE136 completed 93 ops with No 9 Squadron beginning May 1943 and ending with transfer to No 189 Squadron, which reformed as an off-shoot of the former unit at Bardney in October 1944. Final tally of ops numbered 109 and then came 'retirement' to 1659 HCU flogging the circuits with aspiring crews. Finally grounded, this worthy warrior became a ground instruction airframe at No 1 Radio School before being dumped for fire fighting practice at the RAF's Fire School./*W. H. Killner; H. W. Holmes Collection*

Bottom right: **Survivor** Still bearing a long service stripe applied by her ground crew is BIII DV302 'SR-H', here awaiting the axe at 46 MU Lossiemouth in 1946. In cockpit is WO Ron Emeny, one time No 207 Squadron rear gunner and successful evader. DV302 went to No 101 Squadron Ludford Magna from 32 MU St Athan in November 1943 and for many months rivalled BIII DV245 'SR-S' – built on the same production line three months earlier and thus with a head start – in the friendly race to achieve 100 ops. In the event DV245, appropriately named 'The Saint', was first by completing her 'ton' on Hanover 5/6 January 1945 in the hands of Flg Off R. P. Patterson RCAF and crew. 'Howe' followed on 7/8 January when Plt Off J. A. Kurtzer RAAF and crew raided Munich. However such good fortune could hardly last and 'The Saint' succumbed to fate on Bremen 23 March 1945, reputedly her 122nd trip. 'Howe' finished the conflict with her total at 121 and survived until scrapped at Lossiemouth January 1947./*R. T. Emeny*

298

You Aren't the Only One to Come Back

JIM EMMERSON

'Never go back' would be a phrase voiced by most former air and ground crews after they have revisited the airfields once so much a part of their daily life.

The passing years have told on the deserted runways and approaches; Nissen huts once so alive with humanity have long since been turned over to farm storage; Watch Offices stand as gaunt skeletons of crumbling brick. Many of the villages and towns once a haven for high spirited youth have changed, enlarged to keep pace with the increased population, developed in the march of progress.

Canadian Jim Emmerson is among a host of Commonwealth men to make the pilgrimage and here relates his experience, but 10 years after the war – a mixture of emotion and disappointment.

From Georgetown, Ontario, Jim – one of four brothers to serve his country during the war – was a clay press operator in a porcelain factory before enlistment. He returned home soon after VE Day 1945, a 22-year old flying officer, bound for duty with Tiger Force in the Far East. However, the dropping of the Atom bomb put paid to this and he was discharged in December of the same year.

His postwar career has been as a journalist and he is presently fully occupied working on the re-write desk of a Toronto newspaper.

'At the first echoing sound of my footsteps, birds took fright and whirred up through the girders overhead. Rusted remnants of corrugated metal roof creaked eerily in the wind. Framed by the skeletal remains, clouds could be seen high above in the sunlight, drifting as silently as candle flames.

'I stepped from the cavernous, ghostly hangar onto the crumbling tarmac. In every fissure and crack, grass, weeds and flowers struggled to live in the decay that had been the vibrant, thunderous home of two Canadian 6 Group Bomber Command squadrons.

'The airfield at Skipton-on-Swale, almost midway between Ripon and Thirsk in Yorkshire, had been the base of No 424 "Tiger" Squadron (my own) and No 433 "Porcupine" Squadron.

'An assignment in Farnborough by my newspaper, the *Toronto Telegram*, had given me this chance in 1955 to fulfil a long-held dream of revisiting my old operational airfield.

'The 3,000 miles from my Canadian home had disappeared with the speed of a modern air liner. But nothing could turn back the 10 years on the ravaged runways, the derelict buildings.

'In our old crew room – silent as its dust – a loose door slammed fitfully in the breeze.

'Scores of thundering engines had shaken this field. Hundreds of shouting, laughing airmen had enlivened it. Around the field and in the buildings Tannoy speakers had commanded in vibratory tones: "The following crews will report . . ." Now there was silence. The ruin remained for my eyes. But my mind brought back brief glimpses of other scenes:

'It's 11 March 1945. Lancaster "QB-W" screams off the runway at 130mph, 11,000lb of bombs, 1,760gal of gasoline aboard. Smoke drifts up from behind. I glance back to see bomb aimer and navigator surveying a smouldering Gee set. I grab my fire extinguisher and hand it back. Only when we're safely home from Essen do they tell me that in their initial panic they grabbed an explosive oxygen bottle – not an extinguisher – and almost turned that on the fire.

'Nearby Harrogate was a hunting ground for girls when crews enjoyed a stand-down. We're in the Officers' Mess at a meeting to hear angry rebels protest about poor food. In reproach, our commanding officer stresses that the nearby district is constantly searched for choice food items to improve the menu. "Do you realise", he asks, pointing to our pious, innocent-looking messing officer, "that Flt Lt Hallett goes into Harrogate every Saturday to see what he can pick up?"

'Wg Cdr Clyde Marshall is briefing No 424 Squadron crews for a night operation. Recalling that German night fighters had shot up our field the night before, he finishes with an order which will never take its place beside Nelson's "England expects" in the history books. But it is practical. "If Jerry comes tonight and catches us still on the ground",

Above: Jim Emmerson framed in the rear doorway of a former No 6 Group Lanc X staging through Yarmouth, Nova Scotia, August 1945. /*J. W. Emmerson*

says Marshall, "there's only one thing to do: shut down your engines: get out . . . and . . . run like hell!"

'We are over the North Sea on an air-to-sea firing training flight. Regulations call for "low flying" at a minimum of 200ft. Actually, anyone way up there at 200ft is considered at "oxygen level" by crews who prefer to skim the surface. Back at base, fellow pilot Bill Harker is telling me how he got so low "my props were throwing up spray". Assuming a languid look, I replied: "Yes we did that too but found it boring so I put down 30 degrees of flap and surfboarded back!"

'7 March 1945, and four "Sprog" crews set off for Dessau. Two of us come back.

'Bomb aimer Arthur ("Boots") Boothroyd approaches with an urgent plea. He has met a young lady who lives a mile or so off the end of the main runway. Could we impress her by swooping low over her house? I feign shock at such a suggestion, stressing that it's a serious offence to engage in deliberate low flying. Boothroyd's features fall in disappointment, as I add "But, as you know, some of these air-crafts don't climb as well as others." I think we left tire marks on the young lady's roof.

'It's 10 April 1945, and we're over Leipzig in daylight. A Lancaster rolls over in flames and goes down at our right. Tail Gunner Charlie Helsdon announces on intercom: "There's a Hally going down behind us." Both victims hit by flak. I saw no fighters, heard no one mention fighters. I am surprised, therefore, when at de-briefing mid-upper gunner Don More says he had seen a couple of Mustangs mixing it up with a German jet. The

300

Above: **Tell-Tale Tracks** Like gigantic scars, the airfields of yesteryear still dominate the landscape from the air. This is Elsham Wolds circa 1972, revealing the typical layout of a wartime airfield. Local contractors have begun digging up overgrown dispersals, and a GPO repeater now stands at the end of a once busy runway. Since this picture was taken a new road has been cut through the centre of the main runway, and a water treatment plant now occupies permanent acreage within the airfield's perimeter. Former No 103 Squadron Aussie navigator Don Charlwood wrote about his nostalgic return to Elsham in our original *Lancaster At War.*/Grimsby Evening Telegraph

No Weeping Now
J. R. Walsh, 1976

I went back to the lonely Wolds, the fens and the empty sky.
I saw the tall gaunt elms, heard the calling rooks, how time
had passed me by.
Grass had grown on the runways, in the hangars stood rusting
ploughs;
The dispersal points were empty, just starlings and grazing cows.
The Watch Office stood deserted,
Or maybe the ghosts of men:
Stood and watched as I walked remembering,
For I'd said 'I'll come back again'.
The windsock hung in tatters, forlorn in the cold damp air,
Then I thought, 'What does it matter?', there is nobody here to
care.
The crew huts were but ruins, rotting timbers and sagging floors;
Not a voice to break the silence, just the wind and the
creaking doors.
Then I recalled these once were billets,
Full of life and the noise of men:
With the crackling roar of Merlins,
Or the whispering scratch of a pen.
So I stood quite still to listen; was there a message there for me?
In the shadows would they remember, had they left me a sign to see?.
If they had it was too elusive, made dim by the veil of years;
And I recalled all the purpose and courage, till my eyes were
blurred by tears.
I turned away downhearted for this was not the field I had known;
Not the brave bold home of my memories; fool I was for the years
had flown.

interrogation officer stiffens and demands more detail. "Are you sure?" he presses. Taken aback somewhat, More replies: "I'm positive that's what I saw." Then, as a perplexed look comes over his face he adds doubtfully: "Unless the Mustangs were fighting amongst themselves."

' "Give me a course to Consett in Durham County", I asked our navigator Jerry Brown as we set off on some training exercises. From Consett, I fly what I feel is the proper heading and distance to bring us to a place called Crag Head, too tiny to be marked on the map. But soupy smog closes in and try as I might I can't spot the cluster of houses. "What were you looking for up there?" Brown wanted to know when we landed at base. "I was looking for the little mining village my parents came from", I tell him. Brown, never one to exhibit sentimentality, fixes me with a stern stare and declares: "If I had known that – we'd be up there yet still looking!"

'The war is over. We've been detailed to fly unused bombs 70 miles off shore from Whitby and dump them in the sea. The first day, everyone dutifully flies the 70 miles. But then it becomes apparent that those continuing to do so are falling farther behind in the queue for a second and third load. Thereafter, the bomb line seems to move ever and ever closer to England. Fortunately, we run out of bombs before anyone wanting to be first at the pub, begins dropping them on Whitby itself.

'Memories faded and ghosts seemed to be listening in the silence. The Control Tower, littered with glass and debris stood voiceless like a sentinel guarding the past. Once it had been alive, full of bustle, chatter and cryptic radio Jargon: "Shortsight Willie to Briarwood" a No 424 Squadron skipper would call to the station. "Pabob Roger, downwind", a No 433 pilot would announce, alerting Control he was in the downwind leg nearing approach.

'On a gentle slope falling off to the Swale River, cattle grazed. Geese rambled amid ruins of Nissen huts. The hard stand which had been home to our regular aircraft – "W-Willie" – was a crumbling patch of asphalt. On it, a broken-wheeled farm cart lay askew.

'Crops grew between the runways. The runways themselves were losing the battle against weeds, grass and flowers. I drove slowly along the main runway and then to the farmhouse to thank the owner for allowing me to browse around.

'I tried to find words to tell him what had brought me. "You don't have to explain", he cut in. "I get lots of them in here like you. You're not the only one to come back!"

'I switched on the engine of my rented car and drove down his lane to the main road.

'I didn't look back.'

Above left: **They have Gone . . .** ' . . . At the first echoing sound of my footsteps, birds took fright and whirred up through the girders overhead. Rusted remnants of corrugated metal roof creaked eerily in the wind . . .' (*left*) ' . . . on a gentle slope falling off to the Swale River, cattle grazed. Geese rambled amid ruins of Nissen huts . . .'/*Both J. W. Emmerson*

Above: **Keepers of Memories** ' . . . Nothing could turn back the ten years on the ravaged runways, the derelict buildings. In our old crew room – silent in its dust – a loose door slammed fitfully in the breeze . . .' (*above*) Dunholme Lodge in November 1972, the gutted watch office surrounded by rich Lincolnshire farmland. Right foreground is the open-fronted building which once housed the fire engines and blood wagon. (*centre right*) Wickenby September 1973, with Nissen huts, now given over to storing a farmer's trucks and implements, steadily losing the battle against nature.
/*D. Lodge, H. Watson Wickenby; B. Goulding*

Bottom right: **Mute Sentinel** Framed by leaf-shorn trees stands the water tower at Metheringham on a cold April day in 1972, a mute sentinel from a vibrant past. Where once throbbed the heart of an operational squadron lie worn out tractors and discarded iron frames.
/*H. Watson*

Caterpillar Club
Certificate of Membership

SGT. J. NOBLE

is a member of the CATERPILLAR CLUB,
having saved his life by parachute.

SIGNED

HON. SEC. EUROPEAN DIVISION.

IRVIN

AIR MINISTRY, 3 APR 1944 194

IS TO CERTIFY that 1341382 Sgt. J.Noble,

R.A.F. born on 9th May, 1921, at present

a prisoner of war in Stalag Luft 3.

and whose prisoner of war number is 222531 has been

promoted to Temporary Flight Sergeant with effect from

24th August, 1943. and the requisite notification

has been published.

P.407915/43.

The Air Officer in Charge R.A.F. Records.

(*12544) Wt. 19438—588 5m 7/43 T.S. 700
(*13746—12544) Wt. 43822—M328 10m 12/43 T.S. 700

Postlude

Aftermath

THE AFTERMATH

Hamburg street, devastation.
One-legged man, foul amputation.
Leaning on two sticks, he'll stand
Gazing at his battered land.

He thinks of wife and child, both dead;
A thousand sorrows fill his head.
No help at all, for him, to know
That Goering died a week ago.